C0-AOE-038

The social psychology of knowledge

This book is published as part of the joint publishing agreement established in 1977 between the Fondation de la Maison des Sciences de l'Homme and the Press Syndicate of the University of Cambridge. Titles published under this arrangement may appear in any European language or, in the case of volumes of collected essays, in several languages.

New books will appear either as individual titles or in one of the series which the Maison des Sciences de l'Homme and the Cambridge University Press have jointly agreed to publish. All books published jointly by the Maison des Sciences de l'Homme and the Cambridge University Press will be distributed by the Press throughout the world.

Cet ouvrage est publié dans le cadre de l'accord de coédition passé en 1977 entre la Fondation de la Maison des Sciences de l'Homme et le Press Syndicate of the University of Cambridge. Toutes les langues européennes sont admises pour les titres couverts par cet accord, et les ouvrages collectifs peuvent paraître en plusieurs langues.

Les ouvrages paraissent soit isolément, soit dans l'une des séries que la Maison des Sciences de l'Homme et Cambridge University Press ont convenu de publier ensemble. La distribution dans le monde entier des titres ainsi publiés conjointement par les deux établissements est assurée par Cambridge University Press.

The social psychology of knowledge

Edited by
Daniel Bar-Tal and Arie W. Kruglanski

The right of the
University of Cambridge
to print and sell
all manner of books
was granted by
Henry VIII in 1534.
The University has printed
and published continuously
since 1584.

Cambridge University Press
Cambridge
New York New Rochelle Melbourne Sydney

Editions de la Maison des Sciences de l'Homme
Paris

Published by the Press Syndicate of the University of Cambridge
The Pitt Building, Trumpington Street, Cambridge CB2 1RP
32 East 57th Street, New York, NY 10022, USA
10 Stamford Road, Oakleigh, Melbourne 3166, Australia
and Editions de la Maison des Sciences de l'Homme
54 Boulevard Raspail, 75270 Paris Cedex 06

First published 1988

Printed in Great Britain by
Redwood Burn Limited, Trowbridge, Wiltshire

British Library cataloguing in publication data

The social psychology of knowledge.
1. Knowledge, Sociology of 2. Knowledge – Psychological aspects 3. Social psychology
I. Bar-Tal, Daniel II. Kruglanski, Arie W.
306'.42 BD175

Library of Congress cataloguing in publication data

The social psychology of knowledge/edited Daniel Bar-Tal and Arie W. Kruglanski.
p. cm.
Includes index.
ISBN 0 521 32114 X
1. Knowledge. Sociology of. 2. Social psychology. I. Bar-Tal, Daniel II. Kruglanski, Arie W.
BD175. S625 1988
306'.42–dc19 87–27611

ISBN 0 521 32114 X
ISBN 2 7351 0232 7 (France only)

RB

We dedicate this book lovingly to our mothers
Sofia (Zosia) Bar-Tal and Olga (Ola) Oxorn
who provided us with much of our social knowledge

We dedicate this book to [illegible]

[illegible]

who provided us with much of our [illegible] knowledge

Contents

Contributors

Reuben M. Baron Department of Psychology, University of Connecticut
Daniel Bar-Tal School of Education, Tel Aviv University
Yoram Bar-Tal School of Medicine, Tel Aviv University
Patricia G. Devine Department of Psychology, University of Wisconsin
Kenneth J. Gergen Department of Psychology, Swarthmore College
Zvi Ginossar Department of Psychology, Hebrew University of Jerusalem
Carl F. Graumann Psychologisches Institut, University of Heidelberg
David L. Hamilton Department of Psychology, University of California, Santa Barbara
Reid Hastie Department of Psychology, Northwestern University
E. Tory Higgins Department of Psychology, New York University
Denis Hilton Department of Psychology, University College, Cardiff
The late *Joseph M. F. Jaspars*
Arie W. Kruglanski Department of Psychology, University of Maryland at College Park
Cathy McFarland Department of Psychology, Simon Fraser University
Thomas M. Ostrom Department of Psychology, Ohio State University
Kenneth A. Rasinski Department of Psychology, Northwestern University
John K. Rempel Department of Psychology, University of Waterloo
Michael Ross Department of Psychology, University of Waterloo
Thomas K. Srull Department of Psychology, University of Illinois, Urbana–Champaign
Charles Stangor Department of Psychology, New York University
Yaacov Trope Department of Psychology, Hebrew University of Jerusalem
Robert S. Wyer, Jr. Department of Psychology, University of Illinois, Urbana–Champaign
Mark P. Zanna Department of Psychology, University of Waterloo

Preface

The present volume attempts to look at various areas of social cognitive research from a unique conceptual perspective embodied in the notion of human knowledge. The common interest in seriously exploring the "knowledge" perspective brought many of the present contributors to Shefayim, Israel, in the June of 1984. There, we decided to publish a collection of theoretical and empirical essays on various facets of the cognition/knowledge interface.

We felt that the volume as a whole should highlight those aspects of the contributions that specifically pertain to the knowledge construct. Three such broad aspects could be readily discerned. The first aspect concerned the concept of knowledge as such; the way it differs from cognition and the way it is social in character. The second aspect concerned the issue of generality versus specificity in conceptions of social knowledge: are we better off proposing content specific conceptions of knowledge formation (e.g. concerning the formation of attitudinal knowledge, knowledge of the past, causal knowledge, or statistical knowledge), or is it possible to formulate general epistemic models to account for the formation of all knowledge? The third aspect concerned the issue of validity or proof. As compared to "mere cognition", "knowledge" has a distinct feel of reality to it. In other words, we do not know something unless we know it to be true. But, how do we establish the veracity of our knowledge?

The final product, the present book, more than lived up to our expectations. The contents of the chapters range from broad historical and philosophical attempts to elucidate the social psychological significance of knowledge as construct to more narrowly focused ideas on specific aspects of knowledge acquisition. Although the integrative themes are not always explicit, the careful reader will discover that they are at the foundation of every chapter. In this respect the present volume is not to be regarded as a collection of unrelated essays, but as a modest first step at providing a multi-level, multi-topical discussion of the same general problem, the mystery of human knowledge. The redirection of social cognitive research into the problem area of "knowledge" is admittedly deliberate. As will become clear, we regard such a shift in focus as capable of opening up exciting new areas of study as well as refreshingly expanding the scope of social psychological inquiry.

We would like to thank Tel-Aviv University and the Israel Academy of Science for providing the initial funds for the Shefayim conference. We are also grateful to the School of Education and the Department of Psychology at Tel-Aviv University who provided the secretarial help needed for editing this book. In addition, we are especially indebted to Jos Jaspars who played such an active role at the beginning of this publishing venture. It is most sad and unfortunate that he is no longer among us. His death in 1985 is a grave loss both to his friends and to the field of social psychology as a whole.

D.B.T.
A.W.K.

1 The social psychology of knowledge: its scope and meaning

Daniel Bar-Tal and Arie W. Kruglanski

One way to stimulate new research directions in a field of science is to redefine or recategorize its topics of inquiry. Such seemingly semantic shifts may have profound consequences on research directions in the field for years to come. They often expand or reduce the scope of inquiry, refocus the research on new parameters of interest, and introduce different perspectives which may alter old conceptions and research paradigms. As an example, in the last fifteen years or so one field of social psychology has been significantly modified by two such redefinitions. Thus, in the late 1960s and the early 1970s the attribution field emerged, based on the seminal works of Heider (1958), Jones and Davis (1965), and Kelley (1967, 1971, 1972). Attribution research has been concerned with the question of how people in everyday life assign causality for their own behavior, to that of other persons, or to impersonal events in their environment (Frieze and Bar-Tal 1979).

Once posed, the attribution question engendered hundreds of studies on a broad range of social psychological topics (see for reviews Frieze *et al.* 1979, Harvey *et al.* 1976, 1978, 1981, Jones *et al.* 1972, Kelley and Michela 1980, Kruglanski 1980, in press). Attribution became a leading interest area in social psychology, and most contemporary textbooks in the field devote at least one chapter to the burgeoning research activity on attributional issues.

With the advent of the "social cognition" movement in the late 1970s, social psychology has witnessed a new transformation of its subject-matter. Broadly defined (Taylor 1981), social cognition deals with how people perceive their social world and relationships. This movement has been heavily influenced by the theories and research paradigms of cognitive psychology. It implies that the attribution question is only one among many of concern to the social cognition field (cf. Kruglanski, in press). Besides its considerable breadth, the new social cognition movement features a distinctive "information-processing" metaphor, as a result of the cognitive psychology influence. This introduced social psychologists to such new topics as encoding, organization, storage, and retrieval of social stimulus information. In turn, the new interests facilitated the development of appropriately rigorous and sophisticated research methodologies aimed at discriminating among such fine cognitive "microprocesses". While mainstream social psychology has been cognitive in some sense since the 1940s (cf. Scheerer 1954, Zajonc 1968), the new social cognition movement redefined the major issues to be confronted and drew social psychologists' attention to previously unheeded work in cognitive psychology proper. Highly dynamic and active, the social cognition movement provided a new research paradigm for social psychologists to approach their topics of inquiry, and has inspired intense research activity in the past decade (see e.g. Fiske and Taylor 1984, Forgas 1981a, Hastie *et al.* 1980, Higgins *et al.* 1981, Showers and Cantor 1985, Wyer and Srull 1984).

The focus on intrapsychological processes and the heavy influence of cognitive theories and methods fueled the continuing controversy regarding the distinctive nature of social cognition. While some social psychologists do not perceive substantial differences between cognition and social cognition (e.g. Simon 1976), others clearly differentiate between the two (cf. Forgas 1981b, Landman and Manis 1983, Zajonc 1980). The former emphasize that all cognitive phenomena are governed by the same processes. The latter identify specific characteristics of human beings (as simultaneous *objects* of cognition and cognizing *subjects*) that render social cognition and perception qualitatively distinct from the perception of inanimate objects. The social cognition movement has been criticized on several other grounds as well. Some authors objected to the dominance of the information-processing approach (e.g. Baron and Harvey 1980, McGuire 1983), others pointed to the narrow scope of social cognition research which neglects motivation, affect, or behavior (cf. Weary *et al.* 1980, Zajonc 1980), as well as the social context (i.e. social interaction, group behavior, culture) of cognitive phenomena (cf. Doise and Mackie 1981, Forgas 1981b, Neisser 1980).

One purpose of the present volume is to introduce the term "social psychology of knowledge" as a new way to look at the social cognitive domain. Let us consider how "social psychology of knowledge" differs from previous social cognitive paradigms, and along what paths it may guide future research in the area.

The social psychology of knowledge

We view knowledge in a subjective or intersubjective sense as the total sum of beliefs to which an individual or a group may subscribe. Beliefs are accumulated through years of human experience and are stored in the human mind. They constrain persons' reality and in this sense delimit human action. Knowledge is to some considerable extent relative, and what one person (group, culture) considers knowledge may be regarded as superstition by another. The contents of beliefs are of unlimited scope, therefore human knowledge has no a priori boundaries. Accordingly, it is possible to categorize knowledge in any number of ways. For example, Russell (1948) differentiated knowledge by acquaintance and knowledge by description; Ryle (1949) differentiated knowing *how* and knowing *that*; and James (1890) drew a distinction between knowledge of acquaintance and knowledge about.

The "knowledge" label covers such diverse social cognitive terms as "hypotheses", "judgments", "inferences", "attributions", "perceptions", "attitudes", "preferences", "values", "ideologies", "goals", or "intentions". All these could be considered as varieties of knowledge which persons may have. More broadly yet, "knowledge" denotes the shared realities of given communities (e.g. scientific ones) or cultures (see Bar-Tal, in press). In that latter sense, "knowledge", while subsuming "intrapersonal" cognitions, is at the same time thoroughly "interpersonal", or social. Even "intrapersonal" knowledge is social in an important sense. Much of any individual's knowledge is acquired from other people and is based on their beliefs and world views. The "facts" of our experience are social in an important sense. They depend for their meaning on previously constructed cultural concepts and categories in which terms "experience" is framed. In this respect, the acquired knowledge contributes to individual and group differences.

Social psychology of knowledge should, therefore, focus on the contents of knowledge as well as on the social and cognitive processes whereby knowledge forms and changes. In this sense, "social psychology of knowledge" is broader in scope than the field of "social knowing", which implies and emphasizes the *process* of knowing (cf. Baron 1981, McGuire 1983, Neisser 1980), or of "social knowledge", which implies a preoccupation with *contents* (e.g. of causal categories, as in attribution theory). The study of processes is important because it may uncover the general trans-historical and transcultural regularities whereby persons make up their minds on the basis of arguments and evidence. An investigation of knowledge formation processes would undoubtedly include not only informational processing mechanisms, but also affective and motivational factors that probably have impact on our thought processes and lend them intensity and direction (cf. Sorrentino and Higgins 1986). Furthermore, in view of the prevailing assumption that individuals act consistently with their beliefs, the study of social knowledge may open new avenues to the understanding of human behavior. The study of contents may have also other implications. It may allow mapping of individuals' and groups' knowledge, understanding the influence of individuals on other individuals, and explaining the effects of individuals' knowledge on their reactions.

The focus on knowledge may bring social psychologists into contact with alternative disciplines that have had a longstanding interest in explaining knowledge. Philosophers from Plato and Aristotle through Descartes, Locke, or Kant all the way to Russell and Popper have tried to assess the nature of knowledge and to determine its sources and validity. Most recently, non-justificationist philosophers (e.g. Kuhn 1970, Lakatos and Musgrave 1970) have noted the need to reconstruct major aspects of scientific developments in historical, sociological, and psychological terms, as compared to purely rationalistic (e.g. hypothetico-deductive) construction of science.

The latter developments in particular pose an exciting challenge to cognitive social psychologists. The social psychology of knowledge could, thus, provide us with concepts and methods for understanding scientific knowledge and scientific progress at the same time as it sheds light on lay knowledge and its development. Alongside sociologists of knowledge and of science (e.g. Berger and Luckmann 1967, Coser 1968, Merton 1957, Stark 1977), social psychologists of knowledge could make major contributions to interpreting the miracle of modern science. This promises to be a real "bootstrap" operation. Our theories about knowledge acquisition are in themselves types of knowledge, subject to the rules and regularities they themselves articulate. As in Escher's famous drawing, even as we move upward (toward abstractly explaining knowledge) we may finally reach the lowest plane from which we have just set out (i.e. that of knowledge to be explained). Such formal paradoxes only add challenge and excitement to the task of forging a social psychological conception of knowledge.

Themes of the present volume

Contributions to the present volume represent diverse perspectives on the phenomenon of human knowledge. Some chapters address aspects of social knowledge from the information-processing (the social cognition) perspective, others adopt historical, constructivist, ecological, problem-solving, and lay epistemic approaches. Despite the diversity, three general themes can be discerned which run through the volume as a whole, and which are touched upon by the various chapters: the nature of knowledge; the process–contents distinction in knowledge analyses; and the problem of validity of knowledge structures. In what follows we briefly indicate how these principal themes of our volume are addressed by the various individual contributions.

The nature of knowledge

Gergen sets out to elucidate the very concept of knowledge. He distinguishes between two contrasting conceptions of knowledge: the "dualistic" one viewed as representation, and the "monistic" one considered as social construction. According to Gergen the representational conception is essentially individualistic whereas the constructionist conception is inherently social. Furthermore, the representational conception is open to various criticisms (e.g. of infinite regress) and the absence of compelling criteria to distinguish the mental representation of objects from the objects as such. Gergen proceeds to describe recent lines of work within the constructionist perspective, including his own analysis of psychological discourse, as basically circular. Whether the latter conclusion will be widely accepted (or greeted with "lusty enthusiasm" as Gergen puts it), remains to be seen. Yet Gergen's ideas merit close consideration by social psychologists. For example, the implication that social cognition research is necessarily committed to a *representational* conception of knowledge need not go unchallenged. In fact, social cognition research could be conceived as articulating a view of social *construction* in which larger knowledge structures (e.g. associationist networks) are assembled from smaller bits of knowledge (the "stimulus information" being processed). Be that as it may, Gergen's arguments about knowledge (psychological or otherwise) are characteristically intriguing and provocative.

What Gergen calls "representational", Graumann calls "transcendental". Both conceptions allude to a relation between cognition on the one hand and external reality on the other. Unlike Gergen, however, who views contemporary social cognition concepts (e.g. schema) as committed to such a relation (hence as essentially representational), Graumann considers them as more nearly mentalistic or "immanentist". Furthermore, tracing the "cognition" concept from James's (1890) *Principles* to contemporary information-processing models, Graumann suggests that the earlier, Jamesian notion was explicitly more concerned with "knowledge", emphasizing as it does the reality aspect, ascertained via convergence of independent perceivers. Precisely for the latter reason, "knowledge" is a more social concept than "cognition", so the historical trend (which the present volume may help to reverse) has apparently moved the field from knowledge to cognition.

Baron contrasts two major types of knowledge: perceptual and cognitive. Perceptual knowledge takes ontogenetic and phylogenetic precedence over cognitive knowledge. Moreover, the two types of knowledge could be governed by different psychological processes. Perceptual knowledge could be gained via automatic processing, whereas cognitive knowledge could be gained via controlled processing. Perceptual knowledge concerns concrete particulars, whereas cognitive knowledge refers to general categories. Perceptual knowledge is direct whereas cognitive knowledge is constructed. The post-Gibsonian, dual mode epistemology proposed by Baron is reminiscent of other similar dichotomies, e.g. between affect and cognition (cf. Zajonc 1980), or between tacit and explicit types of knowledge (cf. Polanyi 1958).

Bar-Tal and Bar-Tal and Kruglanski define knowledge broadly as the totality of a person's beliefs on various topics. Other contributors do not explicitly define knowledge, yet suggest what knowledge is by dwelling on its particular examples. Trope and Ginossar analyze the acquisition and application of *statistical* knowledge, Zanna and Rempel discuss *attitudes* as knowledge structures; this allows them to integrate the historically incompatible, unidimensional versus tridimensional definitions of attitudes. Both Hamilton and Jaspars suggest that *causal attributions* are types of knowledge, and Ross and McFarland discuss memories of the *past* as types of knowledge.

The process and contents of knowledge formation

The diversity of knowledge types naturally raises the question of whether, in fact, they have anything in common. Put differently, can we hope to uncover a process of knowledge acquisition which applies to all knowledge types, or are these mediated by qualitatively separate processes? Contributors to this volume differ in their stands on this issue. Baron believes that perceptual knowledge is governed by a different process from conceptual knowledge. Gergen implies that a uniform theory of knowledge acquisition is possible, but that its specific nature would depend on the metatheory of knowledge one adopts: a representational theory of knowledge may emphasize the nature of mental processes, whereas a constructionist theory of knowledge may stress, instead, notions of social interaction, negotiation, and influence. This is not to say that the "representationist" and the "constructionist" models do not share important features. To mention one, both representationist and constructionist conceptions imply that knowledge ought to be *consistent* in some sense. For the representationist (or the transcendentalist, in Graumann's sense) the consistency refers to a *correspondence* between cognition and reality, whereas for the constructionist it refers to interpersonal consistency or social *consensus*.

Uniform approaches to knowledge acquisition are proposed by Bar-Tal and Bar-Tal, Kruglanski, and Trope and Ginossar. Bar-Tal and Bar-Tal start with the nonjustificationist assumption (cf. Bartley 1962) that knowledge (including scientific knowledge) is objectively unprovable. Therefore, a useful approach to the study of knowledge is to adopt a subjective or intersubjective perspective. Furthermore, Bar-Tal and Bar-Tal draw the distinction between particularistic and universalistic generalizations in social psychology, and outline several useful functions that a study of cognitive contents could accomplish: contents are indispensable for the testing of process models, they are necessary for predicting specific behaviors from general theories (see also Kruglanski and Klar, in press), and for implementing intervention measures in applied settings.

The distinction between contents of knowledge and processes of knowledge acquisition is also drawn by Kruglanski, who discusses the historical confusion between levels of analysis in previous social cognitive theories. But primarily Kruglanski outlines a judgmental model (the theory of lay epistemology) which integrates informational and motivational factors affecting the epistemic process. In Kruglanski's theory, these two types of factor are functionally complementary and jointly necessary for every bit of epistemic behavior. This is opposed to prevalent "two route" approaches whereby some knowledge is based on informational (or cognitive) influences, other on motivational influences.

A general model of human judgment is also proposed by Trope and Ginossar. These authors adopt the problem-solving perspective to judgment or knowledge acquisition. According to this perspective, a search for a sequence of productions ultimately transforms the initial state of knowledge about the problem into a state in which the goal is satisfied. Production rules are stored in long-term memory and are activated as a function of their accessibility (cf. Higgins and King 1981) and their perceived match to the judgmental problem in question. Systematic application of the problem-solving approach demonstrates that, contrary to previous implications, statistical judgments are governed by the same psychological factors as non-statistical judgments (or "heuristically" based judgments). Thus, the distinction between statistics and heuristics turns out to be one of cognitive *contents* rather than of *process* (see also Kruglanski and Ajzen 1983).

Aspects of the general judgmental process are elaborated in several further contributions to this volume. Zanna and Rempel advance the provocative proposal that attitudinal judgments can be variously based on cognition, behavior, or affect. This analysis is rich in researchable implications. It also raises several theoretical issues of interest. Do the different bases of attitudes fulfill the same *function* in the judgmental process? From the lay epistemic perspective, for instance (cf. Kruglanski, this volume), own behavior toward, or beliefs about, the attitude object could serve as types of "evidence" from which an attitude could be consciously deduced. By contrast, affect toward the attitude object is more likely to represent an unconscious motivational influence which may render a given attitude a desirable or an undesirable knowledge structure. If so, affect may selectively bias the memory search toward affect-congruent beliefs or past behaviors. Thus, Zanna and Rempel's "affect" could represent a "need for specific structure" influencing the formation of an attitude. In alternative cases, attitudes could be based on needs for "nonspecific" structure, based on the desire to act or orient oneself in one's environment. In this broad sense an affective (or a motivational) component might be part and parcel of all attitudes rather than representing a basis for some attitudes.

Higgins and Stangor discuss many ways in which the judgmental context affects the judgments rendered. Some such effects relate to the "informational" *contents* which serve as evidence for a given judgment. For instance, the context of a target's behavior may be taken as evidence against a dispositional attribution of her acts. Other context effects refer to the *process* of judging; they include context-driven accessibility of constructs for encoding stimulus information, and the effects of mood on categorization and reconstructive memory.

Reconstructive memory is also a focal topic for Ross and McFarland. Their data and theorizing could be interpreted to mean that judgments about one's own past differ in contents only from other possible judgments. As with all judgments, those of one's own past seem strongly affected by the accessibility of various constructs or categories. Ross and McFarland allude to such accessible constructs in discussing implicit theories of *stability* and *change* that people may adopt in regard to various topics. Other implicit theories could be similarly involved. One's theory of how Americans felt or behaved in the 1960s could affect one's memory of one's own feelings and behavior during that period. Furthermore, the same motivational factors which affect the rendition of all judgments could have impact on our recall of past events. In some circumstances one could be motivated to "freeze" one's extant theories about the past and be impervious to information inconsistent with those theories. Such freezing could stem from a "need for a nonspecific structure" regarding one's notions about one's past, or from the directionally biased "needs for specific structure". For instance, one could exaggerate the memory of past sins to highlight the magnitude of one's moral improvement. Alternatively, one could idealize past interactions in order to diminish current relationships. In short, the same informational and motivational factors which influence judgments of our present could also affect judgments of "the way we were".

A chapter by Devine and Ostrom examines the process of inconsistency management as investigated by "point on a continuum" models versus contemporary information-processing approaches. According to the authors, inconsistency management is essential to the attainment of coherent social knowledge. Point-on-continuum theories primarily stress the mechanism of discounting as a way of handling inconsistency. By contrast, information-processing models also imply the conditions under which discounting may occur, and suggest, additionally, the consequences of inconsistency management on such aspects of the perceiver's cognitive process as encoding and recall.

Hamilton's chapter examines inconsistency management "at the interface of attribution and person memory research". It is found that, as with other types of information processing, the more time-consuming and cognitively "difficult" the attributional activity, the more effectively it is represented in memory. Furthermore, items of information of which the (attributional) implications are inconsistent with those of other information are particularly likely to be recalled. Hamilton views attribution as a process that "occurs in conjunction with other processes in the course of comprehending, understanding, storing and using information". An alternative view compatible with Hamilton's research would be to regard attribution as representing the application of general information-processing principles to the specific *content domain* of causal judgments.

Jaspars outlines a model of causal attribution that combines subjects' prior "real world" knowledge with the information at hand. The information is encoded in terms of mental categories which the subjects construct, and which need not (although possibly they could) correspond to the "person", "time/modality", and "entity" categories assumed by the attribution theorists. Jaspars's model of causal inference thus appears to be "top-down" or deductive as contrasted with the "bottom-up" inductive models in the attributional literature (cf. Kelley 1967). In this sense at least, Jaspars's approach is not too dissimilar from the problem-solving or hypothesis-testing models proposed by Trope and Ginossar and Kruglanski respectively. Presumably such models apply to the formation of noncausal inferences as well as causal ones.

Similarity between different types of inference, notably scientific and lay inference, is also highlighted in the chapter by Wyer and Srull. These authors suggest that, just like lay persons, scientists go through several stages in processing empirical data. Furthermore, the factors that influence the processing at each stage could be similar for the scientist and the lay person. Construct accessibility, for example (cf. Higgins and King 1981), affects the scientists' interpretation of a phenomenon just as it may affect lay judgments and inferences. Moreover, the procedures lay persons and scientists use for data acquisition may heavily influence the conclusions drawn from the data. In this sense, then, the data can not "speak for themselves". All inferences are "biased" by pre-existing knowledge structures (theoretical hypotheses and methodological assumptions) that influence the data we collect and the way we interpret them.

The validity issue

By definition, the term "knowledge" refers to a state of affairs we hold to be true. Thus, the issue of validity should figure prominently in any discussion of the way social knowledge is acquired or modified. Indeed several chapters in the present volume touch on this theme, whether explicitly or implicitly. Furthermore, several authors discuss the "objective" validity of human judgments, whereas others address the subjective experience of validity. Among the former, Hastie and Rasinski devote a chapter to discussing the "logics" typically used in research on the "objective" accuracy of human judgments and make suggestions as to how such research might be improved. Higgins and Stangor suggest that contextually driven judgments and memories can be "objectively" valid, in the sense of faithfully reflecting the stimulus information on which they were based in the first place.

Objective validity of judgments and perceptions is also addressed by Baron from his "dual mode", neo-Gibsonian perspective. Social perception is assumed to be generally accurate, and to be tested against its pragmatic or behavioral consequences for the organism: the perception that an opening is sufficiently wide is tested by attempting to crawl through it. Baron contrasts such ecological criteria of veridicality with the cognitive models where accuracy is assessed in reference to logical or prescriptive criteria (as Bayesian theorem). Ross and McFarland discuss biases in recall as systematic and subjective deviations from objective facts (hence, as inaccuracies), influenced by individuals' implicit theories and/or their motivational states. Finally, Wyer and Srull imply that the validity of scientific theories is established via the exclusion of competing hypotheses, inconsistent with the theories at issue.

Several contributions to the present volume bear on validity as defined from the knower's subjective perspective. Devine and Ostrom deal with inconsistency management that presumably occurs in order to determine a valid state of affairs. A perceived person cannot be both "honest" and "dishonest". Thus, either one of the two is discounted (the solution favored by point-on-continuum models) or a differentiating explanation is adopted in which the circumstances of honest and dishonest behaviors are identified (the solution stressed by contemporary information-processing approaches). Similarly, Hamilton's research suggests that attributors may attempt to account for causally inconsistent information, supposedly because unresolved inconsistency forestalls a sense of valid knowledge.

The issue of subjective validity is dealt with explicitly in the chapters by Bar-Tal and Bar-Tal and Kruglanski. In both frameworks, the experience of validity is mediated by perceived consistency between one's evidence and one's hypothesis. An inconsistency between evidence and hypothesis, or the accessibility of several inconsistent (competing) hypotheses, signals potential invalidity. A resolution of such inconsistency always involves denial of one of the inconsistent cognitions at least in their original form (cf. Kruglanski and Klar 1987). The denied cognition is thereby pronounced an "error" whereas the remaining one is (tentatively) assumed to represent the veridical state of affairs.

It is of interest to note that some notion of consistency or correspondence is commonly involved in "objective" as well as subjective conceptions of validity. In the case of "objective" definitions, accuracy is defined as correspondence between a judgment and a criterion of some sort, and hence it denotes a consistency between the two. Similarly, inaccuracy is defined in terms of a deviation of the judgment from the criterion, hence denoting an inconsistency. Furthermore, broadly speaking, the "criterion" itself is a judgment to which some ("authoritative" or "knowledgeable") persons subscribe. Viewed in these terms, "objective" accuracy represents consistency, and inaccuracy an inconsistency, *as defined from the "knowledgeable" persons' perspective.* In other words, objective accuracy amounts to *interpersonal* consistency of judgments whereas subjective accuracy represents *intrapersonal* consistency.

The nature of knowledge, the unitary versus manifold nature of the knowledge of process acquisition (the process versus contents issue) and, the issue of veridicality (in its subjective or objective sense) represent some of the broad themes of contributions to the present volume. Beyond those commonalities, however, the chapters are rich in unique conceptual and empirical details that offer numerous exciting possibilities for further research on the social psychology of knowledge.

References

Bar-Tal, D. (in press). *Group beliefs*. New York: Springer Verlag.

Baron, R. M. (1981). Social knowing from an ecological-event perspective. In J. H. Harvey (ed.), *Cognition, social behavior, and the environment*. Hillsdale, NJ: Lawrence Erlbaum.

Baron, R. M. and Harvey, J. H. (1980). Contrasting perspectives on social knowing. *Personality and Social Psychology Bulletin* 6, 502–6.

Bartley, W. W. (1962). *The retreat to commitment*. New York: Knopf.

Berger, P. and Luckmann, T. (1967). *The construction of reality*. New York: Penguin.

Coser, A. L. (1968). Sociology of knowledge. In D. L. Skills (ed.), *International encyclopedia of the social sciences*, vol. 8. New York: Macmillan and Free Press.

Doise, W. and Mackie, D. (1981). On the social nature of cognition. In Forgas 1981a.

Fiske, S. T. and Taylor, S. E. (1984). *Social cognition*. Reading, Mass.: Addison-Wesley.

Forgas, J. P. (ed.) (1981a). *Social cognition*. London: Academic Press.

Forgas, J. P. (1981b). What is social about social cognition? In Forgas 1981a.

Frieze, I. H. and Bar-Tal, D. (1979). Attribution theory: past and present. In Frieze *et al.* 1979.

Frieze, I. H., Bar-Tal, D., and Carroll, J. S. (eds.) (1979). *New approaches to social problems*. San Francisco: Jossey Bass.

Harvey, J. H., Ickes, W., and Kidd, R. (eds.) (1976). *New directions in attribution research*, vol. 1. Hillsdale, NJ: Lawrence Erlbaum.

Harvey, J. H., Ickes, W., and Kidd, R. (eds.) (1978). *New directions in attribution research*, vol. 2. Hillsdale, NJ: Lawrence Erlbaum.

Harvey, J. H., Ickes, W., and Kidd, R. (eds.) (1981). *New directions in attribution research*, vol. 3. Hillsdale, NJ: Lawrence Erlbaum.

Hastie, R., Ostrom, T., Ebbesen, E., Wyer, R., Hamilton, D., and Carlston, D. (eds.) (1980). *Person memory: the cognitive basis of social perception*. Hillsdale, NJ: Lawrence Erlbaum.

Heider, F. (1958). *The psychology of interpersonal relations*. New York: Wiley.

Higgins, E. T., Herrman, C. P., and Zanna, M. P. (eds.) (1981). *Social cognition: the Ontario symposium*, vol. 1. Hillsdale, NJ: Lawrence Erlbaum.

Higgins, E. T. and King, G. (1981). Accessibility of social constructs: information processing consequences of individual and contextual variability. In N. Cantor and J. F. Kihstrom (eds.), *Personality, cognition, and social interaction*. Hillsdale, NJ: Lawrence Erlbaum.

James, W. (1890). *The principles of psychology*, vol. 1. London: Macmillan.

Jones, E. E. and Davis, K. E. (1965). From acts to dispositions: the attribution process in person perception. In L. Berkowitz (ed.), *Advances in experimental social psychology*, vol. 2. New York: Academic Press.

Jones, E. E., Kanause, D. I., Kelley, H. H., Nisbett, R. E., Valins, S., and Weiner, B. (eds.) (1972). *Attribution: perceiving the causes of behavior*. Morristown, NJ: General Learning Press.

Kelley, H. H. (1967). Attribution theory in social psychology. In D. Levine (ed.),

Nebraska symposium on motivation, vol. 15. Lincoln: University of Nebraska Press.

Kelley, H. H. (1971). *Attribution in social interaction.* New York: General Learning Press.

Kelley, H. H. (1972). *Causal schemata in the attribution process.* New York: General Learning Press.

Kelley, H. H. and Michela, J. L. (1980). Attribution theory and research. *Annual Review of Psychology* 31, 457–501.

Kruglanski, A. W. (1980). Lay epistemo-logic – process and contents: Another look at attribution theory. *Psychological Review* 87, 70–87.

Kruglanski, A. W. (in press). *Basic processes in social cognition: A theory of lay epistemology.* New York: Plenum.

Kruglanski, A. W. and Ajzen, I. (1983). Bias and error in human judgment. *European Journal of Social Psychology* 13, 1–44.

Kruglanski, A. W. and Klar, Y. (1987). A view from a bridge: synthesizing the consistency and attribution paradigms from a lay epistemic perspective. *European Journal of Social Psychology* 17, 211–41.

Kuhn, T. S. (1970). *The structure of scientific revolutions*, 2nd edn. Chicago: University of Chicago Press.

Lakatos, I. and Musgrave, A. (eds.) (1970). *Criticism and the growth of knowledge.* Cambridge: Cambridge University Press.

Landman, J. and Manis, M. (1983). Social cognition: some historical and theoretical perspectives. In L. Berkowitz (ed.), *Advances in experimental social psychology*, vol. 16. New York: Academic Press.

McGuire, W. J. (1983). A contextualist theory of knowledge: its implications for innovation and reform in psychological research. In L. Berkowitz (ed.), *Advances in experimental social psychology*, vol. 16. New York: Academic Press.

Merton, R. K. (1957). *Social theory and social structure.* New York: Free Press.

Neisser, U. (1980). On "social knowing". *Personality and Social Psychology Bulletin* 6, 601–5.

Polanyi, M. (1958). *Personal knowledge.* Chicago: University of Chicago Press.

Russell, B. (1948). *Human knowledge.* London: George Allen & Unwin.

Ryle, G. (1949). *The concept of mind.* New York: Barnes & Noble.

Scheerer, M. (1954). Cognitive theory. In G. Lindzey (ed.), *Handbook of social psychology.* Cambridge, Mass.: Addison-Wesley.

Showers, C. and Cantor, N. (1985). Social cognition: a look at motivated strategies. *Annual Review of Psychology* 36, 275–305.

Simon, H. A. (1976). Discussion: cognition and social behavior. In J. S. Carroll and J. W. Payne (eds.), *Cognition and social behavior.* Hillsdale, NJ: Lawrence Erlbaum.

Sorrentino, R. M. and Higgins, E. T. (eds.) (1986). *Handbook of motivation and cognition.* New York: Guilford Press.

Stark, W. (1977). *The sociology of knowledge.* London: Routledge & Kegan Paul.

Taylor, S. E. (1981). The interface of cognitive and social psychology. In

J. H. Harvey (ed.) *Cognition, social behavior, and the environment*. Hillsdale, NJ: Lawrence Erlbaum.

Weary, G., Swanson, H., Harvey, J. H., and Yarkin, K. L. (1980). A molar approach to social knowing. *Personality and Social Psychology Bulletin* 6, 574–81.

Wyer, R. S. and Srull, T. K. (eds.) (1984). *Handbook of social cognition*, 3 vols. Hillsdale, NJ: Lawrence Erlbaum.

Zajonc, R. B. (1968). Cognitive theories in social psychology. In G. Lindzey and E. Aronson (eds.), *The handbook of social psychology*, 2nd edn., vol. 1. Reading, Mass.: Addison-Wesley.

Zajonc, R. B. (1980). Cognition and social cognition: a historical perspective. In L. Festinger (ed.), *Retrospections on social psychology*. New York: Oxford University Press.

2 From knowledge to cognition[1]

Carl F. Graumann

We are seekers for truth but we are not its possessors. (Karl R. Popper)

Introduction

When, years after social psychology has come to be almost synonymous with cognitive social psychology, we are all of a sudden confronted with the title "social psychology of knowledge" the question suggests itself: what is the relationship between cognition and knowledge? Are we presented with another synonymy, so that the social psychology of knowledge *is* cognitive social psychology re-dressed or merely relabeled? Or is the social psychology of knowledge a subdivision of a comprehensive cognitive social psychology? The reader of this volume, and also this author, may or may not be more knowledgeable after reading this book. But, independently, the question of the relationship between knowledge and cognition has its own intrinsic interest both historically and systematically. In order to demonstrate this double interest I shall argue that the psychological concept of cognition has historically undergone several changes the general direction of which, in a nutshell, is: from knowledge to cognition. Not that "knowledge" was the original term and "cognition" its modern successor; it was "cognition" from the beginning. Only the meaning or usage has changed in the indicated direction. Some of these changes have been documented elsewhere (Graumann and Sommer 1984), mainly the changes in emphasis, as from gestalt-like cognitive structures (Scheerer 1954) through cognitive dynamics (Zajonc 1968) to the recent information-processing conception (Wyer and Srull 1980). These changes have been recognized and (partly) acknowledged as progress by others (Markus and Zajonc 1985) and, there-

1 The author is grateful for the critical comments that Daniel Bar-Tal, Ken Gergen, and Arie Kruglanski made on the earlier draft of this chapter.

fore, need not be described again in detail. Only their significance for social psychological thought will later be discussed. Since "knowledge" has never been a technical term in psychology (nor were its German equivalents *Erkenntnis* or *Wissen*), and has only recently been adopted by cognitivists, we are still free to think and to propose what a social psychology of knowledge could be, depending on how broadly or narrowly we prefer to conceive of both knowledge and social psychology. To propose a social psychology of knowledge, however, implies that so far it does not yet exist.

The present situation

For most contemporary social psychologists it goes without saying that social psychology "is" and "is to be" cognitive. Whatever has been named the "cognitive turn" or even the "cognitive revolution" has become such a movement that an historiographer of our discipline is reminded of the behaviorist revolution, and the spokesmen of the new era indulge in the language of power politics when we read that "an ever-increasing cognitive imperialism" (Markus and Zajonc 1985: 141) is reigning now, that cognition dominates social psychology (Zajonc 1980), and that we are under "the sovereignty of social cognition" (Ostrom 1984). It fits the quasi-political scenario that observers now witness (and are amused by) a conspicuous bandwagon effect: there have been those who claim to have been first on the band wagon ever since Lewin, who indeed Americanized his concept of *Erkenntnis* into "cognition". Early adherents, originally influenced by gestalt psychologists, remember that they had emphasized the role of cognition in behavior when other recent cognitivists were still proud to be behaviorists. In addition, they are irritated by those cognitive psychologists who, under the impact of cognitive science, have adopted the information-processing view. Working under the so-called "computational metaphor", they feel and sometimes indicate that only observance of the information-processing paradigm makes a social psychologist really "cognitive". Without counting the various types or tokens of cognitive psychology, their variety is at least as rich as was once that of learning (or S–R) theory.

On the surface it seems possible to reduce the ambiguity of the favorite attribute "cognitive" by introducing the distinction between a procedural and a topical usage. The latter then refers to the field of "cognition" as distinct from other fields like "emotion" or "motivation" or "small group research". The procedural usage, on the other hand, refers to the cognitivist approach to any psychological topic; psychology here becomes almost synonymous with the study of information processing (Lindsay and Norman 1977), and hence a branch of cognitive science.

I agree with Srull and Wyer (1984) that this conceptual distinction is helpful, but a second glance reveals that it is this very distinction that introduces new problems. If cognition were a topic in its own right, i.e. a more or less distinguishable field of psychological research among others, then this distinction would become blurred if all other fields of psychology became "cognitized", i.e. treated as if emotions, evaluations, preferences, and the many modes of motivation were but varieties or "special cases" of information processing. I shall not discuss here whether this is fully possible, but Schachter's theory of emotion (Schachter 1964) and the Atkinson–McClelland–Weiner–Heckhausen theory of motivation (Heckhausen 1980) are suggestive cases of the new cognitivism, which is replacing the old behaviorism. (It would also be interesting to enter into a comparison between the two recent isms; surface differences are more than outweighed by "deep structure" similarities, but this is only a side issue of the present topic; cf., however, Gergen 1985.)

The other reason why the distinction between a topical and a procedural usage of the term "cognitive" is not so helpful as it should be is the fuzziness of the term "cognition". A considerable literature has been accumulating on this topic in the last few years. One essential issue of the controversy is between "information processors" and "ecologists" (Knowles and Smith, 1982)[2] on the nature of *perception* (including social perception). Is it cognitive? Does cognition include perception, is it part of it or superimposed? Or has "cognition" merely replaced the earlier "perception" (Ostrom 1984: 8)? Is it psychologically correct to say that I see a house, a horse, or my friend? Or do I have to say that I "cognize" them? Is it permissible to speak of social perception, person perception, speech perception? All this may be subsumed under cognition, but the distinction between perception and cognition has so far survived the information-processing paradigm.

For Neisser (1976: 4) perception is a "hypothetical" stage of cognition, which term in turn "refers to all the processes by which the sensory input is transformed, reduced, elaborated, stored, recovered, and used", and he adds that these cognitive processes operate even "in the absence of relevant stimulation, as in images and hallucinations". The distinctive feature of all these processes is "*construction*" (1976: 10), as exemplified in the chapters on "visual cognition" dealing with iconic storage, verbal coding, template matching in pattern recognition, etc. Construction is the use made of "stimulus information" by means of internal mechanisms and operations,

2 Also, the larger part of the symposium on "Social Knowing", as represented in vol. 6, no. 4 of the *Personality and Social Psychology Bulletin* (1980), deals with the ecological versus information-processing approach to "social knowing", a term chosen to cover both perception and cognition.

partly borrowed from programming. Although reference is made occasionally to "stimulus information", we do not learn how much "information" is in the stimulus, the proximal as compared with the distal stimulus. Is there information *in* the environment to be picked up by means of our sense organs as Gibson (1979) maintains? Does perceiving include picking up information *from* the environment or is it primarily construction? Gergen (1985: 542) finds Neisser "agonizing" in limbo between the "exogenic" and "endogenic" perspective. For many cognitive (social) psychologists the possible distinction between perception and cognition is no problem at all; they have restricted their models to what is going on between input and output. Information-processing, then, is – to paraphrase Brunswik's critique of Lewin's field approach (Brunswik 1943: 266) – "postperceptual and prebehavioral". Ecological validity is none of their concern.

Not only perception but also *learning* has remained in the twilight zone: textbooks on cognitive psychology and on information processing (e.g. Neisser 1967, Lachman *et al.* 1979) will contain various chapters on memory, but none on learning – an almost compulsory reversal of the former behaviorist textbook bias with lots on learning but almost nothing on memory. But if cognition is held to be synonymous with information processing, is not learning one important way of such processing? Is learning not another word for the acquisition of knowledge? Even if this is not exactly the Hullian or Skinnerian way of putting it, must a cognitivist be as reluctant to deal with learning as a behaviorist was with respect to cognition? The author of "A Glossary of Some Terms Used in the Objective Science of Behavior", William Verplanck, risked a joke when he confessed to remaining ignorant of what a cognition is "so far as he knows, he has never had one, and no one has ever been able to correct him on this, or tell him how to have one, or how to recognize it if he did" (Verplanck 1957, pt. 2). Maybe it is the behaviorist (or S–R) heritage that has placed a kind of taboo on learning for the cognitivist, much as mentalist or introspectionist terms had once been tabooed by the behaviorist.

Similar to the dissociation of perception and cognition, that of learning and cognition may be due to the turn from behaviorist *peripheralism* to cognitivist *centralism*. Although I agree with the late Dalbir Bindra (1984) who questioned the novelty of most "intended meanings" of "cognitive", insisting that behaviorism was not always peripheralist, definitely not in the era of mediationism, it is true that for most behavior theorists the explanatory emphasis was on the environment, in interaction with the sensory and motor periphery of organisms. While in cognitive psychology the acquisition of knowledge is conceived of in terms of information processing *within* a system capable of encoding, recoding, storing, and retrieving information, in the language of behaviorism learning was equivalent "to exhibiting a change in behavior between two successive exposures to the same environment that cannot be attributed to manipulation of drive operations", to disease, growth, physical trauma, etc. (Verplanck 1957, pt. 2: 20). Is it this external view, by contrast with an internal one, which accounts for the seeming incompatibility of the two discourses? If from behaviorist *externalism* the pendulum has swung back to a new kind of *internalism*, we should try to understand the new swing better by comparing it with the old one, from mentalist internalism to behaviorist externalism. Is the movement, if circular, spiral-shaped (Srull and Wyer 1984), ever attaining new levels of knowledge? Or is it, to use a more "behavioral" metaphor, the rotating motion of a treadmill? In any case, the shift from external to internal view has not only happened, it was meant to happen. And it was meant to be as radical as the behaviorist viewpoint. Then, all behavior was in terms of stimuli and responses. Now, "every psychological phenomenon is a cognitive phenomenon" (Neisser 1967: 4). In principle, the new internalist view has become and has remained the perspective of all strictly cognitivist psychologists. Their major (or even exclusive) concern has been the structures and processes by which input is transformed within an information-processing system.

It is from this perspective that we should try to understand what cognition was meant to signify when it was introduced into psychology and what has become of it.

Cognition: the transcending mind

It may be wise to begin with William James. He is not only one of the first psychologists to introduce and to define cognition as a psychological construct. He was influential enough, via his *Principles* of 1890, to be considered as ancestor by such strikingly different psychological schools as behaviorism and phenomenological psychology (Linschoten 1968). But at the same time James had remained a philosopher, at least in some important respects, one of which is that he still cared for conceptual clarity. So when he introduced cognition as a central term of his psychology, he took it from his philosophical heritage. That, however, means that he had to choose between two conceptions of *mind*, cognition being a function of the mind.

One was the conception of an immanent mind, one of a transcending mind. Since I cannot here explore the various philosophical schools that influenced psychological thought in the nineteenth century, I will briefly state that there was the epistemological theory of *immanentism* which placed reality as the correlate of all experience inside our mind or consciousness, which later, in the tradition of Locke, was an immaterial entity containing ideas or any other mental elements or contents. So all objects of knowledge are "in" the mind, and the mind is something "in" the body; both have a quasi-spatial immanence. Immanence never was a very clear and unambiguous term, but the idea of immanence had a strong and lasting impact on psychology. When the latter was established as a science of mind or consciousness, its field of research comprised contents and processes, sought, by means of introspection, *inside*. Ideas, thoughts, feelings, motives were conceived as entities and processes, *contained* in a container-like mind. In modern terms we would have to say that they were all *intra-systemic* events. I emphasize this internalist or immanentist view of the mind as it was held by most mainstream mentalists of the time, since I maintain that modern cognitivism, in its movement away from behaviorism, tends to relapse into the pit of immanentism, from which behaviorism had vainly tried to rescue psychology. If cognition is, again, something occurring *inside* a system, mental or physical, we are epistemologically back where we were one hundred years ago. In this respect (though not in others), cognitivism is but a modern version of immanentist mentalism.

But there was (and for centuries had been) another conception of mind and of cognition, definitely *non*-immanent. It may be tempting to go back to the "dark" Middle Ages and refer to Thomas Aquinas (1980, qu. 2, ar. 5, ag. 15), who in his *Summa theologica* stated "cognitio est media inter cognoscentem et obiectum" ("cognition is the middle between the knowing and the object"), but that would not be quite fair, since the soul was still then thought to be of divine origin and, although living in a mortal body, participating in the divine.

I would rather skip philosophical schools and ask you to look into James's *Principles*, where I think the alternative tradition becomes manifest. James's conception of cognition has to be considered together with his conception of mind or consciousness. In the latter he anticipated, as Linschoten has shown, phenomenology. Consciousness, for example, is characterized as relation with and presence to objects. "In some manner our consciousness is 'present' to everything with which it is in relation" (1890, 1: 214).

It is not *in* our mind or consciousness that we "represent" objects that may or may not exist outside our mind. Mind itself *is* this relation and presence or, to use the awkward term, transcendence – reaching beyond. Our presence to everything with which we are in relation can be of two kinds:

I am *cognitively* present to Orion whenever I perceive that constellation, but I am not *dynamically* present there, I work no effects" (ibid.). Dynamically we are present in any action, viz. by means of our body. By our mind we are related to other objects in terms of *cognitive* or *emotional* relations. The mind *knows* them and "inwardly *welcomes or rejects* them". (James 1890, I: 216)

When James decided to use the term "thought" for consciousness in general he was, on the one hand, following Descartes's usage of the cogito for the whole of mind. On the other hand, he gave as his reason that "thought" suggests the omnipresence of cognition (or reference to an object other than the mental state itself), which he calls the "essence" of mental life (I: 186). Here, in his conception of cognition, James almost literally anticipates the phenomenological definition of intentionality. Later too, in his criteria of the "stream of thought", we find the proposition: "*Human thought appears to deal with objects independent of itself; that is, it is cognitive, or possesses the function of knowing*" (271). Hence, not everything "mental" is cognitive in and by itself; it becomes cognitive (or "knowing") only by reference to independent reality.

But how do we ever attain reality, i.e. get at the extramental existence of what we are referring to? The reasons James gives are in the variety of thoughts having the *same* objects, and in the variety and vividness of relations to our mind something may have (James 1890, II: 298). In the first case, interpersonal judgment attributes cognition and reality: "The judgment that *my* thought has the same object as *his* thought is what makes the psychologist call my thought cognitive of an outer reality" (I: 272). Language or communication is implied here, but not made explicit by James. Yet there is "sameness in a multiplicity of objective appearances" that ultimately establishes our belief in something beyond or outside our acts of believing – something which by virtue of this independence we call "real" (I: 272). Here it becomes evident for the first time that what we call "real" is subjectively constituted as objectively being there. The other way to know an object as real or, more generally, to confer reality on something is the establishment of immediate practical or dynamic relations between an object and ourselves (II: 296). Reality is attained by cognitive or dynamic relations; conversely, cognition is reference to or relation with independent reality.

It is important to see that the autonomy or independence of all things we call "real" and treat as real (cf. Graumann 1974) is of our own constitution. "The fons and origo of all reality, whether from the absolute or the practical point of view, is thus subjective, is ourselves" (II: 296–7). There are degrees or levels of "reality" depending on whether merely cognition or, in addition, emotion, volition, and actions are involved. Since knowing always "supposes two elements, mind knowing and thing known" (I: 218) and hence is an irreducible relation, there are also degrees or levels of knowing.

One distinction worth remembering is between *knowledge of acquaintance* and *knowledge about* (the *kennen/wissen, connaître/savoir* distinction). We may be acquainted with many persons and things, but it is only about a few that we have proper knowledge.

I know the color blue when I see it, and the flavor of a pear when I taste it . . . an effort of attention when I make it; a difference between two things when I notice it; but *about* the inner nature of these facts or what makes them what they are, I can say nothing at all. (I: 221)

If we have to communicate their attributes of reality we are at a loss if we try to describe them. What we can do is to tell people, "Go certain places and act in certain ways, and these objects will probably come" (I: 22). So we tell people what to *do* in order to *know*. Very often knowledge of acquaintance is acquired by acting. Even knowledge about is gained by activity; we subject an object's relation "to a sort of *treatment*" and we "operate upon it with our thought" (I: 222).

The emphasis on acting gives a new perspective to the difference between *feeling* and *thought* as merely gradual: "Through feelings we become acquainted with things, but only by our thoughts do we know about them" (I: 222). There is a cognitive function in feeling, knowing, and acting.

I feel I should stop here: James's *Principles* are a horn of plenty for those forced to live on the meager diet of modern textbooks. What I have tried to show is that cognition when introduced into psychology about one hundred years ago still referred to the processes and products of knowing. Mind, whose nature it is *to be present to* everything we are related to, turned out to be a relational, transcendent term. Reality in its different degrees and modalities of "realness" and testability was part and parcel of the concept of knowledge, rather than knowledge (cognition) being a state of one system and reality an opposed and separate system or mere system environment. Cognition originally means knowing or what is known. We may call this the *epistemic function* of cognition. If knowing refers to something known to exist independently of the act of knowing, knowing ultimately is definable only by including reality terms: we justify our knowledge by acting accordingly, not by any ultimate truths or superior authorities. Ultimately, there are no objective criteria to prove the truth of any cognitions; there is no other "objectivity" than what our own actions will yield as "objectively there".

James was not a founder of a psychological school of thought. After the *Principles* and their *Briefer Course*, "Jimmy" James returned to philosophy. His conception of experience as the cognitive and dynamic presence to all things we are in relation with was continued and elaborated in phenomenology, but remained relatively uninfluential in psychology. The immanentist conception of a consciousness containing elements and their combinations, severed from outer or any reality, was rightly attacked by the behaviorists, who had learned part of their pragmatic attitude from James and the other pragmatists. The deliberate exorcism of all things mental and a preoccupation with animal learning prohibited or inhibited any behaviorist concern with problems of knowledge. But when behaviorism turned cognitive via the various "neo" and "neoneo" variants, cognitions, then labeled mediators or mediating mechanisms and blushingly declared to be mere hypothetical constructs, were as encapsulated in an otherwise black box as were Wundt's and his students' elements of consciousness. Not Skinner's operants, but Osgood's, Bousfield's and Berlyne's mediating r–s sequences were – in spite of the S–R terminology – cut off from any observable reality. There was not even an introspectionist peep-hole to pierce the darkness of the box, which gradually, as the Lachmans have shown (Lachman *et al.* 1979), developed into an information-processing system which may have lost some of this darkness but has retained the containing character of the box. It is true that S and R have been replaced by input and output of information, but the reality beyond, i.e. outside the system, has theoretical existence only as its own representation inside the system.

Unfortunately, there is little concern for the key concept of information among the adherents of the information-processing paradigm. In one of the leading textbooks of psychology, titled *Human information processing: an introduction to psychology* (Lindsay and Norman 1977), the authors do everything to convince their readers that psychology is synonymous with the study of information processing. But they fail to supply a definition of information, nor is it an indexed term. In several other leading texts, information and cognition go undefined. Glass, Holyoak, and Santa (1979: 2), who equate "cognitive psychology" with "the study of knowledge", try to justify why the former may also be called "information-processing psychology" with reference to the alleged synonymity of "information" and "knowledge". Yet are we wrong in assuming that knowledge is not a feature of the external (stimulus) world, but a product of information processing, encoded and stored in persons' memories, whereas information may be picked up from the environment? If information is made synonymous with knowledge it must also be treated in that way, as an intrapersonal or intrasystemic state of affairs (leaving "external memories" aside). But this usage is at variance with the meaning of information that was originally introduced into psychology, for example, by George A. Miller (1951). He had defined information as "the occurrence of one out of a set of alternative discriminative stimuli" (41), still in accordance with the mathematical theory of information (Shannon and Weaver 1949) in which information is the opposite of uncertainty, but nevertheless only a quantity. In spite of the fact that the information processed in computers, which serve as analogues of cognition, still obeys the logic of information theory, one has the impression that the concept of information as used in present cognitivist theorizing is the untechnical everyday word which lay people use interchangeably with "knowledge": *I have no knowledge of x = I have no information about x.* But whereas in ordinary language both information and knowledge have objective reference, i.e. point to the objective world, we miss this referential (or intentional) feature in most recent information-processing models concentrating on the "universe within" (Hunt 1982).

It must be emphasized that the critique of a relapse into immanentism or self-encapsulation is levelled, not against any cognitive theories in general experimental or social psychology, but against those theories which conceive of the human mind as an information-processing system the theory of which does not explicitly account for *the referential character of knowing*, no matter whether the label "cognition" or "knowledge" is used. It is true that some cognitive (social) psychologists do not go along with the "development" from "cognition" to "information processing". But do attribution theorists, for example, theoretically account for the referential character of knowledge? Is not the knowledge *presupposed* that Peter is not under external constraints, that he has the ability to perform a certain act, etc.? Jones and Davis's (1965) theory of "correspondent inferences" is in fact about making inferences, i.e. about internal ("mental" or "cognitive") processing. As such it may be an important contribution to our understanding of inference (and so are related approaches), but it presupposes social knowledge rather than accounting for it. Here exactly is the unfinished task for a social psychology of knowledge which must be able to make use of both traditions in the psychological study of cognition: from the inside and from the outside.

Cognition: from outside

To look for knowledge and cognition inside closed minds and systems has been the rule in mentalism and cognitivism, to conceive of mind as openness and presence the exception. There have been attempts, though, to understand cognition and knowledge from outside which deserve some attention. I am talking about behaviorism, but not of the "neoneo" kind. Two examples will do: Tolman and Skinner. For both, the reality outside is not the social reality of, say, phenomenology; it is the physical environment of stimuli. And whatever is called cognition (in Tolman 1932) or knowledge (in Skinner 1976) is under the control of such environment. So loss of reality or self-encapsulation is not their problem. It is well known that while Tolman dared to speculate about the internal correspondences of behavior–environment contingencies, Skinner tries to remain chaste. Accordingly, for Skinner (1976) knowing is a very restricted term: ultimately, all knowledge is *knowing how to* and is practically synonymous with behavior that someone can execute (151–3). Knowing *about* something for Skinner is knowing how to. "We know about electricity if we can work successfully, verbally or otherwise, with electrical things" (152). Here Ryle's useful distinction between knowing-how-to and knowing-that (Ryle 1949) is behaviorally collapsed. Knowledge is not a disposition. "We do not act by putting knowledge to use; our knowledge *is* action, or at least rules for action" (Skinner 1976: 154). And it makes perfect behavioristic sense to confirm (Francis Bacon and Karl Marx) that knowledge is power: "Operant behavior is essentially the exercise of power: it has an effect on the environment" (Skinner 1976: 154).

I must refrain from critically analyzing the hidden phenomenology of such radical behaviorism (cf. Kvale and Grenness 1975). It is merely the swing of the pendulum that took us to this other extreme of a radical externalization of the knowledge problem, anchoring knowledge and cognition as deeply as possible in the outer world. I would argue that we could even do better than the radical behaviorist by means of a less restrictive, i.e. more ecological, concept of the environment. Tolman (1932) was on the road to such conception when he tried to be a *cognitive* behaviorist. He realized that he could not do without inner determinants of behavior (which, by the way, he called "immanent"). But they had to be inferred from the observed interchange between behavior acts and environmental features ("commerce-with"). The two major classes of such inferred "determinants" of behavior were cognition and purpose. Assuming that Tolman's theory is still well remembered, I need not go into details. But I would like to stress that Tolman's "environment" differed fundamentally from Skinner's. For behavior to be recognized as "cognitive", it must be shown to be contingent upon environmental features of the manipulanda, discriminanda, and means–end relations type.

This means that the environment, physical as it may be, is basically defined in terms of "behavior supports". Gibson (1979) very much later spoke of "affordances" or, more explicitly, of tripartite "signgestalten", i.e. the signified interrelationship between sign objects and signified objects. Cognition, then, as well as purpose, is inferred from a *semiotically* interpreted environment. The art of the researcher is to describe the environment from the organism's or individual's perspective, not from the researcher's own view. (The latter was described by James (1890, I: 196) as the "psychologist's fallacy".)

Again, we discover in Tolman's behaviorism and in his environment-guided conception of cognition a "kryptophenomenology", a term which he later adopted (from W. Köhler) for his own position (Tolman 1959: 147). However "mindless" behaviorism in general tried to become, the more or less radical externalization of all mental states and processes was intentionally one-sided. Yet it was a type of one-sidedness (or bias) that tried vainly to make up for the deficiencies of the complementary one-sidedness of mentalist immanentism.

It is my impression that the so-called "cognitive turn", to the degree that it is a deliberate turning away from the externalism (environmentalism) of behaviorist psychology, is in danger of giving up the positive heritage, one aspect of which was the discovery of what today I would call "the ecology of experience and behavior". The remedy, though, is not another "turn", nor even a return to behaviorism. But unless the new immanentism of information-processing systems is not conceptually and theoretically overcome, the present neglect of ecological validity brings forth a renewed neglect or even loss of reality in psychological science. Cognition, however, which theoretically is not based in the reality we know *about* so much as in the knowing subject, is deprived of its essential function: knowledge, be it knowledge of the world, about the world, or how to cope with the world.

Individual cognition and social knowledge

In conclusion I would like to discuss one very important implication of all forms of immanentism, old or new, hard or soft.[3] It is the social deprivation that normally goes under the name of *individualism*. Without looking back over the long tradition of theoretical and methodological individualism in psychology whose ideological character has recently been critically analyzed by Billig (1982), I will concentrate on modern cognitive social psychology with its overall emphasis on internal processes and structures. In this emphasis, cognitive social psychology is no different from cognitive general experimental psychology, with which it shares many models. Positive as this close relationship is for a unitary conception of psychology, the question to be asked is: "What is social about social cognition?" (Forgas 1981a).

The usual answer given is that we call those cognitions "social" that "represent" other people or maybe social structures and systems. The problem is then reduced to the question whether there is any general difference between, say, *my* cognition of a natural or artificial object and that of my

3 "Hard" refers to the information-processing paradigm, "soft" to the host of other theories and models of social cognition not under the rule of the "computational metaphor".

uncle. If it is only a matter of content, the difference between social and nonsocial cognition is conceptually as trivial as was once the distinction made between a physical and a social stimulus when a social stimulus was a physical stimulus originating in another person, or rather "organism". Also, relationships between cognitions (as of dissonance) do not necessarily refer to social or interpersonal phenomena: they may refer to any "association" of two things or events. Unless we think primarily of *consequences* in terms of social behavior, i.e. behavior with respect to others, there would be no need nor legitimation to assign many of the favorite cognitive theories (on dissonance, self-perception, objective self-awareness, heuristics, lay epistemology, symbolic self-completion, information processing) to a field called social psychology. In and by themselves, these theories are as individual-centered as those of general experimental psychology. It may even be that, as Forgas (1981b: 260) states, "the recently emerging social cognition paradigm turned out to be even more individualistic and psychologistic than its predecessor".

A social psychology of knowledge, however, should be more than a mere extension of the general experimental psychology of cognition. Knowledge itself is social, be it by definition or by usage. I may have ideas, feelings, notions, hunches that I would not call knowledge. To consider something as knowledge presupposes that I know what the criteria or norms of knowledge are, in, I hasten to add, our culture and contemporary society. Not every mental content or rather its resulting utterance will be credited as (indicative of) knowledge. Whatever one's own or other people's reasons are for "acknowledging" a proposition or an activity as knowledgeable, it is these (explicit or implicit) social criteria and norms that make knowledge what it currently is. Currently, of course, means that today's knowledge may be tomorrow's unwarranted belief. We are all aware, since we went to school, that a large part of the knowledge of former times, including that of our own former time, has now to be put between inverted commas.

Sociologists of knowledge have long realized that such changing norms of knowledge, mainly of the "common stock of knowledge" (Schutz 1962), are an essential part of what we may call the social constitution of reality (Berger and Luckmann 1967). To the degree that knowledge is about reality and knowing is, in principle, referring to reality, knowledge is inseparable from its social context. Hence there is no absolute and objective knowledge other than knowledge posited as "absolute" and "objective" by our society. A social psychological concept of knowledge is different from the technical term of abstract epistemology. It cannot be rooted in an individualistic and immanentist cognitive social psychology, but must be conceptualized in accordance with and in the framework of a social theory of knowledge. The social representation approach (Moscovici and Farr 1983) is a promising sign that you do not have to give up psychology in order to investigate social knowledge.

References

Aquinas, Thomas (1980). *Opera omnia*, vol. 3. Stuttgart: Frommann–Holzboog.

Berger, P. and Luckman, T. (1967). *The social construction of reality*. London: Allen Lane.

Billig, M. (1982). *Ideology and social psychology: extremism, moderation and contradiction*. Oxford: Blackwell.

Bindra, D. (1984). Cognition: its origin and future in psychology. In J. R. Royce and L. P. Mos (eds.), *Annals of theoretical psychology*, vol. 1. New York: Plenum.

Brunswik, E. (1943). Organismic achievement and environmental probability. *Psychological Review* 50: 255–72.

Forgas, J. P. (1981a). What is social about social cognition? In J. P. Forgas (ed.), *Social cognition*. London: Academic Press.

Forgas, J. P. (1981b). Epilogue: everyday understanding and social cognition. In J. P. Forgas (ed.), *Social cognition*. London: Academic Press.

Gergen, K. (1985). Social psychology and the phoenix of unreality. In S. Koch and D. E. Leary (eds.), *A century of psychology as science*. New York: McGraw-Hill.

Gibson, J. J. (1979). *The ecological approach to visual perception*. Boston: Houghton Mifflin.

Glass, A. L., Holyoak, K. J., and Santa, J. L. (1979). *Cognition*. Reading, Mass.: Addison-Wesley.

Graumann, C. F. (1974). Psychology and the world of things. *Journal of Phenomenological Psychology* 4: 389–404.

Graumann, C. F. and Sommer, M. (1984). Schema and inference, models in cognitive social psychology. In J. R. Royce and L. P. Mos (eds.), *Annals of theoretical psychology*, vol. 1. New York: Plenum Press.

Heckhausen, H. (1980). *Motivation und Handeln. Lehrbuch der Motivationspsychologie*. Heidelberg: Springer.

Hunt, M. (1982). *The universe within*. New York: Simon & Schuster.

James, W. (1890). *The principles of psychology*. 2 vols. New York: Holt.

James, W. (1892). *Psychology. Briefer Course*. New York: Holt.

Jones, E. E. and Davis, K. E. (1965). From acts to dispositions: The attribution process in social perception. In L. Berkowitz (ed.), *Advances in experimental social psychology*, vol. 11. New York: Academic Press.

Knowles, P. L. and Smith, D. L. (1982). The ecological perspective applied to social perception. *Journal for the Theory of Social Behaviour* 12: 53–78.

Kvale, S. and Grenness, C. E. (1975). Skinner and Sartre: towards a radical phenomenology of behavior? In A. Giorgi, C. T. Fisher, and E. L. Murray (eds.), *Duquesne Studies in Phenomenological Psychology*, vol. 11. Pittsburgh: Duquesne University Press.

Lachman, R., Lachman, J. L. and Butterfield, E. C. (1979). *Cognitive psychology and information processing*. Hillsdale, NJ: Lawrence Erlbaum.

Lindsay, P. H. and Norman, D. A. (1977). *Human information processing. An introduction to psychology*, 2nd edn. New York: Academic Press.

Linschoten, J. (1968). *On the way toward a phenomenological psychology: the psychology of William James*. Pittsburgh, PA: Duquesne University Press.

Markus, H. and Zajonc, R. B. (1985). The cognitive perspective in social psychology. In G. Lindzey and E. Aronson (eds.), *The handbook of social psychology*, 3rd. edn. New York: Random House.

Miller, G. A. (1951). *Language and communication*. New York: McGraw-Hill.

Moscovici, S. and Farr, R. M. (eds.), *Social representations*. Cambridge/Paris: Cambridge University Press/Maison des Sciences de l'Homme.

Neisser, U. (1967). *Cognitive psychology*. New York: Appleton-Century-Crofts.

Neisser, U. (1976). *Cognition and reality*. San Francisco: Freeman.

Ostrom, T. M. (1984). The sovereignty of social cognition. In R. S. Wyer and T. K. Srull (eds.), *Handbook of social cognition*, vol. 1. Hillsdale, NJ: Lawrence Erlbaum.

Ryle, G. (1949). *The concept of mind*. London: Hutchinson.

Schachter, S. (1964). The interaction of cognitive and physiological determinants of emotional state. In L. Berkowitz (ed.), *Advances in experimental social psychology*, vol. 1. New York: Academic Press.

Scheerer, M. (1954). Cognitive theory. In G. Lindzey (ed.), *Handbook of social psychology*, vol. 1. Cambridge, Mass.: Addison-Wesley.

Schutz, A. (1962). *Collected papers*, vol. 1. The Hague: Nijhoff.

Shannon, C. E. and Weaver, W. (1949). *The mathematical theory of communication*. Urbana: University of Illinois Press.

Skinner, B. F. (1976). *About behaviorism*. New York: Random/Vintage.

Srull, T. K. and Wyer, R. S. (1984). Progress and problems in cognitive social psychology. In J. R. Royce and L. P. Mos (eds.), *Annals of theoretical psychology*, vol. 1. New York: Plenum Press.

Tolman, E. C. (1932) *Purposive behavior in animals and men*. New York: Appleton-Century-Crofts.

Tolman, E. C. (1959). Principles of purposive behavior. In S. Koch (ed.), *Psychology: a study of a science*, Vol. 1. New York: McGraw-Hill.

Verplanck, W. S. (1957). A glossary of some terms used in the objective science of behavior. *Supplement to the Psychological Review* 64 (6), pt. 2.

Wyer, R. S. and Srull, T. K. (1980). The processing of social stimulus information. A conceptual integration. In R. Hastie, T. M. Ostrom, E. B. Ebbesen, R. S. Wyer, Jr., D. L. Hamilton, and D. E. Carlston (eds.), *Person memory: the cognitive basis of social perception*. Hillsdale, NJ: Lawrence Erlbaum.

Zajonc, R. B. (1968). Cognitive theories in social psychology. In G. Lindzey and E. Aronson (eds.), *The handbook of social psychology*, 2nd edn., vol. 1. Reading, Mass.: Addison-Wesley.

Zajonc, R. B. (1980). Cognition and social cognition: a historical perspective. In L. Festinger (ed.), *Retrospections on social psychology*. New York: Oxford University Press.

3 Knowledge and social process

Kenneth J. Gergen

If our concern is the understanding of knowledge, it is essential that we give initial consideration to the concept of knowledge itself. What do we take to be the nature of our subject-matter? This question is no mere philosophic précis, for the answer one provides places important limits on the forms of understanding that may subsequently be generated. In the present context we have taken as our aim the generation of knowledge about the nature of knowledge. In elucidating the object of our appraisal (what we wish to know about) we simultaneously establish the grounds upon which our formulation must rest. (I take it to be a form of intellectual mischief to define knowledge as one sort of thing but knowledge of knowledge as quite another.) In effect, the range and variations in the understanding that can be generated by our analyses will be importantly foreshadowed in the account given of the nature of knowledge itself. Most important to our proceedings, the significance we attach to social process will largely depend on how we define the nature of knowledge.

Representational versus constructionist accounts of knowledge

The present paper is hardly a vehicle for a full exegesis on the nature of knowledge; rather it is my essential aim to sketch out a particular view of the social basis of knowledge. It will prove a useful preliminary to this sketch if we consider briefly two contrasting views of the nature of knowledge. Knowledge about the world – including other persons – is commonly said to be represented in the various bodies of propositions about which there is studied assent. Current theories of nuclear fission, genetic coding, electromagnetic propagation, and the like are said to represent bodies of acceptable knowledge, while monetary theory in economics and cognitive theory in psychology hover at the threshold between opinion and knowledge. Yet how are we to understand the genesis of these various bodies of knowledge? The more traditional account, and that embraced by much psychological research, is that these bodies of knowledge are expressions of *mental representations*. That is, through various psychological processes such as sensation, attention, perception, and rational calculation, individuals develop mental representations of the world as it is. When these representations are expressed in linguistic form, and successfully tested by others who rely on their mental skills, we may satisfactorily speak of accumulated knowledge. In effect, this view holds that knowledge is the possession of single individuals (until shared), and is premised on some form of mind–material dualism (a knower and an object of knowledge). From this perspective a distinctly psychological theory of knowledge acquisition is entailed. The explanatory function in one's theory is most congenially carried by mental terms (e.g. concept formation, cognitive heuristics, information retrieval).

In contrast, we may also view these various bodies of discourse as *social constructions*. That is, they are bodies of publicly shared discourse. They may be by-products of the attempt to predict and control nature, but they are not inherently mirrors to nature. To carry out knowledgeable discourse is, on this account, a form of social performance. The implied ontology here is monist (as there is no "mental process" to be considered). Explanatory interest centers on the processes of social interchange from which judgments of the presence or absence of knowledge may proceed. The explanatory burden is likely to be carried by terms referring to various aspects of social process (e.g. negotiation, power, collusion). In effect, depending on how we view the nature of knowledge, we commit ourselves to distinctly psychological as opposed to social theories of its production.

It is also apparent that one's choice of a theory of knowledge must derive from conceptual as opposed to empirical considerations. For each attempt to vindicate a given theory of knowledge would necessarily rely on evidence that was legitimate within its own framework. Neither a representationist nor a constructionist theory of knowledge could rely on "divine inspiration" for its support, for example, as divine inspiration is not recognized as a legitimate basis of justification within either theory itself. By the same token, neither a representationist nor a constructionist could accept as convincing the evidence generated by the opposition. For the representationist all propositions are, by definition, manifestations of the psychological world; they do not exist independently of the mental domain. For the constructionist the same propositions are manifestations of the social world;

there is no mental world to be considered. Thus, by defining the world in its own terms, each side should be able to maintain itself indefinitely without empirical challenge.

For this reason it is important to give preliminary consideration to conceptual or analytic grounds of justification. If a given conception of knowledge proves problematic on analytic grounds, there is little reason to pursue its implications at the level of research. If it is impossible to justify or render intelligible a given view of knowledge in terms of its basic premises, then the ends which research are to serve become obscured.

The problematics of knowledge as representation

It is in this latter vein that Ryle (1949), among others, has raised significant questions concerning the concept of knowledge as mental process. As Ryle contends, such an assumption is an unfortunate legacy from Cartesian metaphysics; it is similar to positing ghosts in machines to understand their operation. Ryle's principal argument is that the concept of mental functioning as antecedent to overt performance ultimately commits one to a form of infinite regress. In particular, if we say that an action has been preceded by a mental process that is either silly or shrewd, intelligent or asinine, then we are forced to give an account of how the character of this process (its intelligence, shrewdness, etc.) came to be. Why is one's thinking, for example, particularly acute in a given case? This account must necessarily make use of preceding mental processes. For example, one might say that the thinking is acute because one paid close attention. In effect, one's attention was wise, or shrewd. Yet why was attention so disposed? Another well-functioning process must be posited, and so on. Or again, in the traditional dualist mode, if an action is judged to be intelligent, such intelligence is attributed to a preceding mental act, e.g. the intelligent *planning* of actions. Yet how are we to account for the fact that such planning was itself intelligent? After all, one can plan in a deficient way. As Ryle argues, the intelligence of the planning must be based on some other process from which its intelligence is borrowed – such as the intelligent consideration of priorities, memory, or foresight. Yet one then confronts the problem of accounting for the intelligence of these operations, and so on, ad infinitum.

Ryle is hardly alone in his critique of the dualistic premise. To his misgivings must be added those of Wittgenstein (1963), Austin (1962), Needham (1972) Coulter (1983), and many others. Most powerful perhaps is Richard Rorty's recent volume, *Philosophy and the mirror of nature* (1979), in which he examines the historical roots and problematic character of assuming the existence of a mind that reflects or mirrors nature.

Among other things, Rorty attempts to show that the concept of knowledge (as mental representation) was born of the attempt (primarily by Kant) to salvage philosophic study. The primary concerns of philosophy had been metaphysical; however, debate in this domain was rapidly being replaced by physical theory. What was required was a foundational discipline that could not be converted to empirical study. This could be accomplished with the doctrine of a priori ideas, said to be foundational to the framing of empirical science itself.

Elsewhere I have also attempted to examine the viability of such terms as "concept" or "mental category" or "schema" in theories of self-knowledge (Gergen 1985). In this case I have attempted to demonstrate the problem of linking mental categories or concepts with external events – on either the stimulus or the response side. At the outset there appears to be no means of understanding how environmental events (including social influence attempts) enter into the category system or schema. If all understanding requires concepts or schemas, then how could such mental dispositions be developed at the outset? Unless the dispositions were innate, there is no means by which the incoming stimuli could be understood. (For example, a mother's punishment would fail to add to a child's understanding unless the child already possessed a concept of punishment.) Similar problems plague the attempt to move from the mental world to that of behavior. How are abstract categories converted to discrete physical movements? If propositions about how one should behave require rules that specify how the propositions apply to any given circumstance, one has entered another infinite regress. Each application rule is also an abstract proposition which itself must be defined. In effect, if mental representation is assumed it is difficult to understand how real world information could enter the system or physical actions might proceed from it.

The social genesis of knowledge

The preceding arguments are not intended to foreclose on the concepts of knowledge as psychological representation. However, they do raise doubt concerning the viability of this option sufficient to invite one to consider other possibilities. In particular, it is intriguing to pursue more fully the possibility of knowledge as propositional networks inherent in a social process. This potential has not gone wholly unrealized, and indeed within recent years the social construction of knowledge has become a topic of focal concern. The intellectual forebears of contemporary inquiry would include Mannheim's (1936) ground-breaking work on the sociology of knowledge, Marx's (1967) critique of the ideological interests of capitalist economic theory, and the work of the Frankfurt school (Jay 1973) examining the class interests underlying various forms of seemingly value-neutral theory. Berger and Luckmann's broad-ranging *The social construction of reality* (1966), Georges Gurvitch's *The social frameworks of knowledge* (1971), and Jurgen Habermas's (1971) assessment of the social interests supporting the generation of scientific knowledge should also be considered fundamental.

However, it is the more recent history of thinking in this area that should be of special interest in the present context. The beginning of the watershed may be properly traced to Thomas Kuhn's *The structure of scientific revolutions* (1970). This volume managed to accomplish two important goals. The first was to offer a reasonably compelling account of scientific revolution that did not rely on empiricist philosophy of science. (Empiricist philosophy of knowledge, it should be apparent, has been the chief grounds for justifying the dualistic view of knowledge as mental representation.) As an historian of science, Kuhn shifted the focus of concern from matters of induction, hypothesis formation, deduction, verification, and refutation (traditional props in the empiricist concept of the accumulation of knowledge) to the social communities of science. Philosophy of science, in Kuhn's analysis, is replaced by a theory of sociohistorical change. Second, and more indirectly, the vast popularity of Kuhn's work has served as a more general signal that empiricist philosophy of science was rapidly becoming moribund. The philosophic assumption that theoretical propositions could be derived from or corroborated through systematic observation had come under blistering attack over the years – first by those like Popper, who remained committed to an altered form of empiricism, and later by a small army of important thinkers, including Quine (1951), Hanson (1958), Taylor (1971), Toulmin (1961), and Feyerabend (1976). There have been defenders of the old tradition but, perhaps because of the multiplicity and plausibility of the criticism, such defenses have not demanded broad attention. Instead, the intellectual community seemed vulnerable to an alternative account of knowledge – and, at least in rudimentary form, this is what Kuhn's volume provided.

With broad interest thus kindled, investigators from wide-ranging disciplines began the more arduous task of furnishing a full and coherent account of the social processes that give rise to the more formal propositions of science. This work should be of special interest to social psychologists because its concerns have largely shifted from the broad sociological level (*à la* Mannheim) to the realm of social microprocesses – that is, the ongoing, concrete relationship among practitioners of science. In effect, such work is often distinctly social psychological. Thus, for example, Barry Barnes (1974) has offered a social account of the concept of rationality in science and how it is used within subcultures of natural scientists. David Bloor (1976) has shown how the utility of formal logic and mathematics in the sciences is subject to social negotiation. Pierre Bourdieu (1975) has demonstrated how the production of scientific papers operates much like a market economy. The attempt within scientific subcultures is to accumulate *symbolic capital* in the form of published books and papers. This symbolic capital may be cashed in for numerous other resources (grants, fellowships, status). Latour and Woolgar (1979) have carried out what amounts to an anthropological field study among biochemist "natives" of the Salk Institute. As these authors contend, the production of evidence in a given scientific paradigm rests on a subtle but vital array of social microprocesses. It is through social practices that scientific order is created from disorder, and through which "a statement can be transformed into an object or a fact into an artifact" (236). In a similar vein, Karin Knorr-Cetina (1981) has carried out an ethnography of a plant protein research laboratory, and has elucidated (much as an exchange theorist might) the ways in which the exchange of resources among research participants influences the path of research. Many additional contributions could be cited – including, I might add, that of Donald Campbell (1986) on belief change in scientific collectivities.

Social construction in psychology

Although much of the work in allied disciplines has gone relatively unnoticed within the experimental wing of social psychology, it has been an important catalyst for those engaged in what may be viewed as social constructionist inquiry in social psychology (Gergen 1985, Gergen and Davis 1985). Inquiry of this sort is premised on the assumption that propositions about the world (including persons) are not (and in principle cannot be) built up inductively from observation. Rather, such propositions largely represent historically contingent conventions of intelligibility. Their truth or falsity, rationality or absurdity, reality or mysteriousness are all matters of social determination. It is in this vein, for example, that Kessler and McKenna (1978) have brought into question the seemingly incontrovertible fact that there are two genders. Averill (1983) has demonstrated how emotions are not built into the nervous system – constituents of the genetic code – but are historically situated performances. Mummendey (1984) and her colleagues have demonstrated how aggression is not a fact of social life, but rather a socially achieved agreement – the product of people negotiating about what has occurred.

A more circumscribed group, tinged in Wittgensteinian hues, has been particularly concerned with the conventions of language in the production of knowledge. Of all the social practices in which scientists are engaged, language is certainly primary. Indeed, one of the chief (some would argue the only) products of formal scientific activity is language specimens (books, papers, lectures). As indicated, these language structures cannot be derived from observation. Rather, existing language conventions form a normative forestructure for the subsequent generation of "scientific facts." Regardless of the form of one's observations in the sciences, one's measuring devices, or one's statistical tools, the final conclusions must ultimately be poured into the preformed mold of intelligible language. Regardless of the processes of social negotiation, collusion, exchange, and manipulation, this language is governed by existing conventions. These conventions will largely determine the contours of the propositions we commonly take to be knowledge.

It is in this vein that Smedslund (1985), for example, has attempted to elucidate the commonsense theorems that underlie much psychological theory. Ossorio (1985) and his colleagues have tried to lay out a set of fundamental propositions required for intelligibility in our understanding of persons. Davis and Todd (1982) have probed the commonsense components basic to accounts of intimacy. Semin and Chassein (1985) have examined the dependency of formal and statistically derived models of personality structure on existing folk models of the mind.

It is largely this form of enterprise that has occupied much of my own attention during the past several years. In particular I have been concerned with psychological discourse, its structure, origins, and functions. If such language does not mirror a world independent of it, how does it function, and what are its limitations? At the outset the attempt was to explore various forms of psychological explanation – to take systematic account of the means by which people (including professional psychologists) explain human actions (Gergen and Gergen 1982), and to ask about the pragmatic and ideological implications of competing explanatory forms. This interest was later expanded to include the study of narrative explanations – both of self and of others (Gergen and Gergen 1983). In this case the concern was with the ways various forms of story are used to inject coherence into accounts of action across time. Additional work has centered on the constraints placed on the existing ontology of mind by the pragmatic aspects of human interchange; here the attempt has been to show that major features of existing theories of mind are necessary by-products of using a verbal language (Gergen 1985a). Finally, attention has been given to both the structure and flexibility of existing ethnopsychologies. In the case of structure, the attempt has been to illuminate the linguistic structure that constrains what may be said about human action (Gergen 1984). In the case of process, we have tried to show how items on mental tests are subject to indefinite renegotiation in meaning (Gergen *et al.* 1986). Thus mental tests operate much as blank slates upon which investigators may inscribe virtually any conclusion they wish to project.

I realize this truncated summary furnishes little substance for the chewing. I thus wish to elaborate on a single thesis of some significance. The problem is an interesting one – and in important ways can be traced to Plato, Locke, and Kant. In its present form it is the problem of how we are to account for the array of commonly accepted assumptions about the relationship between the mind and the external world. We tend to assume, for example, that we possess sensations that reflect the contours of an external reality; concepts that carve the world into categories; motives, intentions, plans, and attitudes that guide or prompt our public conduct, and so on. How do such assumptions emerge in social (and scientific) life? As can be seen, this problem recapitulates an earlier theme. Specifically, the attempt here is to account for "knowing that" from the perspective of "knowing how" – to account for mind–body linkages in the traditional dualistic system by focussing on conventions of discourse. In doing so we shall understand why it is so tempting to believe that mind is interposed between our confrontation with nature and our subsequent actions.

The principle of functional circularity

At the outset one might suppose that initial assumptions concerning the relationship between mind and the external world might emerge from experience. One might build inductively from the particulars of experience to the generalities embedded in the assumptions. Yet a barrage of attacks on the inductive method of building propositions (cf. Popper 1968, Medawar 1960, Hanson 1958) make it clear that such suppositions could not be spun from the raw stuff of experience. It is also exceedingly difficult to account for such suppositions genetically; there is little reason to believe they are built into the genetic code. It is my present contention that propositions relating the mental and the physical world are essentially analytic. That is, they represent the extension of a system of linguistic equivalencies. Their truth value is neither derived from nor dependent upon observation. Rather, it is dependent on and derived from linguistic systems of definition. My proposal, which I shall call the principle of *functional circularity*, can be stated in both a general and a restricted form. The general form is also the stronger of the two: *All reasonable propositions declaring a functional linkage between mental terms and observable events are analytically true*; that is, their truth is derived from the structure of the language as opposed to their relationship to observables. Propositions of this sort might include such statements as "Whenever the volume on my stereo is high my neighbors became irritated," "When people are angry they are likely to become aggressive," or "Whenever Lorna enters the room I am overcome with emotion." The more specific rendering of the functional circularity proposal has specific application to psychological study: *All reasonable propositions declaring a functional relationship between the stimulus world and the psychological domain, or between the latter domain and subsequent action, are true by definition.* Should such a proposition prove viable, we would find the theories and research in psychology which purport to describe processes of perception, language learning, information processing, emotional expression, the relation between attitudes and behavior, the relation between thought and action, and so on are essentially products or extensions of existing language conventions. When these conventions are examined in detail, we would discover that such statements are necessary derivatives of the definitional structure. In effect, propositions within the S-O-R framework may not be fundamentally empirical, but by-products of a linguistic forestructure.

I can understand why the proposal for functional circularity may not be greeted with lusty enthusiasm. Many readers may feel a certain trepidation at this point. If so, the remainder of this chapter will probably be insufficient to win confidence. However, there are three analytic strokes that can be more ably made, and if these prove palatable, one might concede that the general formulations merit more serious consideration.

The first of these supporting proposals is that *the definitional system for psychological terms is essentially self-contained.* Consider at the outset that there is no obvious way by which the definition of a psychological term can be established ostensively, that is, by a process of pointing to a set of mutually observed particulars. One may turn to indirect or inferential observables, but this option too suffers from difficulties. In the indirect case one turns to observable indicators for the definitions of the mental term. Their position is embraced most fully by operationists who proclaim that, for example, intelligence (as a psychological construct) *is* what intelligence tests measure. However, this would be to suggest, for one, that a particular movement of the hand on a particular test form constitutes intelligence, a view that even the most committed operationalist would have to relinquish (as one could be trained or ordered to mark test forms in precisely the same pattern and few would wish to hold such actions as indicative of intelligence). Further, there are numerous alternative explanations available for the same actions (motivation, enculturation, attention, etc.). Indeed, if the earlier cited research is generalizable (Gergen *et al.* 1986), there should be as many plausible explanations for the observable actions as there are psychological trait terms in the language.

With these forms of definition abandoned, we have the remaining possibility of defining mental predicates in terms of other mental predicates. As suggested earlier, mental terms are much like mathematical integers; their meaning is principally derived from the way in which they figure within a set of conventional rules governing the system in which they are a part. If each mental term is defined by yet other mental terms, we are confronted by a full definitional circularity with respect to such terms. For example, if we examine the definition of a mental term such as "purpose," we find (using a standard *Random House Dictionary*) that it is chiefly defined as a "reason." A reason in turn is defined as a "mental power" or "power of mind"; and mind in turn is defined as an agency that, among other things, has the power to reason. The system of definition is essentially closed. In other instances this circularity is more extended. For example, an "attitude" is traditionally defined as a "manner of feeling," which in turn is defined as an "affective state of consciousness." The latter in turn is distinguished by its *not* being a "cognitive state." Cognitive states of mind are essentially those in which reason plays a major role. A reason is in turn a mental power or power of mind, and mind is defined as an agency that, among other things, experiences affective states. (It should also be noted that although dictionary definitions of ostensively defined entities are also linguistic, they are not, as in the case of psychological terms, circular. A "bird," for example, is defined as a "warm blooded vertebrate covered with feathers and forelimbs modified into wings." However, "wings" are defined in turn as "anterior extremities or appendages of the scapular arch." If one then searches for the meaning of such terms as "extremities," "appendages," or "scapular arch" one never returns to the word "bird.")

In this light let us consider now the problem of specifying functional relationships among mental entities. It is often said that our thoughts are biased by our emotions or values, that our reason informs our intention, that our moral beliefs inhibit our instinctive drives for pleasure, and so on. Why are such functional relationships perfectly plausible? As we have seen, they are not grounded in observation. So how are we to account for this compelling validity? And too, other causal relationships among mental entities can be specified which seem less plausible or compelling. Linguistic convention permits one to say that the death instinct influences our moral beliefs, our intentions influence our dreams, or hopes inhibit happiness. Yet, such propositions fail to ring true by contemporary standards. If there is no objective reason to suppose such propositions are invalid, how are we to account for their impotence?

It is my proposal that the degree of apparent validity attached to propositions connecting one mental state to another is dependent on the extent of their definitional circularity (up to the point of simple redundancy). That is, the more closely the causal agent is defined by that entity upon which it acts, the more plausible will be the functional proposition. To be more precise, as term A increasingly shares definitional space with term B, it becomes increasingly plausible to say that A causes B (or vice versa). To the extent that A is defined by the absence of B, it becomes increasingly plausible to say that A inhibits or has a negative effect on B. To illustrate, in the former case it is above suspicion to say that concentration will generally improve one's ability to think logically. Concentration is by definition a constituent part of thought. Thinking is a concentrated effort. By the same token, it is perfectly plausible to say that mental distraction (or failure to concentrate) will decrease one's ability to think logically. The absence of concentration is, by definition, the absence of thought.

For purposes of clarity let us consider a contrasting case. We commonly say "It is difficult for me to think when I am so emotional." However, emotion is by definition the absence of cognition (or thought); the redundancy of the statement contributes to its plausibility. This common belief is also reflected in the psychological literature in the hypothesis that high states of arousal interfere with problem solving. Yet if problem solving is defined as the exercise of reasoning powers, reason is the absence of emotion, and emotion is a state of arousal, then it is true by definitional extension that high arousal and problem solving are mutually exclusive. By conventional standards it would border on cultural nonsense to assert the contrary of such propositions (e.g. I am most logical when I am very emotional, excited, or aroused). More complex propositions could and should be considered. However, given the basic self-containment of psychological terminology, thorough examination should reveal that they are fundamentally circular.

We may now turn to the second supporting proposal, one that is perhaps more succinctly stated than the first. However, its efficiency should not be mistaken for triviality. Indeed, the implications of this second proposal are broadly substantial, and it is only a single implication that we shall examine within the present context. The proposal in this case is that *propositions about the external world may generally be converted or reduced to statements about mental conditions*. The wisdom behind this proposition is amply demonstrated in our common folk wisdom. As we say, "beauty is in the eye of the beholder," or "you *think* I am . . . angry . . . or in love, etc., but it's all in your head." Although a good deal of psychological theory has been based on such reduction, the ultimate implications of doing so have yet to be examined. For example, it has become commonplace at this juncture to say that behavior is a joint function of situation and personality (Magnusson and Endler 1977). Yet for those who take this stance the "situation" is essentially "that which the individual perceives." The "real" situation is thus reduced to perception. At this point one begins to develop an uneasy sense of incoherence, for perceptions of situations are meat and potatoes for a personality psychologist. Thus the concept of a situation, independent of an observer, can (and one might argue, should) be abandoned. As a result interactionism is an unwarranted conclusion; all could be reduced to personality study.

Similar problems emerge in Bandura's (1977) attempt to integrate behaviorist and cognitive approaches to the acquisition of aggressive tendencies. Bandura first endorses the behaviorist tradition; he argues, "The influential role of antecedent events in regulating aggressive behavior is most clearly revealed in experiments that arrange the necessary learning conditions. When aggression is rewarded in certain contexts . . . the level of aggressive responding can be altered simply by changing the contextual events that signal probable outcomes" (63). This account primarily employs the language of the stimulus world; it reifies environmental events and little reference is made to a psychological world. Yet later in his analysis Bandura shifts the focus and adopts the language of internal representation. He argues,

> People do not respond to each momentary item of feedback as an isolated experience. Rather, they proceed and synthesize feedback information from sequences of events over long periods of time regarding the conditions necessary for reinforcement, and the pattern and rate with which actions produce the outcomes. It is for this reason that vast amounts of behavior can be maintained with only infrequent immediate reinforcement. Because outcomes affect behavior through integrative thought, knowledge about schedules of reinforcement can exert greater influence upon behavior than does the reinforcement itself. (97)

Here the external world becomes transformed into a psychological world and this latter domain has the capacity to construct its own ontology. The language of external events has been transformed into a language of internal events. If the implications are pressed, Bandura could abandon the former language in favor of the latter. There is nothing in the former that cannot be translated into the latter.

At this point one may wish to offer rebuttal: earlier the distinction was made between analytic and synthetic definitions – the former dependent on linguistic structure and the latter on the extension to a range of observables. Yet it has now been proposed that the language of observables can be reduced to psychological language. Does this not challenge the distinction between the synthetic and the analytic, and if so, are we to conclude that all propositions describing a functional relationship among events are true by definition? Such conclusions possess only an apparent validity. It has been proposed that "real world descriptors" *can be* reduced to psychological equivalents, not that they must be. They may retain their synthetic character so long as the definition remains ostensive, that is, unconverted to linguistic description. If the definitional process is itself described, the resulting definition lapses into an analytic circularity. Thus, to say that the moon is the earth's natural satellite orbiting the earth at a distance of 238,857 miles is itself uninformative until these definitional terms are linked to actions or ostensive "objects" outside the definitional system itself. One must understand what "orbit" and "miles" are outside the confines of the language. The difference here is between the information contained in the proposition "Let A=A" and "Let A equal that to which I am pointing." It is the latter that enables one to use language for pragmatic purposes outside of language use itself.

Let us now introduce the third and last proposition: *propositions about human conduct may generally be converted or reduced to statements about mental conditions*. This conclusion rests on a line of argument that has taken many forms over the past century – for example, in the works of Max Weber, R. G. Collingwood, Peter Winch, R. S. Peters, and, more recently, Charles Taylor. I have attempted to distill and amplify the arguments in my *Toward transformation in social knowledge* (1982). Without exploring the full line of reasoning, the central point for us here is that if we examine the vocabulary of terms employed for describing persons' actions we find that such terms are not linked to or reflective of the actual spatio-temporal character of people's actions. Rather, such terms typically refer to the motive, intention, or disposition underlying the action. Person description does not index the movement of the body from moment to moment (the velocity, the direction, and so on of each bodily part), but rather the psychological state believed to underlie the movements. The case has become transparent in the history of research on aggression. Although investigators were initially committed to defining aggression behaviorally, it became painfully apparent that it was impossible to do so. The movement of one's arm at a certain velocity did not constitute aggression; nor did it count as aggression if the arm were to strike another in the face, for such an event could occur accidentally or unintentionally; the movement counted as aggression only if one believed the actor *intended* to hurt the target of the blow. And so it is with terms like altruism, exploitation, conformity, and obedience; all refer to the motives, intentions, or the like of the actors. (Why this is the case, and must be so in principle, is explained in Gergen 1982.) The result of this condition is that propositions about human action may generally be considered statements about psychological states. They appear to describe overt behavior, but they actually inform one about states of mind. With this third proposition thus elaborated, let us move over the threshold upon which we are now poised.

If all propositions about reality can be reduced to propositions about mental states, and propositions about human action are also used to index mental states, then it follows that all S-O-R propositions are essentially propositions about mental states. Yet, following our initial argument, mental state language is essentially a closed system of definition; all states are defined in terms of each other. As we have also seen, propositions about relations among mental states generally rely on a definitional unpacking; the more common the definitional space, the greater the plausibility of a causal link. It follows ineluctably that S-O-R propositions are true by virtue of linguistic convention. Further, and more generally, all reasonable propositions relating mental predicates to observable events should be equally circular.

Illustrations may be useful at this juncture. Let us consider first the case of relating psychological concepts to overt behavior. For example, traditional research on the relationship between attitudes and behavior maintains that there is a strong functional relationship between one's attitudes and one's behavior toward a given object, person, or issue (cf. Ajzen and Fishbein 1980). Yet one becomes suspicious of underlying problems when it becomes apparent that the only means of assessing attitudes is through behavior. Thus, the proposition can be read out as a description about relationships among the forms of conduct. People's statements about their behavior are, on this account, related to their behavior. Yet we have also seen that our language for behavior (including people's statements) is an intentional one; that is, it indexes motivational states. One is not interested in the overt sounds of a person's statements, but their underlying intent. It is not people's bodily movements that are important in their joining a protest or using prophylactics, but their intentions in doing so. As a result, we find that what appears to be a proposition about the functional relationship between behaviors is a proposition about the relationship among mental entities. Thus, for example, when a measure of attitudes toward nuclear arms is correlated with voting for or against the President, one has a verbal indicator of affect (or attitude) toward nuclear arms (the attitude measure), and a behavioral indicator (voting) of affect toward the same issue. In effect, one is essentially trying to establish that positive sentiments toward X are related to positive sentiments toward X. The relationship is fully circular.

One might wish to rebut this argument by pointing to imperfect correlations at the empirical level. Do such irregularities not suggest that the research is not circular? Such a rebuttal is of little consequence. Any deviation must be explained, and from the present perspective such explanation will again fall back on circular reasoning. One would in this case have to specify another psychological basis or meaning for a vote for the President, for example, improved economy or national pride. With such specification one commits oneself to a new proposition, for example, positive sentiments toward nuclear arms are related to positive sentiments toward a strong economy, and a supporting explanation such as "nuclear arms programs bolster the economy." Yet, as we see, this new explanation once again reinstates functional circularity. One is essentially arguing once again that positive attitudes toward the economy are related to positive attitudes toward the economy. In effect, the sense we make of "if-then" propositions seems to depend on their inherent circularity.

We confront much the same situation in the case of propositions about the effects of stimuli on psychological states. To propose, for example, that physical beauty engenders attraction is to say little more than that attractive persons are attractive. In the same way, the proposition that similarity breeds attraction becomes circular as soon as an explanation is given for the functional linkage. If one argues that similarity breeds attraction because similar people boost one's esteem, and enhanced self-esteem is considered an attractive or desirable state of mind, then the proposition again reverts to the redundant form: attractiveness is attractive. There is little reason to suppose that the full range of functional propositions from the domain of psychophysics, cognition, and learning are not subject to the same problem. The notorious circularity of the law of effect furnishes good reason to suspect that this is so. The present conceptual analysis furnishes the rationale for why it must be so.

Can the chain of functional circularity be broken through physiological reductionism? For many, the prospect of reducing or translating psychological terms into material terms has been an attractive one, and the dissolution of the present conundrum would only add impetus to such a venture. Yet by extending the implications of the present analysis, we find this option proscribed. In particular, we find that the vocabulary of the mental world is without empirical anchor – it cannot be reduced to or read out in behavioral actions. If so, there is no means of developing reductionist linkages. There are no behavioral entities to be reduced. Consider the search for a physiological basis for depression. In order to determine the physiological correlates one must isolate the existence of depression independent of physiology itself. (If one is limited only to a language of physiology there is simply nothing to reduce.) Yet locating depression independently of physiology confronts us with the same interpretive problem faced in the preceding analysis. One's declaration, "I am depressed" must be interpreted – whether it truly reflects depression or not is opaque. There is virtually no motive state – including joy – that cannot serve as the instigator for proclaiming one's depression. Each further indicator is subject to the same relativity of interpretation. In effect, depression is not a state of mind but an historically situated construction.

If the functional circularity argument can be sustained, a variety of new and interesting questions emerge. For example, if propositions of the kind described here are both pervasive in social life and circular, what is their function within social interchange? If they do not inform us of the world, what role do they serve in personal affairs? And how is it possible to alter the structure of psychological understanding? If the system is self-referring, self-contained, and circular, how can new understandings ever emerge? All are questions for future inquiry.

For the present, however, the purpose of this inquiry has been to demonstrate the efficacy of viewing knowledge not as a possession of individual minds – internal reflections of an external world – but as an artifact of social communities. Rather than a set of internal schemata, rules, or heuristics, propositions about the world are viewed as forms of discourse. And discourse, it is proposed, has its origins in the process of social interchange. In this light the attempt was made to turn the analysis on psychological discourse itself and to explore its dependence on social convention. In particular, how are we to understand why certain propositions about the mind and its relations to the world are intelligible while others are nonsensical? As we find, intelligibility in this case is largely a by-product of tautology. The more closely a proposition approximates circularity of definition (so long as its circularity is not transparent) the more reasonable or valid the proposition appears – a point perhaps worthy of more extended consideration in another context.

References

Ajzen, I. and Fishbein, M. (1980). *Understanding attitudes and predicting social behavior*. Englewood Cliffs, NJ: Prentice-Hall.

Austin, J. L. (1962). *How to do things with words*. New York: Oxford University Press.

Averill, J. (1983). *Anger and aggression: An essay on emotion*. New York: Springer.

Bandura. A. (1977). *Social learning theory*. Englewood Cliffs, NJ: Prentice-Hall.

Barnes, B. (1974). *Scientific knowledge and sociological theory*. London: Routledge & Kegan Paul.

Berger, P. and Luckmann, T. 1966. *The social construction of reality*. Garden City, NY: Doubleday.

Bloor, D. (1976). *Knowledge and social imagery*. London: Routledge & Kegan Paul.

Bourdieu, P. (1975). The specificity of the scientific field and the social conditions of the progress of reason. *Social Science Information* 14: 19–47.

Campbell, D. T. (1986). Science's social system of validity – enhancing collective belief change and the problems of the social sciences. In D. W. Fiske and R. A. Shwader (eds.), *Metatheory in social science*. Chicago: University of Chicago Press.

Coulter, J. (1983). *Rethinking cognitive theory*. New York: St Martin's Press.

Davis, K. E. and Todd, M. J. (1982). Friendship and love relationships. In K. E. Davis and T. O. Mitchell (eds.), *Advances in descriptive psychology*, vol. 2. Greenwich, CT: JAI.

Feyerabend, P. K. (1976). *Against method*. New York: Humanities Press.

Gergen, K. J. (1982). *Toward transformation in social knowledge*. New York: Springer.

Gergen, K. J. (1984). Aggression as discourse. In Mummendey 1984.

Gergen, K. J. (1985a). Social pragmatics and the origin of psychological discourse. In Gergen and Davis 1985.

Gergen, K. J. (1985b). The social constructionist movement in modern psychology. *American Psychologist* 40: 266–75.

Gergen, K. J. and Davis, K. E. (eds.) (1985). *The social construction of the person*. New York: Springer Verlag.

Gergen, K. J. and Gergen, M. M. (1982). Form and function in the explanation of human conduct. In P. Secord (ed.), *Explaining social behavior*. Beverly Hills: Sage.

Gergen, K. J., Hepburn, A., and Comer, D. (1986). The hermeneutics of personality description. *Journal of Personality and Social Psychology* 6: 1261–70.

Gurvitch, G. (1971). *The social frameworks of knowledge*. New York: Harper & Row.

Habermas, J. (1971). *Knowledge and human interest*. Boston, MA: Beacon Press.

Hanson, N. R. (1958). *Patterns of discovery*. Cambridge: Cambridge University Press.

Jay, M. (1973). *The dialectical imagination*. London: Heinemann.

Kessler, S. and McKenna, W. (1978). *Gender: An ethnomethodological approach*. New York: Wiley.

Knorr-Cetina , K. G. (1981). *The manufacture of knowledge*. New York: Pergamon Press.

Kuhn, T. S. (1970). *The structure of scientific revolution*, 2nd rev. edn. Chicago, IL: University of Chicago Press. (Original work published 1962.)

Latour, B. and Woolgar, S. (1979). *Laboratory life: the social construction of scientific facts*. Beverly Hills: Sage.

Magnusson, D. and Endler, N. S. (eds.) (1977). *Personality at the crossroads: current issues in interactional psychology*. Hillsdale, NJ: Erlbaum.

Mannheim, K. (1936). *Ideology and utopia: an introduction to the sociology of knowledge*. New York: Harcourt, Brace & World. (First published in German, 1929–31.)

Marx, K. (1967). *Capital: A critique of political economy*, vol. 1. New York: International Publishers.

Medawar, P. B. (1960). *Induction and intuition in scientific thought*. London: Methuen.
Mummendey, A. (ed.) (1984). *Social psychology of aggression*. Berlin: Springer Verlag.
Mummendey, A., Bonewasser, L. M., Loschper, G., and Linneweber, V. (1982). It is always somebody else who is aggressive. *Zeitschrift für Socialpsychologie* 13: 341–52.
Needham, R. (1972). *Belief, language, and experience*. Chicago: University of Chicago Press.
Ossorio, P. (1985). An overview of descriptive psychology. In Gergen and Davis 1985.
Popper, K. R. (1968). *The logic of scientific discovery*. New York: Harper & Row. (Originally published as *Logik des Forschung*. Vienna: Springer, 1935.)
Quine, W. V. O. (1951). Two dogmas of empiricism. *Philosophical Review* 60: 20–43.
Rorty, R. (1979). *Philosophy and the mirror of nature*. Princeton, NJ: Princeton University Press.
Ryle, G. (1949). *The concept of mind*. London: Hutchinson.
Semin, G. and Chassein, J. (1985). The relationship between higher order models and everyday conceptions of personality. *European Journal of Social Psychology* 15: 1–15.
Smedslund, J. (1985). Necessarily true cultural psychologies. In Gergen and Davis 1985.
Taylor C. (1964). *The explanation of behaviour*. London: Routledge & Kegan Paul.
Taylor, C. (1971). Interpretation and the sciences of man. *Review of Metaphysics* 25 (1).
Toulmin, S. (1961). *Foresight and understanding*. New York: Harper & Row.
Wittgenstein, L. (1963). *Philosophical investigations*, trans. G. Anscombe. New York: Macmillan.

4 An ecological framework for establishing a dual-mode theory of social knowing[1]

Reuben M. Baron

Over the last thirty-five to forty years there has been a progressive weakening of the distinction between perception and cognition in general, and in particular with regard to the relevance of distinguishing between person perception and person cognition (cf. Tagiuri and Petrullo 1958, Fiske and Taylor 1984). The undermining of perception as an epistemic mode distinct from cognition has a long history, going back at least as far as Helmholtz's (1948) doctrine of unconscious inference. In regard to current constructive models, Bruner's role has been central. Specifically, Bruner's (1957a) claim that perception is a categorical decision-making process, in conjunction with the proposition that perception allows us to "go beyond the information given" (Bruner 1957b), have had the effect of severely blurring the boundary between perception and cognition in favor of assimilating perception to higher-order cognitive processes. The progressive undermining of perception as a significant independent epistemic mode has continued with the cognitive revolution, which in effect has relegated perception to an early pre-meaning stage of information processing. According to this view, perceptual level inputs must be constructively enriched through the operation of schema-driven encoding–inference processes before they can serve useful functions in judgment and/or behavior (Neisser 1967, Burnstein and Schul 1982). This type of treatment of perception continues with the adoption by social psychologists of the schema–information-processing model (S-IP). For example, Fiske and Taylor (1984) treat perception as

1 The comments of L. Boudreau, S. Fiske, A. Kruglanski, and L. McArthur on an earlier version of this chapter are gratefully acknowledged. Finally, I absolve Robert Shaw and Michael Turvey, my Gibsonian mentors, of any responsibility for my current revisionist position on Gibson.

"constructive encoding," with the only difference between perception and cognition being whether the organization of inputs occurs early or late in the information-processing sequence, that is, during the registration-encoding stages or during memory-based elaborative processing including decoding-retrieval stages.

At the psychological level, what has occurred is that the nature of perception has progressively shifted from a situation where cognition was assumed to be anchored in perception (cf. Brunswick 1956), as in the adage "seeing is believing," to a situation where "believing is seeing" has become a more appropriate cliché in the sense that perception is ruled by central–categorical structures of a propositional nature (Pylyshyn 1980). At the epistemological–ontological levels the transformation is even more decisive; both perception and cognition are assumed to be limited to a constructive level of knowledge devoid of truth value (Fodor and Pylyshyn 1981, Gergen 1984). Within social cognition an equivalent constructive hegemony has been achieved in regard to the foundations of contemporary theory and research (Markus and Zajonc 1985, Fiske and Taylor 1984).

Given these trends, it is my intention to restore a separate and significant epistemic function for perception, both in general and particularly in regard to the role of perception in the acquisition and utilization of social knowledge. I hope to demonstrate that there is an alternative to having to infer constructively social motives, intentions, and attitudes. Specifically, such dispositions are informationally transparent to an appropriately tuned perceptual apparatus because these states systematically constrain or deform morphological, physiognomic, and kinematic signs.

A second purpose of this chapter is to go beyond the information offered by Gibson's direct perception model. To wit, I offer a revised ecological framework which views perception and cognition as qualitatively distinct modes or strategies of knowing which evolved to deal with a different range of epistemic problems.

An ecological realist perspective on separate functions for perception and cognition

The basic thesis of the present analysis can be stated as follows: when we make a distinction between perception and cognition we are merely describing what nature has already achieved. Contrary to Gibson (1979), I propose that the different modes have evolved to serve different epistemic functions in regard to their relationship to language, social interaction, affect, and consciousness.

Gibson's ecological model of perception

From this perspective the work of J. J. Gibson is critical because it allows us to provide a nonconstructive foundation for perception. In Gibson one can find the most compelling arguments for distinguishing perception from current schema–information-processing models of cognition. Gibson (1979) treats direct perception as in need of *neither* stages of processing *nor* centrally mediated constructive processes. For Gibson it is not necessary to go "beyond the information given" (Bruner 1957) to acquire useful knowledge about the environment. Specifically, under natural conditions the stimulation available to the sensory modalities has been systematically deformed or constrained by the dynamic or dispositional properties of environmental entities. That is, there is information potentially available to be detected by our sensory systems, in the form of higher-order stimulus properties (e.g. Gibson's formless invariants), which specifies the functional utilities or affordances of environmental entities or constellations of entities.

Since the above summary of Gibson's position is highly condensed it requires a certain degree of unpacking in order to establish how it is possible to sustain a nonconstructive model of the acquisition and utilization of information about the world.

The nature of information for the perceptual system: the concept of informational specificity

Baron (1980: 65) describes Gibson's ecological account of informational specificity as follows:

> At the most basic level, we take direct perception to mean that because environmental events structure light (e.g., ambient reflected light), sounds, and other physical parameters in ways specific to their sources in regard to properties of surface and substance, the information available for perception is already sufficiently rich that no additional cognitive elaboration is required to disambiguate its meaning. Such an interpretation transforms perception into an act of discovery or detection as opposed to construction.

According to this view the dispositional, functional properties of entities – that is, their affordances – systematically deform surface stimulus properties (color, shape, texture), as well as how these entities move and change over time in ways which make dispositional or dynamic properties transparent to the perceptual apparatus (cf. Shaw and Pittenger 1977). For example, heavy objects move differently from light ones and, more to the point, animals in sexual heat move and appear differently from their non-aroused counterparts. Consider, for example, how and when it is possible for a male animal to perceive directly whether a female conspecific is in a sexually receptive state. In this regard let us consider a species where sexuality is largely under direct hormonal control. For such a species when a mature male animal is in sexual heat, only certain environmental entities will be perceived as suitable objects for reproductive mating. In ecological perception terms, such an animal is resonating to the external invariant for female sexual receptivity. Thus, one source of direct perception is the fit between the perceiver's preparedness state and the range of suitable objects in the world. Direct perception is possible in this example because in species where hormonal factors closely govern reproductive behavior, *receptive* conspecifics *look*, *smell*, and *behave* differently from nonreceptive ones. Given this situation, *receptivity can be known perceptually* because receptivity objectively constrains the stimulus properties of females in ways to which the male's perceptual system can resonate. In such species receptivity is *unequivocally* linked to certain properties of the stimulus display.

On the other hand, staying with this sexual example, consider a species where hormonal control over sexual behavior is highly variable: humans. Specifically, in humans we have a situation where for a large portion of their life-span males are in a perpetual state of sexual preparedness and where, to make things more complex, female receptivity is not invariably tied to a particular set of sensory signs. *Here we have a situation which I hypothesize will induce a switch from a perceptual to a conceptual strategy of knowing*. That is, one possible epistemic solution to a situation where perceptual knowledge is uncertain is to treat females stereotypically, dividing them, for example, into whores and virgins. Moreover, in regard to the issue of preparedness mode it might be argued that within humans social competence and/or sexual experience moderates the relative use of perceptual and conceptual strategies for achieving knowledge of female receptivity. That is, more socially competent males will stereotype less because they are more able perceptually to differentiate individual variations in receptivity.

The implications of informational specificity are very radical – it is possible under certain circumstances to see, as opposed to infer, so-called hidden causes in both the social and the nonsocial environment. Thus it is informational specificity which allows Gibson to argue that perception need not go beyond the information given. However, the existence of informational specificity does not guarantee that such information will be detected and utilized. What is required in order for structured information to be resonated to is a model of how this structure is unlocked. Here we make use of additional aspects of the Gibsonian model, the concept of attunement, and the proposition that perception is for doing. Taken together, attunement and the yoking of perception to active exploration and manipulation of the world make it possible for perceptual level meaning to be *data-driven* – a matter of *detecting and preserving knowledge* rather than constructing it from the top down. Further, it is the attunement process that shifts the issue of selectivity from a problem in the availability of schemata in the head to a problem of the differentiation of structure in the world (see below).

Getting information out of the world: the mechanisms and meaning of attunement

For Gibson, the acquisition of perceptual knowledge or perceptual learning is a matter of the animal increasing its differentiation of the nested information structures that constitute the physical and social environments. Gibson (1966) uses the analogy of a radio or TV receiver resonating to particular wavelengths and not to others. The concept of attunement is given an ecological flavor because Gibson emphasizes the mutuality of perceptual knowledge, in the sense that the attunement metaphor implies that an animal can detect only what it is prepared for in regard to its sensory-motor capabilities, its current needs, and its history (McArthur and Baron 1983).

The Gibsonian account of attunement provides a radically different view of the nature of selectivity in knowledge acquisition; instead of treating selectivity as a problem in the availability of internal knowledge structures, i.e. schemata, it assumes (1) that sensorimotor attunements can accommodate to changes in environmental conditions on-line, as when a predator recalibrates its trajectory for leaping to compensate for the evasive movements taken by a prey, (2) that action over time leaves a record in the world that can be detected or noticed by a properly attuned animal, thereby obviating the need to assume an internal structure for storing perceptual experience. For example, change is viewed as leaving a characteristic trail of traces. This record can be tracked by an appropriately attuned perceptual apparatus much as an experienced guide uses a trail of footprints and/or broken twigs to establish where an animal has been as well as where it is going; for example, an experienced male rat may detect where a sexually responsive female rat has been, using a trail of olfactory cues.

The availability of such objective change information to the perceptual system has been interpreted by Robert Shaw and his associates (cf. Shaw and Pittenger 1977) to mean that the *same* topological growth transformation that characterizes the actual growth or aging of biological forms can be used by perceivers to detect the relative age in a variety of entities. These include human faces, as well as the relative age of birds, monkeys, and even VWs! These studies speak to the epistemic *sufficiency* of higher-order geometric information to detect change. Further, the same cardiodal strain transformation used by Shaw and his asssociates (Shaw and Pittenger 1977) to study the perception of aging apparently also provides information for the social judgment of dependency in regard to perceived needs for nurturance or help (Alley 1981). Thus there appears to be an evolutionarily based arrangement which allows the perceptual mechanism to detect slow change information.

With relatively transient needs, however, an equally "real" but fast changing system of information pickup is needed. Fortunately there is a series of studies, using Johansson's point (patch) light technique, which appear to demonstrate informational specificity for fast change. The general principle underlying informational specificity in such studies has been dubbed the KSD principle by Runeson and Frykholm (1982), meaning that *kinematics* (i.e. the locomotor and expressive movement of animals) *specify* (i.e. make available to the perceptual apparatus) the informational invariants, which reveal the underlying *dynamics* or dispositional states (Gibson's affordances). Specifically, it may be claimed that the kinematics of movement involving rate, trajectory, and smoothness of motion may be systematically constrained by dispositional states such as the intentions of the target person. For example, people who intend to deceive may move more jerkily, or people who are depressed may adopt a slower, more leaden gait than persons in a happy mood. In such situations dispositional states become transparent to perception by systematically distorting or deforming a wide range of *observable expressive* parameters, including gait, posture, facial expression, and various types of paralinguistic information. If the case of the detection of chronic need states illustrates how "form follows function," in the present case of fast change we may say the "medium is the message" or we "wear our hearts on our sleeves." Specific examples include Cutting's demonstrations (Cutting 1978, Cutting *et al.* 1978) that patch-light movements specify gender and personal identity, Runeson and Frykholm's (1981, 1982) studies of the patch-light information for perceived heaviness of a lifted object and intent to deceive, as well as Bassili's (1978, 1979) demonstrations that point-light mappings of facial expressive movements specify the informational invariants for primary emotions.

The above examples all make a case for the specificity of social stimulus information to its dispositional sources. At the simplest level, it might be said that one can invoke a perceptual interpretation whenever important social properties are mapped onto overt gestures, expressions, or behaviors that are available as stimulus information for the perceiver. (See pp. 60–1 for a detailed elaboration of this position.)

Attunement and context effects

The attunement model also offers a different perspective on context effects from that suggested by the constructionist encoding position. Specifically, contexts from an ecological perspective do not create new meanings by priming or making differentially accessible schemata for encoding purposes; rather, they serve an *attunement* or *differentiation of structure function* in guiding the *discovery* of stimulus information by making salient different aspects of structure which already exist in the environment.

To clarify just how radical a difference in the meaning of selectivity I have in mind, let me use two examples. Asch (1952), in a series of prestige suggestion studies, presented subjects with an identical passage on revolution. For half the subjects this passage is attributed to Lenin while the other half are told it was authored by Jefferson. Selectivity enters the picture in regard to how we treat the strong finding that these sources elicited radically different interpretations of this identical passage. Asch posed the problem in just the terms that are currently at issue when he suggested that there were two ways to conceptualize the data. (1) The subjects' interpretations could be viewed as a change in the *judgment of the object*. In current schema–information-processing terms this implies that selectivity was a matter of constructive encoding, in the sense that the input took on a different meaning depending upon whether the passage was fitted into a "democratic" or a "communist" schema for revolution. The ecological attunement–differentiation view, on the other hand, is anticipated by Asch's proposition that the different contexts changed the *object of judgment*; that is, the effective stimulus was changed – for example, people may have focused their attention on different words, sentences, or paragraphs.

However, since the use of a *verbal* medium tends to tilt the epistemic mode toward a more conceptual level of processing, a much better empirical example is provided by Massad, Hubbard, and Newtson's (1979) attempt to change subjects' interpretations of the Heider–Simmel (1944) paradigm. In this study subjects were given instructional sets designed to change the typical view of the big triangle as the "bad guy" and the little square as the "good guy." These different instructions *only* resulted in different judgments when they led to differences in how the film was *unitized* or *partitioned* in terms of where the boundaries were put for sequences, rates, and trajectories of the movements of the geometric entities. To the extent that such different partitions may be seen as *changing the stimulus information*, we may interpret Massad *et al.*'s data as fitting Asch's change in *object of judgment* model. In the Gibsonian view it would be claimed that the different instructions, by *directing* the person to notice different organizations of the stimulus, were revealing different affordances. For example, a given sequence of arm movements may, depending on which aspect of the trajectory I focus on, look more like throwing or reaching; or it may change to looking like a greeting if I also observe certain reciprocal waves from one other person.

In sum, from the ecological perspective selectivity is a matter of tuning the perceptual–motor apparatus so that it is able both to notice the nested levels of structured information that already exist in the world to be detected, and to generate new structured information by inducing change through goal-directed movements and actions in the world. From this perspective, context is merely a special case of preparedness and as such is viewed as fine-tuning the resonance-differentiation process. In this regard it should be noted that, although Neisser (1976) conceptualizes preparedness in schema terms, his treatment of the relationship between schemata and perception follows an attunement rather than a schema-priming constructive model. That is, for Neisser schemata do not construct perceptual meanings vis-a-vis an encoding process; rather, they guide the distribution of attention in regard to partitioning or differentiating the stimulus array. Finally, although the traditional Gibsonians do not conventionally pose the problem in these terms, we see a fundamental difference between the constructive encoding and ecological perspective in regard to assimilation–accommodation. That is, the constructive schema model drives the animal towards epistemic *assimilation* in order to maximize the likelihood of holding onto one's existing schemata. On the other hand, a perceptual attunement model is more open and accommodative in the Piagetian sense of attuning the animal to changes in environmental properties (cf. Neisser 1976).

Activity as a means of detecting structure

Gibson (1979) begins his last work by commenting that "perception is for doing." In the present context it is primarily through *doing* that structure is unlocked. From this perspective perception is a "hands-on," blue-collar type of experiential way of learning about the world, which is limited to those aspects of the environment within our direct sensory grasp or what we can directly encounter or explore by seeing, touching, hearing, feeling, and smelling. In Bertrand Russell's (1948) apt terms, it is limited to first-hand knowledge or *knowledge by acquaintance*.

Specifically, it is through actively exploring and manipulating the world that we are able to distinguish what is important. As we attempt to do things with entities we produce prospectival transformations and integrate information from separate sensory modalities into a perceptual system which is able to resonate to higher-order invariants in the world. That is, it is the movements of the observer and/or the stimulus events that organize the optic array and create the changes necessary for the extraction of invariants. Thus, we do not know what is invariant about an entity unless we can say which aspects change and which do not change as we actively explore it and/or observe its changes over time. Similarly, in regard to person perception we may need to see people in different settings and roles before we can extract invariant person properties.

The crucial role of actively perceiving in the detection of invariants is important at another level. It is often incorrectly claimed that it is the relative contribution of the perceiver as opposed to the contribution of the stimulus that differentiates perception from cognition (cf. Markus and Zajonc 1985). From the ecological viewpoint the perceiver's contribution is just as important, albeit of a different order. That is, the perceiver for Gibson is active in the world, while the schema-driven information processor is active internally, with regard to various inferential coding processes.

The argument for a neo-Gibsonian view

From my perspective, Gibson's major contribution to epistemology is building a foundation for a nonconstructive model of perception. Largely because of Gibson we no longer have to view perception as "parasitic on cognition." For example, Fiske and Taylor (1984) are merely reflecting the current cognitive Zeitgeist when they describe perception as "constructive encoding" which only differs from cognition in that organizational processes operate early as opposed to late in the information-processing sequence. Unfortunately, also from my perspective, Gibson does not use this insight the way I would have preferred. Instead, because of his interest in closing "the gap between perception and cognition," Gibson (1979) turns reductionist himself by (in effect) making *cognition parasitic on perception.* That is, he argues that (1) both perception and cognition involve the extracting and abstracting of invariants, (2) cognition is an inferior epistemic mode because (*a*) seeing comes before and constrains cognizing, (*b*) cognizing involves a loss of information relative to perceiving because cognition typically involves a verbally driven stereotyping process whereby the rich information available in the stimulus array is compromised vis-a-vis processes of categorical encoding.

Specific reasons for adopting a dual as opposed to a unitary epistemic mode theory

My own view is to reject a reductionist, unitary process model at both ends; I do not want to reduce perception to cognition nor cognition to perception. Why? Let me count the ways:

The developmental argument

I propose that at the levels both of phylogeny and of ontogeny a developmental hierarchy exists; perceptual knowing is hypothesized to have evolved prior to conceptual knowing. Specifically, basic perceptual functioning is assumed to rest only upon the availability of sensori-motor systems. On the other hand, conceptual knowing, or cognition, is assumed to be a higher-order development largely contingent upon the availability of symbolic structures. In this regard, it may be noted that Piaget's sensorimotor schemata are assumed to develop *prior* to the existence of high-order cognitive–symbolic grouping operations. Further, Odom's (1978) perceptual salience research suggests that many of the "basic and significant changes that occur in psychological development are primarily or exclusively based on the perceptual system's changing sensitivity to relations in the environment rather than on the cognitive processes that evaluate those changes" (128). Consistent with the primitive character of such developing perceptual functions is Vygotsky's (1962) finding that children are able to perceive correctly what they can do with an object earlier than they can label the object.

Moreover, it appears possible to argue that the organization of the brain itself reflects a similar hierarchic developmental progression, with perception being initially yoked to the more primitive brain structures involved in the reptilian and paleomammalian brains, whereas conceptual knowing does not "kick in" fully before the development of the neomammalian brain particularly in regard to the linguistic–analytic capacities of the left hemisphere. In this regard it may also be noted that emotion theorists such as Leventhal (1980) and Buck (1985) have associated more primitive emotional states with perceptual–sensory as opposed to conceptual–symbolic modes of processing.

The language–social communication argument

I believe that a case can be made for the development of language being the major source of the bifurcation between perception and cognition. I propose that there may well be a basic linkage between cognition and the development of verbal–linguistic systems, at the level both of phylogeny and of ontogeny. Specifically, I hypothesize that in prehistory there was a progression from direct perception to conceptual knowing which was mediated by the evolution of language. Moreover, I believe children pass through a similar developmental sequence, with all of us beginning as Gibsonians. That is, as Gibson (1979) observes, you have to see it before you can say it.

There are two issues I would like to address in regard to language. First is the information specificity–iconicity problem. If direct perception depends upon informational specificity, it would appear that, in general, there is a continuum from actual events, to video or films, to pictures, to purely linguistic descriptions, with words being the lowest in informational specificity. For example, C. E. Cohen (cited in Markus and Zajonc 1985) argues that a set of words or verbal descriptions provides less structure or fewer constraints, that is, is less "stimulus bound," than a film that shows an individual engaging in a series of behaviors, thereby setting up a situation which, according to Markus and Zajonc (1985: 168), "may well exaggerate the impact of schemas as the immediate cause of information processing." Vygotsky (1962: 5) goes even further, stating: "A word does not refer to a single object but to a group or class of objects. Each word is therefore already a generalization." On the same page he goes on to make a qualitative distinction between perception and cognition in this respect: "generalization is a verbal act of thought and reflects reality in quite a different way than sensation and perception."

Similarly, Gati and Tversky (1984) propose that verbal and pictorial events elicit different epistemic modes, with verbal stimuli eliciting a search for *common* features while pictorial stimuli often call for the discrimination of *distinctive* features. They go on to interpret these effects as possibly related to the fact that words designate objects while pictures depict them. That is, verbal codes are conventional or arbitrary symbols for objects, whereas pictures share many features of their referents. Specifically, "there is a sense in which pictorial stimuli are 'all there' while the comprehension of verbal stimuli requires retrieval or construction" (368).

It is, however, important to observe that all verbal descriptions are not created equal. Thus, whereas there may be qualitative epistemic differences *between* perception and cognition, there may also be quantitative variation *within* each system. For example, a realist landscape is certainly more perceptual than a surrealist dreamscape. Similarly, within the arena of verbal labels one can find variations in the extent to which labels are tied to the properties of their referents in the world. For example, whereas the trait label of warmth may readily be manifest in expressive gestures, the label of conscientiousness may not be. Specifically, if one's social construct is an arbitrary, conventional one which is symbolized in the form of a verbal label, all that one can observe is whether different people share the same conventional rule system. For example, if people are asked to judge whether Paul is evil or conscientious, these are abstract social labels of low iconicity. Unfortunately, people who are evil do not generally walk or talk differently from the rest of us.

On the other hand, judgments of whether Paul is a warm person or a hostile person, even when framed verbally, are using constructs which are closer to icons or signs in the sense that *they are tied to perceptually discriminable referents in the world.* Thus I would argue that such concepts are more like pictures in that they are closer to depicting (i.e. indexing) than representing their referents. I suggest the term *perceptionoid* for such iconic labels, and hypothesize that because their groundings are less arbitrary, there should be greater intersubjective consensus regarding judgments of their existence in people. Moreover, the consensus process is different; arbitrary labels are merely indicative of common rule usage; *perceptionoid* labels indicate common points of perceptual discrimination. (See Brown 1985 for an excellent discussion of the role of iconicity in language.) Stated more broadly, in the depictive–iconic case the verbal label is not what is carving up nature; rather we have a situation where the observed distinctions in the phenomena call out to be labelled. That is, highly iconic labels are in effect data-driven, while labels of low iconicity are imposed more to satisfy the requirements of cognitive efficiency in regard to communication and perhaps ease of storage (see below). Finally, it should be emphasized that when talking of spoken words there are paralinguistic sources of information that may be treated as having high informational specificity, in the same sense that gait or facial expression may directly specify underlying dispositions. For example, the pause patterns and pitch of highly anxious people appear directly to map internal states of anxiety.

The role of social communication

However, up until now I have left out a critical part of the story – what motivates the language–conceptual knowing development? Here I would suggest an important role for social communication. What I hypothesize is that, as the social unit becomes more complex and people now have to communicate their experiences with the world to relative strangers, direct perception and nonverbal gestures simply will not do. Specifically, verbal categorizations are easier to communicate than idiosyncratic, albeit rich, sensory experiences. Thus, as social complexity increases in the form of expected interaction with strangers, it collectively motivates people to develop language as a means of sharing experiences, thereby creating modes of knowing that are more abstract and stereotypic. It is of interest in this regard that the first written languages appear to have been pictographs

(Egyptian hieroglyphics, for example), thereby suggesting the slow shift from perception to cognition under the pressure of needs to interact and communicate. Further, these speculations specifically fit Vygotsky's view that the prime motivation for initial perceptual–cognitive development is social communication–social contact (cf. Vygotsky 1962: 19).

Recent research carried out by Hoffman, Mischel, and Baer (1984), as well as work carried out within my own laboratory, strongly suggests that the specificity–generality of impression formation is strongly influenced by social communication demands in the service of actual and potential social interaction. Specifically, as predicted above, when we move from individualistic impressions formed without communication expectancy, to increasing levels of expected social communication–interaction – including, in my own research (Baron *et al.* 1986a), actual interaction – the impression formation process becomes more stereotypic in the sense that behavioral detail or individual complexity is lost in favor of polarized trait-type categories. Two other findings clarify the boundary conditions for trait usage. First, Hoffman *et al.*'s (1984) findings indicate that this effect is attenuated when the expected communication is in a nonverbal mode, that is, when subjects expect to draw a picture of the other person. Second, Baron, Boudreau and Oliver (1986b) found that asking subjects mentally to image or to visualize the target in the behavioral scenes *decreases* the use of traits relative to behavioral descriptions.

Perception and cognition as epistemic strategies for dealing with variations in the equivocality of input

It would appear that stimulus manipulations based upon verbal descriptions (what Russell (1948) refers to as secondhand knowledge or knowledge by description in contrast to knowledge by acquaintance) provide a weaker set of constraints on the input side. That is, verbal descriptions provide less stimulus binding; or, to put it more generally, words with certain exceptions bear equivocal or arbitrary relationships to their referents in the world. We may generalize this point by proposing an *evolutionary* argument to the effect that perception is the preferred epistemic strategy when signs are iconic; i.e., when stimulus properties are reliably linked to their dispositional referents or hidden motives, intentions, emotions (or affordances in the general case) – that is, when there is *informational specificity*, as when a female rat's sexual receptivity is reliably revealed by olfactory cues. On the other hand, when signs of receptivity are not iconic – that is, when there is an *equivocal* or symbolic relationship between signs and their referents, or low informational specificity (as is the case with receptivity in human females) – a different and more constructive–inferential *epistemic strategy* is demanded. For example, Goffmanesque verbal self-presentations require constructive decoding (cf. Swann 1984). This argument will be developed in detail when we examine the implications of the present analysis for social knowing (see pages 69–78).

Why perceptual equivalence classes differ from conceptual ones

Having rationalized in general terms why a distinction between perception and cognition is needed, I will now attempt to specify in greater detail how Gibson's concepts must be modified if they are to be useful in clarifying current problems in social knowing. In order to establish a firm foundation for my version of an ecological position, it is necessary to refute Gibson's claim that perception and cognition are identical at the process level, given that both involve the extracting and abstracting of invariants. I will offer three classes of reason against Gibson's process reductionism:

(1) I will argue that the detection of external invariants involves a process which is fundamentally different from inferentially deriving invariants top down;
(2) I will propose that perceptual equivalence classes are particularistic whereas conceptual ones are stereotypic, that is, I will try to demonstrate that while a rose is not a rose, a flower is a flower,
(3) I will argue that, while explicit verbal labeling is crucial to the construction of a conceptual equivalence class, it is not necessary for the recognition of a perceptual equivalence class: that is, I will propose that perceptual knowing yields tacit knowledge whereas conceptual equivalence classes low in iconicity may acquire meaning largely through the act of explicit verbal labeling.

Detecting external invariants versus constructive encoding

I propose that external invariants are discovered rather than inferred constructively because such invariants exist in the world, much as a *melody* can be viewed as an invariant property of a musical composition which unfolds as it is being played. If I am correct, discovering a perceptual equivalence class means something analogous to diagnosing whether someone has the flu. Specifically, one looks for a symptom syndrome involving the infection of an interrelated organ system by the flu virus. Viewed in this way, the flu virus is an external invariant whose growth generates the symptom syndrome. I would like to argue that the detection of perceptual equivalence classes such as affordances follows a similar process. An example from social perception for this type of resonance discovery process is the demonstration that there may be a separate mode in the perceptual system which only resonates to faces. That is, "it resonates to any face (but to nothing else) and does so regardless of the identity, expression, orientation or illumination" (Shepard 1984: 434). Moreover, such high-level modes may resonate to an abstract external invariant directly; its excitation need not depend on excitation of modes that are lower in hierarchy and that correspond to more elementary features of the external object or event (Shepard 1984: 434). I would also claim that the Johansson type of point-light studies of Runeson and Frykholm (1981, 1982) which I cited earlier make a similar point; namely, that there are external invariants which are mapped onto movement systems in ways which make transparent to perception attributes such as gender, emotion, and intention. This process would appear to be very different from establishing or identifying a stimulus as an instance of a schema or category. That is, here the processes are a matter of establishing from the top down whether the stimulus attributes are sufficient – i.e. constitute a family resemblance – to make an *equivalence* judgment or match. This mode of establishing invariants tells us a great deal about how information is encoded but little about what informational constraints exist in the world.

Particularizing versus generalizing

I believe that Gertrude Stein was wrong when she said a rose is a rose is a rose. Rather, she should have said a flower is a flower is a flower, because flowers are abstract, general, and cognitively constructed whereas roses exist in the world to be discovered. That is, particular roses allow the possibility for individuated knowing. A flower in this example is analogous to a stereotype. Indeed, for someone who dislikes nature, it may be just as apt to say all flowers are alike (a flower is a flower is a flower) as it is for someone who is prejudiced against blacks to say all blacks are alike (a black is a black is a black).

Further, it appears that perceptual equivalence classes generate different products from those produced by the stereotyping of cognition. For example, consider the avid gardeners who give proper names to their favorite specific types of flower, talk to them, and refer to them as "my children." All of these actions rest upon highly differentiated perceptual knowing.

Perceptual knowing is individuated or particularistic at a number of levels. The first level stems from the link between perception and doing. Exploratory actions or manipulations of the environment yield sensory equivalence classes as the information yielded from different sensory modalities is tied together by the fact that smelling, touching, hearing, and looking jointly resonate to certain stimulus properties but not to others. Viewed thus, perceptual equivalence classes tell us "more and more about less and less" because the range of events that can be directly encountered at a "hands-on" level are relatively limited. Second, perceptual equivalence classes are particularistic because they are typically tied to particular goals of particular animals. Specifically, perceptual equivalence classes generally are organized along principles of functional cooperation of responses; that is, the parts of the affordance category are related or functionally equivalent in terms of their equifinality regarding a particular goal or purpose. *Such concepts lack the hierarchic organization found in conceptual equivalence classes.* For example, linguistic metacategories such as birds and flowers clearly are more general than their respective subcategories such as robins or roses. Viewed in these terms, conceptual equivalence classes are vertically organized whereas perceptual categories are horizontal (cf. Vygotsky's (1962) distinction between clusters and concepts).

Third, perceptual equivalence classes are particularistic at the level of the species because affordances are *animal referenced* in the sense that perceptual equivalences are defined jointly over the preparedness of the species and the constraints of the niche. That is, something serves a particular function only in regard to the ability of a given type of animal to perform certain actions with certain entities but not others – e.g. walls afford walking for flies but not humans.

In sum, perceptual equivalence classes tell us what the environment is like in regard to what a particular animal can do with different aspects of it, given a situation where the properties to be known have high informational specificity in the sense that environmental cues or signs are highly iconic; that is, they reliably signal their sources.

Before resting the case for why perception is particularistic and conception oriented towards generalizing, I wish to comment on what may seem a paradoxical aspect of this claim. Specifically, the skeptical reader may say, "But how do you reconcile the particularism of perception with the fact that we typically locate properties in the stimulus when there is general agreement or consensus regarding how people respond to it – e.g. if most people judge O to be hostile we are more likely to assume hostility is in the stimulus O than if there is lack of consensus regarding judgments of O's hostility?"

The answer to this paradox, I think, is that in one case we are defining our terms from the perspective of the perceiver or actor and in the other from that of an observer. Specifically, when I claim that perception is particularistic whereas cognition serves a generalizing function (as in stereotyping), I am adopting the perspective of the perceiver and focusing on whether the perceiver treats different entities as equivalent (a stereotypic view) or treats entities distinctively, a perspective tied to his/her recognition of the complex particulars of different entities within a category. It is in this sense that a rose is not a rose because an individual is capable of distinguishing his/her experiences with different roses. Similarly, the mere fact that there is cross-cultural consensus on what stimulus displays indicate the primary emotions (an observer orientation) does not mean that I cannot or do not differentiate when different people are in different states of emotion. Indeed, it is when we assume that all blacks are happy-go-lucky that we are stereotyping. That is, at the perceiver level a stimulus orientation occurs precisely when we do not treat all professors as serious or all blacks as carefree. Indeed, in attribution research the preference of actors for distinctiveness information and observers for consensus information may speak to this very point (cf. Kassin 1979). Such an analysis suggests that Kelley (1967) may have unintentionally conflated actor and observer perspectives, a confusion which becomes a problem when there are "real" actors who have had extended perceptual experiences with the entities in question and hence are likely to trust their own experiential knowledge more than the consensual judgments of strangers (cf. Jones and Nisbett 1972).

There is another reason to distrust the consensus criterion. Specifically, just because consensus is low, as when perceivers in the classic study by Dornbush *et al.* (1965) show low agreement regarding a common stimulus person's attributes, that does not necessarily mean we have to abandon a stimulus-based interpretation. As Schneider *et al.* (1979) point out, it is possible that this stimulus person *looked or acted differently with some of the perceivers.* When this occurs the personality attribute becomes no less real, but what Athay and Darley (1981) would characterize as a property of the perceiver–environment relationship, or (in the present terminology) a social affordance (see below, "Applications to current problems in social cognition").

Perceptual versus cognitive learning

For those readers who are still not convinced that perception is primarily a particularizing and cognition a generalizing mode, let me say that there is one sense in which my account is oversimplified. At the level of learning we may say that perceptual learning moves from the particular to the general whereas cognitive learning moves from the general to the particular. Specifically, if we take stereotypes as our point of departure, cognitive learning would consist of people learning to discriminate or differentiate between the properties of the category and a particular member of the category; for example, as Huck's friendship with Jim grows, Jim becomes a complex particular who stands on his own rather than just another poor black. From this perspective cognitive learning involves leavening general stereotypes with the particularistic information of perception.

On the other hand, perceptual learning, from my perspective, involves the problem of getting cognition into perception in order to achieve some of the advantages of generalization such as decontextualization (cf. Vygotsky 1962). One way to conceptualize such an achievement is to draw an analogy between such learning and what occurs when a basketball player becomes a coach. As a player, much of what he knew about playing may have been at the level of tacit perceptual knowledge. In order to communicate effectively to others in his new role as coach it becomes necessary to filter such perceptual knowledge through linguistically labeled concepts. For example, he must transform perceptually achieved information about the invariants controlling accuracy of shooting to general principles or rules that go beyond the information that was directly given to him/her by sensory information.

The above analysis, in addition to pointing to how the generalizing and particularizing functions of perception and cognition may become blended, implies that explicit labeling processes are important and play different roles in perceptual as opposed to conceptual processes.

Explicit labeling versus tacit recognition

While I would certainly grant that not all cognitive processes involve explicit, conscious processes, I would claim that (1) the greatest differences between perception and cognition occur when we focus on conscious cognitive processes, and (2) perception is essentially an automatic, nonconscious mode.

The implications of consciousness

The claim that perception is essentially automatic whereas cognition functions in both automatic and conscious modes is crucial to the argument for qualitatively distinguishing perception from cognition at a number of levels. First, in support of this distinction, Marcel (1983a: 199) explicitly points out that the aspects of visual perception emphasized by Gibson involve visual processing which is "necessarily carried out automatically and without awareness." Kassin and Baron (1985) take a similar position and propose that this automaticity is tied to the online character of perceptual processing, since the pickup of higher-order invariants in real time is likely to require a speed of processing incompatible with mindful, reflective processes. Moreover, it is unlikely that formless invariants can be verbally categorized in any explicit way, although such inputs can inform and direct action systems below the level of conscious awareness (Turvey 1977).

The automaticity of perception is, in turn, likely to have a number of important implications. First, Marcel (1983b) assumes that "while unconscious automatic processes are not bound by capacity limitations, those associated with consciousness are" (252). Further, Mandler (1984) proposes that it is when cognition is in its conscious mode that information processing is most constructive. Thus, at the level of process the sharpest difference between perception and cognition is likely to occur when cognition is treated as a conscious mode. From this perspective, for example, Kruglanski's (1980) lay epistemology model, which is probably a reconstruction of conscious cognitive processes, may be more different from Gibsonian perception than traditional, information processing models (cf. Fiske and Taylor 1984, Anderson 1980). That is, traditional models have a strong automatic component and hence share an important process characteristic with Gibsonian perception. On the other hand, *both* Kruglanski's model and traditional IP models are strongly wedded to verbal representations, a situation which in and of itself appears to create an epistemic bifurcation. That is, grounding cognitive processes in words achieves an abstract level of generalization at the price of compromising particularistic knowledge. For example, Vygotsky (1962) offers a cogent analysis of how language brings greater flexibility into cognition by decontextualizing epistemic processes. That is, when words became largely symbolic they have meanings which hold over specific situations, whereas perceptually based knowledge, according to Vygotsky, is strongly context-dependent or contextualized (cf. Wertsch 1985).

In support of this line of reasoning Johnson and Raye (1981) find that memories based on actual experience with events possess greater *contextual and sensory detail* than memories based on thinking about events. Moreover, perceptual knowledge may be stored at the level of the motoric as a hard, analogue representation, e.g., in the fingers, which is likely to be retrieved in the form of visual–pictorial images. It is perhaps the basis of what we call "tacit knowledge" in the sense that it is in regard to perceptual knowledge that we can indeed claim "we know more than we can say" (Polanyi 1964), whereas it is in regard to conscious conceptual processes that we often "say more than we can know" (Nisbett and Wilson 1977).

Finally, I would like to propose that, for cognition but not for perception, the labelling process itself may be a top-down process in a very fundamental sense in that conceptual equivalence classes which have no or little perceptual grounding may only come into being when they receive a verbal label. For example, the proposition that blacks are more dangerous than whites may not exist for children either black or white until they are exposed to the categorical stereotype. That is, dangerous at this point comes to exist in the eyes of the beholder child whereas it had no previous perceptual status (which is *not* to say that it will not affect *future* perceptions).

There is, for example, evidence in the research of Vygotsky (1962) that certain events can be recognized, and reacted to correctly prior to children's ability to label such events. On the other hand, it appears to be the basic property of certain higher-order linguistic categories that meaning is largely independent of perceptual roots but is instead a matter of their being linked to other concepts. For example, higher-order concepts such as Machiavellianism receive their meanings from abstract, logical links between concepts such as political adroitness, treating people as means and not ends, and conventional definitions of good and evil.

Perceptual equivalence classes, on the other hand, as we have noted earlier, exist in the world whether they are labeled or not. Thus, whether or not we label a disease the flu it will produce the same symptoms, although our ability to tolerate such symptoms may be decreased or increased by the labeling process. For example, a flu label may be reassuring because it suggests that more serious conditions are not causing our discomfort. Similarly, a child may recognize he or she is being neglected whether or not they can label how they are being treated.

This type of analysis suggests that perception is a powerful, though limited, special-purpose system which achieves an in-depth, direct knowledge of concrete particulars at the cost of a breadth of epistemic knowledge, particularly in regard to "going beyond the information given." From this perspective, perception is to cognition what the photojournalism of *Life Magazine* is to the highly interpretive, intellectual essays of the *New York Review of Books*. In this regard, perceptual-level knowing is probably most useful in regard to capturing the meaning of two very different contexts: (1) in spontaneous, non-self-monitored behaviors which occur automatically, and thereby allow people to "wear their hearts on their sleeves"; (2) in slow-change systems where "form follows function," in the sense, for example, that parameters of appearance have been deformed systematically over time by the chronic activation of certain states. Classic examples of this type of effect have been studied by Shaw and his students regarding properties such as aging and dependency. Other candidates would be the chronic activation of certain emotions leaving certain lines on the face, as in the case of frowning leaving sadness lines around the mouth.

A developmental perspective on the relationship between perception and cognition

Another very critical reason for distinguishing perception from cognition echoes one of Zajonc's (1980) reasons for arguing for separating affect from cognition – the possibility of studying interactions between these systems. I would now like to illustrate the value of such an interaction perspective by looking at the interaction between perception and cognition developmentally.

Earlier I observed that perception precedes cognition in development of ontogeny as well as phylogeny, using the work of Piaget (1952), Odom (1978), and Vygotsky (1962), to buttress this argument. Now I would like to broaden this argument by claiming that one has to distinguish the way perception operates prior to the development of cognition from how it functions afterward. Specifically, for both better and worse I would argue that perception, even Gibsonian perception, will never be the same once man (or woman) has sampled the apple from the tree of symbolic knowledge; thus, at the risk of being too cute, I will refer to perception after cognition as the Adam and Eve effect.

This "after the fall' interpretation clarifies certain conceptual problems in the neo-Gibsonian literature that have always bothered me: (1) Did Neisser (1976) really distort Gibson's position? (2) Where does Shepard's (1984) analysis of the impact of ecological perception on central representations fit in? First, in regard to Neisser's (1976) treatment in which he attempted to reconcile the schema concept with Gibsonian direct perception, it is now clear to me why Neisser's position has been misunderstood. To wit, from the present view he is talking about perception *after* cognition has developed, as in the case of adults or older children. Where Neisser's contribution is particularly important in this regard is that he provides a role for schema functioning which is nonreductionistic in regard to direct perception. Specifically, Neisser (1976) treats schemata as structures which *guide* direct perception or fine tune the perceptual apparatus, *without* usurping its discovery of structure function by assimilating it to a schema-mediated constructive encoding principle (cf. Fiske and Taylor 1984). That is, perceptual meaning for Neisser is, as for Gibson, a matter of a differentiation of structure. The major difference between Gibson and Neisser as I see it is that Neisser is dealing with a cognitively experienced animal whereas Gibson (1979), again from the present view, is *dealing with how perception functions either in a relatively noncognitive animal or a cognitive animal before cognition develops to a sophisticated level.*

Shepard's (1984) analysis deals with a different stage in this process which focuses on how the properties of schemata may be influenced by *prior* perceptual development. That is, Shepard's paper deals with how "pure ecological" perception affects the *formation* of internal representations, whereas Neisser deals with how internal representations influence perception. Consider, for example, the behavior of a chess master compared to an ordinary chess player. Neisser (1976) points out that chess masters actually look at the chessboard more often than less adroit players. However, it is unlikely that eye movements guided by a highly developed cognitive structure function the same way as the eye movements of a relative novice. That is, the master's chunking or unitizing of the board is likely to be very different. For example, the master may organize the board top-down in terms of a linguistic label referring to some classic overall strategy, whereas the novice's attention is likely captured "bottom-up" in terms of the specific current organization of pieces on the board.

Applications to current problems in social cognition

The general nature of affect–emotion

The general domain of affect is perhaps the best place to argue specifically for the relevance of a separate perceptual level strategy, because it is here that the clearest case can be made for our ability to "see" as opposed to infer the hidden dispositional states lying behind social behavior. That is, it is in the perception of emotion that the clearest case emerges for "form following function," in the sense that the different primary emotions appear to take on expressive forms which yield consistent and accurate judgments at a pan-cultural level (cf. Ekman *et al.* 1969). The high stimulus specificity of the primary emotions is also indicated by Bassili's (1978) demonstration that a dynamic visual facial display which only relies on point-light information is sufficient for the accurate recognition of primary emotions. Such data support the role of a resonance to external invariants mechanism in social knowing. The likelihood of a biological foundation for emotion–resonance effects is supported by findings which suggest it is extremely difficult to countercondition such meanings. For example, attempts to pair smiling faces with shock and then use such faces as negative reinforcers have been markedly unsuccessful (Ohman and Dimberg 1978).

Further, even when emotional signs lack species-level biological preparedness, they still appear to display a high level of informational specificity. For example, emotional states such as anxiety and depression appear to be strongly mapped onto external expressive signs, as in the depressive's leaden gait or the hesitant speech patterns characterizing high anxiety.

Affect and cognition

The above considerations would appear to have clear implications for the problem of the relative primacy of affect versus cognition raised by the Zajonc–Lazarus debate (see Zajonc 1980, Lazarus 1982, Zajonc 1984, Lazarus 1984). From the present ecological perspective I would argue that whereas affect may indeed come before cognition, it does *not precede perception.* The present model can be used to clarify the relationship as follows. I offer two possible scenarios which frame the relationship among perception, affect, and cognition.

One possible scenario is that it is the perceptual detection of an affordance that instigates an affective response as the initial adaptive reaction. For example, perceiving that a predator affords threat to survival may directly key a fear response followed either immediately by flight or, with humans, perhaps an appraisal of the situation and then action. Alternatively, the direct perception of the affordance of danger and the elicitation of a fear response may occur simultaneously, suggesting the possibility that the direct perception of affordances and the occurrence of affect might be regarded as *complementary descriptions of the same event.* That is, they are parallel but different types of reactions to the same event. Specifically, both direct perception and primary affect may be seen as analogue processes which serve as signs or signals which are linked to environmental events in a natural or *nonarbitrary way.* In Peirce's (1931–5) classic terms, they are indices rather than symbols.

For example, spontaneous emotion displays may function as signs that the person has encountered certain types of environmental event, as in Buck's (1979) demonstrations that observers can accurately judge whether a stimulus person seen on a video monitor has just been exposed to a sexual, disgusting, surprising, or scenic slide. This type of spontaneous sign communication appears to be fundamentally different from what occurs with explicit verbal communication, where one often has to decode the message by separating out the real intention from the verbal content. For example, people who are racially prejudiced will often say the "right things" in terms of the content message but reveal a negative tone paralinquistically which can be readily detected (cf. Buck 1979). From the ecological perspective the paralinguistic cues are perceived directly, in the same sense that a leaden gait may be a sign of depression. In such a situation the affect produced by direct perception may precede cognition or the constructive encoding–decoding of the explicit verbal message.

Implications for the study of attitudes

One of the major implications of the ecological realist perspective is that it suggests a radical change in the way we view attitudes. First, given the close ties attitudes have to emotion in regard, for example, to classical conditioning and to acquisition of phobias, it is likely that at least the direction of a person's attitude would be perceptually transparent, particularly in regard to directly acquired attitudes. For example, one can probably perceive whether a given person likes another by observing their body-slant and their preferred distance from that person (cf. Hall 1966, Patterson 1982). More importantly, the realist ecological perspective in regard to attitude formation provides a systematic framework for deriving the Fazio and Zanna (1981) findings that directly acquired attitudes are better predictors of behavior than indirectly acquired attitudes. If directly acquired attitudes can be equated to perceptually rich and those indirectly acquired to verbally mediated, I would qualify the Fazio–Zanna position as follows: directly acquired attitudes will do a better job of predicting concrete, specific behaviors whereas indirectly acquired attitudes will do better predicting global, categorical criteria of a stereotypic nature. For example, in Swann's (1984) terms, directly acquired attitudes allow a high level of circumscribed accuracy in prediction, but do poorly in regard to global accuracy – that is, across perceivers, settings, and over extended periods of time.

The ecological perspective also provides a clear framework for describing how attitudes form and change and why different routes of attitude change may occur (Petty and Cacioppo 1981). Essentially, I would argue that the types of directly acquired attitude described above are likely *affective reactions* to *directly perceived affordances*. For example, affordances which signify nurturance or caring will elicit positive affect; affordances signifying ugliness or danger will elicit negative affect. The basic argument is analogous to the Rosenberg–Peak (Rosenberg 1956) perceived instrumentality model of attitude structure and formation, whereby affect was predicted to be positive if the person's values were inferred to be furthered by the attitude object and negative when the target was viewed as blocking the attainment of a value.

The ecological realist model also offers a new perspective on the meaning and determinants of attitude change, and in the course of so doing suggests a new functional theory of attitude change. First, as an overarching perspective it is assumed that perceptually acquired knowledge is open and provisional. Perception is stimulus-driven and accommodative in Piaget's sense. It is a *soft mold* which is constantly refashioned by contact with the multiple structuralizations of reality offered by the external world. From this perceptual learning perspective, attitude change could be treated as a process of increasing the differentiation or detection of structure in the world. In Asch's (1952) terms, what occurs is a change in the *object of judgment*. Gibson's (1979) contribution to Asch's analysis is to imply that what changes with differentiation may be the ability to see *different affordances*.

As applied to the literature on attitude change, this perceptual learning model suggests that the most basic meaning of attitude change might be a change in the perceived affordance structure and that, in effect, the most powerful way to produce change is to allow the perceiver spontaneously to observe new affordances for the target. Such an idea is implicit in certain field studies of attitude change motivated by the "contact hypothesis" (cf. Amir 1969). That is, direct equal-status contact is likely to facilitate the direct pickup of new affordances as the attitude target is progressively differentiated over time.

On the other hand, current models of change as a constructive, self-generated elaboration of pro and con arguments elicited by a verbal message make sense for *indirectly acquired attitudes devoid of a strong perceptual experiential base*. Thus the dichotomy drawn by Petty and Cacioppo (1981) between central and peripheral routes to change is, in effect, half right. It is a good model for changing indirectly acquired attitudes with a short-term verbal communication. It is, I believe, however, very inadequate for attitudes which are directly acquired and involve a long-term direct exposure to the target *in vivo*. Here I would argue that change of a much longer-lasting nature follows an automatic as opposed to a central route. That is, I would argue that centrally mediated, constructive verbal processes only make for more stable, longer-lasting change when "words" dominate the formation and change processes. Returning to our earlier argument, so-called peripheral variables such as communication properties and medium parameters become highly significant from the ecological perspective. For example, different communicators will lead people to partition the same message differently (the "change in object of judgment" argument). Further, the medium is the message in the sense that verbal persuasive communication likely produces change vis-a-vis conceptual–inferential processes, whereas extended face-to-face encounters with the attitude object are likely to produce change vis-a-vis a change in the perceived affordances of the target. Such changes will facilitate stable long-term change so long as direct contact occurs on a regular basis; that is, so long as concrete particulars dominate over stereotypic inference.

This analysis does *not* equate the central route with constructive processes and the peripheral route with perception. What it does do is suggest that it is not necessarily true that centrally induced change processes will be longer-lasting than the peripheral route. Specifically, when the automatic processes are perceptual in the sense that new affordances are detected, thereby changing the object of judgment, I predict long-term change *without* the involvement of central processes. Such shifts in perceived affordances need to be distinguished from automatic peripheral processes such as pairing persuasive communications with drinking Coke, which are indeed *not* likely to produce lasting change. In this regard communicator variables such as variations in credibility appear particularly likely to modify perceived affordances in a manner analogous to Neisser's (1976) treatment of schemata guiding the differentiation of the environment.

The development of an adult social relationship

In this section I would like to develop further the theme of how perceptual and cognitive factors interact in a developmental sequence, although now my focus will be on *interpersonal development*, as in the development of a relationship.

The first essential point to be understood is that, while moving from an intrapersonal to an interpersonal perspective means an *increase* in the complexity of the information to be processed from a constructionist perspective, it means something very different from an ecological point of view. Specifically, *scaling up the complexity* of a social situation may actually simplify the task of perceptual social knowing so long as complexity means an increase in structured information. Specifically, the information derived from social interaction is often richer in structure than the information available from individual actions because such interaction data contains temporally extended relational–contextual constraints derived from *joint* patterns of action. For example, consider the problem of deciding whether P is a dominant person. If P is viewed in isolation it is clear we have to resort to inference; we must, in effect, construct this property on the basis of comparing what P looks like and says with our schema of what a dominant person is like. However, once in an interaction, domination becomes a relationally defined social affordance perceivable from how P's actions affect O's. That is, dominance becomes specified in how P's actions lead O's actions over time. Specifically, dominance rests on behavioral asymmetry; that is, it may be said that the affordances of dominance are instantiated in behavior to the extent that asymmetry in one direction becomes characteristic of a relationship, be it in terms of biases in turn-taking, pace, pauses, or other parameters of an *extended* social interaction. For example, P is perceivably dominant over O when (1) O's responses lag behind P's, (2) O models or reciprocates the nature of P's responses more than P does for O's; (3) P is more likely to interrupt O than O is P; (4) P's response rate or pace "entrains" or captures O's rhythm of response. Viewed thus, joint, asymmetric action produces a structured context which *both* generates *and* reveals higher-order invariances which allow people to perceive a relational social affordance such as dominance.

Further, such perceptual social knowing is *relatively free of capacity limitations* because the information that is detected in the forms of social affordances is likely to be *utilized on-line* rather than stored. Moreover, if it is stored it is likely to be stored in analogue form involving little or no transformation of mode. This type of perceptual knowing is likely to be automatic, given the requirement that during social interaction it must function on-line; that is, it requires rapid detection of fast events available in a transient flow of information. Specifically, an effortful, conscious, cognitive process would be dysfunctional. On the other hand, conceptual knowing within a social interaction context essentially functions in the gaps and in regard to the conscious processing of verbal inputs. Specifically, interaction processing is mindful and constructive (1) when a set of role definitions or self-images are being negotiated at the beginning of a relationship or interaction, (2) when already established scripts break down and must, therefore, be repaired.

The boundaries for perceptual and conceptual processes within a social interaction

The specific contributions of perceptual and conceptual processes within the formation of a social relationship may be described in terms of a phase or stage-type model as follows: (1) prior to actual contact, gross physiognomic and expressive properties (e.g. physical attractiveness, the emotional state given by facial expressions, gait, and posture) provide an initial informational matrix which is rich in stimulus information; (2) at the beginning of actual contact when "identities are negotiated" we have a more or less conscious constructive "battle of the wills" (these terms are used by Swann 1984). However, what Swann in his constructive zeal leaves out is that this negotiation process is only transitory in a "good" relationship or interaction. It is simply too effortful to have to constantly negotiate. Thus, what happens as a relationship stabilizes (or moves into a maintenance phase) is that it goes on "automatic," creating a situation where one's attention gradually becomes educated perceptually to the meaning of one's partner's smallest gesture; for example, one can tell from a good friend or partner's facial expression, gait, or posture what mood they are in and whether or not it is a good time to interact or to leave them alone. Further, I hypothesize that the major difference between perceptual knowing *before* contact and this maintenance stage is that perceiving at the early level of contact is likely to involve a biologically prepared sensitivity to adaptively significant signs (cf. Kassin and Baron 1986) whereas the properties of gesture and expression detected after stabilization are likely to be the product of schema-directed perceptual learning in the Neisserian sense and hence be highly idiosyncratic and relationship-specific rather than working from signs which have cross-cultural generality.

This is not to say that during the *maintenance stabilization* phase there is not *also* constructive processing going on; it is to say that post-cognitive perceptual knowing becomes a way to get around stereotypic and largely vacuous polite social talk. That is, perception may allow us to disambiguate deceptive messages which, while facilitating communication at a superficial level, tend to hide real intentions and motives. In this regard, for example, high self-monitors may show a greater gap between the intent conveyed verbally and nonverbally than do low self-monitors.

Finally, it is proposed that if a relationship deteriorates, just as when a script is disrupted, there will be a return to a more conscious, constructive level of processing (cf. Mandler 1984). That is, in general it is postulated that social information processing is most constructive when one is building a relationship, given that generalized expectations are vulnerable to disconfirmation because of the lack of a direct, concrete, perceptual knowledge base, and when a relationship deteriorates because script-derived specific expectations have been disconfirmed. In both cases cognitive processes fill in the gaps either by constructing new, better-fitting schemata or by retrieving old schemata which are more appropriate than the current ones.

Viewed thus, perception and cognition complement one another at a number of levels. For example, direct perception may allow us to work from species-specific nonverbal cues, whereas cognitively prepared perception allows us to know where to direct our attention when social signs are equivocal. Also, while the automaticity of perceptual functioning may free the perceiver from capacity limitations, the ability to switch back to constructive, conscious cognitive processes may be essential when the environment fails to live up to our expectations.

Implications for the problem of veridicality in social knowing

In regard to accuracy or veridicality the ecological position, whether Gibsonian or neo-Gibsonian, strongly argues for the accuracy of ordinary social perception in the objective sense. Specifically, the criteria for perceptual accuracy are pragmatic and achievement-oriented (McArthur and Baron 1983, White 1984, Swann 1984). This means that the accuracy of what one takes to be a given social perception is tested behaviorally by the consequences of the perceptually entailed actions. For example, my perception that this opening is wide enough to afford crawling through is accurate if I can successfully get through it by crawling. Similarly, a person's perception that a given other person affords "helpfulness" is tested when a gesture of dependency or need that is made towards that person is successful; for example, when a baby's hunger cry leads to the quick availability of a breast. The ecological view that veridicality is tested pragmatically contrasts sharply with cognitive models which define accuracy in terms of logical, prescriptive criteria such as whether a person's judgment fits Bayes' theorem (cf. Nisbett and Ross 1980). Thus, while perception in the Gibsonian mode is clearly tied to an instrumental *truth value* criterion of accuracy, cognition is more likely to fall into a *logical normative framework* regarding whether or not inferences are logically biased as, for example, in the domain of cognitive heuristics (Kahneman and Tversky 1973).

Further, I would claim that these two different models of error treat bias and specificity very differently. From the perspective of a pragmatic, perception-based model, whether or not bias leads to error is an empirical as opposed to a logical issue. For example, a bias to turn right in a maze when looking for food only leads to error when the food is typically on the left side. On the other hand, a bias to under-utilize base-rate information is an error by definition within the constructive–normative model of error. In this regard it may also be noted that, while focusing on the concrete particular case as against general normative information leads to error within the constructive mode, it may facilitate accuracy within the ecological framework. To wit: if I am to decide whether or not to buy a used car from a friend who is a mechanic, I would be better advised to learn of his experiences with this particular car as opposed to reading *Consumer reports* about the average performance rating of this model. *Consumer reports* are only the most appropriate source when I am making a categorical decision such as which brand of car to buy. Veridicality of decision in the specific case will rest upon how well this particular car runs. The above analysis flows from the neo-Gibsonian distinction between the particularizing and the generalizing functions of perception and cognition, especially in regard to what we have discussed as the Gertrude Stein problem. It is also related to the issue I previously raised regarding distinguishing between a perceiver–actor perspective and an observer perspective on judging stimulus-based effects. That is, as perceivers we are likely to prefer our own experiences over *Consumer reports*, whereas experimenter–observers seek consensual data.

It should also be noted that accuracy in social knowing is undoubtedly tied to two other features of the present analysis: (1) It is highly likely that in realms where there is high informational specificity there will be more accuracy, for example, in judging primary affects as opposed to judging higher-order, more conventionalized affects such as guilt or sarcasm. (2)

Within the *trait-impression formation* realm it matters whether a person is asked to judge whether George is conscientious or whether he is a warm person. If the social attribute is low in iconicity – that is, if it is an arbitrary, conventional symbol – all one can observe is whether different people share the same conventional rule system. In this regard it may be noted that Kenrick and Stringfield (1980) and Cheek (1982) found that attributes judged to have observable referents elicited higher levels of cross-situational agreement among judges.

Finally, the present analysis has relevance for the veridicality of implicit theories of personality (IPTs) – the idealism–realism issue in impression formation. The neo-Gibsonian view suggests that we adopt a realism view under two sets of conditions. First, to the extent that trait combinations reflect the operation of an external invariant, implicit theories of personality are rooted in reality, as in my flu virus example. For example, if Eysenck (1967) is correct and introversion–extroversion differences are rooted in differential brain functioning, it is quite possible that the relationships we observe among social withdrawal, social anxiety, and lack of social skills are not constructed but reflect a response syndrome that exists in the world because introverts possess lower levels of important neurotransmitters than extroverts.

Further, it is possible to argue that the reason IPTs are viewed as constructive is that the individualistic and verbal simulation contexts of assessment do not allow perceivers to see how certain combinations of attribute emerge on-line during an actual social interaction. That is, certain trait packages may be real when observed in a relational context. In such situations self-presentation motives and/or roles may generate socially real combinations of traits (cf. Athay and Darley 1981).

Concluding statement

The central theme of this exposition is that the consistent application of an ecological perspective to the acquisition and utilization of knowledge in general, and social knowing in particular, strongly requires that a qualitative distinction be made at the level of process between perception and cognition. In this regard perception has been treated as a direct, hands-on, behaviorally connected mode of knowledge acquisition focusing on concrete particulars, whereas cognition has been treated as indirect, inferential, constructive, and oriented towards generalization. We have gone beyond merely elaborating this distinction and attempted to specify conditions which may influence when one or another of these epistemic strategies will predominate. In this regard we have emphasized the role of communicative–linguistic factors deriving from the constraints of social interactions as well as the iconicity or informational specificity of social signs. From this dual-mode perspective perception is viewed as a more basic, earlier developing, and more narrow, special-purpose system perhaps specialized for the pickup of the functional meanings of iconic nonverbal information. Further, perceptually relevant information is likely to be heavily saturated in affect, to be strongly action- and interaction-oriented, and to require in many cases rapid, real-time, on-line processing.

In sum, it is important to recognize that in opting for a dual mode epistemic strategy, I am rejecting *both* the constructive reductionism which treats perception as parasitic on cognition *and* Gibson's own brand of reductionism which treats cognition as derivative from and inferior to direct perception. I have in effect adopted an ecological position which is *different* from Gibson's because it is *post-cognitive*. I have taken this tack because I believe it is necessary if we are to make the most effective use of the ecological perspective in clarifying current problems in social knowing.

References

Alley, T. R. (1981) *Caregiving and the perception of maturational status*. Unpublished doctoral dissertation, University of Connecticut.

Amir, Y. (1969). Contact hypothesis in ethnic relations. *Psychological Bulletin* 71: 319–42.

Anderson, J. R. (1980). Concepts, propositions, and schemata: what are the cognitive units? *Nebraska Symposium on Motivation*. Lincoln: University of Nebraska Press.

Asch, S. E. (1952). *Social psychology*. Englewood Cliffs, NJ: Prentice-Hall.

Athay, M. and Darley, J. M. (1981). Toward an interaction centered theory of personality. In N. Cantor and J. F. Kihlstrom (eds.), *Personality cognition and social interaction*. Hillsdale, NJ: Lawrence Erlbaum.

Baron, R. M. (1980). Social knowing from an ecological event perspective: a consideration of the relative domains of power for cognitive and perceptual modes of knowing. In J. Harvey (ed.), *Cognition, social behavior, and the environment*. Hillsdale, NJ: Lawrence Erlbaum.

Baron, R. M., Boudreau, L. A., and Oliver, P. V. (1986a). *Effects of expectancy to communicate on trait utilization in person description*. Paper presented at the annual meeting of the APA, Washington, DC.

Baron, R. M., Boudreau, L. A., and Oliver, P. V. (1986b). *A modification of the communication expectancy effect on descriptive trait usage through visual imagery instructions*. Unpublished manuscript, University of Connecticut.

Bassili, J. N. (1978). Facial motion in the expression of faces and of emotional expression. *Journal of Experimental Psychology: Human Perception and Performance* 4: 373–9.

Bassili, J. W. (1979). Emotion recognition: the role of facial movement and the

relative importance of upper and lower areas of the face. *Journal of Personality and Social Psychology* 37.
Brown, R. (1985). *Social psychology*, 2nd edn. New York: Free Press.
Bruner, J. S. (1957a). On perceptual readiness. *Psychological Review* 64: 123–49.
Bruner, J. S. (1957b). Going beyond the information given. In H. Gruber, G. Terrell, and M. Wertheimer (eds.), *Contemporary approaches to cognition*. Cambridge, MA: Harvard University Press.
Brunswick, E. (1956). *Perception and the representative design of psychological experiments*, 2nd edn. Berkeley and Los Angeles: University of California Press.
Buck, R. (1979). Measuring differences in the nonverbal communication of affect: the side viewing paradigm. *Human Communication Research* 6: 47–57.
Buck, R. (1985). *The communication of emotion*. New York: Guilford Press.
Burnstein, E. and Schul, Y. (1982). The informational basis of social judgments: operations in forming an impression of another person. *Journal of Experimental Social Psychology* 18: 217–34.
Cheek, J. M. (1982). Aggregation, moderator variables, and the validity of personality tests. A peer rating study. *Journal of Personality and Social Psychology* 43: 1254–69.
Cutting, J. E. (1978). Generation of synthetic male and female walkers through manipulation of a biomechanical invariant. *Perception* 7: 317–72
Cutting, J. E., Proffitt, D. R., and Kozlowski, L. T. (1978). A biomechanical invariant for gait perception. *Journal of Experimental Psychology: Human Perception and Performance* 4: 1357–72.
Dornbush, S. A., Hastorf, A. H., Richardson, S.A., Muzzy, R. E., and Vreeland, R. S. (1965). The perceiver and the perceived: their relative influence on the categories of interpersonal perception. *Journal of Personality and Social Psychology* 1: 434–41.
Ekman, P., Sorenson, E. R., and Friesen, W. V. (1969). Pan-cultural elements in the facial displays of emotion. *Science* 174: 86–8.
Eysenck, H. J. (1967). *The biological basis of personality*. Springfield, IL: Charles C. Thomas.
Fazio, R. H. and Zanna, M. P. (1981). Direct experience and attitude–behavior consistency. In L. Berkowitz (ed.), *Advances in experimental social psychology*, vol. 14. New York: Academic Press.
Fiske, S. T. and Taylor, S. E. (1984). *Social cognition*. Reading, MA: Addison-Wesley.
Fodor, J. A. and Pylyshyn, Z. W. (1981). How direct is visual perception? Some reflections on Gibson's "ecological approach." *Cognition* 9: 139–96.
Gati, I. and Tversky, A. (1984). Weighty common and distinctive features in perceptual and conceptual judgment. *Cognitive Psychology* 16: 341–70.
Gergen, K. (1984). The social constructionist movement in modern psychology. *American Psychologist* 40: 255–65.
Gibson, J. J. (1966). *The senses considered as perceptual systems*. Boston: Houghton Mifflin.

Gibson, J. J. (1979). *The ecological approach to visual perception*. Boston: Houghton Mifflin.

Hall, E. T. (1966). *The hidden dimension*. New York: Doubleday.

Heider, F. and Simmel, M. (1944). An experimental study of apparent behavior. *American Journal of Psychology* 57: 243–54.

Helmholtz, H. von (1948). Concerning perceptions in general. In W. Dennis (ed.), *Readings in the history of psychology*. New York: Appleton-Century-Crofts.

Hoffman, C., Mischel, W., and Baer, J. S. (1984). Language and person cognition: effects of communicative set on trait attribution. *Journal of Personality and Social Psychology* 46: 1029–43.

Johnson, N. S. and Raye, C. I. (1981). Reality monitoring. *Psychological Review* 88: 67–85.

Jones, E. E. and Nisbett, R. (1972). The actor and observer: divergent perceptions of the causes of behavior. In E. E. Jones *et al.*, *Attribution: perceiving the causes of behavior*. Morristown, NJ: General Learning Press.

Kahneman, D. and Tversky, A. (1973). The psychology of prediction. *Psychological Review* 80: 237–51.

Kassin, S. M. (1979). Consensus information, prediction and causal attribution: a review of the literature and issues. *Journal of Personality and Social Psychology* 37: 1966–81.

Kassin, S. M. and Baron, R. M. (1985). Basic determinants of attribution and social perception. In J. Harvey and G. Weary (eds.), *Attribution in contemporary psychology*. New York: Academic Press.

Kassin, S. M. and Baron, R. M. (1986). On the basicity of social perception cues: developmental evidence for adult processes? *Social Cognition* 4: 180–200.

Kelley, H. H. (1967). Attribution theory in social psychology. In D. Levine (ed.), *Nebraska Symposium on Motivation*. Lincoln: University of Nebraska Press.

Kenrick, D. T. and Stringfield, D. O. (1980). Personality traits and the eye of the beholder: crossing some traditional philosophical boundaries in the search for consistency in all of the people. *Psychological Review* 87: 88–104.

Kruglanski, A. W. (1980). Lay-epistemologic processes and contents. *Psychological Review* 87: 70–87.

Lazarus, R. S. (1982). Thoughts on the relations between emotion and cognition. *American Psychologist* 37: 1019–24.

Lazarus, R. S. (1984). On the primacy of cognition. *American Psychologist* 39: 124–9.

Leventhal, H. (1980). *Toward a comprehensive theory of emotion*. In L. Berkowitz (ed.), *Advances in experimental social psychology*, vol. 13. New York: Academic Press.

McArthur, L. Z. and Baron, R. M. (1983). Toward an ecological theory of social cognition. *Psychological Review* 90: 215–38.

Mandler, G. (1984). *Mind and body: psychology of emotion and stress*. New York: Norton.

Marcel, A. J. (1983a). Conscious and unconscious perception: experiments on visual masking and word recognition. *Cognitive Psychology* 15: 197–237.

Marcel, A. J. (1983b). Conscious and unconscious perception: an approach to the relations between phenomenal experience and perceptual processes. *Cognitive Psychology* 15: 238–300.

Markus, H. and Zajonc, R. B. (1985). The cognitive perspective in social psychology. In G. Lindzey and E. Aronson (eds.), *Handbook of social psychology*. New York: Random House.

Massad, G. M., Hubbard, M., and Newtson, D. (1979). Selective perception of events. *Journal of Experimental Social Psychology* 15: 513–32.

Neisser, U. (1967). *Cognitive psychology*. Englewood Cliffs, NJ: Prentice-Hall.

Neisser, U. (1976). *Cognition and reality*. San Francisco: Freeman.

Nisbett, R. E. and Ross, L. (1980). *Human inference: strategies and shortcomings of social judgement*. Englewood Cliffs, NJ: Prentice-Hall.

Nisbett, R. E. and Wilson, T. D. (1977). Telling more than we can know: verbal reports on mental processes. *Psychological Review* 84: 231–59.

Odom, R. D. (1978). A perceptual salience account of decalage relations and developmental change. In C. J. Brainard and L. S. Siegal (eds.), *Alternatives to Piaget: critical essays on the theory*. New York: Academic Press.

Ohman, A. and Dimberg, U. (1978). Facial expressions as conditioned stimuli for human autonomic responses. *Journal of Personality and Social Psychology* 36: 1251–8.

Patterson, M. L. (1982). A sequential functional model of nonverbal exchange, *Psychological Review* 89: 231–49.

Peirce, C. S. (1931–5). *Collected papers*, ed. C. Hartshorne and P. Weiss. Cambridge, MA: Harvard University Press.

Petty, R. E. and Cacioppo, J. T. (1981). *Attitudes and persuasion*. Dubuque, Iowa: Brown.

Piaget, J. (1952). *The origins of intelligence in children*. New York: International University Press.

Polanyi, M. (1964) *Personal knowledge: toward a postcritical philosophy*. New York: Harper.

Pylyshyn, Z. (1980). Computation and cognition: issues in the foundations of cognitive science. *Behavioral and Brain Sciences* 3: 111–69.

Rosenberg, M. J. (1956). Cognitive structure and attitudinal affect. *Journal of Abnormal and Social Psychology* 53: 367–72.

Runeson, S. and Frykholm, G. (1981). Visual perception of lifted weight. *Journal of Experimental Psychology: Human perception and performance* 7: 733–40.

Runeson, S. and Frykholm, G. (1982). Kinematic specification of dynamics as an informational basis for person and action perception: expectation, gender recognition and deceptive intention. *Uppsala Psychological Reports* 324. Uppsala, Sweden: Department of Psychology, University of Uppsala.

Russell, B. (1948). *Human knowledge, its scope and limit*. New York: Simon & Schuster.

Schneider, D. J., Hastorf, A. H., and Ellsworth, P. C. (1979). *Person perception*. Reading, MA: Addison-Wesley.

Shaw, R. and Pittenger, J. (1977). Perceiving the face of change in changing faces:

implications for a theory of object perception. In R. Shaw and J. Bransford (eds.), *Perceiving, acting, and knowing*. Hillsdale, NJ: Lawrence Erlbaum.

Shepard, R. N. (1984). Ecological constraints on internal representations: resonant kinematics of perceiving, imagining, thinking, and dreaming. *Psychological Review* 91: 417–47.

Swann, W. B. (1984). Quest for accuracy in person perception: a matter of pragmatics. *Psychological Review* 91: 457–77.

Tagiuri, R. and Petrullo, L. (eds.) (1958). *Person perception and interpersonal behavior*. Stanford, CA: Stanford University Press.

Turvey, M. T. (1977). Preliminaries to a theory of action with reference to vision. In R. Shaw and J. Bransford (eds.), *Perceiving, acting, and knowing*. Hillsdale, NJ: Lawrence Erlbaum.

Vygotsky, K. (1962). *Thought and language*. Cambridge, MA: MIT Press.

Wertsch, J. V. (1985). *Vygotsky and the social formation of mind*. Cambridge, MA: Harvard University Press.

White, P. (1984). A model of the layperson as pragmatist. *Personality and Social Psychology Bulletin* 10: 333–48.

Zajonc, R. B. (1980). Feeling and thinking: preferences need no inferences. *American Psychologist* 35: 151–75.

5 A new perspective for social psychology[1]

Daniel Bar-Tal and Yoram Bar-Tal

In the last four decades, social psychology has emerged as a distinguished and important field in psychology. Although it has grown and changed in the scope of investigated topics and theoretical conceptions, its basic foundation has remained the same. This direction of development has continued in spite of the increased criticism of the field arising during the last decade and a half. The present chapter will first describe in brief the foundation of social psychology and present the principal critiques of the field. Then it will suggest an alternative perspective which may provide solutions to some of the criticized problems of social psychology. These problems stem, in our opinion, from the nature of its foundation.

The positivistic foundation of social psychology

The foundation of social psychology is based on the positivistic approach as reflected especially in logical positivism (see Gergen 1979, Hendrick 1977 for a more extensive analysis of the positivistic foundation of social psychology). The positivistic approach to science emerged as a fairly definite outlook in philosophy about fifty-five years ago (for a broader description of logical positivism and logical empiricism see Achinstein and Barker 1969, Ayer 1956, 1959, Carnap 1936, Cohen and Nagel 1934, Feigl 1956). This approach accepts only scientific knowledge as valid. Scientific knowledge is demarcated from nonscientific knowledge by the fact that the former is verifiable while the latter is not. This is the heart of what is called the justificationist position (Weimer 1979), since it justifies science as a method for the attainment of genuine knowledge and considers

1 The authors would like to thank Anat Biletzki, Kenneth Gergen, Reid Hastie, and Arie Kruglanski for their valuable comments on an earlier draft of this chapter.

it the authoritative source of knowledge. Accordingly, scientific knowledge is accumulated through accurate observations of behavior. The rules of collecting these observations are defined by scientific methods. On the basis of the collected observations, scientists may in turn be able to construct a theory to explain the observed behavior. Thus the progress of science is made through inductive logic which allows for generalizations derived from particular observations.

The following basic principles are direct derivations of the positivistic foundation in social psychology: (*a*) the use of the experimental method to perform observations, and (*b*) the attempt to generate laws on the basis of collected observations.

The positivistic approach implies that science has advanced chiefly through accumulation of facts by empirical generalization and by rigorous efforts to exclude speculation. Facts are, therefore, collected ideally through objective quantified observations under carefully controlled conditions. On the basis of the positivistic approach, in an attempt to adapt the presumed methods of investigation in the natural and physical sciences, experimentation has become the hallmark of social psychology. As Klineberg (1965a) has noted, "a laboratory is essential and should become standard equipment. There are, of course occasions when experiments can be conducted in an institution outside the university... The field of experimental social psychology is perhaps ours par excellence, the clearest and most direct trademark of our discipline" (10). In line with this tradition, the experimental method has become the dominant procedure of collecting data. Most of the experiments have been carried out in a laboratory setting within university walls where college students have served as subjects. Although in recent years social psychologists have increased their use of field experiments which have been carried out in real-life settings with individuals who are naturally present, nevertheless, in both methods social psychologists have manipulated a limited number of variables, assuming that their meaning is contained in the operations which they can measure.

With regard to the second principle, an important assumption of the positivistic approach is that general scientific laws can be induced from these observations. According to this view, the task of social psychology is to discover laws governing human social behavior, as was indicated by Mills (1969) for example, "social psychologists want to discover causal relationships so that they can establish basic principles that will explain the phenomena of social psychology" (412). Similarly, Jones and Gerard (1967) stated: "Science seeks to understand the factors responsible for stable relationships between events" (42). The attempt to formulate general laws implies that social psychologists have assumed that it is possible to discover universal principles of social behavior applicable to all persons.

Indeed, the typical writings in social psychology as reflected in textbooks, books, or journals treat the majority of specific findings or theorizing as if they were universal generalizations.

Critiques of social psychology

During the last fifteen years, social psychology has been the recipient of criticism which has dealt with various problems of the field (e.g. Armistead 1974a, Duck 1980, Elms 1975, Harré and Secord 1972, Gergen 1973, 1982, Israel and Tajfel 1972, McGuire 1973, Strickland *et al.* 1976). Among the accumulated criticism we would like to focus on the following two critiques: (*a*) the shortcomings of the experimental method, and (*b*) the obstacles regarding the generation of universal rules of social behavior.

The first critique consists of problems indicating a deficiency of experimentation. Over the years, a number of shortcomings associated with the experimental method have been noted. Some of the examples are the tendency of the subjects to respond to demand characteristics of the experimental situation (e.g. Orne 1962, 1969); the effect of experimenters' expectations on subjects' reactions (e.g. Rosenthal 1966); the artifact of subjects' characteristics caused by volunteering participation in experiments (e.g. Rosenthal and Rosnow 1975); the predominant preoccupation with manipulations of deceptions (e.g. Ring 1967); the artifact of experimenters' characteristics (e.g. Sattler 1970), or the violation of professional ethics in dealing with subjects (e.g. Kelman 1972, Vinacke 1954). Smith (1972) noted in this vein that "the predominant experimental tradition in the field has contributed rather little for serious export in enlarging and refining our views of social man" (94).

The second critique, which has been especially voiced during the last decade, is that it has become more and more apparent that social psychology is experiencing difficulty in generating general laws of social behavior. Inconsistent results in the same areas of research and the inability to replicate the findings indicate that the nature of social behavior is more complicated than it was formerly thought to be. Already, almost twenty years ago, Klineberg (1965b) observed that: "The more recent experiments by social psychologists have rightly attracted considerable attention, but unfortunately many of the results have not stood up under replication" (117). Allport (1968), in analyzing the historical background of social psychology in the 1968 handbook, pointed out that "many contemporary studies seem to shed light on nothing more than a narrow phenomenon studied under specific conditions. Even if the experiment is successfully repeated there is no proof that the discovery has wider validity. It is for this reason that some current investigations seem to end up on elegantly polished triviality – snippets of empiricism, but nothing more" (68). On this basis Smith's (1972) remarks can be evaluated. "After three decades of industrious and intelligent effort, the case for cumulative advance in experimental psychology remains open to reason" (88). These criticisms are of special importance since they undermine the fundamental objective of social psychology as a science, according to the positivistic approach.

At least three causes have been identified to account for the difficulty described above in generating universal laws: (1) historical effect, (2) cultural relativity, and (3) inability to control variables. The first argument has been advanced by Gergen (1973, 1982) who asserted that social psychology cannot make any lasting discoveries since social psychological laws are time-bound. In his opinion, therefore, social psychology should be considered an historical science. The second limitation derives from the argument stating that social behavior is largely culturally relative (e.g. Triandis, 1972, 1975, 1976). Accordingly, many of the variables studied by social psychologists are culture-specific, reflecting "subjective culture". In other words, they characterize a group's way of perceiving its social environment – particularly its norms, roles, and values. Finally, social psychologists have realized that the experimental method cannot completely reconstruct the complexity of real-life situations and control the various variables which affect the subjects in the investigated situation. As a result, many findings are confounded with uncontrolled variables and, therefore, generalizations cannot be generated (Cronbach 1975). As Janis (1975) has pointed out, "Time and again the social psychologist's laboratory findings on main effects and simple interactions that are expected to be dependable generalizations turn out to be will-o-the wisps because they fail to stand up in conceptual replications or turn out to be the product of higher order interactions with 'relatively' trivial variables that are specific to the experimental setting" (111).

In view of the critiques outlined, which have inspired the feelings that social psychology faces a crisis, we would like to present, in the next part of the chapter, an alternative perspective of social psychology. In our opinion this perspective may suggest some solutions to the criticisms and may even provide the beginning of a new foundation for social psychology.

A new perspective

The new perspective is constituted from three bases: nonjustificationist philosophy, subjectivism, and the distinction between universal and particularistic generalizations. These bases are known and have been used by different social psychologists, but they have yet to be supplied in a coherent way to benefit the social psychological endeavor. We view them as complementary and interwoven at the same time, and they will be presented as such.

Nonjustificationist philosophy

The nonjustificationist approach to science, which maintains that all of our knowledge, including scientific knowledge,[2] is conjectural and uncertain, has established itself in philosophy during the last few decades (see for example Bartley 1962, Feyerabend 1981, Kuhn 1970a, Lakatos 1968, Lakatos and Musgrave 1970, Popper 1959, 1963, Weimer 1979). According to this approach, knowledge can neither be proven true nor justified by an appeal to any ultimate authority, and therefore it consists of information in the form of opinions or conjectures. This view suggests that:

> knowledge claims, whether scientific or otherwise, are always fallible; anything in both common sense and the body of science is subject to criticism and consequent revision or rejection, at all times for all time... Thus science is a comprehensively critical endeavor; all its conjectures including the most fundamental standards and basic positions, are always and continually open to criticism. (Weimer 1979: 39–40)

The nonjustificationist approach places rationality in criticism rather than in justification (Bartley 1962, Popper 1963). Since we neither have objective criteria (such as empirical facts) to prove, nor appropriate epistemological authority to convince, we must reject the notion that knowledge has to be proven in order to be genuine or that the maintenance of proof necessarily implies truth. The rationale behind the nonjustificationist rejection of truth-by-proof lies in the conviction that factual evidence is created by the theories we hold. Popper (1959) originated this argument by suggesting that "We can utter no scientific statement that does not go far beyond what can be known with certainty 'on the basis of immediate experience'... Every description uses universal names (or symbols, or ideas); every statement has the character of a theory, of a hypothesis" (94–5).

The chapter of Wyer and Srull in the present volume provides impressive evidence, in the domain of social cognitive research, how scientists often attempt to acquire information with particular objectives in mind, then accordingly select procedures for acquiring it, and finally draw conclusions (see also Greenwald *et al.* 1986).

2 The term "knowledge" is used in this chapter as a psychological concept describing a total number of beliefs, including scientific ones, which individuals hold. Beliefs are defined as propositions in which individuals believe beyond a certain minimal threshold of confidence. But at the same time the existence of truthful knowledge is recognized, though it can never be proved to have been obtained.

With this basis in mind, it has also been suggested that scientists focus on only a few of the limitless features of the environment when they investigate a phenomenon, since their observations are always based on their own limited knowledge (Popper 1963).

In addition, nonjustificationist philosophy rejects the idea that inductive inference provides the logic for creating valid new knowledge. As Popper (1959) pointed out, "it is far from obvious, from a logical point of view, that we are justified in inferring universal statements from singular ones, no matter how numerous, for any conclusion drawn in this way may always turn out to be false" (27).

Popper (1982) does suggest that deductive inference is the logic behind the criterion which demarcates between scientific theory and any other type of knowledge, called by him "pseudo-science". This criterion is testability of the theory by its potential falsification. As he writes:

> I see our scientific theories as human inventions – nets designed by us to catch the world. To be sure, these differ from inventions of the poets, and even from the inventions of the technicians. Theories are not only instruments. What we aim at is truth: we test our theories in the hope of eliminating those which are not true. (42)

Testing according to Popper is aimed at correcting possible mistakes. However, it does not mean that testing necessarily brings us to truth or that a theory that has not been tested is incorrect. "To sum up, it is true – as emphasized in my L.Sc. D. – that even falsifications are never absolute, or quite certain" (Popper 1983: 187).

Consequently, later nonjustificationist philosophy does not even provide an alternative logic, but suggests that ultimate sources of knowledge or epistemological authority simply do not exist. Naturally based distinctions between theoretical and empirical levels cannot be found, and therefore everything becomes an equally potential and authoritative source of knowledge (of special relevance to this argument is Gergen's chapter in the present volume). In this view the rationality of science can be expressed, not by any method of proof or falsification, but rather by criticizing or testing the consistency between any relevant empirical and theoretical information and the position that one entertains at the time. As Lakatos (1978) noted:

> If factual propositions are unprovable then they are fallible. If they are fallible then clashes between theories and factual propositions are not "falsifications" but merely inconsistencies . . . The demarcation between the unproven "theories" and the hard proven empirical basis is non-existent; all propositions of science are theoretical and incurably fallible . . . Propositions can only be derived from other propositions, they cannot be derived from facts. (16)

According to this view, testing can in principle go on forever without being able to establish or refute something conclusively. Testing, according to Popper (1959), "is merely a very important aspect of the more general ideal of intersubjective criticism, or, in other words, of the idea of mutual rational control by critical discussion" (44). This is not to say that knowledge's validity is not defendable – "however the defense of such a claim is not an attempt to prove it, but rather the marshaling of 'good reasons' on its behalf. And the 'good reasons' are never justifications of the claim, only conjectures that are relevant to its assessment" (Weimer 1979: 41).

The belief that scientific observations, including experimental findings, do not have a monopoly on the formation of truthful knowledge implies that laboratory experimentation is only one of many possible ways through which it is possible to generate new knowledge. New knowledge can also be generated by different ways of collecting information as well as by creative thinking. Rigid adherence to laboratory experimentation has prevented social psychologists from developing and using other ways of collecting knowledge. Although a number of social psychologists have called for use of other scientific methods (e.g. Bar-Tal 1984a, Gergen 1978, McGuire 1973, Tajfel 1972), experimentation has still remained the dominant method of research (Higbee *et al.* 1976). For example, observations, content analyses, interviews, or the use of questionnaires are recognized methods which are used by other scientific disciplines as means of knowledge collection. It would be far-fetched to claim that knowledge about competition and cooperation (Mead 1937) collected by anthropologists through observation, or knowledge about voting behavior (Lazarsfeld *et al.* 1944) collected by sociologists through surveys, or knowledge about a relationship between beliefs and behavior (Holsti 1967) collected by a political scientist through content analysis is of less significance than results obtained by the classic works of experimental social psychology.

The point we wish to stress here transcends the criticism of laboratory experimentation as lacking internal and/or external validity (e.g. Adair 1973, Kruglanski 1975, Orne and Evans 1966, Rosenthal and Rosnow 1969). It also goes beyond advocating the use of other methods mentioned before, or the creation of alternative research methods such as social experimentation (Saxe and Fine 1981), treating subjects as informants (Gadlin and Ingle 1975), or allowing individuals to behave spontaneously and freely in experiments (Harré and Secord 1972). Both the rejection of certain methods and an endorsement of specific research methods represents the search for an ultimate epistemological authority. In line with nonjustificationist philosophy, we suggest that no method holds superiority in the acquisition or validation of knowledge, and inductive inference does not necessarily provide the logic for the formation of true facts. Research methods allow greater confidence in the validity of the conclusions because they may eliminate alternative explanations. The fewer alternative explanations scientists have for a given conclusion, the more confidence they feel about it. But since it is impossible to determine a priori what kind of alternative explanations should be eliminated without considering the specific case, it is impossible to decide a priori which method is better for studying that case (Kruglanski and Kroy 1976).

Scientific knowledge grows in different ways since there are various ways to develop knowledge. The variety of standards and motives that characterize different scientists gives rise to plurality in methods and theories (Feyerabend 1981; see also the chapter by Wyer and Srull in this volume). At the same time, observed facts through scientific methods cannot be considered as providing ultimate truth or as being superior to theory as a source of knowledge. Let us not forget that some of the most important psychological revelations were brought to light on the basis of "unsystematic" observations. Piaget formulated the most influential theory of cognitive development on the basis of observing his three children, and Freud proposed a comprehensive theory of personality, development, and pathology on the basis of a few cases he had treated. This is not to say that their observations brought them necessarily to the truth; but we want to emphasize that their observations are not necessarily inferior to any other ways of achieving the true knowledge.

Furthermore, the new perspective not only calls for the use of multiple ways of collecting information, but also calls for greater utilization of armchair psychology. Through insights, introspections, memories, or creative thinking, social psychology can benefit and expand. (See for example the guidelines of Gergen (1982) for the development of "generative theory".) The most significant contributions to social psychology were reached on the basis of armchair theorizing (for example, Heider 1958), which only later was followed by research (see Rakover 1983).

As Heider (1958) suggested: "We shall make use of the unformulated or half-formulated knowledge of interpersonal relations – this source will be referred to as common sense or naive psychology; we shall also draw upon the knowledge and insights of scientific investigation and theory in order to make possible a conceptual systematization of the phenomena under study" (4).

We believe that nonjustificationist philosophy liberates social psychologists from adherence to traditional research methods (especially experimentation) as exclusive sources of knowledge. This avenue hinders the development of social psychology. The new perspective, which does not recognize an ultimate authority for knowledge collection or for its recognition as truth, encourages creative thinking on the basis of any type of observation for the sake of new knowledge formation. The evaluation of new knowledge will come through the examination of its consistency with observations and/or with theoretical beliefs, as recognized by social psychologists. That is, social psychologists, like all other individuals, validate their conclusions by examining the consistency of the entertained hypotheses and alternative explanations with their available knowledge (see the chapter by Kruglanski). In our view, what makes social psychologists scientists is (*a*) their continuous and systematic efforts to extend their own knowledge about social psychology, (*b*) their devotion to the attempt to develop new social psychological knowledge and organize it systematically, and (*c*) their commitment to open-mindedness and new discoveries which is reflected in their constant skepticism, challenge, and criticism of the collected knowledge.

Subjectivism

The second basis of the new perspective is subjectivism. We accept the assumption, especially elaborated by phenomenologists, that reality is subjective and that it is constantly changing (e.g. Husserl 1962, Lauer 1978, Merleau-Ponty 1962, Natanson 1970, Spiegelberg 1966). The subjectivity tenet centers around the consequence of the unique set of experiences that each individual goes through. On the basis of their own experiences, individuals perceive "their own world" and attach to it their own meaning (Schutz 1972). Each individual, therefore, perceives, understands, and experiences the world in his own way. According to this view, there is no such thing as objectivity, since each person, including a scientist, is a captive of his own perspective. Social actions, therefore, have subjective meaning which is inaccessible to any other individual. As Schutz (1972) noted, "the meaning I give to your experiences cannot be precisely the same as the meaning you give to them when you proceed to interpret them" (93).

This subjective perspective is not stable. Throughout their lives, individuals encounter new experiences and may change their perceptions and understandings at any time. In this respect, our perspective suggests a dynamic view of individuals' reality. In this vein, Gurwitsch (1970), the phenomenologist, explained the psychological basis of the subjectivity tenet:

> the schemes of apperception and apprehension play a determining role in and for perception; they contribute essentially toward making the things encountered such as they appear in perceptual experience. As a result of the elimination of the reference to scientific explicability and an ideal mathematical order, we are not reduced to perceptual experience in its pristine purity, that is to say, yielding primary and secondary qualities only. Rather the things perceived present themselves as defined by the purpose they serve, the use that can be made of them, the manner in which

they are to be handled and so on, briefly as determined by schemes of apprehension. (50)

Of special interest for social psychology is the recognition by phenomenologists that, although individuals form their own unique reality, there also exists common reality. Individuals who have similar experiences by being members of the same group also form common perceptions and understandings, in addition to their own. Gurwitsch (1970) referred to such perceptions and understandings as the cultural world of a sociohistorical group.

The tenet of subjectivity is not alien to social psychology (see MacLeod 1947). Numerous social psychologists have recognized that individuals' knowledge is subjective and that it influences their collection and processing of information (e.g. Asch 1952, Brunswick 1956, Harré 1980, Heider 1958, Krech and Crutchfield 1948, and in this vein see Graumann's chapter in this volume). This means that the world that individuals perceive is the world that exists uniquely for them. As Krech *et al.* (1962) noted, "Man acts upon his ideas, his irrational acts no less than his rational acts are guided by what he thinks, what he believes, what he anticipates. However bizarre the behavior of men, tribes, or nations may appear to an outsider, to the men, to the tribes, to the nations their behavior makes sense in terms of their own world views" (17).

Thus the way a person reacts towards social stimuli depends on how he perceives, interprets, and evaluates the information contained in that stimulus or situation.[3] The perception, interpretation, and evaluation depend in turn on the knowledge that this individual has, and knowledge which consists of beliefs regarding various objects is accumulated through an individual's life. (See the chapters by Devine and Ostrom, Hastie and Rasinski, Higgins and Stangor, Jaspars, and Ross and McFarland in this volume.)

The new perspective assumes that understanding of an individual's reaction is contingent on knowing his beliefs, since individuals mostly behave consistently with their knowledge. As Heider mentions (1958), "If a person believes that the lines in his palm foretell his future this belief must be taken into account in explaining certain of his expectations and actions" (5).

It is, therefore, not surprising that a number of social psychologists have emphasized the cognitive nature of social psychology, assuming that a study of social behavior should be carried out through the investigation of the individual's knowledge (e.g. Eiser 1980, Fiske and Taylor 1984,

3 A basic assumption that underlies many of the propositions in the present chapter is that much of human social behavior is mediated by the cognitive repertoire of the behaving person.

Harvey and Smith 1977, Manis 1977, Markus and Zajonc 1985, Mischel 1979, Ostrom 1984, Wyer and Srull 1984, Zajonc 1980).

An important implication of this position is that neither in the formulation of a theory nor in the investigation of social behavior should social psychologists impose their "objective" definition of the contents of individuals' beliefs in the specific case. On the contrary, social psychologists need to recognize that the contents of beliefs are of unlimited scope, and that individuals differ in regard both to the beliefs that they maintain and to the accessibility of those beliefs at any given moment. Thus, individuals participating in social psychological studies are active knowers who perceive, experience, process information, and behave according to their own definition of the situation which is based on their own knowledge (see also Harré 1974, Secord 1977). Therefore, social psychologists should consider "reality" from the point of view of investigated individuals (see also Buss 1975, Armistead 1974b).

In this vein, it should be noted that the described analysis is also grounded in nonjustificationist philosophy, since the latter rejects the notion of the objectivity of science because scientists, like other individuals, develop scientific knowledge on the basis of their own biases, limited knowledge, and tendencies. According to nonjustificationist philosophy, any content of knowledge is potentially biased and any scientific or statistical method is a mere conjecture of ultimate unknown veridicality.

This principle should be applied to social psychological research as well as to theorizing. For example, the measurement of attitude–behavior relations should result in asking the subjects what types of behavior are perceived by them as implied by the relevant attitude. It should not be assumed that there is any specific behavior which is necessarily implied by a given attitude (e.g. Salancik 1982). Along the same lines, Abelson (1976) proposed that the relationship between attitude and behavior depends substantially on scripts that individuals have or can construct about social events. With regard to attribution research, Taylor (1976) noted that "the fact that in experimental studies only person-oriented questions are asked of subjects and a liberal criterion for what constitutes a person attribution is set leaves the experimenter little choice about what conclusions to reach. Open-ended questions, for example, lead one to very different conclusions about the process of person perception" (74).

Similarly, researchers studying causal perceptions of success and failure should first establish the cognitive repertoire of utilized causes and their meaning (e.g. Bar-Tal *et al.* 1984) and not assume that individuals use only four causes which can be classified dichotomously on two dimensions. Also, when dealing with consistency between cognitions, as in the case of dissonance research (Festinger 1957), we should not assume that any given cognition has the same relevancy and applications for all human beings. When individuals do not perceive implications of cognitions as contradicting each other, attitude change, as predicted by dissonance theory, may not occur.

Another important implication of subjectivity refers to the tendency of social psychologists to determine situational factors which influence behavior or cognition. But it cannot be assumed that situational variables have stable and universal qualities for all individuals; that is, that all individuals perceive, interpret, and evaluate the situational stimuli in the same way. For example, research on leadership tends to predict the behavior of followers on the basis of such characteristics as task structure, leader's personality, organizational environment, or power structure (see Bar-Tal 1985, Hunt and Larson 1974) out of many possible variables and possible ways of their perception. Similarly, in the area of helping behavior, social psychologists have assumed that certain situations trigger certain cognitions which lead to certain behaviors (see Bar-Tal 1984b).

The same argument can also be applied to personality research. The assumption behind conceptions of personality traits such as locus of control (Rotter 1966), anxiety (Shedletsky and Endler 1974), or self-monitoring (Snyder 1979) is that individuals who possess certain personality traits maintain certain types of cognition in every situation, at all times. This assumption implies that individuals possess stable cognitions. In contrast, the new perspective suggests that we cannot assume that the same cognitions are available to everyone all the time. Cognitions are dynamic and may change from time to time and from situation to situation. Any assessment of cognitions requires knowledge of the cognitive repertoire existing in the "phenomenological field" of the individual. On the basis of the revealed repertoire, it is possible to construct measurement instruments (e.g. Bar-Tal *et al.* 1978, Gergen *et al.* 1986). Researchers need to be aware of the problems in arbitrarily assigning cognitive contents to the investigated population, and need to recognize instead the subjective and changeable nature of human cognition.

The subjective and changeable nature of individuals' reality makes it difficult for social psychologists to formulate rules on how an individual will react to specific situations. Even if social psychologists do make observations in one situation, any change of individuals participating in a study, or change of the features of the situation, may also change the findings, since new cognitions may differently influence the behavior (the latter point has been extensively explored by Higgins and Stangor in the present volume). Even so, this perspective does not imply that no commonality can be found in human groups. As phenomenologists have recognized the essence of the cultural world of a sociohistorical group, social psychologists also have recognized that individuals who pass through common experiences form similar beliefs (e.g. Lonner 1979, Pepitone 1981, Triandis 1978). Advancing this point, Gergen (1982) has pointed out that, as

> [the] individual is capable of transforming the meaning of stimulus conditions in an indeterminant number of ways, existing regularities must be considered historically contingent – dependent on the prevailing meaning systems or conceptual structures of the times. In effect, from this perspective the scientist's capacity to locate predictable patterns of interaction depends importantly on the extent to which the population is both homogeneous and stable in its conceptual constructions. (17)

In this vein, for example, Bar-Tal (in press) has proposed the concept of "group beliefs", indicating that group members do form common beliefs. This is one of the tasks of social psychologists – to find out the common beliefs of a group which constitute its reality and thus influence group members' social behavior.[4]

Universalism versus particularism

According to the new perspective it is necessary, in social psychology, to differentiate between what can be universally generalized and what can be applied only to a particular case. Universal generalization involves generalization over individuals, places, situations, and times, while particularistic generalization is limited to certain individuals, situations, and places. The former generalization allows for universal laws which can be used in a description of human behavior in any place, time, or situation. The latter generalization is limited to individuals who are known to maintain a similar repertoire of beliefs and therefore may behave similarly in the same situations, or to certain situations which may affect similarly different individuals. The acceptance of universal generalizations does not imply that induction justifies universal statements, since there is no method or logic to determine a priori which generalization is universal. Nevertheless, once a universal principle is proposed, its universality should be examined with the available evidence in accordance with the consistency principle described before. That is, as long as scientists do not find exceptions, the formulated principle can be considered as universal.

On the basis of the above distinction between the two types of generalization, we would like to suggest that, in many cases, while social psychologists attempted to formulate universal generalizations, they in fact often theorized and performed studies which enabled them to derive only parti-

4 That is not to say that membership in any given group necessary implies any specific cognition. Rather, we suggest that familiarity with group beliefs is useful for an understanding of a behavior that group members may perform.

cularistic generalizations. The literature of social psychology is filled with examples of specific conclusions which are treated as providing universal laws. For instance, attitude similarity leads to attraction; physically attractive individuals are perceived as good; aggression is enhanced by heat, crowding, noise, and even various scents; observation of a helping model increases this behavior; mere presence of others increases arousal; groups take riskier courses of action than individuals; individuals compare themselves to similar others, etc. (For specific analyzed examples see Bar-Tal 1984b, Cartwright 1973, Wispé 1980.) These described "laws" cannot be universally generalized. They may characterize only specific populations in given situations.

How individuals would behave in certain situations depends on how they would perceive, interpret, and evaluate given stimuli. Since cognitive processes are dynamic, the availability of specific cognitions may change from time to time and from situation to situation, and since individuals differ in their cognitive repertoire it is difficult to predict which cognitions will be triggered by specific individuals in a given situation. Therefore, different individuals have different cognitions and exhibit different behaviors in different situations. In order to elicit the same behavior from different individuals we have to assume that specific situations would trigger similar cognitions. The problem social psychologists have run into is that they have assumed that the triggered cognitions of individuals in certain situations, times, and places can be generalized to other situations, times, and places (Faucheux 1976, Jahoda 1979, Smith 1978). But any change of individuals, situations, places, or times may alter the cognitions and therefore also change the behavior (see for examples studies by Kruglanski *et al.* 1984, Kruglanski and Freund 1983 which illustrate this point).

In view of the problems described above, a number of social psychologists have expressed doubts as to whether it is possible to discover universal laws in social psychology (e.g. Gergen 1973, Thorngate 1976). Gergen (1973), for example, has suggested that: "Unlike the natural sciences ... [social psychology] deals with facts that are largely nonrepeatable and which fluctuate markedly over time. Principles of human interaction cannot readily be developed over time because the facts on which they are based do not remain stable" (309).

According to our view, unsuccessful attempts to develop universal theory in social psychology should not lead us to the conclusion that social psychology cannot be a science (e.g. Gergen 1973). Rather, we should avoid the mistake of confusing what can be particularistically generalized with what can be universally generalized (Bar-Tal 1984b).

In order to explore further the difference between universal and particularistic generalization, we suggest an examination of their meaning in the context of *content* and *process* distinction. *Contents* refer to cognitions that individuals use to characterize people, behaviors, topics, events, objects, places, or situations. *Processes* refer to sequences of operations performed by individuals which describe principles of overt and covert behaviors. Both contents and processes can be found on different levels of universality. It is possible to find contents which may be held by an individual in a certain situation and time and it is possible, as well, to identify contents which may be held by a large portion of the human population or even by all human beings. In the same way, it is possible to describe particular processes of specific behaviors that pertain to certain individuals, times, or situations, and it is possible to describe a general underlying process of a behavior category that pertains to all human beings. We would like to suggest that it is less feasible to formulate universal laws on the basis of contents than on the basis of processes. That is, while even the identification of universal content does not imply that it is always accessible and therefore cannot always be used in explaining and predicting human behavior, a universal process that underlies a given behavior can be always used to explain and predict that behavior. This is so because universal processes are not dependent on contents that may or may not be in an individual's (the naive person's) repertoire. Instead, they describe sequences of operations in general and abstract terms. Therefore, they do not have to be in every individual's head, but are used only by the analyst of human behavior. Moreover, through the study of universal processes it is more probable to develop causal understanding of social behavior than through the study of universal contents. The former direction explicitly focuses on the explanation of behavior principles, while the latter does not necessarily provide causal explanations. This distinction is similar to Manicas and Secord's (1983) suggestion of differentiating between studying general causal properties of configured structures and studying the particular changing configurations.

The studying of universal process in social psychology has two functions. First, it provides parsimonious and general explanations of social behavior. These explanations are suitable for any specific behaviors that the given process underlies and thus may provide an integration of knowledge collected in social psychology. Second, it allows us to make specific predictions when specific relevant contents of the behavior are known. The mere knowledge of contents does not enable us to describe the course of behavior people will take.

Of special interest for the present approach, which greatly emphasizes individuals' knowledge as a determinant of human reactions, is the distinction between contents of knowledge and the epistemic process of knowledge acquisition. This distinction between contents of knowledge and the epistemic process involves the question of the ability to formulate universal laws of social behavior. According to Kruglanski (1979, 1980), who formulated the lay epistemology theory, contents of knowledge refer to all the propositions whose validity a person may wish to ascertain. Contents of knowledge are of unlimited scope and may be related to a particular culture, at a certain place in a given situation, and over a specific period of time. In contrast, the epistemic process that he suggests is universal. It describes the sequence of cognitive operations performed by individuals on their way to a given bit of knowledge, irrespective of specific contents. Kruglanski (1980 and the chapter in the present volume) proposed that the process of knowledge acquisition consists of two phases: first, the cognitive generation stage wherein the contents of knowledge come into existence in our mind; second, the cognitive validation stage which concerns assessment of the degree of confidence that is attributed to the generated contents. The former phase occurs within the stream of associations and it depends on the salience of various stimuli, momentary availability of various ideas, and the person's mental capacities such as intelligence or creativity. The latter phase is accomplished via deductive logic based on the consistency principle, which assumes that the acceptance of knowledge depends on the consistency of one's conclusion with one's premises (see also the chapters by Trope and Ginossar and by Devine and Ostrom in this volume).

This description is presented as content-free and universal because so far no exceptions to the presented principles have been found. Kruglanski has successfully demonstrated how it encompasses specific contents of attribution theory (Kruglanski 1980) and various consistency theories (Kruglanski and Klar 1987). Recently, the described process model has even been applied to specific analyses of behavior, still in a universal way. Thus, Bar-Tal *et al.* (in press) have suggested a process model describing interpersonal interaction, and Bar-Tal and Bar-Tal (1985) have proposed a description of the process of helping behavior performance.

It should be noted that very often social psychologists argue that general theories in social psychology are useless because they do not allow us to make general and accurate (valid) predictions. Thorngate (1976) expressed this position by stating: "It is impossible for an explanation of social behavior to be simultaneously general, simple and accurate" (126). The fallacy in such statements stems from the confusion between accuracy and specificity. It is possible, in our view, to explain and predict very accurately from general and relatively simple principles. Accurate predictions can be derived from universal process descriptions because they do not have exceptions. The description of universal process is in general and abstract terms and it is possible to predict accurately on its basis. For example, according to the lay epistemology theory individuals, in order to make a decision, will select an alternative which will be consistent with their beliefs available at the moment of making the decision. However, specific predictions refer to actual contents of cases of certain individuals in certain circumstances. In order to make specific predictions, one has to be familiar with specific contents relevant to the predicted case. In our previous example, it is necessary to be familiar with the specific beliefs of the individual to be able to predict what actual decision he will make.

Most of the middle-range theories in social psychology do not require familiarity with all the specific contents related to the prediction because they are based on the implicit assumption that certain contents are universal and that, therefore, it is not necessary to measure them in each group. Such theories provide a "stereotypic" approach to the problem. The use of this stereotypic approach may lead to errors. Predictions in social psychology, as well as in real-life cases, require knowledge of specific contents involved. But since, as social psychologists, we want to explain and not just specifically predict, we have to find the universal process which underlies the relevant behavior.

An important point which should be emphasized is that the present perspective does not preclude the study of contents, but rather indicates the limitation of this research direction. According to our view the study of contents has three main objects: (*a*) elucidating and examining universal processes, (*b*) performing particularistic descriptions, and (*c*) enabling social intervention. The first objective is concerned with examination of any universal process. Universal process is described in abstract terms and is used as a universal principle. Any examination of universal process, however, has to be done within a content-bound framework – that is, specific variables have to be inserted into the abstract concepts if one intends to study process or describe a specific case of an individual's behavior. The particularistic direction of research focuses on the study of contents in order to characterize certain individuals, groups, or situations. Particularistic studies, for example, may attempt to map the repertoire of cognitions of a certain group in a specific domain in order to describe cognitions triggered in a specific group in a given situation, or to study the relationship between cognitions and behavior of a group in a given situation (see for example D. Bar-Tal 1986, Klar 1987 in press, Lamiell 1981, Runyan 1983). Finally, social intervention with groups cannot be done without knowing the relevant contents which characterize the target population in the specific situation. Only on the basis of this knowledge is it possible to understand the antecedents and outcomes of behavior of a certain group and thus plan the direction of intervention and its effects (see Y. Bar-Tal 1986).

In this vein, content-bound research is not intended to generate universal laws of behavior, but rather to describe the behavior of specific individuals or groups functioning in a specific time, place, and situation (see for example Bar-Tal, in press). Even so, it is possible that certain contents may characterize a number of groups or even be universal. A number of social psychologists who recognize the limitations of contentual research have attempted to search for the universal contents of social behavior (e.g. Berry 1979, Jahoda 1978, Lonner 1979, Triandis 1978). The major effort of social psychology today, however, is directed at particularistic, content-bound theory and research. As long as social psychologists recognize the limitation of such endeavors, their objectives will remain realistic.

Summary

The three bases of the presented perspective for social psychology are complementary and should be seen as reinforcing one another in the construction of the new foundation for the field. Specifically, the nonjustificationist approach suggests that there are no objective ways to determine truthful knowledge. In other words, there are no objective ways to assess the truthfulness of any contents of beliefs, including so-called scientific ones. As a result, we can only refer to contents of beliefs from the subjective point of view of the perceiver. Also, in light of the nonjustificationist rejection of induction via scientific observations, as the right way of constructing truthful theories, it is suggested that findings pertaining to specific contents do not necessarily help to develop general theory. All these arguments imply that social psychologists have to differentiate between what can be universally and what can be particularistically generalized. While focus on specific contents limits our ability to generate universal knowledge, the study of universal processes not only allows for the generation of general theory but also provides an explanation of social behavior.

Nonjustificationist philosophy, the subjective nature of human behavior, and the distinction between particularistic and universal generalizations provide a new outlook for social psychology. The new perspective "allows" social psychologists to derive their knowledge about social behavior from various sources. The recognition that all knowledge is fallible, that there is no ultimate authority to validate it, that scientific methods are only additional ways to collect knowledge, and that scientists' research and theorizing is guided by subjective beliefs with no monopoly on objectivity – this recognition encourages social psychologists to attempt different means of observation. Accordingly, social psychologists are free to use their own thinking capacities to theorize and investigate to further the development of new social psychological knowledge.

Social psychologists' specialization in collecting knowledge about social behavior is a result of their training and work. The scope of their knowledge about social behavior is greater than that of other psychologists. This accumulated knowledge, together with the incoming information collected through observations, serves as a basis for new insights and discoveries. The acceptance of any idea as part of accumulated knowledge always depends on its consistency with one's premises. But social psychologists, in their acquisition of knowledge, must exercise constant criticism and challenge the presented beliefs. Skepticism, together with the attempt to explain inference (Weimer 1979), the striving to discover new knowledge (Lakatos 1970), the will to solve the puzzle of knowledge (Kuhn 1970b), and the attempt to falsify the collected knowledge and to learn from mistakes (Popper 1959), can all contribute to making the social psychologists' endeavor more fruitful.

The proposed perspective focuses on the knowledge of human beings which in turn functions as a basis for social behavior. Knowledge consists of numerous beliefs about various subjects. Human beings actively process information and, on this basis, form their beliefs. The knowledge of each individual is unique, subjective, and potentially biased. It is not static, but dynamic. Not only does an individual's knowledge change through the years, but in addition the accessible beliefs at any given moment may vary. Nevertheless, together with an emphasis on the individual's uniqueness, the present perspective allows the possibility that individuals living in social groups and sharing common experience also form common beliefs. These common beliefs may be the basis for similar behaviors which are so often observed among members of a group.

Finally, the proposed perspective outlines the directions that social psychologists can take in studying the universal and the particular. Universal generalizations can be expressed in terms of the processes which underlie social behavior, irrespective of the specific contents. The discovery of these processes is a necessary objective if social psychologists desire to explain and predict social behavior. But the elucidation of the processes is only one necessary direction of social psychologists' contributions. A study of specific groups in a specific milieu is another important task. When following this direction of research, social psychologists should rely on the relevant contents of the studied group. Any progress in studying contents, however, must be based on an understanding of the processes which underlie social behavior. The latter contribution is limited in that the acquired knowledge about a specific group may be only particularistically and not universally generalized.

In sum, the perspective suggested here would change old bases, assumptions, and premises (as reflected in the way social psychologists have adopted positivistic tenets) which have failed to lead to the construction of a discipline for which many of us strove. The crises that we often go through demonstrate the fallacies of the old direction and strengthen the need to look for alternatives. The proposed perspective offers solutions to some of the problems encountered in the last decade. We feel, if this is not too presumptuous, that the presented perspective provides a new paradigm in the Kuhnian sense, since it views social psychological accomplishments in an alternative way and suggests a different foundation for social psychology's future endeavors.

References

Abelson, R. P. (1976). Script processing in attitude formation and decision making. In J. S. Carroll and J. W. Payne (eds.), *Cognition and social behavior*. Hillsdale, NJ: Lawrence Erlbaum.

Achinstein, P. and Barker, S. F. (eds.) (1969). *The legacy of logical positivism*. Baltimore: Johns Hopkins University Press.

Adair, J. G. (1973). *The human subject: The social psychology of psychological experiment*. Boston: Little, Brown.

Allport, G. W. (1968). The historical background of modern social psychology. In G. Lindzey and E. Aronson (eds.), *The handbook of social psychology*, 2nd edn., vol. 1. Reading, Mass.: Addison-Wesley.

Armistead, N. (ed.) (1974a) *Reconstructing social psychology*. Harmondsworth: Penguin.

Armistead, N. (1974b). Experienced in everyday life. In Armistead 1974a.

Asch, S. E. (1952). *Social psychology*. Englewood Cliffs, NJ: Prentice-Hall.

Ayer, A. J. (1956). *The problem of knowledge*. Baltimore: Penguin.

Ayer, A. J. (ed.) (1959). *Logical positivism*. New York: Macmillan.

Bar-Tal, D. (1984a). American study of helping behavior: what, why and where. In E. Staub, D. Bar-Tal, J. Karylowski, and J. Reykowski (eds.), *Development and maintenance of prosocial behavior: international perspective*. New York: Plenum.

Bar-Tal, D. (1984b). *The limitations of investigating contents: the case of helping behavior*. Unpublished manuscript.

Bar-Tal, D. (1986). The Masada syndrome: a case of central belief. In N. Milgram (ed.), *Stress and coping in time of war*. New York: Brunner/Mazel.

Bar-Tal. D. (in press). *Group beliefs*. New York: Springer.

Bar-Tal, D., Bar-Tal, Y., Geva, N., and Levin-Yarkin, K. (in press). Planning and performing interpersonal interaction: a cognitive–motivational approach. In W. H. Jones and D. Perlman (eds.), *Perspectives in interpersonal behavior and relationships*. Greenwich, Ct.: JAI Press.

Bar-Tal, D., Goldberg, M., and Knaani, A. (1984). Causes of success and failure and their dimensions as a function of SES and gender: a phenomenological analysis. *British Journal of Educational Psychology* 54: 51–61.

Bar-Tal, D., Leinhardt, G., and Bar-Tal, Y. (1978). Effect of an innovative science program on perceptions of locus of control and satisfaction. *Science Education* 62: 349–57.
Bar-Tal, Y. (1985). *Viewing leadership from the followers' perspective: a comparison with contingency models*. Unpublished dissertation, Boston University.
Bar-Tal, Y. (1986). *Toward an applicable social psychology: a nonjustificationistic perspective*. Unpublished manuscript.
Bar-Tal, Y. and Bar-Tal, D. (1985). *Performance of helping behavior: process and content*. Unpublished manuscript.
Bartley, W. W. (1962). *The retreat to commitment*. New York: Knopf.
Berry, J. W. (1979). A cultural ecology of social behavior. In L. Berkowitz (ed.), *Advances in experimental social psychology*, vol. 12. New York: Academic Press.
Brunswick, (1956). *Perception and the representative design of psychological experiments*, 2nd edn. Berkeley: University of California Press.
Buss, A. R. (1975). The emerging field of the sociology of psychological knowledge. *American Psychologist* 30: 988–1002.
Carnap, R. (1936). Testability and meaning. *Philosophy and Science* 13: 419–71.
Cartwright, D. (1973). Determinants of scientific progress: the case of research on the risky shift. *American Psychologist* 28: 222–31.
Cohen, M. R. and Nagel, E. (1934). *An introduction to logic and scientific method*. New York: Harcourt, Brace & World.
Cronbach, L. J. (1975). Beyond the two disciplines of scientific psychology. *American Psychologist* 30: 116–27.
Duck, S. (1980). Taking the past to heart: one of the futures of social psychology? In R. Gilmour and S. Duck (eds.), *The development of social psychology*. London: Academic Press.
Eiser, J. R. (1980). *Cognitive social psychology*. London: McGraw-Hill.
Elms, A. C. (1975). The crisis of confidence in social psychology. *American Psychologist* 30: 967–76.
Faucheux, C. (1976). Cross-cultural research in experimental social psychology. *European Journal of Social Psychology* 6: 269–322.
Feigl, H. (1956). Some major issues and developments in the philosophy of science of logical empiricism. In Feigl, H. and Scriven, M. (eds.), *Minnesota studies in the philosophy of science*. Minneapolis: University of Minnesota Press.
Festinger, I. (1957). *A theory of cognitive dissonance*. New York: Harper & Row.
Feyerabend, P. K. (1981). *Problems of empiricism*, vol. 2. Cambridge University Press.
Fiske, S. T. and Taylor, S. E. (1984). *Social cognition*. Reading, Mass.: Addison-Wesley.
Gadlin, H. and Ingle, G. (1975). Through the one-way mirror: the limits of experimental self-reflection. *American Psychologist* 30: 1003–9.
Gergen, K. J. (1973). Social psychology as history. *Journal of Personality and Social Psychology* 26: 309–320.

Gergen, K. J. (1978). Toward generative theory. *Journal of Personality and Social Psychology* 36: 1344–60.

Gergen, K. J. (1979). The positivistic image in social psychology. In A. R. Buss (ed.), *Psychology in social context*. New York: Irvington.

Gergen, K. J. (1980). Towards intellectual audacity in social psychology. In R. Gilmour and S. Duck (eds.), *The development of social psychology*. London: Academic Press.

Gergen, K. J. (1982). *Toward transformation in social knowledge*. New York: Springer.

Gergen, K. J., Hepburn, A., and Fisher, D. C. (1986). Hermeneutics of personality description. *Journal of Personality and Social Psychology* 50: 1261–70.

Greenwald, A. G., Pratkanis, A. R., Leippe, M. R., and Baumgardner, M. H. (1986). Under what conditions does theory obstruct research progress? *Psychological Review* 93: 216–29.

Gurwitsch, A. (1970). Problems of the life-world. In Natanson 1970.

Harré, R. (1974). Blueprint for a new science. In Armistead 1974a.

Harré, R. (1980). Making social psychology scientific. In R. Gilmour and S. Duck (eds.), *The development of social psychology*. London: Academic Press.

Harré, R. and Secord, P. (1972). *The explanation of social behaviour*. Oxford: Blackwell.

Harvey, J. H. and Smith, W. P. (1977). *Social psychology*. St Louis: Mosby.

Heider, F. (1958). *The psychology of interpersonal relations*. New York: Wiley.

Hendrick, C. (1977). Social psychology as an experimental science. In C. Hendrick (ed.), *Perspectives on social psychology*. Hillsdale, NJ: Lawrence Erlbaum.

Higbee, K. L., Lott, W. J., and Graves, J. P. (1976). Experimentation and college students in social psychology. *Personality and Social Psychology Bulletin* 2: 239–41.

Holsti, O. R. (1967). Cognitive dynamics and images of the enemy. In D. J. Finlay, O. R. Holsti, and R. R. Fagen, *Enemies in politics*. Chicago: Rand McNally.

Hunt, G. J. and Larson, L. L. (ed.) (1974). *Contingency approaches to leadership*. Carbondale: Southern Illinois University Press.

Husserl, E. (1962). *Ideas: general introduction to pure phenomenology*. New York: Macmillan.

Israel, J. and Tajfel, H. (eds.) (1972). *The context of social psychology*. London: Academic Press.

Jahoda, G. (1978). Cross-cultural perspectives. In H. Tajfel and C. Fraser (eds.), *Introducing social psychology*. Harmondsworth: Penguin.

Jahoda, G. (1979). A cross-cultural perspective on experimental social psychology. *Personality and Social Psychology Bulletin* 5: 142–8.

Janis, I. L. (1975). Field experiments on the effectiveness of social support for stressful decisions. In M. Deutsch and H. Hornstein (eds.), *Problems of applying social psychology*. Hillsdale, NJ: Lawrence Erlbaum.

Jones, E. E. and Gerard, H. B. (1967). *The foundations of social psychology*. New York: Wiley.

Kelman, H. C. (1972). The rights of the subject in social research: an analysis in terms of relative power and legitimacy. *American Psychologist* 27: 989–1016.

Klar, Y., Bar-Tal, D., and Kruglanski, A. W. (1987). Conflict as a cognitive schema. In W. Stroebe, A. W. Kruglanski, D. Bar-Tal, and M. Hewstone (eds.), *The Social psychology of intergroup conflict*. New York: Springer.

Klineberg, O. (1965a). The place of social psychology in a university. In O. Klineberg and R. Christie (eds.), *Perspectives in social psychology*. New York: Holt, Rinehart & Winston.

Klineberg, O. (1965b). Some philosophical and methodological problems in social psychology. In B. Wolman (ed.), *Scientific psychology*. New York: Basic Books.

Krech, D. and Crutchfield, R. S. (1948). *Theory and problems of social psychology*. New York: McGraw-Hill.

Krech, D., Crutchfield, R. S., and Ballachey, E. L. (1962). *Individual in society*. New York: McGraw-Hill.

Kruglanski, A. W. (1975). The human subject in the psychological experiment: fact and artifact. In L. Berkowitz (ed.), *Advances in experimental social psychology*, vol. 8. New York: Academic Press.

Kruglanski, A. W. (1979). Causal explanation, teleological explanation: on radical particularism in attribution theory. *Journal of Personality and Social Psychology* 37: 1447–57.

Kruglanski, A. W. (1980). Lay epistemologic process and contents. *Psychological Review* 87: 70–87.

Kruglanski, A. W. and Ajzen, I. (1983). Bias and error in human judgment. *European Journal of Social Psychology* 13: 1–44.

Kruglanski, A. W. and Freund, T. (1983). The freezing and unfreezing of lay-inferences. Effects on impressional primacy, ethnic stereotyping, and numerical anchoring. *Journal of Experimental Social Psychology* 19: 448–68.

Kruglanski, A. W., Friedland, N., and Farkash, E. (1984). Lay persons' sensitivity to statistical information: the case of high perceived applicability. *Journal of Personality and Social Psychology* 46: 503–18.

Kruglanski, A. W. and Klar, Y. (1987). A view from a bridge: synthesizing the consistency and attribution paradigms from a lay epistemic perspective. *European Journal of Social Psychology* 17: 211–41.

Kruglanski, A. W. and Kroy, M. (1976). Outcome validity in experimental research: a re-conceptualization. *Representative Research in Social Psychology* 7: 166–78.

Kuhn, T. S. (1970a). *The structure of scientific revolutions*, 2nd edn. University of Chicago Press.

Kuhn, T. S. (1970b). Logic of discovery or psychology of research? In Lakatos and Musgrave 1970.

Lakatos, I. (ed.) (1968). *The problem of inductive logic*. Amsterdam: North-Holland.

Lakatos, I. (1970). Falsification and the methodology of scientific research programmes. In Lakatos and Musgrave 1970.

Lakatos, I. (1978). *The methodology of scientific research programmes*, vol. 1. Cambridge University Press.

Lakatos, I. and Musgrave, A. (eds.). (1970). *Criticism and the growth of knowledge*. Cambridge University Press.

Lamiell, J. T. (1981). Toward an idiothetic psychology of personality. *American Psychologist* 36: 276–89.

Lauer, Q. (1978). *The triumph of subjectivity*, 2nd edn. New York: Fordham University Press.

Lazarsfeld, P. F., Berelson, B., and Gaudet, H. (1944). *The people's choice: how the voter makes up his mind in a presidential campaign*. New York: Duel, Sloan, and Pearce.

Lonner, W. (1979). The search for psychological universals. In H. C. Triandis and W. W. Lambert (eds.), *The handbook of cross-cultural psychology*, vol. 1. Boston: Allyn & Bacon.

McClelland, D. C. (1955). The psychology of mental content reconsidered. *Psychological Review* 62: 297–320.

McGuire, W. J. (1973). The Yin and Yang of progress in social psychology. *Journal of Personality and Social Psychology* 26: 446–56.

MacLeod, R. B. (1947). The phenomenological approach to social psychology. *Psychological Review* 54: 193–210.

Manicas, P. T. and Secord, P. F. (1983). Implications for psychology of the new philosophy of science. *American Psychologist* 38: 399–413.

Manis, M. (1977). Cognitive social psychology. *Personality and Social Psychology Bulletin* 3: 550–66.

Markus, H. and Zajonc, R. B. (1985). The cognitive perspective in social psychology. In G. Lindzey and E. Aronson (eds.), *Handbook of social psychology*, vol. 1. New York: Random House.

Mead, M. (ed.) (1937). *Competition and cooperation and primitive people*. New York: McGraw-Hill.

Merleau-Ponty, M. (1962). *Phenomenology of perception*. New York: Humanities Press.

Mills, J. (1969). The experimental method. In J. Mills (ed.), *Experimental social psychology*. New York: Macmillan.

Mischel, W. (1979). On the interface of cognition and personality. *American Psychologist* 34: 740–54.

Natanson, N. (ed.) (1970). *Phenomenology and social reality*. The Hague: Nijhoff.

Newell, A. and Simon, H. A. (1972). *Human problem solving*. Englewood Cliffs, NJ: Prentice-Hall.

Orne, M. T. (1962). On the social psychology of the psychological experiment. With particular reference to demand characteristics and their implications. *American Psychologist* 17: 776–83.

Orne, M. T. (1969). Demand characteristics and the concept of quasi-control. In R. Rosenthal and R. L. Rosnow (eds.), *Artifact in behavioral research*. New York: Academic Press.

Orne, M. T. and Evans, F. J. (1966). Inadvertent termination of hypnosis on hypnotized and simulating subjects. *International Journal of Clinical and Experimental Hypnosis* 14: 61–78.

Ostrom, T. M. (1984). The sovereignty of social cognition. In R. Wyer and T. Srull (eds.), *Handbook of social cognition*. Hillsdale, NJ: Lawrence Erlbaum.

Pepitone, A. (1981). Lessons from the history of social psychology. *American Psychologist* 36: 972–85.

Pivcevic, E. (1970). *Husserl and phenomenology*. London: Hutchinson.

Popper, K. R. (1959). *The logic of scientific discovery*. New York: Harper & Row.

Popper, K. R. (1963). *Conjectures and refutations*. New York: Harper & Row.

Popper, K. R. (1982). *The open universe, an argument for indeterminism*. London: Hutchinson.

Popper, K. R. (1983). *Realism and the aim of science*. London: Hutchinson.

Rakover, S. S. (1983). Hypothesizing from introspection: a model for the role of mental entities in psychological explanation. *Journal for Theory of Social Behaviour* 13: 211–30.

Ring, K. (1967). Experimental social psychology: some sober questions about some frivolous values. *Journal of Experimental Social Psychology* 3: 13–123.

Rosenthal, R. (1966). *Experimenter effects in behavior research*. New York: Appleton-Century-Crofts.

Rosenthal, R. (1976). *Experimenter effects in behavioral research*. New York: Irvington Publishers.

Rosenthal, R. and Rosnow, R. L. (1969). The volunteer subject. In R. Rosenthal and R. L. Rosnow (eds.), *Artifact in behavioral research*. New York: Academic Press.

Rosenthal, R. and Rosnow, R. L. (1975). *The volunteer subject*. New York: Wiley.

Rotter, J. B. (1966). Generalized expectancies for internal versus external control of reinforcement. *Psychological Monographs* 80 (1, whole no. 609).

Runyan, W. M. (1983). Idiographic goals and methods in the study of lives. *Journal of Personality* 51: 413–37.

Salancik, G. R. (1982). Attitude–behavior consistencies as social logics. In M. P. Zanna, E. T. Higgins, and C. P. Herman (eds.), *Consistency in social behavior*, vol. 2. Hillsdale, NJ: Lawrence Erlbaum.

Sattler, J. M. (1970). Racial "experimenter effects" in experimentation, testing, interviewing and psychotherapy. *Psychological Bulletin* 73: 137–60.

Saxe, L. and Fine, M. (1981). *Social experiments*. Beverly Hills, Ca.: Sage.

Schlenker, B. R. (1974). Social psychology and science. *Journal of Personality and Social Psychology* 29: 1–15.

Schutz, A. (1972). *The phenomenology of the social world*. London: Heinemann.

Secord, P. (1977). Social psychology in search of a paradigm. *Personality and Social Psychology Bulletin* 3: 41–50.

Shedletsky, R. and Endler, N. S. (1974). Anxiety: The state–trait model and the interaction model. *Journal of Personality* 42: 511–27.

Smith, M. B. (1972). Is experimental social psychology advancing? *Journal of Experimental Social Psychology* 8: 86–96.

Smith, M. B. (1976). Social psychology, science, and history: so what? *Personality and Social Psychology* 2: 438–44.

Smith, R. J. (1978). The future of an illusion: American social psychology. *Personality and Social Psychology* 4: 173–6.

Snyder, M. (1979). Self-monitoring processes. In L. Berkowitz (ed.), *Advances in experimental social psychology*, vol. 12. New York: Academic Press.

Spiegelberg, J. (1966). How subjective is phenomenology? In M. M. Natanson (ed.), *Essays in phenomenology*. The Hague: Nijhoff.

Spiegelberg, H. (1975). *Doing phenomenology*. The Hague: Nijhoff.

Strickland, L. H., Aboud, F. E., and Gergen, K. J. (eds.) (1976), *Social psychology in transition*. New York: Plenum.

Tajfel, H. (1972). Experiments in a vacuum. In Israel and Tajfel 1972.

Tajfel, H. and Fraser, C. (1978). Social psychology as social science. In H. Tajfel and C. Fraser (eds.), *Introducing social psychology*. Harmondsworth: Penguin.

Taylor, S. E. (1976). Developing a cognitive social psychology. In J. S. Carroll and J. W. Payne (eds.), *Cognition and social behavior*. Hillsdale, NJ: Lawrence Erlbaum.

Thines, G. (1977). *Phenomenology and the science of behaviour*. London: Allen & Unwin.

Thorngate, W. (1976). Possible limits on a science of social behavior. In Strickland *et al.* 1976.

Triandis, H. C. (1972). *The analysis of subjective culture*. New York: Wiley.

Triandis, H. C. (1975). Social psychology and cultural analysis. *Journal for the Theory of Social Psychology* 5: 81–106.

Triandis, H. C. (1976). Social psychology and cultural analysis. In Strickland *et al.* 1976.

Triandis, H. C. (1978). Some universals of social behavior. *Personality and Social Psychology Bulletin* 4: 1–16.

Vinacke, W. (1954). Deceiving experimental subjects. *American Psychologist* 9: 155.

Weimer, W. B. (1979). *Notes on the methodology of scientific research*. Hillsdale, NJ: Lawrence Erlbaum.

Wispé, L. (1980). The role of moods in helping behavior. *Representative Research in Social Psychology* 11: 2–15.

Wyer, R. S. and Srull, T. K. (eds.) (1984). *Handbook of social cognition*. Hillsdale, NJ: Lawrence Erlbaum.

Zajonc, R. B. (1980). Cognition and social cognition: a historical perspective. In L. Festinger (ed.), *Retrospections on social psychology*. New York: Oxford University Press.

6 Knowledge as a social psychological construct

Arie W. Kruglanski

Like Molière's M. Jourdain, most social psychologists may have been "talking knowledge all their lives" without realizing it. This assumption is a basic premise of the present chapter in which the construct of knowledge in social psychological research is discussed and analyzed. The relevance of knowledge to social psychology spans several separate levels of analysis. Some social psychologists have been interested in *contents* of specific knowledge structures, others in the *process* whereby knowledge structures in general are formed or modified, yet others in a mix of the two. In the first part of this chapter, I discuss the level of analysis problem in social cognitive psychology and the pitfalls it might pose for research in the area. The second part describes my lay epistemic model of knowledge acquisition, formulated in part to differentiate between levels of social cognitive analysis. The third section describes several recent lines of experimental work guided by the model's derivations. The paper concludes by considering the theoretical and empirical implications of the present approach, and by noting its possible future directions.

The level of analysis problem in social cognitive psychology

Content-bound research

Some types of social psychological research have dealt with specific contents of knowledge structures. An example would be Lerner's well-known study of the "belief in a just world" (Lerner 1980). While possibly widely shared, such belief still pertains to a specifically circumscribed set of cognitive contents. Besides believing in justice, people may believe in God, Love, Power, Fate, and so on. Each of those beliefs and many others could become an intriguing topic of social psychological inquiry, with possible implications for important interpersonal phenomena.

Another example of content-bound social cognitive research is the field of attribution, where different causal contents were involved in reference to different domains of effects. Whereas initial attributional formulations (Heider 1958, Jones and Davis 1965, Kelley 1971) stressed the internal–external distinction between causes, subsequent analyses focused on more refined contents of possible causal categories. Thus Weiner and his associates (Weiner 1979, Weiner and Litman-Adizes 1980, Weiner 1985a) proposed that, in achievement settings, persons may ascribe their successes and failures to causes which are "internal" or "external", "stable", or "unstable", and "controllable" or "uncontrollable".

Further attributional work identified other causal dimensions of occasional interest to lay persons. Abramson, Seligman, and Teasdale (1978) identified the attributional dimension of "globality" in addition to "internality" and "stability". Orvis, Kelley, and Butler (1976) identified the attributional dimension of "intentionality" as well as thirteen categories of explanation used by members of young couples to account for their own or partners' behaviors. Kruglanski (1975) distinguished between "endogenous" and "exogenous" attributions of actions, in which the former refers to action perceived as "an end in itself" and the latter to action perceived as "a means to a further end".

Some social psychological topics have concerned broader content categories of knowledge structures. A case in point is attitudes which can be considered as beliefs with affective or evaluative *contents*. Thus the domain of attitudes pertains to a particular category of knowledge structures whose defining feature is *evaluative* content. For instance, positive attitude towards New York may represent a belief that one "loves New York", that "New York is a 'great' city", etc. For recent analyses of attitudes as knowledge structures see Fazio *et al.* 1983, Kruglanski (in press, a: ch. 6), and Zanna and Rempel in this volume.

Process-bound social cognitive research

In contrast to social psychological research about various knowledge contents, important domains of social psychological inquiry addressed cognitive phenomena applicable across contents. The recently burgeoning field of social cognition falls into this latter category, as does my own model of lay epistemology described later. For instance, effects of schemata on recall (Cantor and Mischel 1977, Markus 1977), effects of construct accessibility (Higgins *et al.* 1977, Higgins and King 1981, Higgins *et al.* 1985, Higgins and Stangor, this volume), saliency (Taylor and Fiske 1975, 1978; McArthur and Ginsburg 1981), memory (Wyer and Srull, in press, Hamilton, this volume), or epistemic motivations (Kruglanski, in press, a) may hold across diverse possible contents of cognitions.

In a sense, the processes studied by many social cognitive psychologists may be described as cognitive rather than as socially cognitive, i.e. as applicable to object perception as well as to social perception. In other words, "inanimate objects" and "persons" represent two content categories of cognitions to which the same general judgmental process may apply. This is not to deny that object and person perception may also differ (cf. Fiske and Taylor 1984, Sorrentino and Higgins 1985). But their commonalities as cognitive contents suggest that general cognitive models may be applicable to both. This implies the potential utility of such models for explaining various social psychological phenomena at the core of which are persons' knowledge structures of various kinds.

Multi-level (hybrid) theories in social cognitive psychology

Occasionally, social cognitive theories appear undecided as to the level of analysis at which they aim. A case in point is attribution theory, which both purports to describe how lay persons render causal explanations *in general* and also dwells on *specific contents* of causal categories. Consequently, attribution theory contains constructs on a variety of levels. A construct like "covariation", for example, pertains to all cases of causal assignment, whereas constructs like "internal" or "endogenous" attribution pertain to specific cases of causal assignment (for a more extensive discussion, see Kruglanski, in press).

If attribution theory mixes different levels of analysis *contemporaneously*, dissonance theory has shifted from more to less abstract formulations *over time*. In the original statement of the theory, Festinger (1957) defined a dissonant relation as one in which the obverse of one cognitive element follows from the other. This definition is content-free, or applicable across cognitive elements irrespective of content. However, in time the definition of dissonance has changed and become tied to several content elements: Brehm and Cohen (1962) interpreted dissonance as bound to cognitions concerned with making a decision, an interpretation seconded by Festinger (1964). Further interpreters have suggested that simply making a decision is not enough. Additional cognitions may be necessary, in particular "having exercised one's volition", "being responsible for the decision", and the decision yielding "highly negative consequences" (Collins and Hoyt 1972, Cooper and Fazio 1984). Thus, while in attribution theory multiple levels of analysis continue to coexist, in the case of dissonance a "shrinkage" has occurred from a more to a less general level of analysis.

But what is wrong, anyway, with having different levels of analysis represented in the same theoretical formulation? A major pitfall is redundancy. In particular, the same higher-level construct might reappear repeatedly "under the guise" of diverse lower level constructs, without the commonality being officially stated or recognized. This makes for a proliferating theory in which the same (higher-level) idea is unwittingly proposed over and over again, thus "rediscovering the wheel". For example, Kelley's (1967) attributional criteria conjoin the (higher-level) concept of "covariation" to several lower-level concepts, notably "person", "entity", "time", and "modality" (for a detailed demonstration see Kruglanski, in press, a). Yet the essential role of "covariation" in the "criteria" generally goes unrecognized, and the two concepts are typically regarded as separate.

Similarly, the notion of "discounting" (cf. Kelley 1971) is generally considered separate from the "number of non-common effects" hypothesis (Jones and Davis 1965), although both pertain to the same idea that an individual's confidence wanes when presented with competing alternative hypotheses (Kruglanski 1980). Cognitive balance (Heider 1958) has been defined in terms different from cognitive dissonance (Festinger 1957), and the "cognitive inconsistency" in both has not been explicitly articulated or analyzed despite considerable amounts of research.

The fascination of social cognitive psychologists with contents of cognitions is not hard to fathom. In a sense, it is the study of cognitive contents which sets apart social cognitive from "purely" cognitive psychologies. It is the contents which are "social"; they are admittedly affected by culture, socialization, and learning, whereas the cognitive process is presumably governed by culture-free laws of inference and information-processing constrained by all persons' physiological "hardware".

Perhaps that is why even the generally content-free "social cognition" movement has time and again injected the study of cognitive contents, implying that these represent exceptions to general laws of information-processing, and should therefore be regarded as moderators of such laws. In a recent review Higgins and Bargh (1987) consider several lines of research, all departing from the proposal that particular cognitive content categories are processed uniquely, notably the "self", the "human target" (versus the "situational context") of perceived actions, and "statistical" (or aggregate) as opposed to "case-specific" (or individuating) information. Thus it has been claimed that information encoded as self-referent is remembered better than information encoded via alternative modes (notably semantic, phonemic, and structural modes: cf. Rogers *et al.* 1977).

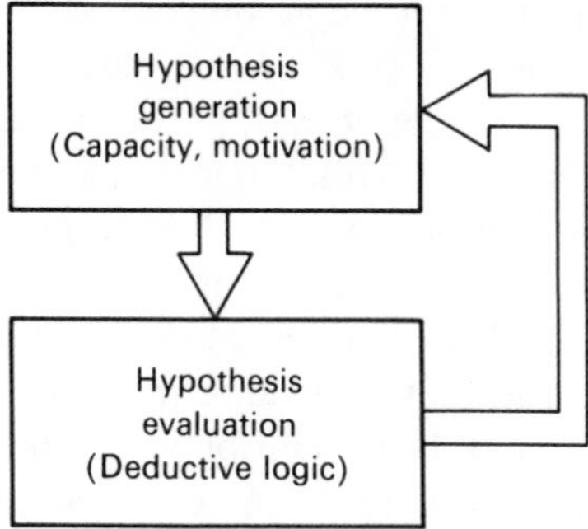

Fig. 6.1

Similarly, it has been hypothesized that "context" information is typically under-utilized as compared with "target information" (Ross 1977), and that statistical (e.g. base rate) information is typically under-utilized as compared with case information (cf. Kahneman and Tversky 1973). Instructively, in all three cases the putative uniqueness of given cognitive (informational) categories has been dispelled by subsequent research, and the seemingly "unique" effects originally claimed for content variables appear now reducible to cognitive process variables (for an elaboration of this conclusion, see Higgins and Bargh 1987).

An alternative to stalking the elusive concept of the uniquely social cognitive level of analysis may be to explore how the cognitive level of analysis (admittedly applicable to nonsocial contents as well) may enrich our understanding of phenomena. In addition, numerous cognitive content categories of interest (whether universally held or restricted to specific groups, cultures, or situations) could be explored separately, without mixing them with the more general level of analysis. The latter approach has guided my own social cognitive research within the lay epistemic paradigm (Kruglanski, in press). This theory originated from an attempt to distinguish between content and process elements in attribution theory (cf. Kruglanski *et al.* 1978, Kruglanski 1980). In the next section the lay epistemic model is described in some detail, followed by a review of recent research conducted under its aegis.

The epistemic sequence

According to the theory of lay epistemology (see, for example, Kruglanski and Ajzen 1983, Kruglanski and Klar 1987, Kruglanski, in press, a), the process whereby all knowledge is formed or modified involves a two-phase sequence in which hypotheses are generated and validated (see Fig. 6.1).

Hypothesis validation is assumed to be accomplished deductively. The individual departs from a premise linking (in an *if–then* fashion) a given category of evidence with a given hypothesis, and proceeds to infer the hypothesis on affirming the evidence. This is not meant to imply that lay persons are skillful deductive logicians or that they do not err on logical tasks (cf. Wason and Johnson-Laird 1972). Rather, it is suggested that the *form* of validation is typically deductive. People infer their conclusions *from* evidence; this suggests that they had subscribed to a prior premise whereby *if* the evidence was found the conclusion would be warranted.

However, the deductive validation of hypotheses has no unique point of termination. In principle, one might always come up with further alternate hypotheses compatible with the same body of evidence. This poses the following dilemma for a theory of knowledge acquisition. On the one hand the epistemic sequence could continue indefinitely. On the other hand, at most times we seem to possess a variety of definite knowledge, that is, things we "know for sure". This suggests that in those numerous instances the epistemic sequence *did* come to a halt. And we need to find out how this came about – that is, to identify the mechanisms effecting the cessation (or conversely, the initiation or continuation) of the epistemic sequence. The lay epistemic model recognizes two such general mechanisms, respectively based on the notions of cognitive *capacity* and epistemic *motivation*.

Capacity notions: availability and accessibility

Two types of cognitive capacity, long-term and momentary, are sometimes discerned in the social cognitive literature. Long-term capacity to generate hypotheses on a given topic has to do with construct *availability* (cf. Higgins *et al.* 1982). This refers to the individual's general repertoire of social knowledge stored in long-term memory. Consider a person whose car stalled in the middle of a highway. To the extent that this individual was knowledgeable in the automotive domain, (s)he might have numerous available notions to draw on, and hence might continue generating numerous alternate hypotheses to account for the car's failure. Conversely, an individual with a more restricted set of automotive notions might be compelled to stop the hypothesis generation process much sooner.

Short-term capacity to generate hypotheses on a topic has to do with construct *accessibility* (Higgins and King 1981). Suppose that an individual has just read an issue of the *Car and Driver* magazine. This might contextually prime numerous automotive concepts, resulting in a greater number of alternate hypotheses being generated by our individual.

The second category of braking (starting) mechanisms affecting the epistemic sequence relates to the person's epistemic needs. Three types of motivational force are assumed to be relevant to the epistemic process: respectively the needs for nonspecific structure, specific structure, and ambiguity.

The need for nonspecific structure

The need for nonspecific structure represents the desire for a definite answer concerning some issue, *any* answer as opposed to confusion and ambiguity. A heightened need for nonspecific structure is likely to trigger intense epistemic activity, where no initial knowledge existed, and to bring such activity to a halt once some plausible hypothesis has been advanced and supported by extant evidence. In this sense, the need for nonspecific structure is said to promote epistemic "freezing".

The need for nonspecific structure could spring from *heterogeneous motivational sources*. Self-esteem and social approval concerns might elicit one's interest in various topics (the arts or world affairs, for example), potentiating needs for nonspecific structures in the relevant domains. Control strivings could arouse a need for nonspecific structure, where knowledge was assumed to facilitate control. A need for nonspecific structure could be similarly based on power strivings, craving for affection, etc.

The need for specific structure

The need for nonspecific structure is assumed to be unbiased toward particular types of knowledge. It refers to cases where persons are interested in an answer without prejudice as to the answer's special properties. At times, however, persons might harbor strong preferences among kinds of knowledge. These pertain to our second epistemic need type, labeled a *need for specific structure*. A need for specific structure could stem from any of the structure's properties – for instance, its particular contents, that may be flattering or otherwise desirable. It could further stem from its novelty, its apparent creativity, or from any other feature that might appear attractive.

If the need for *nonspecific* structure may generally promote epistemic "freezing", that for a *specific* structure might promote either "freezing" or "unfreezing", depending on whether current knowledge or hypothesis was congruent with one's particular desires. For example, a person entertaining the possibility that (s)he contracted a dangerous illness, or that (s)he is about to lose an attractive job, might intensely seek out new evidence to contradict the undesirable conclusions. By contrast, a person surmising that (s)he is about to receive a desirable job offer, or that (s)he did well on an exam, might often be resistant to contrary evidence, and be quick to dismiss alternative, less sanguine interpretations of available information.

In other words, the present notion of "need for specific structure" refers to a directionally *biased* influence on the epistemic process. Such influence may steer the process away from undesirable knowledge structures and towards desirable ones. Again, needs for specific structures are assumed to be *diversely determined*. For instance, esteem concerns might render ego-protective or enhancing attributions more attractive than their alternatives. The need for control might induce preferences for "controllable" or "important" features of causal categories, etc.

The need for ambiguity

A third motivational force assumed relevant to the epistemic process is the "need for ambiguity". The "need for ambiguity" pertains to situations where ambiguity is valued or desired for some reason. This might occasionally occur where the individual experiences a high "fear of invalidity", stemming from the appreciable expected costs of a mistaken judgment. Where the erroneous commitment to a judgment appears costly, persons might value ambiguity and inconsistency, or at least tolerate it, as a means for ultimately lowering the likelihood of a mistake.

The "need for ambiguity" might also stem from the unwanted *restriction of potential* imposed by a definite judgment. Snyder and Wicklund (1981) furnish an illuminating discussion of cases where definite self-knowledge might connote predictability and dullness; in such instances persons might well seek ambiguity and eschew structure. The "need for ambiguity" may occasion intense epistemic activity where definite knowledge was "in danger" of forming. This might increase sensitivity to new information possibly inconsistent with the current hypothesis, and/or increase the tendency to generate competing alternatives to the hypothesis. Furthermore, when one's initial state is ambiguity, a "need for ambiguity" might suppress further epistemic activity "threatening" to bring about unwanted clarity. Generally, then, the "need for ambiguity" may be said to promote epistemic "unfreezing".

The "need for ambiguity" might originate from *diverse* motivational sources, for example, having to do with manifold possible costs of a judgmental error (stemming from self-esteem concerns, possible economic losses, danger to one's physical safety, and so on), or diverse possible reasons for "intrinsically" valuing ambiguity (such as romance, unpredictability, or adventure). Finally, the "need for ambiguity" is assumed to be *unbiased* in its effects on the epistemic process. It may steer epistemic activity away from structure in general rather than toward any particular structure.

Experimental studies of epistemic behavior

The epistemic model has been applied to several research topics in cognitive social psychology. This work can be classed in accordance with three categories of factors assumed to affect judgmental behavior: (1) epistemic motivations, (2) the deductive logic of hypothesis validation, and (3) contents of specific knowledge structures. Let us consider those topics in turn.

Motivational effects on epistemic behavior

Subjective confidence

Mayseless and Kruglanski (1987) investigated subjective confidence as it might be affected by the need for (nonspecific) structure and the fear of invalidity. In previous research, subjective confidence has been typically assumed to depend on the degree of consistency between one's hypothesis and one's evidence: confidence in a hypothesis was assumed to be high to the extent that the available evidence was consistent with the hypothesis, and low to the extent that it was inconsistent (Kruglanski 1980).

For instance, in attribution theory (Kelley 1967) subjective confidence in ascribing an effect to an external entity is assumed to be high when the informational criteria (of distinctiveness, consistency, and consensus) are *consistent* with an entity attribution. Similarly, in Bayesian analyses of inference (Edwards 1982), posterior subjective probability in a hypothesis increases upon the receipt of data *consistent* with the hypothesis (or data whose assumed probability given the hypothesis is high) and decreases on the receipt of data *inconsistent* with the hypothesis.

According to the present analysis, however, the individual's readiness to consider inconsistent data or hypotheses is not static. Rather, it is dynamically affected by the various epistemic motivations. This means that the same data may affect differently the confidence of different individuals in the same hypothesis, or the confidence of the same individual on different occasions. In particular, given high fear of invalidity a person might (temporarily) tolerate ambiguity, and generate numerous competing interpretations for every received item of information. In turn, consideration of multiple competing (hence, inconsistent) hypotheses may well cause the confidence in any given hypothesis to wane (Kelley 1971, Kruglanski 1980, Kruglanski, in press, a). By contrast, given high need for (nonspecific) structure, individuals' tendency to consider alternate hypotheses might be low, and their confidence correspondingly high. It follows that subjective confidence should be negatively affected by individuals' fear of invalidity, and positively by their need for (nonspecific) structure.

To test those predictions, Mayseless and Kruglanski (1987) engaged subjects in a tachistoscopic recognition task of identifying barely visible digits flashed on the screen. In the *fear of invalidity* condition, subjects were promised extra-experimental credits for correctly identifying nine out of the ten digits. In the *need for structure* condition, subjects were given verbal instructions stressing the importance of forming unambiguous, clear-cut opinions, ability said to correlate with "high mental concentration and intelligence". In addition, a *neutral control* condition was included where no motivational induction was attempted.

Subjects' confidence in their initial hypothesis, the magnitude of confidence shifts (upward or downward) occasioned by each successive stimulus presentation, and their extent of informational search (the number of times they operated the tachistoscope) were significantly lower in the fear of invalidity condition than in the need for structure condition, with the neutral control condition falling in between those two. These findings conform to predictions of the lay epistemic analysis.

Hypothesis generation

It has been suggested that the between-condition variability in confidence observed in the Mayseless and Kruglanski (1987) research may have been mediated by subjects' differential tendencies to entertain alternative interpretations of the information provided. To test this idea, subjects in an additional experiment were presented with unusual-looking photographs of parts of common objects. As expected, subjects in the fear of invalidity condition generated more hypotheses concerning the objects' identity than subjects in the neutral condition who, in turn, generated more hypotheses than subjects in the need for structure condition.

Thus the Mayseless and Kruglanski (1987) research provides suggestive evidence that persons' subjective confidence may be a function of their epistemic motivations, and that this might be mediated by differential tendencies to engender many rather than few alternatives to their current hypotheses. Further work on the motivational underpinnings of subjective confidence could profitably relate it to various social psychological phenomena in which personal self-assurance may be expected to play a significant role – phenomena such as shyness (Zimbardo 1977), social influence, or leadership.

Primacy effects in impression formation

Primacy effects in impression formation (Asch 1946) consist of the tendency to base impressions of a target more on the early than on the late information. Such effects could represent the phenomenon of epistemic "freezing", because they signify early closure and relative insensitivity to subsequent information. If so, primacy effects should be augmented by a heightened "need for nonspecific structure", and reduced by a heightened "need for ambiguity".

In an experiment designed to test those predictions, Kruglanski and Freund (1983) presented subjects with serial information about a target, and had them rate this person's attractiveness as a job candidate. In some cases, positive target information came first followed by negative information; in other cases the order was reversed. "Need for nonspecific structure" was manipulated via degrees of time pressure. We had assumed that time-pressured individuals would experience a heightened need for nonspecific structure as structure makes fewer demands on one's time than ambiguity.

The "need for ambiguity" was manipulated via *fear of invalidity* aroused via evaluation apprehension. In the high condition, subjects expected their judgments to be compared with those of professional psychologists. In the low condition, subjects were told that the evaluation method was at a pilot stage and its validity was unknown. Primacy effects were significantly higher with high (versus low) need for (nonspecific) structure and significantly lower with high (versus low) fear of invalidity.

Replicating the effects of epistemic motivations on impressional primacy

Freund, Kruglanski, and Schpitzajzen (1985) replicated the effects of epistemic motivations on impressional primacy with different operational definitions of the need for (nonspecific) structure and the fear of invalidity. In one replication, the need for structure was operationalized via demands for unidimensional (and hence global and undifferentiated) versus multidimensional judgments, and the fear of invalidity via potential costs *to the target person* of the subject's judgmental mistake. In the second replication, fear of invalidity was manipulated as in the first experiment, and need for structure was manipulated via degrees of time pressure. Finally, in the third replication need for structure was manipulated as in the first experiment and fear of invalidity, via degrees of evaluation apprehension. All three designs strongly replicated the original findings of Kruglanski and Freund (1983) where primacy effects were consistently more pronounced under high (versus low) need for structure and under low (versus high) fear of invalidity.

Anchoring effects

Tversky and Kahneman (1974) identified persons' tendency to anchor numerical estimates in initial values without sufficiently adjusting those estimates in the light of subsequent information. According to the present analysis, "anchoring" could represent epistemic "freezing" in which information-processing comes to a halt after an initial estimate has been made and slightly adjusted. If so, anchoring tendencies should be strengthened by a heightened need for (nonspecific) structure, and weakened by a heightened fear of invalidity. Those predictions were tested by Kruglanski and Freund (1983: study 3).

In estimating the probabilities of compound (conjunctive or disjunctive) events, subjects may often use as anchors the probabilities of their component simple events (Bar-Hillel 1973). If so, the anchoring tendency could lead to an *overestimation* of the probabilities of conjunctive events, as these are smaller than the probabilities of their constituent simple events. Similarly, anchoring could result in an *underestimation* of the probabilities of disjunctive events which are larger than probabilities of the component simple events. Following a procedure developed by Bar-Hillel (1973), Kruglanski and Freund (1983) asked subjects to choose from pairs of events the one more likely to occur. Some pairs contrasted conjunctive events with simple events, while other pairs contrasted disjunctive events with simple ones. Need for structure was manipulated via degrees of time pressure, and fear of invalidity via evaluation apprehension. Subjects' tendency to overestimate the likelihood of conjunctive events, and to underestimate that of disjunctive events (both indicative of anchoring) increased, as predicted, under high (versus low) need for structure and decreased under high (versus low) fear of invalidity.

Stereotypic judgments

Research described thus far examined the effects of epistemic motivations on the formation of *new* knowledge structures. But the same motivations might also affect persons' tendency to base judgments on pre-existing knowledge, or to be "theory-driven" rather than "data-driven" *Pre-existing* knowledge affords a ready base for launching a given judgment. Thus, under high (versus low) need for nonspecific structure, individuals might be more disposed to base their judgments on pre-existing structures. Conversely, under high (versus low) fear of invalidity, subjects might be less inclined to do so, and might instead assign more weight to situational information. Consistently with those notions, Kruglanski and Freund

(1983: study 2) found that Israeli subjects' tendency to assign higher grades for a literary composition of authors believed to be of Ashkenazi (versus Sephardi) origin was totally eliminated under a combination of a high fear of invalidity and a low need for structure.

When prejudice leads to discrimination: "freezing" on pre-existing attitudes

"Freezing" might also be involved in cases of acting on one's prejudices rather than on the information at hand. In a recent study (Bechtold and Zanna 1985), subjects known for their prejudice against women in management ranked résumés of men and women on their attractiveness for a given position. Based on pilot work, it had been ascertained that the two types of résumé did not systematically differ in attractiveness. A very different judgment was reached by the prejudiced subjects, but only when their need for structure may have been aroused! Specifically, under time pressure those persons rated the men's résumés as significantly more attractive than the women's, exhibiting considerable discrimination in line with their prejudicial attitudes. Virtually no sex-typed discrimination, however, was manifested by similarly prejudiced subjects in the absence of time pressure. To the extent that these results were mediated by the need for structure, this construct could represent one of the factors affecting the degree to which prejudice may lead to discrimination, or more generally, the degree to which specific judgments are "frozen" on pre-existing knowledge structures.

Interactive effects of epistemic motivations and initial confidence

In research thus far, the need for (nonspecific) structure has appeared to inhibit epistemic activity, and the need for ambiguity (induced via a fear of invalidity) appeared to facilitate such activity. However, those effects may be moderated by the degree to which an individual starts out with a fairly crystallized knowledge structure versus a relative ambiguity: a person under high (versus low) need for (nonspecific) structure who departs from crystallized knowledge has already what (s)he desires, and hence might be unmotivated to engage in a further informational search. Accordingly, in previously described studies, curtailment of epistemic activity has typically occurred *after* some preliminary knowledge (for example an ethnic stereotype, an early impression, or an initial estimate) had been already formed.

The case might be very different where the individual starts out with relative ambiguity. In such circumstances, a person under high (versus low) need for (nonspecific) structure might be considerably motivated toward informational search, which might lead to the coveted state of "knowledge". Opposite effects might be observed with persons with high (versus low) need for ambiguity. Specifically, where the individual starts out with a fairly crystallized knowledge, while what (s)he prefers (if only temporarily) is ambiguity, (s)he might well be motivated to conduct further informational search. However, if the same person *begins* with ambiguity, (s)he might be unmotivated to "jeopardize" it via additional search. The above notions were investigated in a pair of recent studies by Peri, Kruglanski, and Zakai (1986).

Experiment 1: Need for structure effects. Subjects were presented with five series of drawings. Each series contained either two or four *standard* drawings on a given topic ("man", "woman", or "tree") each produced by a different person, and a *criterion* drawing on a different topic (invariably, a "house") drawn by *one* of the persons who had prepared the standard drawings. The task was to identify for each series the particular standard drawing by the individual who has done the criterial drawing. The time allotted was three minutes. Subjects stated their *interim judgment* after one minute and during the remaining two were given the opportunity to compare socially with previous subjects in the same experiment. This was accomplished by turning over some (or all) of the standard drawings, on the reverse side of which were inscribed the percentages of previous subjects choosing them as correct answers.

The design of the study was a 2×2 factorial with the independent variables of (1) need for structure (high versus low) and (2) initial confidence in the hypothesis (high versus low). Need for structure was manipulated via degrees of task clarity: in the *low* condition, subjects received guiding criteria for assessing the drawings' similarity. Those were based on pilot work, and comprised linear quality of the drawing (whether thick or thin, strong or weak, continuous or discontinuous), the drawing's size and location on the page (whether big or small, centered or off-center), its degree of elaboration (detailed and elaborate or simplistic and unadorned), and perspective (containing depth or flat). Subjects in the high need for structure condition received no comparable criteria for assessing drawings' similarity. We had assumed that in the absence (versus presence) of criteria, subjects would be unpleasantly confused, and hence under a need for (nonspecific) structure regarding the nature of their task.

Initial confidence was manipulated via the number of choices presented to subjects. In the high condition there were two alternatives, in the low condition four. Two dependent variables were used both designed to tap

Table 6.1. *Mean extent of social comparison as function of initial confidence and need for structure*

		Initial confidence	
		High	Low
Need structure	High	2.60*	3.52
	Low	4.37	2.82

* Extent of comparison was based on number of cards turned over, corrected for the available number of cards. To yield a uniform index, that number was divided by a factor of 2 in the high confidence condition and by a factor of 4 in the low confidence condition.

Source: Peri *et al.* 1986.

Table 6.2. *Mean latencies (in seconds) of first comparison as function of initial confidence and need for structure*

		Initial confidence	
		High	Low
Need structure	High	60.39	33.67
	Low	19.47	49.01

Source: Peri *et al.* 1986.

subjects' tendency to engage in informational search: (1) the *number* of standard drawings they turned over to ascertain the percentages of other people choosing them as correct answers, and (2) the *latency* of turning over the first standard drawing. The relevant results are displayed in Tables 6.1 and 6.2.

As may be seen, our predictions were supported. In the high initial confidence condition the average number of standard drawings turned over by subjects under high need for structure is lower than the corresponding number turned over by subjects under low need for structure. This trend is reversed in the low initial confidence condition. Furthermore, in the high initial confidence condition the latency of turning over the first standard drawing is longer for subjects under high (versus low) need for structure, a trend which is reversed, again, in the low initial confidence condition.

Experiment 2: Need for ambiguity effects. The procedure of our next experiment was essentially identical to that of the previous study, as was our manipulation of initial confidence and measurement of the dependent variables. The only difference concerned the way in which subjects stated their final choice. Specifically, they did so by distributing ten coins (of equal value) across some (or all) of the standard drawings, in proportion to their perceived likelihood of representing the correct choice.

The experimental design was a 2×2 factorial in which two levels of initial confidence (high versus low) were manipulated orthogonally to two levels of the need for ambiguity. Our predictions stated that in the high initial confidence condition subjects influenced by high (versus low) need for ambiguity would tend more to engage in informational search. By contrast, in the low initial confidence condition we expected subjects influenced by high (versus low) need for ambiguity to engage less in informational search.

Need for ambiguity was manipulated via degrees of the fear of invalidity. In the high condition subjects expected their overall performance to be evaluated against other subjects. This was to be accomplished in accordance with the number of coins a subject placed on the correct drawings across the five series. In principle, a subject's score could range from 0 (in case (s)he did not place any "bets" on the correct drawings in any of the five series) to 50 (for placing ten coins on the correct drawings in all five series).

In addition, subjects in the high need for ambiguity condition were constrained in the number of coins they could bet "safely" on any one drawing. To the extent that they placed more than five coins (in the low confidence condition), or more than seven coins (in the high confidence conditions) on the wrong drawing they would lose all of their points for that particular series. Thus subjects in the high need for ambiguity condition were discouraged from making a definite commitment to any particular judgment. Such commitment might have resulted in a loss of valuable points, and hence lower their total score.

Subjects in the low need for ambiguity condition were not informed of an evaluative scoring system, nor were they constrained in distributing their bets across different standard drawings. The main experimental results are displayed in Tables 6.3 and 6.4. As may be seen, the data generally support our predictions. In the high initial confidence condition subjects under high (versus low) need for ambiguity turned over more drawings on the average. This trend is reversed in the low initial confidence condition.

Furthermore, in the high initial confidence condition subjects under high (versus low) need for ambiguity manifested shorter information-search latencies, whereas the opposite trend showed in the low initial confidence condition.

In sum, the findings of Peri *et al.* (1986) suggest that epistemic motivations interact with the epistemic point of departure in affecting persons' extent of informational search. With a fairly confident knowledge to start with, high (versus low) need for structure suppresses further informational search and high (versus low) need for ambiguity intensifies it. By contrast,

Table 6.3. *Mean extent of social comparison as function of initial confidence and fear of invalidity*

		Initial confidence	
		High	Low
Fear invalidity	High	3.94*	3.00
	Low	2.62	3.60

* Extent of comparison was based on number of cards turned over, corrected for the available number of cards. To yield a uniform index, that number was divided by a factor of 2 in the high confidence condition and by a factor of 4 in the low confidence condition.

Source: Peri *et al.* 1986.

Table 6.4. *Mean latencies (in seconds) of first comparison as function of initial confidence and fear of invalidity*

		Initial confidence	
		High	Low
Fear invalidity	High	37.01	47.84
	Low	65.11	39.79

Source: Peri *et al.* 1986.

with ambiguity to start with, high (versus low) need for structure intensifies informational search whereas high (versus low) need for ambiguity apparently suppresses it.

Behavioral consequences of disconfirmed expectancies

Persons' reactions to disconfirmed expectancies may be affected by their epistemic motivations. A disconfirmed expectancy may upset the person's sense of knowledge. Thus, if individuals' need for nonspecific structure is high (versus low) and/or their need for ambiguity is low (versus high), they might be upset more by a disconfirmed expectancy. Furthermore, if the disconfirmation is congruent with a person's need for specific structure it should generate less upset than if it does not. The above notions were tested in a recent study conducted at Tel-Aviv University.

Following the procedure developed by Aronson and Carlsmith (1962), subjects experienced a series of failures followed by an unexpected success. Specifically, they viewed sets of three drawings each, and identified the one drawing in the set which belonged to a person with some unique property (either a mentally disturbed or an artistically gifted individual). On the first three series of ten trials subjects received failure feedback (of three, two, two, and three correct identifications respectively out of a possible ten). On the fourth series of trials subjects received success feedback, whereby they made correct identifications in eight out of the ten cases.

Half the subjects were placed under high need for structure and low need for (or tolerance of) ambiguity, whereas the remaining half were under low need for structure and high need for (tolerance of) ambiguity. Furthermore, half the subjects in each condition regarded success on the task as highly desirable whereas the remaining half regarded it as less desirable.

The experimental manipulations were accomplished as follows. All subjects expected to fill out a questionnaire concerning their perceived ability to make the requisite identifications. In the high need for structure/low tolerance for ambiguity condition, subjects expected to have limited time in which to respond to the questionnaire and were not given specific instructions concerning accuracy. In the high tolerance for ambiguity/low need for structure condition, subjects expected to have unlimited time and were urged to reach the most accurate assessments possible.

In the high success desirability condition, subjects were told that the task consists of identifying drawings prepared by mentally disturbed individuals. It was expected that, for psychology students, who served as our subjects, success on such task would appear highly desirable. By contrast, subjects in the low success desirability condition were told that the task consists of identifying the drawings of artistically gifted persons. Success on such a task was not expected to appear particularly desirable to psychology students.

Under the pretext that the experimenter had mistakenly failed to time the last, fourth series of trials, this series was repeated and the number of changes made by subjects was recorded. This number was higher in the high need for structure/low tolerance for ambiguity condition than in the low need for structure/high tolerance for ambiguity condition. Furthermore, the number of changes was lower with high (versus low) success desirability. Thus it appears that the degree to which a disconfirmation of an expectancy is rejected, and the expectancy is reconfirmed, may depend on an individual's epistemic motivations with reference to which a disconfirmed expectancy may or may not be upsetting.

Comparisons with similar and dissimilar others

The lay epistemic analysis has implications for conditions under which individuals might wish to compare with others whose opinions are similar or dissimilar to their own. According to Festinger's (1954) theory of social comparison processes, similarly minded others are often preferred for comparison purposes over dissimilar others. This general prediction may be qualified by motivational considerations suggested by the lay epistemic theory. In particular, a preference for similar others may be manifest when the individual is high on a need for nonspecific structure and/or a need for specific structure with which a current opinion is *congruent*. However, the opposite preference, for dissimilar others, might be manifest when the individual is under a high need for ambiguity and/or a high need for specific structure with which a current opinion is *incongruent*.

These notions were recently tested in a series of studies by Kruglanski and Mayseless (in press, b). In one study, subjects whose fear of invalidity was experimentally aroused (via an induced expectation of a monetary prize for a correct answer) predominantly chose to compare with dissimilarly minded others. By contrast, subjects whose need for self-confirmation (or defensiveness) was aroused chose more to compare with similarly minded others. Finally, in a neutral control condition subjects selected about equal proportions of dissimilar and similar opinions for comparison.

Two further studies tested the combined effects on comparison similarity of the need for (nonspecific) structure and the fear of invalidity. The experiments differed considerably in the tasks employed. In one study the task involved the resolution of a cognitive inconsistency, whereas in the other study it involved perceptual judgments of relative length. Furthermore, in one study the fear of invalidity was manipulated via an expectation of a prize (a candy bar) for an accurate answer whereas in the other study it was manipulated via degrees of evaluation apprehension. Also, in both studies the need for (nonspecific) structure was manipulated in various ways via degrees of time pressure. The results of the two studies were highly similar. In both cases subjects under high (versus low) need for structure tended to choose for comparison partners whose opinions were similar to their own. By contrast, under high (versus low) fear of invalidity subjects preferred more to compare with dissimilar others.

In sum, it appears that the direction of comparison (whether toward a similar or a dissimilar other) may be importantly affected by the individual's epistemic motivations. Specifically, influenced by high need for nonspecific structure or a specific structure congruent with the person's wishes, (s)he may prefer comparison with a similar other expected to provide support for his/her opinions. However, a high need for ambiguity (for example, induced by a fear of invalidity), or a high need for specific structure incongruent with the person's wishes, may impel an individual to prefer comparison with dissimilar others who may provide alternative points of view, and hence create the ambiguity desired.

Collective decision-making: "group think" and the "freezing" effect

Evidence reviewed thus far supports the view that the various epistemic motivations may affect individuals' tendency to "freeze" or 'unfreeze" their opinions. However, "freezing" may characterize group decisions just as it does individual decisions. In an insightful analysis of political decisions by several US administrations (for example, in the Bay of Pigs fiasco, the October missile crisis, or the bombing of North Vietnam), Irving Janis (1972) coined the term "groupthink" to describe a "freezing" by cabinet members on their collective policies, and their aggressive rejection of dissenters. According to Janis, the degree to which *different* groups may succumb to "groupthink" may differ according to their degree of cohesion or "we feeling". Our present motivational analysis suggests additionally that for the *same* group, the tendency to "freeze" may depend on such momentary pressures as nearness of the decision deadline.

With the deadline relatively remote, group members' prepotent motivation might be to safeguard the validity of their decision. This might induce relative open-mindedness to divergent ideas, and increase the tolerance of ambiguity produced by dissenting views. With the deadline near, however, the group's overriding motivation might be to reach consensus. Such need for structure might well intensify the group's tendency to "freeze" or engage in "groupthink". In turn, this might reduce the group's tolerance for dissent, and enhance its tendency to reject deviates.

In a field experiment which put those ideas to a preliminary test, groups of Tel-Aviv (boy and girl) scouts were presented with a decision where to spend their annual "work-camp" of two weeks' duration. One choice was an affluent, centrally located kibbutz with such attractive "props" as swimming pool, tennis courts, and color TVs. The other choice was a "fledgling" borderline kibbutz "in the middle of nowhere" and lacking such basic conveniences as well appointed bathrooms.

Despite what might appear to some the obvious choice, the idealistic scouts predominantly preferred the rugged little settlement over its comfortable alternative. However, unbeknownst to the other group members, the investigators asked one of the scouts to appeal (fictitiously) for the opposite choice, and do so either early on in the deliberation process or toward the very end, near the designated deadline. When the dissenting view was voiced early, the member expressing it was evaluated relatively positively and not significantly differently from members expressing a conforming opinion. However, when the dissent came late, the evaluation was considerably more negative. This result may indicate the group's tendency to "freeze" in a proximity of deadline, and to consequently reject the deviate.

In sum, research described above supports the various motivational derivations of the lay epistemic model. In particular, it illustrates the model's applicability to social psychological phenomena as apparently diverse as impression formation, social comparison, stereotyping, and group decision-making. Thus, the present findings are compatible with a major tenet of the lay epistemic approach whereby diverse topics of social psychological inquiry differ in the *contents* of lay knowledge to which they pertain, while they are similarly affected by various parameters of the knowledge acquisition *process*, such as the epistemic motivations.

The deductive element in epistemic behavior

The bulk of research within the lay epistemic framework has so far focused on the effects of epistemic motivations. However, remaining aspects of the model have researchable implications as well. The following section reviews some studies of the deductive aspects of epistemic behavior.

The assumption that people validate their inferences deductively has far-reaching implications for a social psychology of knowledge. Primarily, it provides the conceptual link for integrating various hitherto separate social cognitive formulations. According to this analysis, contrary to the prevalent view, cognitive consistency models are closely akin to the attributional models. As shown in detail elsewhere (Kruglanski and Klar 1987), all cases of cognitive inconsistency contain a core of *logical inconsistency* in which epistemic effect, the undermining of beliefs, may under the appropriate motivational conditions cause upset and aversive arousal (cf. Cooper and Fazio 1984). By contrast, attributional theories highlight the consequences of *logical consistency* between specific informational patterns (including distinctiveness, consistency, and consensus information) and given causal hypotheses (for example, concerning attribution of an effect to an external entity). Such consistency of one's conclusion with (its deducibility from) one's premises may augment one's sense of confidence, a central dependent variable of attribution theorists. Thus, rather than representing incompatible images of the lay person (as an irrational or a rational creature respectively), consistency theories and attributional models appear to address the same process even if they approach it from opposite sides of the logical consistency issue.

The "deductive reasoning" aspect of the epistemic process has empirical as well as theoretical implications. Consider Heider's (1958) balance theory. According to the present interpretation the classical triad "p likes o", "p likes x", and "o does not like x" could be imbalanced because it contains a logical contradiction. The sentence "p likes o" may often imply that p "approves of" or "agrees with" o's preferences, attitudes, and opinions. Thus, to find out that p likes o yet disapproves of o's preferences regarding x contains a contradiction which could foster unpleasantness, unreasonableness, and perceived instability predicted by balance theory.

However, not all positive sentiments may imply approval or agreement. And when they do not, imbalance may not result in upset. These notions were tested in a study by Klar and Pol (1980) at Tel-Aviv University. In the first research phase, native speakers of English judged the extent to which different sentiment terms implied agreement, that is, the extent to which a given sentiment felt by p toward o implies that p and o would share the same sentiment toward x. Examples of sentiments rated as having strong agreement implication are "approves of", "venerates", or "is proud of". Sentiments rated to have medium agreement implication are "likes", "cherishes", "is impressed by"; and those with weak agreement implications are "fancies", "longs for", or "is charmed by".

In the second phase, a different group of subjects was exposed to balanced and imbalanced triads with sentiment terms in each of the strong, medium, and weak implicational categories. The dependent variables used by Klar and Pol were those employed traditionally in balance theoretic research: (1) the rated pleasantness of the situation depicted, (2) its rated reasonableness, and (3) stability. As expected, significant implication by balance interactions appeared on all the dependent measures. More specifically, balance effects (that is, differences between balanced and imbalanced triads) were strongest with sentiments in the strong implication category, weaker with sentiments in the medium implications category, and weakest with those in the low implication category. These findings support the present proposal whereby the effects of cognitive inconsistency (in this case, the effects of cognitive imbalance) are mediated by the epistemic consequences of logical contradiction.

Inconsistency resolution via information search

The present analysis has implications for ways of resolving a cognitive inconsistency. A logical contradiction can be resolved by denying or rejecting one of its "horns". By definition, A and not A cannot both be true. One of them has to be false. If an inconsistency is to be resolved, one of the contradictory cognitions must therefore be rejected or denied. The same analysis also points to the likely direction of the rejection or denial. Simply, the cognition more likely to be denied is that which is less clearly "undeniable", or is held with less confidence.

But what about the case where both inconsistent cognitions are held with approximately equal confidence? In such a situation the individual might be at a loss as to which of the incompatible cognitions is to be denied. If nonetheless motivated to reduce the ambiguity, (s)he might conduct an informational search which might suggest a way out. Thus the epistemic model predicts that individuals whose confidence is distributed evenly over the two contradictory cognitions would be more likely to engage in an informational search than individuals whose confidence is distributed unevenly.

The above ideas were supported by aspects of the Mayseless and Kruglanski (in press, b) research mentioned earlier. In one experiment, some subjects were given ample evidence supporting a target hypothesis, creating high initial confidence. Other subjects were given considerably less supportive information creating low initial confidence. All subjects were then presented with an item of information which contradicted the target hypothesis. The main dependent variable was subjects' tendency to seek the opinions of others before reaching a judgment. The results were clearcut: 65 per cent of subjects in the high confidence condition and only 30 per cent of subjects in the low confidence condition expressed the wish to consult with others. In accordance with the present analysis, it appears that when subjects have low confidence in a proposition, they have less difficulty resolving the contradiction between this and another (credible) proposition (presumably by rejecting the less confidently held of the two) than when they have high confidence in both contradictory propositions.

Hypothesis testing

The notion that lay persons test their hypotheses deductively has implications concerning the question whether they predominantly employ confirmatory (Snyder and Swann 1978) or diagnostic (cf. Trope and Bassok 1983) strategies of searching for information. A confirmatory strategy refers to searching for features which are highly probable under a given hypothesis (for example, searching for instances of extrovert behaviors when testing the hypothesis that someone is an extrovert). By contrast, a diagnostic strategy refers to searching for features which best discriminate between the hypothesis and some alternative (for example, searching for behaviors characteristic of a politician and not an actor when testing the alternative hypotheses that a target is a politician or an actor, but not both, as occasionally happens).

According to the present analysis, whether persons seek characteristic ("confirmatory") or diagnostic information should depend on the *implicational linkages* which (in their mind) connect a given type of information and a hypothesis of interest. Among other factors, this could depend on whether they considered the target hypothesis in isolation (or singly) or in the context of competing hypothesis (or hypotheses). For instance, when testing the hypothesis that a given celebrity is a politician, the "knower" may look for information about behaviors characteristic of a politician (for instance public appearances, interest in public affairs). However, when testing the competing hypotheses that the celebrity is a politician or a high-ranking army officer, the "knower" may look instead for information about diagnostic features that may help discriminate between the two alternatives being considered.

These notions were tested in a series of studies conducted recently by Kruglanski and Mayseless (in press, a). In one study (experiment 1), subjects tested the (single) hypothesis that a given target is an architect, the (single) hypothesis that (s)he is a painter, or the competing hypotheses that (s)he is an architect *or* a painter. As predicted, in the single hypothesis conditions subjects exhibited strong preferences for characteristic (versus non-characteristic) information. Subjects testing the *architect* hypothesis preferred questions about features characteristic of an architect over those about non-characteristic features. Similarly, subjects testing the *painter* hypothesis preferred questions about features characteristic of a painter over questions about less characteristic features. Finally, subjects testing the *painter versus architect* hypotheses did not exhibit preferences for characteristic features of architects or painters. Instead, they exhibited a significant preference for diagnostic (versus nondiagnostic) features demarcating the painter and the architect hypotheses.

Whether an individual tests a hypothesis singly or in the context of competing alternatives may depend, among other things, on this person's motivational orientation. For instance, the generation of alternative hypotheses should be more likely when the individual has high tolerance of ambiguity, and less likely when (s)he has a high need for (nonspecific) structure. To test those notions Kruglanski and Mayseless (in press, a: experiment 3) had subjects test the hypothesis that an interviewee is a painter. A subtle priming of an alternate hypothesis was attempted by casually noting that "the interviewee could, of course, be a member of a different profession, for instance an architect". As predicted, subjects in whom the tolerance of ambiguity was elevated (via instructions stressing the value of accuracy) exhibited greater preference for questions diagnostic with regard to the painter–architect pair than subjects placed under high need for structure (induced via instructions stressing the value of clarity).

Thus it appears that the information which persons may seek in order to test their hypotheses depends on the informational and motivational context in which a given hypothesis is evaluated – all presumably depending on the implicational representations that, for a given individual, render specific item(s) of information relevant to the hypothesis (or hypotheses) being tested. It is because of such considerations of implicational or deductive relevance (cf. Kruglanski 1980) that "characteristic" information may be sought when a hypothesis is tested singly, whereas diagnostic information may be preferred when a hypothesis is tested against competing alternatives.

Content-bound research in the lay epistemic framework

The lay epistemic model suggests a two-pronged approach to social cognitive research. On the one hand, a general model of the judgmental process is proposed and its relevance to a variety of social psychological problems is explored. All the preceding research belongs in that category, including studies which applied the model to social comparison phenomena, ethnic stereotyping, the prejudice–discrimination relation, or social hypothesis testing. As has been stressed repeatedly, the power of the model derives from the assumption that the same epistemic (or judgmental) process applies to all contents of knowledge. Thus, the general principles demonstrated in the lay epistemic model should apply to seemingly unconnected social psychological phenomena, the differences among which stem from the separate content domains to which they refer.

On the other hand, the present approach strongly implies the desirability of "pure" content-bound research, focused on specific contents of knowledge structures of demonstrable interest. Rather than confounding separate levels of analysis, and mistaking special categories of judgment for the judgmental process, it is proposed to study *separately* particular contents of knowledge structures of special consequence or utility.

A recent study by Muzfir (1984) has aimed to "unconfound" judgmental process and contents in reference to the relation between attitude extremity and resistance to change. According to some theories (in particular, Osgood and Tannenbaum 1955), an attitude's resistance to change is positively related to its extremity. One explanation for such correlation may be that extreme attitudes are held with greater confidence than less extreme ones (cf. Insko 1967, Kelley and Lamb 1967). However, while attitudinal extremity and confidence may be often correlated, the two variables are conceptually separate. Extremity refers to the attitude's content, as a more extreme attitude differs in its content from a less extreme attitude. By contrast, confidence is a parameter of the judgmental process: one could be more or less confident in propositions of all possible contents including more or less confident attitudes. Furthermore, resistance to change should depend on one's confidence in a proposition (inversely related to its "deniability") and not on the proposition's content.

Muzfir's (1984) experiment employed a 2×2 design in which attitude extremity (high and low) was orthogonally manipulated to attitudinal confidence (high and low). Subjects in the low extremity condition were presented with a vignette depicting a mild crime (pickpocketing), whereas those in the high extremity condition were presented with a vignette depicting a severe crime (rape and murder). Subjects in all conditions were presented with a sketch of a suspect as he appeared in court and with a composite drawing of the criminal based on a witness' description. In the high confidence condition the composite drawing was highly similar to the sketch, and in the low confidence condition it was somewhat dissimilar.

The initial attitude measure concerned subjects' punitivity toward the defendant. As expected, subjects in the high extremity condition recommended higher punishment on the average than did subjects in the low extremity condition. No differences in punitivity separated the high and low confidence groups. Also as expected, subjects in the high confidence condition were significantly more confident in the recommended punishment than subjects in the low confidence condition, whereas no differences in confidence separated the high and low extremity groups.

To induce attitude change, subjects in all groups were presented with evidence inconsistent with the defendant's culpability, notably another composite drawing portraying a face highly unlike the defendant's and based on a second witness's testimony. Subjects were then asked to make a final recommendation as to the appropriate punishment. The degree of change from the first to the second recommendation served as a measure of attitude change. As predicted, subjects in the high confidence condition exhibited a lesser degree of change than those in the low confidence condition, whereas subjects in the high versus low extremity conditions did not significantly differ in amount of attitude change. Thus, it seems that an attitude's resistance to change depends on a judgmental process element, notably confidence, rather than on a judgmental content element, notably extremity.

According to the lay epistemic perspective, attitudes refer to a particular content domain of knowledge structures which specifically deals with *evaluative* statements. Their formation and change should, therefore, be affected by the same factors which govern the formation and change of innumerable alternative knowledge structures unrelated to evaluation. The present perspective on evaluative statements should have researchable implications of interest. For instance, the finding that *evaluative inconsistencies* are processed more extensively, and are therefore more efficiently recalled than *descriptive inconsistencies* (cf. Wyer 1974), might be reducible to differences in process variables with which the descriptive evaluative distinction may have been confounded in past research. A typical instruction to subjects to form an impression of the target might have been often understood as an instruction to form an evaluative impression. If so, better recall of evaluative (versus descriptive) inconsistencies could stem from higher arousal of the need for structure concerning an evaluation (versus a description) of the target person. This possibility could be profitably pursued in subsequent research.

Self-ascribed epistemic authority. Muzfir's research above demonstrates the utility of drawing a clear distinction between epistemic contents and process; however, it does not in itself focus on epistemic contents *per se*. Yet the specific contents of persons' knowledge structures should importantly affect behavior and performance in various situations. Recent studies by Ellis (1984) of "self-ascribed epistemic authority" illustrate a possible direction in which such content-bound research could be taken.

The construct of "epistemic authority" (cf. Kruglanski and Jaffe 1986) relates to a classical topic in the social psychology of communication having to do with source characteristics (such as expertise and trustworthiness). Unique to the present approach is the focus on *subjects' beliefs* concerning the epistemic authority (i.e. reliability) of various sources, including the self. Thus we are assuming that individuals may differ in their beliefs concerning the epistemic authority of different sources in a given domain of interest. Furthermore, we are assuming that tapping the contents of those beliefs may help us predict persons' reactions in various social influence situations.

More specifically, Ellis (1984) hypothesized that an individual's beliefs concerning his or her own epistemic authority in a given domain may moderate the benefits for this person of *experiential learning* versus *frontal lectures*. In an experiential learning situation persons interpret by themselves the meaning of their experiences. Individuals whose own epistemic authority in a domain is low may experience little confidence concerning their interpretations. Consequently they may have difficulties in forming confident knowledge from those experiences, and benefit little from the experiences relative to listening to a frontal lecture, where interpretations are offered by an external authority. By contrast, an individual whose own epistemic authority is high may benefit more from experiential (versus frontal) learning situations.

To test the above ideas, Ellis constructed questionnaires of perceived own epistemic authority for two separate topics, mathematics and interpersonal skills respectively. In each case the questionnaires tapped the degree to which subjects trusted their own authority in making sense of information regarding the domain at issue.

In the course of the research, individuals who scored above or below median on own epistemic authority in a given domain were exposed to experiential learning or a frontal lecture on a pertinent topic. Thus, in the mathematical study high or low scorers on own epistemic authority in mathematics were assigned to experiential learning or frontal lecture conditions designed to impart the same set of mathematical principles. Similarly, in the interpersonal skills study, persons high or low on own epistemic authority in interpersonal skills were assigned to experiential learning or frontal lecture conditions designed to impart a set of interpersonal (notably empathic) skills.

When subsequently tested, individuals with high own epistemic authority who had been previously exposed to experiential learning did consistently better than those who had been exposed to the frontal lecture condition, whereas in the mathematics study the lows did about equally well in the two learning situations, and in the interpersonal skills study they actually did worse in the experimental (vs. frontal) condition. The same pattern of results obtained in the two separate studies dealing with mathematics and interpersonal skills respectively. This implies the generality of the "epistemic authority" construct as a variable of relevance to learning and performance.

Conclusions

The research reviewed above demonstrates the epistemic model's broad range of applicability. In part, this stems from the model's general level of analysis directed at the cognitive (judgmental) process at large. Hence the model has implications for diverse social cognitive phenomena which represent aspects of the judgmental process conjoined to various content areas of interest. In this sense, the epistemic model constitutes an integrative framework which subsumes as its special cases numerous "intermediate range" social psychological frameworks as various attributional models (Kruglanski 1980), cognitive consistency formulations (Kruglanski and Klar, 1987), attitude-change theories (Kruglanski, in press, a), social comparison theory (Kruglanski and Mayseless, in press, a), and so on.

Besides an integration *between* models, the present epistemic framework offers a *within-models* integration. Specifically, it assigns a definite and complementary place in the judgmental process to both informational and motivational variables. In this sense it bridges a dichotomy that has split social cognitive psychology into the "hot" and "cold" cognition camps (cf. Sorrentino and Higgins 1986). The present approach recognizes that all information-processing is motivated and all motivational influences on the cognitive process operate in informational contexts and are governed by rules of information-processing. This highlights neglected motivational aspects in such cognitively "cold" models as attribution theory (Kruglanski, in press, a) and equally neglected informational aspects in putatively "hot" models such as dissonance theory (for more extensive discussions see Kruglanski and Klar 1987; and Kruglanski, in press, a). By bridging the "cold"–"hot" gap within a unitary conceptual paradigm, it is hoped that the epistemic approach would open up novel avenues of research on classic social psychological problems.

Clear separation between judgmental process and contents underscores the value of pure "content-bound" research of social psychological significance. Such research could be conducted on various levels of specificity including levels restricted to particular cultures, groups within cultures, individuals within situations, etc. By contrast with process-bound research which is typically nomothetic in nature, content-oriented research is openly ideographic. Rather than aiming at the discovery of transhistorical and transcultural generalities, such research might be primarily guided by the (conceptual, empirical, or applied) interest value of given belief clusters. For instance, the ideological contents of various groups' beliefs (cf. Billig 1978, Bar-Tal, in press) or life philosophies of significant social figures would qualify as legitimate exemplars of content-bound social psychological research.

The legitimation of content-oriented research in social psychology might instigate methodological developments for mapping out areas of relevant belief contents. Important cross-fertilization in this regard may occur with neighboring disciplines (such as clinical psychology, sociology, or cultural anthropology) which may share with social psychology an interest in the contents of people's knowledge structures.

Finally, applying a theory of the epistemic process to particular contents of knowledge may suggest useful ways of modifying those contents in various desirable directions. For example, Higgins *et al.* (1985) applied cognitive process notions of construct accessibility (cf. Higgins and King, 1981) to activate subjects' chronic notions of self-discrepancy in ways that render them amenable to treatment. Kruglanski and Jaffe (1988) suggested how various "frustrative hypotheses" of neurotic patients may be "unfrozen" and modified in the course of cognitive therapy, and Klar *et al.* (in press) applied the epistemic theory to various "conflict schemata" in order to show how interpersonal or intergroup conflicts may be abated or resolved. Conjunction of a process theory of knowledge acquisition to contents of particular knowledge structures thus promises to become a useful applied tool for the social cognitive psychologist.

References

Abramson, L. Y., Seligman, M. E. P., and Teasdale, J. D. (1978). Learned helplessness in humans: critique and reformulation. *Journal of Abnormal Psychology* 87: 49–57.

Aronson, E. and Carlsmith, J. M. (1962). Performance expectancy as a determinant of actual performance. *Journal of Abnormal and Social Psychology* 65: 178–82.

Asch, S. E. (1946). Forming impressions of personality. *Journal of Abnormal and Social Psychology* 41: 258–90.

Bar-Hillel, M. (1973). On the subjective probability of compound events. *Organizational Behavior and Human Performance* 9: 396–406.

Bar-Tal, D. (1984). The limitations of investigating contents: the case of helping behavior. Unpublished manuscript.

Bar-Tal, D. (1986). The Masada Syndrome: a case of central belief. In N. Milgram (ed.), *Stress and coping in time of war*. New York: Brunner/Mazel.

Bar-Tal, D. (in press). *Group beliefs*. New York: Springer.

Bechtold, J. and Zanna, M. P. (1985). Unpublished data. Waterloo University.

Billig, M. (1978). *Fascists: a social psychological view of the National Front*. London: Harcourt Brace Jovanovich.

Brehm, J. W. and Cohen, A. R. (1962). *Explorations in cognitive dissonance*. New York: Wiley.

Cantor, N. and Mischel, W. (1977). Traits as prototypes: effects on recognition memory. *Journal of Personality and Social Psychology* 35: 38–49.

Collins, B. E. and Hoyt, M. F. (1972). Personal responsibility for consequences: an integration and extension of the "forced compliance" literature. *Journal of Experimental Social Psychology* 8: 558–93.

Cooper, J. and Fazio, F. H. (1984). A new look at dissonance theory. In L. Berkowitz (ed.), *Advances in experimental social psychology*, vol. 17. New York: Academic Press.

Edwards, W. (1982). Conservatism in human information processing. In D. Kahneman, P. Slovic, and A. Tversky (eds.), *Judgment under uncertainty: heuristics and biases*. Cambridge, MA: Harvard University Press.

Ellis, S. (1984). The effect of self-epistemic authority on the relative efficacy of cognitive change methods in different subject matters. Unpublished doctoral dissertation, Tel-Aviv University.

Fazio, R. H., Powell, M. C., and Herr, P. M. (1983). Toward a process model of the attitude–behavior relation: accessing one's attitude upon mere observation of the attitude object. *Journal of Personality and Social Psychology* 44: 723–35.

Festinger, L. (1954). A theory of social comparison processes. *Human Relations* 7: 117–40.

Festinger, L. (1957). *A theory of cognitive dissonance*. Stanford, CA: Stanford University Press.

Festinger, L. (1964). *Conflict, decision and dissonance*. Stanford, CA: Stanford University Press.

Fiske, S. T. and Taylor, S. E. (1984). *Social cognition*. Reading, MA: Addison-Wesley.

Freund, T., Kruglanski, A. W., and Schpitzajzen, A. (1985). The freezing and unfreezing of impressional primacy: effects of the need for structure and the fear of invalidity. *Personality and Social Psychology Bulletin* 11: 479–87.

Heider, F. (1958). *The psychology of interpersonal relations*. New York: Wiley.
Higgins, E. T. and Bargh, J. A. (1987). Social cognition and social perception. *Annual Review of Psychology* 38: 369–425.
Higgins, E. T., Bargh, J. A., and Lombardi, W. (1985). The nature of priming effects on categorization. *Journal of Experimental Psychology: Learning, Memory and Cognition* 11: 59–69.
Higgins, E. T. and King, G. (1981). Accessibility of social constructs: information processing consequences of individual and contextual variability. In N. Cantor and J. Kihlstrom (eds.), *Personality, cognition and social interaction*. Hillsdale, NJ: Lawrence Erlbaum.
Higgins, E. T., King, G. A., and Mavin, G. H. (1982). Individual construct accessibility and subjective impressions and recall. *Journal of Personality and Social Psychology* 43: 35–47.
Higgins, E. T., Rholes, W. S., and Jones, C. R. (1977). Category accessibility and impression formation. *Journal of Experimental Social Psychology* 13: 141–54.
Higgins, E. T., Straumann, T., and Klein, R. (1986). Standards and the process of self-evaluation: multiple affects from multiple stages. In Sorrentino and Higgins (eds.) 1986.
Insko, C. A. (1967). *Theories of attitude change*. New York: Appleton-Century-Crofts.
Janis, I. (1972). *Victims of groupthink*. Boston: Houghton Mifflin.
Jones, E. E. and Davis, K. E. (1965). From acts to dispositions: the attribution process in person perception. In L. Berkowitz (ed.), *Advances in experimental social psychology*, vol. 2. New York: Academic Press.
Kahneman, D. and Tversky, A. (1973). On the psychology of prediction. *Psychological Review* 80: 237–51.
Kelley, H. H. (1967). Attribution theory in social psychology. In D. Levine (ed.), *Nebraska Symposium on Motivation*. University of Nebraska Press.
Kelley, H. H. (1971). Attribution in social interaction. In E. E. Jones, D. E. Kanause, H. H. Kelley, R. E. Nisbett, S. Valins, and B. Weiner (eds.), *Attribution: Perceiving the causes of behavior*. Morristown, NJ: General Learning Press.
Kelley, H. H. and Lamb, T. W. (1967). Certainty of judgment and resistance to social influence. *Journal of Abnormal and Social Psychology* 55: 137–9.
Klar, Y., Bar-Tal, D., and Kruglanski, A. W. (in press). Conflict as a cognitive schema: an epistemological approach. In W. Stroebe, A. W. Kruglanski, D. Bar-Tal, and M. Hewstone (eds.), *Social psychology of intergroup and international conflict*. New York: Springer.
Klar, Y. and Pol, I. (1980). Imbalance effects as functions of agreement implication. Unpublished data, Tel-Aviv University.
Kruglanski, A. W. (1975). The endogenous–exogenous partition in attribution theory. *Psychological Review* 81: 387–406.
Kruglanski, A. W. (1980). Lay epistemologic–process and contents: another look at attribution theory. *Psychological Review* 87: 70–87.

Kruglanski, A. W. (in press, a). *Basic processes in social cognition: a theory of lay epistemology*. New York: Plenum.

Kruglanski, A. W. (in press, b). Motivations for judging and knowing: implications for causal attribution. In E. T. Higgins and R. M. Sorrentino (eds.), *Handbook of motivation and cognition*, vol. 2. New York: Guilford Press.

Kruglanski, A. W. and Ajzen, I. (1983). Bias and error in human judgment. *European Journal of Social Psychology* 13: 1–44.

Kruglanski, A. W. and Freund, T. (1983). The freezing and unfreezing of lay inferences: effects on impressional primacy, ethnic stereotyping, and numerical anchoring. *Journal of Experimental Social Psychology* 19: 448–68.

Kruglanski, A. W., Hamel, I. A., Maides, S. A., and Schwartz, J. M. (1978). Attribution theory as a special case of lay epistemology. In J. H. Harvey, W. J. Ickes, and R. F. Kidd (eds.), *New directions in attribution research*, vol. 2. Hillsdale, NJ: Lawrence Erlbaum.

Kruglanski, A. W. and Jaffe, Y. (1986). Curing by knowing: a lay epistemic approach to cognitive therapy. In L. Abramson (ed.), *Social and personality perspectives in clinical inference*. New York: Guilford Press.

Kruglanski, A. W. and Klar, Y. (1987). A view from a bridge: synthesizing the consistency and attribution paradigms from the lay epistemic perspective. *European Journal of Social Psychology* 17: 211–41.

Kruglanski, A. W. and Mayseless, O. (in press, a). Contextual effects in hypothesis testing: effects of competing hypotheses and epistemic motivations. *Social Cognition*.

Kruglanski, A. W. and Mayseless, O. (in press, b). Motivational effects in the social comparison of opinions. *Journal of Personality and Social Psychology*.

Lerner, M. J. (1980). *The belief in a just world: a fundamental delusion*. New York: Plenum.

McArthur, L. Z. and Ginsburg, E. (1981). Causal attributions to salient stimuli: an investigation of visual fixation mediators. *Personality and Social Psychology Bulletin* 7: 547–53.

Markus, H. (1977). Self schemas and processing information about the self. *Journal of Personality and Social Psychology* 35: 63–78.

Mayseless, O. and Kruglanski, A. W. (1987). What makes you so sure? Effects of epistemic motivations on judgmental confidence. *Organizational Behavior and Human Decision Processes* 39: 162–83.

Muzfir, M. (1984). Unpublished data. Tel-Aviv University.

Orvis, B. R., Kelley, H. H., and Butler, D. (1976). Attributional conflict in young couples. In J. H. Harvey, W. J. Ickes, and R. F. Kidd (eds.), *New directions in attribution research*, vol. 1. Hillsdale, NJ: Lawrence Erlbaum.

Osgood, C. E. and Tannenbaum, P. H. (1955). The principle of congruity in the prediction of attitude change. *Psychological Review* 62: 42–55.

Peri, N., Kruglanski, A. W., and Zakai, D. (1986). Interactive effects of initial confidence and epistemic motivations on the extent of informational search. Unpublished manuscript, Tel-Aviv University.

Rogers, T. B., Kuiper, N. A., and Kirker, W. S. (1977). Self-reference and the encoding of personal information. *Journal of Personality and Social Psychology* 35: 677–88.

Ross, L. (1977). The intuitive psychologist and his shortcomings: distortions in the attribution process. In L. Berkowitz (ed.), *Advances in experimental social psychology*, vol. 10. New York: Academic Press.

Snyder, M. and Swann, W. B. (1978). Hypothesis testing processes in social interaction. *Journal of Personality and Social Psychology* 36: 1202–12.

Snyder, M. L. and Wicklund, R. A. (1981). Attribute ambiguity. In J. H. Harvey, W. J. Ickes, and R. F. Kidd (eds.), *New directions in attribution research*, vol. 3. Hillsdale, NJ: Lawrence Erlbaum.

Sorrentino, R. M. and Higgins, E. T. (eds.) (1986). *Handbook of motivation and cognition: foundations of social behavior*. New York: Guilford Press.

Trope, Y. and Bassok, M. (1983). Information gathering strategies in hypothesis testing. *Journal of Experimental Social Psychology* 19: 560–76.

Tversky, A. and Kahneman, D. (1974). Judgment under uncertainty: heuristics and biases. *Science* 185: 1124–31.

Wason, P. C. and Johnson-Laird, P. N. (1972). *Psychology of reasoning: structure and content*. Cambridge, MA: Harvard University Press.

Weiner, B. (1979). A theory of motivation for some classroom experiences. *Journal of Educational Psychology* 71: 3–25.

Weiner, B. (1985a). "Spontaneous" causal thinking. *Psychological Bulletin* 97: 74–84.

Weiner, B. (1985b). An attributional theory of achievement motivation and emotion. *Psychological Review* 92: 548–73.

Weiner, B. and Litman-Adizes, T. (1980). An attributional expectancy–value analysis of learned helplessness and depression. In J. Garber and M. E. P. Seligman (eds.), *Human helplessness: Theory and applications*. New York: Academic Press.

Wyer, R. S. (1974). *Cognitive organization and change: an information processing approach*. Hillsdale, NJ: Lawrence Erlbaum.

Zimbardo, P. G. (1977). *Shyness: what it is, what to do about it*. Reading, MA: Addison-Wesley.

7 Understanding social knowledge: if only the data could speak for themselves[1]

Robert S. Wyer, Jr., and Thomas K. Srull

Hundreds if not thousands of experiments address the question of how humans acquire knowledge about their social environment. In conducting and evaluating this research, however, it is sometimes easy to forget that we as scientists are ourselves guided by processes very similar to the ones we are attempting to investigate. Scientists, like lay people, are governed by a set of rules and procedures for acquiring knowledge. Just as it is important to understand the processes that govern information acquisition by people in general, so is it necessary to understand the rules that govern the acquisition of *scientific* information in order to evaluate the conclusions that are drawn and their implications for subsequent scientific behavior (the design of future experiments, the degree to which alternative interpretations of data are entertained, whether there is thought to be a cumulative development of knowledge in a given domain, and so on).

There appears to be a rather direct analogy between the process of acquiring scientific information and the process of acquiring knowledge in general. For example, an individual who receives information about someone with a particular goal in mind is often assumed to activate a set of concepts and cognitive procedures that are relevant to the attainment of this objective. These concepts and procedures will heavily determine which of all the available information is attended to, how it is interpreted, the implications drawn from it, and the way in which it is integrated with existing knowledge. In the process of pursuing this goal or objective, a general representation of the target person will be formed and stored in memory. This

1 The preparation of this chapter was supported by grants BNS83–02105 from the National Science Foundation and MH3–8585, BSR from the National Institute of Mental Health. Appreciation is extended to Galen Bodenhausen, Reid Hastie, Tom Ostrom, and the editors of this volume for penetrating comments on an earlier draft of this manuscript, and to the University of Illinois Social Cognition Group for stimulating many of the ideas and criticisms that underlie the issues we have raised.

representation may then be used for later judgments and decisions, and this will often occur independently of the episodic facts that led the representation to be formed in the first place (see e.g. Wyer, Srull, and Gordon 1984). Consequently, the goals and procedures that are initially activated at the time knowledge is acquired can have a substantial influence on the types of conclusion that are later drawn on the basis of it. Moreover, this influence can persist long after the original processing took place (for more formal explanations of these phenomena, see Higgins and King 1981, Srull and Wyer 1986, Wyer and Srull 1984, 1986).

The acquisition of scientific knowledge may be viewed similarly. For example, a scientist often attempts to acquire information with particular objectives in mind, and selects procedures for acquiring it that are assumed to be relevant to these objectives. The information acquired, and the conclusions drawn from it, are heavily influenced by these initial decisions. Moreover, the conclusions are usually *generalizations* and are drawn in the context of at least a vague theoretical formulation of the phenomena observed. This formulation will then influence the acquisition and interpretation of subsequent information, often independently of the empirical data that led to its initial development.

As the above discussion implies, the analogy between the scientific acquisition and use of knowledge and its acquisition and use by the layperson exists at many different stages. For example, when a layperson receives information about people and events in his or her social environment for the purpose of making a judgment or behavioral decision, several mediating stages of processing are theoretically involved (Wyer and Srull 1986). These stages include:

(1) the interpretation of new information in terms of previously existing concepts;
(2) the organization of new information into a coherent representation of its referent, based at least in part on general world knowledge of the *type* of referent it describes;
(3) the storage of such a representation in memory;
(4) the retrieval of the representation from memory at the appropriate time, along with other knowledge about the referent that may be relevant to the judgment or behavioral decision;
(5) the integration of multiple implications of the knowledge retrieved for the judgment or decision to be made; and
(6) the generation of some overt response.

A scientist's acquisition of knowledge involves a similar sequence of steps:

(1) the interpretation of an observed phenomenon in terms of theoretical concepts deemed relevant;

(2) the incorporation of these interpreted observations into a general theoretical formulation of the phenomenon and the entities involved in it, based in part on general (scientific) knowledge of the properties of these entities and their interrelatedness;
(3) the transfer of this formulation, as modified by the observed phenomenon, to "scientific memory";
(4) the subsequent retrieval of the formulation, along with other scientific knowledge for use in new experimentation;
(5) an integration of the implications of this retrieved scientific knowledge to arrive at a prediction or conclusion concerning phenomena to which the knowledge is relevant; and
(6) the public reporting of this conclusion (e.g. in a journal article).

It is interesting to speculate that not only the stages of knowledge acquisition and use, but the factors that influence the processing of information at each stage, are analogous in the case of the layperson and the scientist. For example, as laypersons' interpretation of an observed phenomenon may be biased by concepts that happen to be most accessible in memory at the time the observation is made (cf. Bargh 1984, Higgins and King 1981, Wyer and Srull 1981), so may scientists' interpretation of a phenomenon be biased by the theoretical concepts they happen to apply. Just as laypersons' overt responses may be influenced by implicit rules of communication and perceptions of what the recipient of the communication already knows and considers acceptable (cf. Grice 1975, Kraut and Higgins 1984, Wyer 1981), so may scientists' reports of findings and the interpretation they give to them be biased by formal and implicit rules of scientific communication, and by the scientific zeitgeist that makes certain subsets of possible conclusions more or less easily accepted (Weimer 1979).

Unfortunately, a detailed discussion of this analogy at all stages of knowledge acquisition and use is beyond the scope of this chapter. Therefore, we will focus on a particular concern that the analogy makes salient. Specifically, the data that are attended to, the interpretations that are placed on them, and the general conclusions that are drawn are critically dependent on which goals and procedures were initially activated at the time the data were acquired. Moreover, once a general cognitive representation is formed (by the scientist as well as the layperson), it may constrain the types of information one subsequently seeks and the way that this new information is interpreted. This can occur independently of (*a*) the general procedures that were initially used to collect the information and (*b*) the specific empirical results that originally led the cognitive representation to be formed.

A recognition of the fact that the conclusions based on scientific knowledge are affected by the assumptions that guide its acquisition is of course not new (cf. Weimer 1979). In the present chapter, we examine some of the assumptions that often underlie the scientific study of *social* knowledge. In doing so, we distinguish between two general sorts of assumptions. One sort concerns the nature of the social *phenomenon* being considered, independently of the procedures used to investigate it. Thus, for example, the tendency to report attitudes that are consistent with a position one has recently agreed to advocate may be interpreted differently depending on whether one invokes the assumptions of cognitive dissonance theory (Festinger 1957) or those of self-perception theory (Bem 1972). The merits of such alternative interpretations are typically a major focus of scientific inquiry and investigators are well aware of their existence. At another level, however, theoretical assumptions may also underlie the *procedures* that are commonly selected by investigators for use in collecting data and the measures that they derive from them. In many instances, the selection of these procedures seems based largely on convenience rather than any a priori theoretical considerations. Thus, the theoretical assumptions that necessarily underlie the use of these procedures, and the interpretation of data obtained through their use, are often not explicitly stated by the investigator and in many instances appear not to be recognized.

This chapter reviews several procedures that are commonly used in research on social information-processing. In our discussion of these procedures, we will attempt to point out that the conclusions drawn about a phenomenon are heavily dependent upon the assumptions that underlie the procedure used to investigate it. In addition, we will point out instances in which the use of a particular procedure may itself alter the phenomenon that the acquired information is intended to explain.

In order to provide an organization for our discussion, we will generally consider a prototypic situation in which subjects receive stimulus information about themselves, other persons, or events that take place in their social environment, and then make a judgment or behavioral decision on the basis of this information. The focus of social cognition theory and research is on the cognitive processes that mediate the effects of such information on overt behavior, and the situational factors that influence these processes. Several mediating stages of information-processing are potentially involved, including those noted in our earlier discussion. Most if not all of these stages of processing come into play regardless of whether the ultimate response being investigated is a measure of memory, a social judgment, or a specific behavioral decision. A major thesis of the present chapter is based on a recognition of this fact. That is, many of the memory measures used in social cognition research are often assumed to reflect the results of a particular stage of processing. In fact, however, the responses that enter into these measures, like the behavior they are intended to explain, are often the consequence of processing at several different stages. Therefore, the effect of a particular experimental variable on these responses may be susceptible to alternative interpretations, depending on one's assumptions about the particular stages of processing involved. Put another way, the selection of a specific response measure is not arbitrary; it necessarily carries with it a specific set of assumptions about the processes that underlie the responses one obtains. These assumptions are often based on theoretical considerations, the validity of which are sometimes very controversial. Thus, when the measure used to investigate a particular phenomenon is selected without a full understanding of these assumptions and their implications, considerable theoretical and empirical confusion can result.

In the pages that follow, we attempt to point out some of the implicit and explicit assumptions that underlie the use of various methods of data acquisition in social information-processing, and give some examples of the ambiguities that can arise from applying certain methods without considering their underlying assumptions. Our discussion will not provide a detailed treatment of the measures themselves, or the complete range of their applicability (for an extensive discussion of social information processing methodology, see Srull 1984). Nor will it be a detailed theoretical exposition of the phenomena to which the measures are applied (for such treatments, see Wyer and Srull 1984, 1986). Rather, we will concentrate on the theoretical bases for using each measure, and will give examples that demonstrate the need to consider these underpinnings very carefully in drawing conclusions that are defensible. Our discussion will be divided into four sections. The first three sections focus on the types of measure often used to evaluate the cognitive mediators of social judgment: recall, recognition, and response time. In the last section, we will discuss judgment data themselves and the problems encountered in interpreting them as reflections of the processes that underlie behavioral decisions.

Free recall measures

A common type of experiment in social information-processing is one in which subjects receive information about a person or event with instructions to use it for a particular purpose (to learn the information, to form an impression of its referent, to make a particular type of judgment, etc.). They are then asked at some later time to recall as much of the information as possible. A researcher might then compute any of five different types of index:

(1) the total *amount* of information recalled;

(2) the *type* of information units that tend to be recalled;
(3) the *order* in which the various items are recalled;
(4) the number of *intrusions*, or the reporting of items that were not actually specified in the original information;
(5) the *implications* of the recalled information for a particular judgment or decision.

These indices are typically used to draw conclusions about three separate questions: (*a*) the extent to which the information was initially learned, (*b*) the content and organization of the mental representation formed of the object described by the information, and (*c*) the particular aspects of the information that are used as a basis for judgments and decisions.

We will discuss the potential uses of recall data for addressing each of these issues. However, it is first necessary to describe several alternative sets of assumptions that are often made about the processes that underlie the recall of information.

General considerations

The successful recall of information is often assumed to depend on its prior association with cues that are also present at the time of retrieval. Such cues can take nearly any form. For example, they might be concepts that were used to interpret the information when it was first received. They might also be past personal experiences that were thought about at the time of information acquisition, or other items that were received earlier in the experiment. Aspects of the physical environment (e.g. the color of the walls or the type of lighting) or internal states (e.g. one's mood or level of hunger) can also serve as effective retrieval cues.

Suppose a subject learns that John got drunk and spilled guacamole dip on the white living-room rug. If the person interpreted John's behavior as "clumsy" at the time it was first described, this trait concept might then serve as a retrieval cue for the behavior if it is activated at the time of recall. Alternatively, the event "John got drunk" may serve as a retrieval cue for the causally related consequence of John's faux pas. John's mishap might also be cued by thinking about a prior personal experience with similar features (e.g. spilling coffee over a white tablecloth).

Nearly all theories of free recall suggest that the concepts and attributes activated in a recall situation cue the retrieval of whatever information one reports. However, many of them differ with respect to the assumptions they make concerning (*a*) the nature of the underlying representation of information in memory, and (*b*) the processes that allow isolated components of this representation to be retrieved.

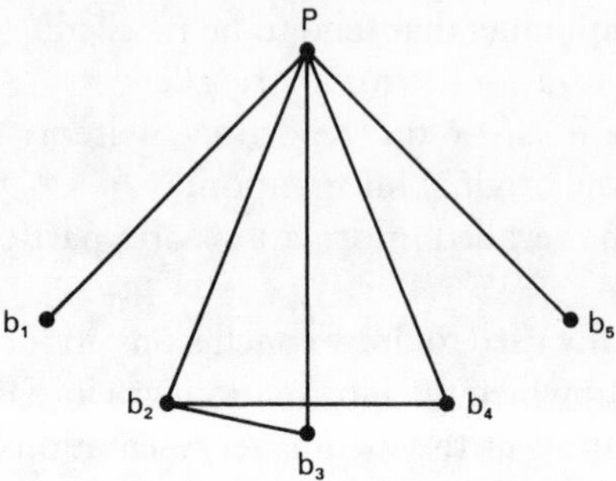

Fig 7.1. Network representation of a person (P) and five behaviors manifested by P ($b_1 - b_5$)

Associative network formulations. Many models conceptualize the representation of information in memory as an associative network of concepts and relations (e.g. Anderson and Bower 1973, Collins and Loftus 1975; in the area of social information-processing, see Wyer, Bodenhausen, and Srull 1984, Wyer and Carlston 1979). Concepts in such a network are represented by nodes, and associations by pathways connecting them. However, the nodes themselves are assumed to have no *internal* structure. Associations are presumably the result of contemporaneous representations of the concepts in working memory (rehearsing two items together, thinking about concepts in relation to one another, and so on). Thus, according to this view, a subject who learns that a person P is described by a set of behaviors might form a representation of the person of the type depicted in Fig. 7.1. This particular network assumes that the subject not only thinks about each behavior in relation to the person who manifests it (P), but also thinks about certain behaviors in relation to one another, resulting in direct associations between them.

How is information retrieved from such a network? Two general alternative sets of assumptions have been proposed. One type of model assumes there is a *serial* directed search of the network. Once the concept represented by a particular node is activated, other concepts are retrieved by progressing from node to node along the pathways that have been established in the network (for minor variations on this approach, see Anderson 1972, Hastie 1980, Srull 1981, Srull *et al.* 1985).

A second type of model assumes a *parallel* search of the network. This is best exemplified by various spreading activation formulations (e.g. Anderson 1976, Collins and Loftus 1975, Wyer and Carlston 1979). This type of model assumes that once a concept node is activated, the excitation created by thinking about the concept spreads simultaneously from this node down all the pathways that are connected to it. When the excitation reaches a terminal node, it begins to accumulate; if the amount of this excitation reaches some threshold value, the new node is then activated. The excitation that results from thinking about this newly activated concept then spreads to other nodes, and so on.

It should be clear that associative network models tend to put all of the conceptual weight on the relations between concepts, and they de-emphasize the internal structure of new episodes that are encoded into memory (for example, they treat each behavior as a single unit, rather than assume that the behaviors themselves are composed of more elementary features that have important psychological significance). A second general class of models takes nearly the opposite approach. It is to these that we now turn.

Retrieval models. As a general class, retrieval models make minimal assumptions about how a newly encoded episode is "organized" and represented in relation to other things that are known (for specific examples of this approach, see Anderson 1976, Eich 1985, Gillund and Shiffrin 1984, Hintzman and Ludlum 1980, Murdock 1982, Ratcliff 1978, Tulving 1983). That is, they de-emphasize any relations that may exist between concepts. They do, however, make elaborate assumptions about the *internal* structure of any encoded event. In most cases, a vector or matrix format is used to represent the structure of new events that are encoded into memory. Each event is broken up into a set of elementary features (which include self-generated associations) and the "values" of such features are the components of the vector or matrix that is used to represent the event. Each vector or matrix is stored independently of all of the others.

A common element in all of these models is that a retrieval cue (either presented by the experimenter or internally generated) can also be broken down into more elementary features and represented in vector or matrix format. The effectiveness of any cue will be a function of the "similarity" of its own vector (matrix) with the vector (matrix) of the to-be-recalled event. This provides one explanation of why a cue is effective *only if some or all of its features were thought about at the time of encoding*, as implied by the principle of encoding specificity (Tulving and Thomson 1973).

As noted, several different versions of this type of model have been proposed. However, a slightly simplified characterization of Ratcliff's (1978) theory can be used to illustrate the general process. According to this model, features of the information one acquires are encoded and represented in terms of one of more existing semantic concepts. If several features are subsequently thought about that are similar to those that represent the encoded event, they will cause the item to "resonate." If the level of this resonance is of sufficient magnitude, the item will be activated in consciousness (i.e. recalled).

An attractive feature of many retrieval models is their potential for taking into account differences in the *strategy* that subjects decide to use in retrieving information at the time they are asked to do so (for a very nice illustration of this, see Norman and Bobrow 1979). The use of a retrieval strategy can be viewed as the intentional compilation of a set of retrieval cues that are likely to activate the information for which one is searching in memory. When trying to recall the fifty United States, for example, one might adopt a strategy of proceeding geographically or alphabetically, or one might use a personal drive across the country or knowledge of college athletic conferences as heuristics. It is important to note that each strategy may elicit only a subset of the States, and so several different strategies might ultimately be employed. In contrast to associative network conceptualizations, retrieval models place a heavy emphasis on factors that exist at the time of output as well as those that take place at the time of input. The importance of this will become clear later in this section.

Reconstructive models. The third type of model is particularly powerful in conceptualizing the dynamics that result in the intrusion of general world knowledge into the recall of specific information. There are two general versions of this model. One postulates the existence of previously learned knowledge structures (scripts, schemata, etc.) that function as configural units and are used to interpret raw information whose features can be instantiated in terms of them. For example, one may have a previously formed prototypic representation of a lawyer, or of the sequence of events that occurs when eating at a restaurant. When specific information is received about a particular person or event sequence that exemplifies such a prototype, this information is not directly stored. Rather, only a "pointer" to the prototype is actually retained, along with equivalence rules for translating specific features of the new information into prototypic ones and back again. This representation is sufficient to permit the new information to be reconstructed later, even though its details are not uniquely stored. However, because of this same process, one would expect to find many intrusions of unspecified features in subjects' recall protocols as well.

As an example, it would be possible for one to reconstruct information that Susan went to China Inn, ate chop suey, and paid $13.45 for the meal on the basis of a "restaurant" script and the equivalence rules: customer = Susan, food = chop suey, check = $13.45, and so on. Moreover, such an underlying representation permits features that were not specifically described in the information (e.g. the fact that Susan looked at the menu) to be inferred. These inferences would ordinarily be scored as intrusions. (In practice, of course, not all aspects of the information will have "slots" in any single script or knowledge structure. Such aspects of the information are appended to the schema as tags; see Graesser and Nakamura 1982,

Minsky 1977, Norman and Bobrow 1976, Schank and Abelson 1977.)

A second general type of reconstructive model also assumes that new information is interpreted with reference to a pre-existing knowledge structure. However, it assumes that once the information is organized and encoded in terms of this prior knowledge, it is stored in memory as a conceptual unit rather than as simply a pointer to the prototype used to interpret it (e.g. Bransford and Franks 1973, Wyer and Srull 1986). The different implications of these two versions of the reconstructive model for the interpretation of recall data will be noted shortly.

Amount-of-processing models. A fourth conceptualization places special emphasis on the amount of cognitive activity involved in processing information at the time it is encoded. In general, the model assumes that more extensively processed information becomes more accessible in memory and therefore is more likely to be recalled (Craik and Lockhart 1972, Wyer and Hartwick 1980). This may be true because thinking more extensively about information leads it to be more elaboratively encoded in terms of previously formed concepts, thereby making these concepts more effective retrieval cues (Anderson and Reder 1979, Jacoby and Craik 1979). Another possibility is that more extensively thought-about information becomes more strongly associated with contextual (situational) cues available at the time it is received, and therefore is more likely to be retrieved in any later situation in which those same cues are present (Raaijmakers and Shiffrin 1980, 1981, Tulving 1983).

In both of the above cases, amount-of-processing effects on memory can clearly be conceptualized in terms of retrieval and/or associative network models of the sort described earlier. However, such models imply that amount of processing will affect memory only when the concepts or situational cues that exist at learning are also present at the time of recall. Other conceptions of amount-of-processing effects do not require this assumption. For example, Wyer and Srull (1986) postulate that more extensively processed information may enter into a greater number of independently formed and stored representations of the person or event to which it pertains, and therefore is relatively more likely to be retrieved. Moreover, more extensively processed information may often be more *recently* processed, which may also give it a memory advantage independently of other stored information (Wyer and Srull 1980, 1986). As these considerations imply, amount-of-processing models often require more fundamental assumptions about the reasons why amount of processing should in fact have an influence on memory. Nonetheless, amount of processing per se has been postulated as a factor underlying recall sufficiently often for it to warrant consideration in its own right.

Much more formal statements of the types of conceptualization outlined above are obviously possible. However, the descriptions we have provided are sufficient for our present purpose. This is simply to indicate that any interpretation of recall data will depend substantially on which of several sets of assumptions one is willing to make. We will demonstrate this more explicitly in the pages that follow.

Recall as an index of learning and knowledge

The role of processing objectives. It may seem obvious upon first consideration that the total amount of information one can recall reflects the degree to which the information has been learned. It may seem equally self-evident that the harder one tries to remember the information at the time it is first received, the better the information should be learned and therefore the better it should be recalled. However, the application of such reasoning has some ironic implications for the interpretation of existing data.

Consider, for example, a study by Hamilton *et al.* (1980). Subjects read a list of behaviors and were told either to learn and remember them as well as possible, or to form an impression of what the target would be like. Subjects who were told to learn the information subsequently recalled less of it than those who were told to form an impression (despite the fact that it was a *surprise* recall test for these latter subjects). This finding, which has been replicated many times since (Srull 1981, 1983, Srull and Brand 1983, Srull *et al.* 1985, Wyer and Gordon 1982), is ironic in terms of the logic outlined above. Specifically, it would suggest either that people learn information better when they try not to do so, or that recall is not an adequate index of learning. Both conclusions seem unlikely.

1. The above finding is most often interpreted in terms of an amount-of-processing model. The *assumption* is that an impression formation objective leads the behavioral information to be more extensively processed. Because it is more extensively processed, it is more accessible for recall at a later time. One piece of evidence in support of this is that the impression set seems to maintain its superiority over relatively long delay intervals (Srull 1981, Wyer and Gordon 1982). However, the model leads to circular reasoning unless one can construct an *independent* criterion for inferring amount-of-processing differences other than the memory measure they are postulated to affect. Otherwise, recall differences not only wind up being explained in terms of amount-of-processing differences but are used as a basis for inferring that differences in amount of processing exist. Thus far, no such index has been uncovered (see Baddeley 1978).

2. An associative network approach also emphasizes how processing objectives may alter encoding mechanisms at the time of input. The *as-*

sumption of this model is that subjects with the goal of forming an impression are more likely to think of the various behaviors in relation to one another. Relative to the memory objective conditions, this results in an associative network that is more highly interconnected – in other words, one that provides more retrieval routes to each individual item. Can such an assumption be independently validated? Some evidence suggests that it can. For example, performing a secondary task at the time of encoding can completely eliminate the advantage normally observed for impression objective subjects (Srull 1981, Srull *et al.* 1985). Moreover, when multiple targets are used the advantage is sometimes seen only within a single target (Srull 1983), and when multiple trait categories are used the advantage sometimes occurs only within certain trait categories (Wyer and Gordon 1982).

Two points are important for our purposes. First, as noted above, the empirical evidence suggests limits to the generality of memory differences across all items. Second, one can postulate different network structures to account for the results obtained. Independent evidence for the validity of these knowledge structures needs to be amassed in order to prevent the reasoning from becoming circular here as well.

3. A third, very different account of the findings of Hamilton *et al.* (1980) is provided by a retrieval model. Unlike the associative network theory, which assumes that the processing objectives serve to change the nature of the encoding mechanism, the retrieval model begins with the *assumption* that all the items in both the memory-objective and impression-objective conditions are encoded into long-term memory (i.e. they are "learned" equally well in both cases). It is, therefore, also assumed that any differences observed in recall must be due to some retrieval process. The most likely candidate in the Hamilton *et al.* study is the type of retrieval cue that subjects have available at the time of recall. For example, subjects with an impression formation set may encode the individual behaviors in terms of a relatively small number of trait concepts that are relevant to the general objective of forming a coherent impression. If subjects then think about one or more of these traits at the time of recall, each trait will serve as a retrieval cue for the several behaviors that were encoded in terms of it. In contrast, subjects who are explicitly told to remember the behaviors may *not* encode the information in terms of higher-order trait concepts. Consequently, these organizing concepts are not available to use as cues at the time of retrieval, and so the recall of the behaviors is relatively poor. Such an analysis is consistent with evidence that cues at retrieval are most effective when they contain features that were also encoded at the time of input (see Tulving and Thomson 1973).

Thus, of the four general types of model we have considered, only the reconstructive model seems inapplicable in accounting for the relatively better memory for behaviors by subjects who have read them with an impression formation objective.[2] This does not mean that it is impossible to discriminate among such theories. We have dealt in this section with only a single experiment, and it is not too surprising that its results can be interpreted in different ways. However, it would also be a mistake to assume that "the data speak for themselves." They do not. The results of any single experiment can only be interpreted in the context of an explicit set of assumptions. And different assumptions will always provide alternative interpretations of the same data.

Is there any way out of this conundrum? Yes. The first step is to refine in much more detail the assumptions that are being made. Exactly *how* is the network more elaborate and interconnected? Exactly *how* do the features of the cue interact with the features of the encoded item? Once this is done, more subtle implications of the assumptions can be tested empirically. The general point is that no single experiment, no matter how elegant or ambitious, can be interpreted in isolation. Discriminating among competing theories, as in the example above, is difficult but not impossible. It does require, however, extended programs of research that systematically examine as many of the underlying assumptions as possible (cf. Laudan 1977). Articulating the assumptions to the point where they have specific empirical consequences is the major challenge that researchers in this, or any other, field must confront.

The role of category set size. Another phenomenon with ironic implications for the use of recall as an index of the amount of learning is the effect of category set size. Suppose subjects are asked to form an impression of two persons, A and B, based on ten behaviors of A and twenty behaviors of B. If subjects are later asked to recall the information, they will typically

2 The "pointer plus tag" version of the reconstructive model would seem to imply that once subjects identify the type of person being described by a set of behaviors, they will store only a pointer to a prototypic representation of this person they have acquired as part of general knowledge, and will not store the individual behaviors that led the prototype to be applied. Not all of these behaviors can typically be reconstructed on the basis of the prototype alone. (For example, information that someone stole a wallet may lead the person to be designated a prototypic "dishonest person." However, this particular behavior is not characteristic of all such persons, and thus it may not be reconstructed from the prototype per se.) Moreover, some reconstructed behaviors are likely to differ from those that were actually presented. Thus, this version of a reconstructive model would predict poorer memory for presented behaviors under impression formation conditions than under memory-objective conditions (in which a prototype is not activated and used as a basis for the memorial representation of the information presented). Moreover, it would predict more intrusions in the former conditions, which does not in fact occur (cf. Wyer and Gordon 1982).

recall a greater proportion of A's behaviors than of B's (Srull and Brand 1983).

All but the reconstructive model provide interpretations of this finding. According to an amount-of-processing model, the extensiveness with which each item is processed is negatively correlated with the total number of items that pertain to any single target. Thus, in the example above, A's behaviors would be processed more extensively (on average) than B's and thus a higher proportion of them should be recalled. An implicit assumption in this model is that the retrieval process itself is equally efficient in both cases; any observed difference is due to differential encoding.

A second theoretical interpretation of this finding is based on the associative network conceptualization of memory. The spreading activation version of this model is illustrative. In the present context, the model assumes that all behaviors of a particular person are stored in memory and are associated with a central concept of the person. When a subject is later asked to recall the behaviors, he/she activates the central person node, and activation spreads down the various pathways connecting it to the behavior nodes. However, because the activation transmitted along any given pathway is less when the number of pathways is large than when it is small, the probability of recalling any given behavior is less in the former condition than in the latter. The serial version of this model generates the same prediction (see Rundus 1973). Implicit in the associative network approach, however, is the assumption that items in each category are learned equally well at the time of input. This is in direct contrast to the amount-of-processing model.

The retrieval model described earlier offers yet a third interpretation. This model also assumes that all items are learned equally well. However, the internal structure of the items will systematically vary. Specifically, one prominent feature of each item will be the target person to whom it pertains (sometimes referred to as a superordinate or category cue). At the time of recall, the subject will need to generate retrieval cues to aid in the search of memory. In the present example, the most obvious are the names of the two people. However, the more items become associated with a single cue, the less powerful that cue becomes in eliciting any one of them. This is the principle of *cue overload* (Watkins 1979). In the present example, A's name is associated with ten items, whereas B's name is associated with twenty items. Thus, according to the principle of cue overload, a greater proportion of A's behaviors should be recalled than of B's behaviors. This prediction rests solely on the assumed internal structure of the items and the retrieval cues that are likely to be used at the time of recall.

In sum, the same empirical phenomenon (recall of a greater proportion of category members when the total number presented is small than when it is large) could be interpreted as due to differences in initial learning (the amount-of-processing model), differences in the way in which the items are related to one another in memory (the associative network model), or differences in the effectiveness of various cues as a function of the internal structure of the individual items (the retrieval model).

The role of intrusions. Still other confusions in the use of recall as an index of learning arise in interpreting intrusions of material that was not actually presented. To see this, suppose a subject who has been told about a particular person's visit to a specific Chinese restaurant recalls being told that the person looked at the menu, although this was not actually stated. Such intrusion errors are typically accounted for on the basis of reconstructive models of memory. (The other three types of model have no a priori implications for these intrusions.) However, the implications of these errors for learning depend on which type of reconstructive model one uses. For example, the schema-pointer-plus-tag model (Graesser *et al.* 1979) assumes that subjects do not actually store a representation of the original information in memory. Rather, they store only a pointer to a prototype from which it can be reconstructed. According to this view, intrusions occur because subjects report prototypic features in the process of reconstructing the information from the prototype at the time of *retrieval*. In contrast, other models (e.g. Bransford and Franks 1971, 1973) assume that subjects *do* store a representation of the specific information they receive once they have organized and interpreted it in terms of their prototypic knowledge. According to this model, intrusions reflect inferences about unmentioned features of the information that subjects add to the representation they form at the time of *encoding*. Thus, the implications of intrusions for learning depend on which conceptualization one assumes. In the first case, intrusion errors might be interpreted as indications of a failure to attend carefully to details of the actual information presented, and therefore of poor learning. In the second case, they would be interpreted as an indication of an effective integration of the information presented into a meaningful unit, and therefore an indication of a very functional learning process.

Summary. The examples described in this section all make a similar point. The amount of information recalled, as well as the presence of intrusions in recall, can often be interpreted in terms of several different theoretical formulations of the recall process. The models presented were described in relatively "pure" form. However, social cognition researchers often modify these approaches to fit a particular domain (person memory, group stereotyping, etc.). Indeed, many of the models in social cognition appear to be hybrids of these various approaches. In any event, when a particular index of recall is applied out of the context of a specific process model of the phenomena reported, theoretical conclusions drawn on the basis of these phenomena may often be impossible to evaluate.

Recall as an index of cognitive organization

A great deal of research has been directed toward understanding the mental representations that are formed of people and events. Questions about both content and organization have been asked. Conclusions about these matters are typically based on both the *type* of information recalled and the *order* in which it is recalled. To date, most theories of person memory have been guided by associative network models. These models have been used to construct a reasonably clear picture of how social information is organized. However, the construction of this picture has required several different types of data that *converge* on a set of conclusions about the phenomena at hand. Any given study that is considered in isolation is susceptible to multiple interpretations. However, by conducting a systematic program of research, the entire set of findings can potentially provide evidence that converges in favor of one interpretation over the others.

As a concrete example, Hamilton *et al.* (1980) have reported that, when subjects are given behavioral information about a particular target person for the purpose of forming an impression, the behaviors they recall tend to be clustered in terms of the personality traits the behaviors exemplify. This does not occur, however, when subjects receive the information with a memory set. The conceptual question is why this is so. When the data are considered in isolation, the answer depends on which memory model one wishes to adopt.

An associative network interpretation of such results is very straightforward. Subjects who learn about a target's behavior with the objective of forming an impression are *assumed* to encode spontaneously and organize the behaviors in terms of personality trait concepts. As a result, trait–behavior clusters are formed of the sort shown in Fig. 7.2 (*a*), where each central node (T_1 or T_2) represents a trait concept, and the peripheral nodes (denoted b_1, b_2, etc.) refer to the behaviors that exemplify them. The pathways connecting any given behavior and trait reflect associations formed as a result of interpreting the behavior as an instance of the trait. These trait–behavior clusters are assumed to be stored independently in memory. At the time of recall, subjects access each cluster in turn and report the behaviors contained in it, leading to a clustering of the recalled behaviors in terms of the trait categories. In contrast, subjects with the objective of remembering the information do not encode and organize the behaviors in terms of more general trait concepts. Therefore, a clustering of behaviors at the time of recall does not occur under these conditions.

a. Trait-based organization
of behaviors of person P

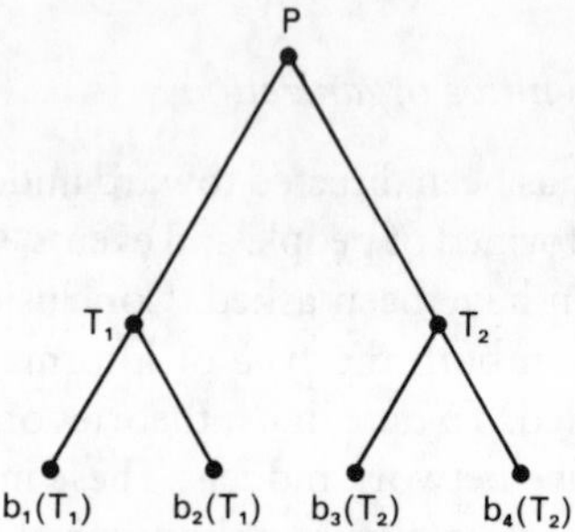

b. Independent storage of
behaviors of person P

Person P

$b_1(T_1)$
$b_3(T_2)$
$b_2(T_1)$
$b_4(T_1)$

Fig. 7.2. Representation of person (P) described by two behaviors (b_1 and b_2) interpreted as exemplifying trait T_1 and two behaviors (b_3 and b_4) interpreted as exemplifying trait T_2, based on (*a*) an associative network model and (*b*) a retrieval model assuming independent storage of behaviors. (The trait encoding of each behavior is denoted parenthetically beside each behavior.)

A retrieval model can also be used to interpret these clustering results. Subjects with an impression formation set are still expected to encode the behaviors in terms of the traits they exemplify. However, no organization between them is postulated. Rather, it is assumed that each behavior is stored independently in memory, similar to the way shown in Fig. 7.2 (*b*). However, when subjects are later asked to recall the behaviors, they will need to begin the search with certain retrieval cues. These are likely to be the various trait concepts. For example, they may begin with "dishonest," and then use this as a retrieval cue for all the behaviors that were encoded in terms of it. Having done this, they will then select another retrieval cue, and so on. This process will also lead to a clustering of the recalled behaviors. However, all the conceptual weight is placed on the internal structure of the encoded representations of the individual behaviors, and none at all on the (potential) associations among these behaviors.

It is clear that quite different conclusions would be drawn from evidence of clustering in free recall data, depending on which general model of recall processes one wishes to adopt. According to one model, it would reflect the organization of the items in memory. According to the other, it would have no implications whatsoever for the cognitive organization of the information.

Associative network models of recall are most often assumed in person memory research (cf. Wyer and Gordon 1982, Wyer and Unverzagt 1985). However, the retrieval model may actually provide a better account of clustering data. For example, the network conceptualization outlined above would seem to imply that trait clustering should be nearly perfect, with one trait–behavior cluster being exhausted before another is searched. In fact, although trait-related behaviors are recalled in succession more often than would be expected by chance, other "unrelated" behaviors are interspersed with a reasonably high frequency.

The most direct evidence bearing on this issue was obtained by Gordon (1982). In some conditions of her study, subjects were presented with behaviors of a person that exemplified three different traits. However, the behaviors associated with each trait occurred in three different situations. The order in which subjects subsequently recalled these behaviors suggested that the recall of one behavior cued the recall of others that were related to it. However, the particular aspects of the behavioral descriptions that had this cueing function varied over the sequence of recalled behaviors in a way that would not be easily accounted for by an assumption that subjects had organized the behaviors in terms of *either* traits *or* situations. For example, suppose the traits exemplified by the behaviors are A, B, and C, and the situations in which they occurred are denoted 1, 2, and 3. Then, a typical sequence of recalled behaviors might be:

A1, B1, B2, C2, C1, C3, A3, A2 . . .

In other words, each behavior shares one feature with the behavior that precedes it, suggesting that certain features of one behavior cued the recall of others that were semantically related to it. However, this does not seem to result from a prior categorization of the behaviors in terms of traits or situations at the time of input. The pattern of recall is most consistent with a retrieval model. That is, a subject may code the behaviors in terms of both traits and situations at the time he/she receives them, but may not organize them in terms of either set of features. Later, the subject's recall of one behavior may make one of its coded features particularly salient, and this leads the subject to search for and retrieve a second behavior that has this same feature. This second behavior, once retrieved, may call a different feature to mind, leading the subject to use this new feature as a retrieval cue. This implies that the order of recalling behaviors is a result of applying changing retrieval strategies at the time of recall and does not necessarily reflect their organization in memory.

In any event, the above considerations make the point that whatever interpretation one wishes to give to a clustering measure requires a commitment to a particular set of assumptions about the encoding, organization, and retrieval processes that underlie recall. Moreover, once this theoretical commitment is made, it may have additional implications that require different measures to evaluate.

This point of course applies to other recall measures as well. A second example drawn from person memory research is illustrative. Specifically, when subjects are told to form an impression of someone on the basis of information about his behavior, and have been given a trait-based expectancy for what the person is like, they show better recall of behaviors that are inconsistent with the expectancy than behaviors that are consistent with it. One interpretation of this (cf. Hastie 1980, Srull 1981) is that subjects think about the inconsistent behaviors in relation to others the person has manifested in an attempt to explain their occurrence, and this leads to the establishment of associations between these inconsistent behaviors and other (both consistent and inconsistent) ones. This cognitive activity does not occur when a consistent behavior is received. Consequently, the number of associative pathways leading from (and therefore *to*) the inconsistent behaviors is greater, on average, than those leading to the consistent behaviors, giving the former behaviors a recall advantage. One ironic implication of this formulation is that inconsistent behaviors become better integrated into the representation formed of the target person than do consistent ones.

However, considered in isolation, this result obviously has other interpretations. Based on an amount-of-processing formulation, for example, one might assume that the inconsistent behaviors are simply thought about more, independently of other behaviors presented about the person. This would lead the inconsistent behaviors to have a recall advantage for reasons that have nothing to do with their organization in memory. To interpret these data in terms of an associative network formulation rather than an amount-of-processing formulation, a number of additional criteria must be used.

For example, if only inconsistent behaviors stimulate the cognitive activity that leads interbehavior associations to be established, there should be few if any associations between one consistent behavior and another. Therefore, the probability of recalling a consistent behavior immediately following another consistent one should be much less than the probability of recalling a consistent behavior following an inconsistent one. Moreover, if subjects are asked to recall behaviors orally rather than in writing, the time required to recall a consistent behavior immediately following another consistent one should be greater than the time to recall a consistent behavior following an inconsistent one. In addition, situational factors that distract subjects from performing the cognitive work required to reconcile inconsistent behaviors should not appreciably affect the recall of consistent ones. Research by Srull (1981; Srull *et al.* 1985) has supported all three of these implications. Finally, the recall advantage of inconsistent behaviors is not evident when a trait-based expectancy is not activated until after the behaviors are presented (Wyer, Bodenhausen and Srull 1984). This latter finding indicates that the recall differences do not result from different retrieval strategies activated at the time of recall.

In this particular area of research, therefore, an associative network model of person memory seems better able to handle the data *as a whole* than any of the alternative conceptualizations. However, no single piece of evidence alone could be used to support one model over the others.

The series of studies described above exemplify several important points. First, the interpretation of a particular type of free recall data carries with it implicit (and, on rare occasions, explicit) assumptions about the encoding, organization, and retrieval processes that underlie the recall of information more generally. Second, a commitment to these assumptions has implications for other phenomena and response measures that must be evaluated in order to gain confidence in the validity of the assumptions. Finally, without an explicit statement of the process model one assumes to underlie the measure used, theoretical conclusions drawn on the basis of the measure may often not be very meaningful.

Recall as an index of the basis of judgments

A third use of recall measures in social cognition, as in social psychology more generally, has been to diagnose the cognitive mediators of judgments. In fact, there is typically very little correlation between the implications of the judgment-relevant information one can recall and judgments that are presumably based on it. This finding is pervasive in several research areas, ranging from communication and persuasion (Greenwald 1968) to person perception (Anderson and Hubert 1963, Carlston 1980, Dreben *et al.* 1979, Wyer, Srull, and Gordon 1984), attribution of responsibility (Fiske *et al.* 1979), and behavioral decision-making (Loken 1984). It seems reasonable to question why this lack of correlation exists. However, the better question might be why the relation *should* exist.

The hypothesis that judgments are related to the implications of recalled information requires an inordinate number of more fundamental assumptions about the processes that underlie recall, the processes that underlie judgments, and the similarity between them. As we have pointed out, assumptions concerning the basis for information recall must be made with reference to a particular theoretical model of encoding, organization, and retrieval processes. Analogous model-based assumptions must be made concerning the processes that underlie *judgments*. The existence (or absence) of a relation between recall and judgments can be interpreted meaningfully only if the two sets of assumptions are explicit.

Again, an example drawn from research on person memory may help to demonstrate this point. Suppose subjects are told to form an impression of someone on the basis of a list of behaviors the person has manifested. Later, they are asked to report their impression of the person along a series of evaluative dimensions (likeableness, for example) and trait dimensions, and are finally asked to recall the original behavioral information. At least three alternative sets of assumptions might be made.

1. An associative network model would assume that subjects with an impression-formation objective extract an evaluative, trait-based concept of the person from the initial behaviors presented. These and subsequent behaviors are then associatively linked to this central concept. However, behaviors that are *inconsistent* with the central concept also become associated with other behaviors presented as a result of trying to reconcile their occurrence. If subjects are asked to recall the behaviors, they engage in a sequential search of the behaviors by progressing along the pathways connecting them, and therefore they are likely to recall a high proportion of inconsistent than consistent behaviors. However, suppose subjects are asked to judge the person. Then they are likely to use the implications of the central concept they have formed, without reviewing the specific behaviors connected to it (cf. Wyer, Srull, and Gordon 1984, Wyer and Budesheim 1987). Thus, according to this conceptualization, there is no reason to expect a positive relation between the judgments that are made and the evaluative implications of the behaviors recalled. This is because *subjects use different components of the representation as a basis for recall and judgment.*

2. One possible version of a retrieval model assumes that subjects with an impression-formation objective form a general concept of the person being described that is based upon the person's behaviors but is stored independently of these behaviors. Moreover, the individual behavior items themselves are stored independently of one another. Later, if subjects are asked to make a judgment of the person, the statement of this task objective may lead them to retrieve the central concept of the person and use it as a basis for the judgment. However, if they are asked to recall the behaviors themselves, the retrieval cues they use to access them may be quite unrelated to the central person concept. If these behaviors are retrieved nonsystematically, there will be no necessary relation between the implications of the behaviors and the implications of the central person concept on

which the judgments are based. This conceptualization therefore predicts a lack of relation between recall and judgments because *different sets of information are retrieved under the two task objective conditions.*

3. A related possibility does not require the assumption that a central person concept is formed at all at the time the behavioral information is presented. Rather, it simply assumes that the behaviors are individually stored in memory, and are later sampled randomly in order to respond to the specific task demands at hand (to recall the behaviors or to make a judgment). According to this view, subjects may use the same retrieval strategy in both cases, and therefore may sample behaviors from the same population. However, a subject who is asked to make a judgment may actually use only a small subset of the judgment-relevant information he/she would recall if asked explicitly to do so. Alternatively, the subject may use all of the information he/she can recall, but may weight the implications of some pieces more heavily than others. In either case, the simple sum or average of the implications of the information would be a poor index of the judgment the subject makes. According to this view, therefore, a relation between judgments and the implications of recalled information does in fact exist. However, the failure to observe it may result from the theorist's inability to specify *a priori* precisely how much of the recalled information subjects actually used and how they weighted its implications.

The examples above serve several functions. First, they point out that there are *a priori* grounds for assuming that the amount and implications of recalled information are often unlikely to be appropriate indices of the knowledge that subjects consider in making judgments. This is true even when the information recalled is objectively relevant to the judgment. Second, the examples also point out that the conclusions one draws as to why judgments and recalled information are often uncorrelated depend very heavily on the specific assumptions one makes about the processes that underlie both responses. That is, the lack of relationship could be attributable to factors that occur at the encoding, organization, retrieval, or integration stages of processing, depending on the particular theoretical framework one adopts. Moreover, the lack of relation is not of particular interest except in terms of its implications for a particular theoretical framework. Some attempts have in fact been made to provide an adequate conceptualization (Lichtenstein and Srull 1985, Wyer and Srull 1986, Wyer and Unverzagt 1985), and hypotheses based on it have been supported empirically (Lichtenstein and Srull 1985, Wyer and Budesheim 1986, Wyer and Unverzagt 1985). However, when considered in the absence of a clear model, *any* relation between recall and judgment measures will be completely uninformative. Parameters of the experimental situation, which provide the context for observing such a relationship, may or may not be important from the perspective of any given theory, and the data observed simply cannot speak for themselves.

Recognition

Measures of recognition memory, like the free-recall measures discussed in the previous section, are often used as an index of learning and retention. However, the conclusions one draws from these measures are probably even more dependent on the theoretical assumptions one makes about the processes that underlie the responses being measured.

In a recognition paradigm, subjects who have previously been exposed to a set of stimulus items are then presented with each of several "test" items and asked to decide whether each item was among the ones they had seen earlier. Some of the test items were actually presented before, and others ("distractors") were not. Three indices are often considered: (*a*) the likelihood of correctly identifying a stimulus item as having been presented (*hit* rate), (*b*) the likelihood of stating that a distractor had been presented when it had not (*false alarm* rate), and (*c*) the time required to make these judgments. In this section, we will focus primarily on the first two measures (for a discussion of how response time can provide additional information in a recognition memory paradigm, see Srull 1984).

Quite different theories exist concerning the processes that underlie recognition responses. One view is that free recall, cued recall, and recognition all lie along a single continuum. That is, they are not qualitatively different from another (Tulving and Watkins 1975, Watkins 1979). In a free-recall paradigm, there is only one cue and it tends to be very general (e.g. "recall everything you can from *the list*"). In a cued-recall paradigm, there are usually multiple cues and they tend to be much more specific (e.g. "remember that there are items related to *hostility, intelligence, conscientiousness,* and *politeness*"). According to this model, a recognition paradigm is very similar. In recognition, many of the cues that are provided to subjects to aid recall are duplicates of the original items (these are called *copy cues*). However, the underlying retrieval process is no different than in cued recall, or free recall for that matter. According to this model, the critical determinant of recognition responses (like all others) is the association of the stimulus items stored in memory with the retrieval cues available at the time of recognition. In other words, recognition involves a retrieval process that is no different from that in free recall.

An alternative view is proposed by Gillund and Shiffrin (1984). They postulate that the primary criterion for a recognition response to an item is the item's subjective "familiarity." That is, a test item will be responded to affirmatively if it seems "familiar" in the situational and informational context in which the item is presented. According to this model, search and retrieval processes, which play the dominant role in free recall, are simply bypassed when recognition memory measures are used.

A third, less well formalized conceptualization incorporates features of both the above models. According to this view, a subject who receives a recognition test item will first use its features as cues to probe long-term memory for an item that has these same features. If the search is successful, a "yes" response will be given. However, if the subject does not find an item, he/she will have to "guess" whether the test item was included in the original list. This guessing process will be based on some index of subjective familiarity, which is assumed to be a function of the similarity of the item in question to other items the subject does remember as having been presented.

The conclusions drawn from a given set of recognition data will often depend on which of these general sets of assumptions is implicitly made. Some examples drawn from social cognition research demonstrate the ambiguities involved.

In one early study, Cantor and Mischel (1977) gave subjects a list of trait adjectives describing a person that in some cases conveyed extraversion and in other cases introversion. Later, they gave subjects a recognition memory test containing both the original stimulus adjectives and distractors that also conveyed either introversion or extraversion. Subjects typically recognized correctly the items that were actually presented. However, they more often reported that a distractor had been presented if it was semantically consistent with the actual stimulus items than if it was not. Several conclusions could be drawn from this finding, depending on one's assumptions about the processes underlying recognition responses.

1. Suppose one assumes that recognition responses depend on the extent to which features of the test item cue the retrieval of items contained in memory. Then Cantor and Mischel's findings would suggest that distractors with implications similar to the original stimulus items were actually contained in the mental representation that subjects formed from these items. For example, subjects who read about a person described by extraverted items may infer that the person is a prototypic extravert. The mental representation they form of this person may therefore consist of not only the attributes specifically described in the stimulus information but also other, unmentioned attributes that are part of the prototype. Subjects' subsequent recognition responses will therefore be based on both sets of attributes. This model would predict both (*a*) a high hit rate for presented stimulus items, and (*b*) false alarms to distractors that are semantically

similar to the stimulus items and therefore are likely to be contained in the prototype. The conclusion drawn on the basis of this conceptualization is, therefore, that subjects did in fact form a prototype-based representation of the person about whom they received information, that this representation did contain both stated and unstated features of the prototype, and that the unstated features intruded on subjects' memory for the actual stimulus information presented.

2. Now assume that recognition responses are primarily a function of the subjective familiarity of the items. Given this assumption, conclusions drawn from Cantor and Mischel's study would not necessarily have any implications at all for the content of the representation formed of the person described by the stimulus information. For example, subjects who receive a list of adjective descriptions implying extraversion may, in fact, interpret them as extraverted. This will add an increment of subjective familiarity to items on the subsequent recognition task that can also be interpreted as extraverted, regardless of whether they were actually presented initially. This fact alone would predict a higher false alarm rate for extraverted distractors than for intraverted ones. Thus the only conclusion one would draw from Cantor and Mischel's findings, based on this set of assumptions, is that the individual stimulus items were often encoded as "extraverted" or "introverted" at the time they were received. These encodings would presumably occur prior to the organization of the encoded features in terms of a prototype. In fact, one would not need to postulate the activation and use of a prototype at all.

3. Finally, consider a "guessing" interpretation of the recognition responses. According to this conception, differences in the false alarm rate may simply reflect subjects' guessing strategy under conditions in which they cannot remember whether the test item had been presented or not. Specifically, subjects may judge the target person to be an extravert on the basis of the extraverted adjectives describing him, but store the original stimulus items independently of this judgment. If, on the subsequent recognition test, subjects cannot remember whether the item to be judged was or was not presented, they will then make a guess based on the item's semantic consistency with the (extraverted) impression of the person. This interpretation suggests that the greater false alarm rate for consistent than inconsistent items reflects a response strategy that occurs at the time of output.

Similar ambiguities exist in a study by Cohen (1977) on the effects of stereotyping. In this study, subjects who were told that a target person was either a waitress or a librarian observed a videotape of the person containing features and behaviors that were sometimes stereotypic of a waitress and sometimes stereotypic of a librarian. On a subsequent forced-choice recognition task, subjects showed a greater tendency to choose items that were consistent with the occupation-activated stereotype than items that were inconsistent with it, regardless of whether the items described had actually been observed. This consistency bias could be attributed to the fact that the stereotype-consistent items were included in a memorial representation of the target whereas stereotype-inconsistent items were not, and thus the former were better remembered later on. However, it could also be attributable to a guessing bias that occurred at the time of output, that is, a tendency for subjects to guess that the items they were unsure of were more likely to be there if they were consistent with the occupational stereotype than if they were not. Evidence that the effects of stereotypes on subjects' recognition responses increased over time (i.e. as memory for the actual items decreased) would also be implied by this latter interpretation (see also Cohen 1981).

Thus the conclusions drawn from recognition data depend very much on a theoretical interpretation of the recognition measure itself. Moreover, only one of the interpretations outlined above assumes that recognition responses have direct implications for the actual content of the memorial representation formed on the basis of the original information presented. It is obviously difficult to assess the merits of these alternative interpretations on the basis of recognition data considered in isolation. However, if recognition measures reflect the actual content of the memorial representation formed of the target on the basis of the original information, they should be related to experimental manipulations of this content in much the same way as other memory measures (e.g. recall). This does not appear to be the case. For example, Srull (1981) found that although inducing a trait-based expectancy for a target person increased the recall of behaviors that were inconsistent with these expectancies, it had no effect at all on recognition responses to these behaviors. More recently, Wyer, Bodenhausen, and Srull (1984) reported that the recall advantage of inconsistent information depended substantially on whether the target was a person or a group, whether a trait-based expectancy for the target was induced before or after behavioral information was presented, and the precise point at which instructions to form an impression of the person were given. In contrast, subjects showed generally greater recognition memory for trait-consistent behaviors under *all* conditions, regardless of these factors.

The differences above make salient a general confusion that has pervaded the social cognition literature. That is, some persons (e.g. Cantor and Mischel 1977, Cohen 1977) have concluded that expectancy-consistent information is better "remembered," whereas others (Hastie 1980, Srull 1981, Srull *et al.* 1985) have concluded that expectancy-inconsistent information is better "remembered." This difference is primarily, if not exclusively, attributable to the fact that the first group of researchers based their conclusions on recognition measures and the second group on free recall measures.

There is one point on which conceptualizations of recognition memory typically agree. That is, nearly all of them assume that if subjects extract a more abstract trait or evaluative concept from the information presented, this concept will affect the tendency to respond affirmatively to items that are consistent with its implications. To this extent, recognition measures can often be used to determine whether or not a particular type of concept has been extracted from the information, independently of its role in organizing this information.

A study by Hartwick (1979) provides an example of this. Subjects read a list of trait adjectives with instructions either to remember them or to form an impression of a person described by them. Later, they were given a recognition task containing distractors that varied both in their descriptive consistency with the original adjectives (whether they descriptively implied the same trait or the opposite trait) and in their evaluative consistency with the adjectives (whether they were similar or different in favorableness). Thus, if a stimulus adjective was "bold", the distractors might be "adventurous" (descriptively and evaluatively inconsistent), "rash" (descriptively consistent but evaluatively inconsistent), "cautious" (descriptively inconsistent but evaluatively consistent), and "timid" (descriptively and evaluatively inconsistent). Subjects responded more affirmatively to distractors that were consistent with the original items presented than to distractors that were inconsistent with them, regardless of the criterion for consistency. More important, instructions to form an impression of the target increased the effect of evaluative consistency (relative to memory set conditions) but did *not* affect the influence of descriptive consistency. This indicates that subjects with an impression set extracted an evaluative theme from the information, and that this theme affected their subsequent recognition responses. This conclusion would be valid regardless of which more specific interpretation of the recognition measure is given.[3]

In any event, it is important to bear in mind that the conclusions drawn from recognition data, like those drawn from recall data, depend on the assumptions one makes about the processes that underlie recognition responses. We currently tend to favor the view that recognition is based primarily on subjective familiarity, and does not reflect differences in the retrievability of the original items being judged (cf. Wyer, Bodenhausen, and Srull 1984). This helps to account for the striking differences between

3 Although Hartwick used signal detection methodology, the design of his study precluded a clear conclusion concerning whether the differences obtained were due to differences in the content of the representation, as reflected in *d'*, or differences in guessing bias at the time of output.

results obtained using recall measures and those obtained using recognition measures. However, it is undoubtedly possible to assume that recognition is a special case of recall, and to account for the same differences in terms of the effectiveness of different retrieval cues in the two memory task conditions. Gaining additional evidence in favor of one view over the other would be a useful objective of future research.

Response-time measures

It seems reasonable to assume that the time required to respond to a stimulus is some function of the time required to perform each of the component stages that underlie the generation of this response. Moreover, if one has a precise theory of the stages of processing that underlie judgments in a particular situation, and if one postulates factors that independently affect the different stages of processing, these factors should have independent and additive effects on overall response time (Sternberg 1969, 1975). If effects are not additive, it implies either that (*a*) the experimental factors do not affect the stages of processing one assumes, or (*b*) the stages themselves are nonindependent.

There is often an inherent ambiguity in interpreting response-time data. This is particularly true when the responses being made require assumptions about both (*a*) the structure and organization of the cognitive material on which the response is based, and (*b*) the nature of the retrieval and use of this material. As Anderson (1978) and others have pointed out, it is often impossible to localize the exact source of response-time differences. That is, a given pattern of response times may be accounted for equally well by (*a*) postulating differences in the structure and content of memory, but assuming a single search and retrieval process for accessing it, or (*b*) assuming a single memorial representation and postulating different search and retrieval processes. In many instances, these alternative interpretations must be evaluated in terms of their relative plausibility or parsimony rather than their consistency with the data.

Three types of tasks of relevance to social information-processing employ response-time methodology.

(*a*.) priming research, in which one wishes to infer the effects of activating one concept on the accessibility of other, theoretically related concepts;

(*b*.) recognition memory, in which the time required to verify that a stimulus item has previously been presented is assumed to reflect the ease of retrieving the item from memory; and

(*c*.) judgment tasks, in which the time required to judge one or more stimuli with respect to a particular attribute is assumed to reflect the time required to perform certain cognitive operations that underlie the judgment.

We will consider each application in turn.

Priming research

Associative network models of memory typically assume that activating a concept increases the accessibility of other concepts that are associated with it, and therefore increases the likelihood that these associated concepts can be recalled and used as well. This prediction is most often based on spreading activation models (e.g. Collins and Loftus 1975, Meyer and Schvaneveldt 1971). Such models assume that each concept in memory has an activation threshold, and that in order for the concept to be activated and used, excitation must build up at the memory location corresponding to the concept until this threshold is reached. The excitation that activates a concept may be generated in part by external stimuli whose features are similar to the concept's. Thus, for example, presentation of the word "bread" generates excitation that leads the concept of bread to be activated. However, once a particular concept (e.g. "bread") is activated, excitation spreads from it to other, associated concepts (e.g. "butter"), and thus the additional excitation required to activate these latter concepts is less. Consequently, subjects can respond to the word "butter" more quickly in a word identification task if they have previously responded to "bread" than if they have not (Meyer and Schvaneveldt 1971).

One conclusion drawn from the use of response-time methodology to evaluate priming effects is that the effect of priming a concept on responses to an associated concept is unlikely to be detected if more than a few seconds has elapsed between activation of the first (priming) concept and presentation of the second (target) concept. In terms of a spreading activation model, this implies that the excitation existing at an activated concept node decays very rapidly once the concept is deactivated. However, research using other response measures suggests that priming effects are often of very long duration. For example, Tulving, Schacter, and Stark (1982) found that exposing subjects to a list of uncommon words facilitated their performance on a word-fragment completion task in which the words were embedded, and that this effect persisted over a period of several days (even when subjects could no longer report accurately whether or not they had seen the words in the original list). In a quite different type of situation, Srull and Wyer (1979, 1980) found that priming a trait concept in a sentence-construction task affected the interpretation of behavioral information presented in an unrelated impression-formation task. Moreover, although the effect decreased over the time interval between priming and stimulus presentation (consistent with a spreading activation model), it was still significant as much as twenty-four hours after the concepts had been primed. Therefore, these data suggest that the effects of priming a semantic concept on the likelihood of accessing and using it can last a long time.

The different results obtained in these two paradigms provide a graphic example of how conclusions about the same theoretical issue can differ when they are based on alternative research methodologies. In this particular case, it seems clear that the processes that are being tapped by response-time measures are different in important respects from those that are tapped by other indices of a priming effect. Moreover, conclusions drawn about the duration of priming effects are restricted to the particular measure that one chooses to consider, and the particular types of stimulus and judgment domain that one happens to study.

Verification time

The speed with which one can verify that a particular item was included in the information one has received may reflect the ease of retrieving the item from memory (cf. Norman and Wickelgren 1969). To this extent, one might expect that conclusions based on verification time differences would be similar to those based on free-recall measures, which are theoretically also used to evaluate the accessibility of information in memory. However, whether this is so depends on the theoretical assumptions about both the processes underlying verification and those underlying free recall.

For example, associative models of free recall assume that the individual items to be recalled have become associated with one another as a result of encoding and organizational processes that occur at the time they are learned. As a result, the recall of these items is not independent; one item often directs the search to others that are associated with it. To the extent that verification time is also a function of the accessibility of the stimulus items in memory, a spreading activation version of an associative model would predict similar effects. That is, the process of verifying one item should lead excitation to build up at locations corresponding to other items in the stimulus list that have become associated with it, and therefore should decrease the time required to verify these latter items.

On the other hand, it should be noted that *verification* tasks are essentially *recognition memory* tasks. That is, subjects are given a test item and asked to decide whether or not it had previously been presented. To this extent, any of the alternative conceptualizations of recognition memory noted in the previous section may be applicable. In particular, suppose one assumes that responses to an item are not based on the retrieval of the item per se, but rather on a more global judgment of its familiarity. There would then be no reason to suppose that any clear relationship exists between response times to an item on a verification task and the likelihood of reporting it in a free-recall task.

These considerations again make it clear that the use of verification times as a memory index is highly contingent on the a priori assumptions one wishes to make about the process that underlies them. When one is willing to make a particular set of a priori assumptions, however, some useful conclusions can be drawn. An example is provided by Sentis and Burnstein (1979) in an investigation of subjects' tendency to organize information in memory in a manner implied by cognitive balance theory. Subjects received sets of three affective relations among persons and objects that were theoretically either balanced or imbalanced. Then they were presented with configurations of one, two, or three relations from the original materials, and were asked to verify whether they were among the relations they had learned. Sentis and Burnstein postulated that subjects would store the relations in imbalanced triads independently of one another, and therefore that the time required to verify a configuration would increase with the number of relations presented. However, subjects were expected to organize the relations contained in balanced sets into integrated units rather than storing them as independent entities. They were therefore expected to verify a balanced configuration more quickly when all three of the relations it comprised were presented than when only a subset was presented. In short, the time required to verify the relations contained in imbalanced sets was expected to increase with the number to be verified, whereas the time required to verify the relations contained in balanced sets was expected to decrease with the number of relations presented. The results supported both hypotheses.

The Sentis and Burnstein study contrasts with the bulk of social cognition research in which a response measure is chosen because of convenience, tradition, or simple curiosity. In this case, the response measure chosen was the direct result of a specific set of a priori assumptions about how various types of information are presented. It is important to note, however, that these same assumptions can have implications for other response measures as well. For example, if subjects store balanced sets of relations in memory as units rather than as individual items, they should not only remember the relations better but should also tend to report unstated relations that are consistent with the representation formed. Both of these predictions received empirical support in a study by Picek, Sherman, and Shiffrin (1975). In combination, these studies exemplify a conceptually driven approach to research in which a given theoretical formulation is used to derive predictions that are specific to a particular response measure. Unfortunately, other examples of this in the social cognition literature are rare.

Judgment processes

Judgments of a stimulus are often assumed to require the retrieval of judgment-relevant information from memory. The time required to make these judgments is assumed to reflect this retrieval time. However, it may reflect the time required to complete other stages of information-processing as well. For example, suppose a subject is asked to decide if a person has a certain trait on the basis of information about the person's behaviors. The judgment may often involve the retrieval of specific information that bears on it. However, it may also involve (*a*) an initial reading and interpretation of the question being asked, (*b*) an encoding of the behavior in terms either of the trait to be evaluated or of its polar opposite, (*c*) the integration of the implications of these encodings into a single subjective judgment, and (*d*) a transformation of this judgment into the response language one is given to use in reporting it. The overall time the subject takes to report the judgment may be a composite function of the times to complete each of these component processes. Therefore, without specifying precisely what factors theoretically affect the times required to perform each of these component processes in any given instance, and establishing these effects empirically, the interpretation of judgment times is inherently ambiguous. That is, several alternative assumptions about the underlying processes can account for the same pattern of effects. Three examples of this ambiguity are used in illustration.

Trait judgments based on observed behavior. In a very provocative study by Allen and Ebbesen (1981), subjects observed a videotape of a person's behavior in a particular situation. The tape varied in length over experimental conditions, but was constructed in such a way that each segment of the original tape occurred the same proportion of times in each condition. After viewing the tape, subjects were asked to verify details of the person's behavior, and also to make trait judgment of the person. These traits were of two types. Some "abstract" traits were those that subjects typically believe require several behaviors to verify, whereas other "concrete" traits were those that can often be inferred on the basis of a single instance of behavior. The time required to judge each type of trait was computed separately.

Three findings are of particular interest. First, the time required to verify behavioral details increased with tape length. Second, the time required to judge "abstract" traits also increased with tape length. However, the time required to judge "concrete" traits was independent of tape length. The question is what these results imply for both the representation of the information in memory and the processes of retrieving it and making judgments. There are at least three possibilities.

1. Suppose first that one assumes that differences in trait judgments reflect differences in the encoding of the behaviors exemplified by the traits. One might then interpret Allen and Ebbesen's results as follows. Subjects store a linear representation of the behavioral sequence they observe. In addition, when they encounter a behavior that has clear trait implications, they spontaneously code this behavior in terms of the trait, and ultimately combine these spontaneous encodings to form a separate, trait-based representation of the target person. When subjects are subsequently asked to verify a behavioral detail, they mentally review the behavioral sequence, and thus their verification time increases with tape length (i.e. with the average temporal position of the detail to be verified). When they are asked to judge a trait that required many behaviors to verify (i.e. a trait that is not contained in their spontaneous trait-based representation of the target), they again review the behavior sequence, and so their time to make these judgments also increases with tape length. However, suppose subjects are asked to judge a "concrete" trait, which they have already inferred on the basis of the target's behavior. They then make the judgment on the basis of this prior encoding without consulting their representation of the event sequence, and so their judgment time is not dependent on tape length.

2. Now suppose one assumes that differences in judgment time reflect differences in the time required to search and retrieve specific information relevant to the judgment. Then, to interpret the difference between abstract and concrete judgment times, one might postulate that subjects form only a *single* linear representation of the observed event sequence, and that all judgments are based on the content of this representation. However, if a concrete trait can be verified on the basis of a single behavior, and if the likelihood of such a behavior is the same at each point in the sequence, the position of the first relevant behavior in the sequence will be independent of tape length. Therefore, the time required to make their judgment should not vary with the length of the tape. In contrast, an exhaustive search of the representation is required when the presented trait requires many behaviors to verify it, and so judgment time should increase with the length of the tape.

3. Finally, one may wish to assume that the time required to make judgments is primarily a function of *integration* time, or the time necessary to combine the implications of the information in order to arrive at a single

subjective value. That is, subjects may break the event sequence they observe into units, but may store these units independently of one another in memory. The units and the information contained in them may be equally accessible. However, the number of these units increases with tape length. If the judgment of a concrete trait is based on a single (randomly retrieved) behavior, the time required to make the judgment would not vary with tape length. In contrast, the judgment of an abstract trait requires an integration of the implications of all relevant behaviors one has observed. If integration time increases with the number of pieces to be integrated, this could also account for the judgment-time difference reported by Allen and Ebbesen.

Still other interpretations of Allen and Ebbesen's data are possible (cf. Wyer and Gordon 1984). The point, however, is that any one of several alternative interpretations could be made of the response-time difference reported, depending on one's assumptions about which stage of processing the measure is tapping.

Use of oneself as a basis for judging others. A question often raised in the literature on social information-processing concerns the relation between self-judgments and judgments of others. For example, it seems likely that, at least under some circumstances, people will use their self-perceptions, or beliefs about how they would personally behave in a situation, as a basis for judging others or predicting what others would do (see Ross *et al.* 1977). In other cases, however, the direction of inference may be reversed. That is, a person may consider how others are likely to behave, or the attributes others are likely to have, and use them as bases for self-judgments (cf. Festinger 1954). Thus both considerations imply that subjects' self-judgments will often be similar to their judgments of others. The question is how to determine which alternative process underlies this relation.

One general approach for answering this question was proposed by Lynch (1981). He argued that if self-judgments are used as a basis for judging others, subjects should make these latter judgments more quickly when they have previously been asked to judge themselves (and thus the underlying basis for their judgment has already been established). On the other hand, self-judgments should also be made more quickly if subjects have previously been asked to judge others. This is because self-judgments are theoretically made spontaneously *in the process* of making the initial judgment of others, and thus they do not have to be recomputed at the time they are explicitly requested.

To see this more clearly, suppose t_s is the time to judge oneself, t_o is the time required to judge another person *given that the self-judgment has been made*, and the time required to perform all other components to the judgment process is a constant, t_r. Then the time required to make self- and other-judgments in the two possible orders is as follows:

	Judgment of self	Judgment of other
Judge self first	$t_r + t_s$	$t_r + t_o$
Judge other first	t_r	$t_r + t_s + t_o$

These considerations predict an interaction of response type and response order. Specifically, the difference in time required to make self-judgments and other-judgments should be greater when the other is judged first than when the self is judged first.

If judgments of others are used as a basis for self-judgments, however, the pattern would be:

	Judgment of self	Judgment of other
Judge self first	$t_r + t_s + t_o$	t_r
Judge other first	$t_r + t_s$	$t_r + t_o$

Here, the difference in response times to make the two judgments should be greater when self-judgments are first. In fact, Lynch reported data that were more consistent with the first possibility, and concluded that self-judgments probably mediated other-judgments rather than the reverse.

To draw this conclusion, however, one must assume that response times under the conditions investigated are primarily a function of the time required to compute judgments (e.g. integration time). In other words, it requires the assumption that t_r is constant over all conditions. Suppose this is not the case. Then Lynch's results could be explained even if self-judgments and other-judgments are completely independent! To see this, suppose the times required to judge oneself and to judge others are constant over conditions, but that other judgments take longer to compute than self judgments ($t_o > t_s$). Suppose in addition that some time is required to read and comprehend the question being asked and the particular attribute to be judged, and that this time is greater the first time a particular attribute is asked about ($t_{r,1}$) than the second time it is asked about ($t_{r,2}$). Then,

	Judgments of self	Judgments of other
Judge self first	$t_{r,1} + t_s$	$t_r + t_o$
Judge other first	$t_{r,2} + t_s$	$t_{r,1} + t_o$

Therefore, if $t_{r,1} > t_{r,2}$ and $t_o > t_s$, the difference in response times when the other is judged first would be greater than the time required when the self is judged first. Therefore, an independent judgment model that takes into account potential differences in reading/comprehension time can account for Lynch's results as well.

Judgments of temporal order. Suppose subjects are given two events they have learned about and are asked which occurred first. If sequences of events are represented cognitively in a linear, "comic strip" fashion (cf. Abelson 1976), this comparison might be made by first identifying the location of one of the two events to be compared, and then progressing either forward or backward in the sequence until one finds the other. If this is the case, it should take longer for persons to judge two events that are temporally distant than events that are close together. In fact, however, the opposite is true. That is, temporal-order judgments are *faster* when the events are far apart (Galambos and Rips 1982, Nottenburg and Shoben 1980).

The question is why this is so. The answer depends on what assumptions one wishes to make about the primary determinants of response time under the conditions investigated. On one hand, one might assume that response times are primarily a function of the time required to search for and retrieve the two events being compared from memory. Given this assumption, the results would raise serious questions about the validity of the hypothesis that the events are organized in memory in a linear (temporal) fashion. However, an alternative assumption is that events are retrieved independently of one another, and with equal speed, regardless of where in memory they are located. In other words, response-time differences do not reflect differences in search and retrieval time, but instead reflect differences in the time required to compare the features of the events and compute their order once they are retrieved. Because events are likely to be more distinctive when they are far apart, their temporal order may be computed more quickly. This set of assumptions could account for the findings described above, and suggest that such results have no implications whatsoever for the temporal organization of the events in memory.

This example therefore provides yet another case in which different conclusions can be drawn, depending on what assumption one wishes to make concerning the phase of information-processing that response-time measures are tapping. It turns out that in this particular example, the second set of assumptions described above is more viable than the first. But this is only because *other* types of data can be better accounted for on the basis of these assumptions. For example, subjects who read about events that are not described in chronological order nevertheless recall them chronologically, and are often unable to reconstruct their presentation order when asked explicitly to do so (Wyer and Bodenhausen 1985). However, the response-time measures alone are insufficient to allow any conclusions at all to be drawn.

Judgment measures

Memory measures of the sort described in the preceding sections are often used by social cognition researchers in the hope of elucidating the processes that mediate social judgments. However, their interest in judgments is, in turn, based on the assumption that judgments of an object summarize cognitions that have important implications for overt behavior. Indeed, the extensive literature on the relation between attitudes and behavior (see e.g. Fazio and Zanna 1981, Fishbein and Ajzen 1975) exemplifies the desire to obtain a clear understanding of the relationship between a particular type of judgment and the class of behaviors it is assumed to affect. However, the existence of a relationship is often assumed implicitly when the determinants of social judgment are investigated. For example, most people would have little interest in the factors that affect judgments that someone is "likeable" if such judgments were not correlated with overt behavior toward the person being judged. Similarly, research on social attribution would be less extensive if attributions were not assumed to mediate behavioral decisions.

However, much of the research in which subjects' reported judgments are used to infer the mediators of social behavior implicitly assumes that the judgments reported by subjects reflect ongoing processes that occur regardless of whether the judgments are actually reported. The question is whether this is actually so. There are two components of this question. One is whether the procedures that are introduced in order to assess judgments and to understand their determinants affect the cognitive processes that are used to generate the judgments. To the extent that this occurs, conclusions drawn about the nature of these judgmental processes are limited to the specific conditions in which these assessment procedures are employed. The second aspect of the question is whether an explicit request to form and report a particular type of judgment intrudes upon the cognitive processing of information on which the judgment is based. To this extent, requesting subjects to report a judgment may lead them subsequently to behave differently from the way they would otherwise have done. In either case judgment tasks, and the data obtained through their use, may not reflect the results of cognitive processing of the sort that typically mediates behavior and decisions. Rather, these tasks may actually *create* processes that would otherwise not occur (cf. Bem 1972). The examples we will draw upon in considering this possibility will come largely from the areas of attribution and person perception. However, the issues are obviously much more general ones.

Impression formation and information integration

Much of the research in social cognition to date has focused on the way in which people use information to make judgments of themselves and others.

However, a general concern with these processes is hardly of recent vintage, stemming at least from the work of Asch (1946). One issue stimulated by Asch's work concerns the manner in which trait-adjective descriptions of a person combine to affect overall evaluations of the person. Until recently, the conceptual basis for much of the work on this question, and the methodology used to investigate it, was guided by the information integration theory developed by Norman Anderson (1971, 1981). Although it is not widely recognized, Anderson's model incorporates many of the component processes we have postulated as underlying judgments and decisions. Specifically, it assumes that a subject who receives trait-adjective descriptions of a person first encodes each individual adjective in terms of its implications for the person's likeableness, assigning a "scale value" to it that reflects these implications. Then, these implications along with those of an "initial impression" (a reflection of the judge's world knowledge about people in general) are integrated to arrive at a subjective estimate of the person's likeableness. This estimate is then transformed to a response along a scale provided to the subject for reporting his/her judgment. Therefore, at least three components of the judgment process-encoding, integration, and response generation – are taken into account by the Anderson model.

The most controversial aspect of the model, at least as it is often applied, is an assumption that the implications of each individual piece of information (e.g. trait adjective) do not depend on the nature of the information accompanying it. If this assumption is correct, the overall judgment of a person can be predicted as a simple algebraic function of the separate, context-independent implications of each piece of information considered separately. To evaluate this possibility, a fairly standard procedure is used. Subjects are typically asked to make judgments of a person described by (for example) pairs of trait adjectives that are formed by combining each adjective in one set (A) with each adjective in a second (B). If the adjectives in each set vary systematically in normative likeableness, this design permits the independent and interactive effects of the two sets of adjectives to be evaluated (Anderson 1970, 1971). Results typically show that the adjectives with unfavorable implications receive greater weight in the integration process than adjectives with favorable implications (Birnbaum 1974). However, a model that assumes that the implications of each adjective presented is independent of its context provides a very good account of the data (Anderson 1966, Anderson and Lampel 1965), and attempts to demonstrate the existence of context-induced changes in meaning using the same research paradigm have typically not been definitive (cf. Hamilton and Zanna 1974, Watkins and Peynircioglu 1984, Wyer 1974, Wyer and

Watson 1969). Therefore, the conclusion typically drawn from this body of research is that pieces of information about a person are encoded independently of one another, and that any difference in the effect of this information on judgments in different conditions is due to differences in the relative weights attached to its constituents – and not to differences in the perceived implications of these constituents.

However, this conclusion is quite different from that based on research performed with other paradigms. Particularly noteworthy is the research noted earlier on the effects of concept accessibility on the encoding of information (for reviews, see Bargh 1984, Higgins and King 1981, Wyer and Srull 1981). This research shows that activating a trait concept as a result of performing one task affects the interpretation of behavioral information presented in a later, ostensibly unrelated task, and that these interpretations, in turn, affect judgments of the person described by the information. The fact that the effect of concept activation on judgments is mediated by its effect on the *interpretation* of the information is suggested by the fact that concepts activated *after* the behavioral information is presented have no influence on judgments (see Srull and Wyer 1980). Given that the interpretation of information about a person is affected by concepts that are activated in a totally different context, it seems very unlikely that it is not also affected by other information about the same person that is presented in the same context. Thus the two bodies of research generate quite different conclusions.

As Wyer and Carlston (1979) point out, the differences may be attributable to differences in the research paradigms used to investigate the phenomena. That is, any particular judgment task may activate a set of processes that are specific to the task, and may lead the information to be treated differently at the various stages of processing. The information presented to subjects in the Anderson paradigm is typically manipulated in a factorial design, with each piece presented in several different contexts to the same subject. Moreover, subjects are often told to assume that each piece of information presented is contributed by a different acquaintance of the person being judged. This procedure may lead subjects to treat each individual piece of information as a separate entity, to construe its implications in isolation, and to use a mechanistic integration rule to combine these implications into a single judgment. In other words, the procedure used to evaluate the Anderson integration model may not actually reflect a general process of impression formation, but rather may *create* a process that is specific to the procedures used to investigate it. To this extent, the generality of the conclusions drawn may be limited. In fact, pieces of information about a person *do* appear to be assigned different meanings in different contexts when this information is presented, and judgments are made, in a more natural social situation (see Aronson *et al.* 1966).

The effects of making prior judgments on behavior

The example above raises the possibility that the general research paradigm used to investigate an existing social phenomenon may, in fact, create a *new* phenomenon that is paradigm-specific. Consequently, the procedure itself may lead to conclusions being drawn that are irrelevant to the conceptual questions that initially led the procedure to be used. The next issue to be raised is whether the mere *reporting* of a judgment has an intrusive effect on the processes that the judgment is intended to reflect, and therefore also changes the overt behavior that is likely to result.

In other words, the judgments that subjects report in an experiment are generally assumed to reflect the results of spontaneous inference processes. It is further assumed that these same processes also mediate various types of behavioral decision. In fact, evidence from a variety of areas suggests that these assumptions may often be invalid. That is, subjects may *not* spontaneously engage in the processes that underlie the judgments they report. Rather, these processes may only occur on demand, when subjects are explicitly required to make a judgment. (For a theoretical account of this possibility in the area of self-perception, see Bem 1972.) On the other hand, once the judgment is made, it may affect subjects' subsequent judgments and behavior. To this extent, a situation arises of the sort noted above. That is, asking subjects to report a judgment may lead them to respond subsequently in ways that otherwise would not have occurred.

Evidence of this is fairly well established in research on the effects of interpolated judgments on other subsequent judgments. These effects, which have been the focus of much research and theorizing (see e.g. Carlston 1980, Lingle and Ostrom 1979, Schwarz and Wyer 1985, Wyer and Hartwick 1980, Wyer *et al.* 1984), will not be reviewed here. Rather, we will restrict our attention to a few experiments in which the request to make a judgment appears to have interfered with the effect of experimental variables on overt behavioral decisions.

1. Sherman, Ahlm, Berman, and Lynn (1978) asked subjects to rate the importance of several social issues that in some conditions were very important and in other conditions were unimportant. Later, a confederate approached the subjects and asked them to help out on a recycling project. When recycling had not been among the issues they had rated, subjects volunteered more help when the issues they did rate were important than when they were unimportant. This is presumably because rating important issues

activated feelings of social responsibility. However, when recycling was included among the issues subjects had rated, the *opposite* effect occurred. That is, subjects volunteered *less* help in the "important issue" condition. This is because the context issues had a contrast effect on subjects' overt ratings of recycling, and these ratings were then retrieved out of context and used as a basis for their decision of whether to help. Thus, asking subjects to make explicit ratings of recycling substantially altered the effect of experimental manipulations on their subsequent behavior.

2. In a quite different study by Sherman and his colleagues (Sherman *et al.* 1981), subjects first were arbitrarily asked to explain either why they might succeed on an anagrams task or why they might fail. Then some subjects were asked to predict how they would actually do before performing the task, whereas others performed the task without making any predictions. Subjects who performed the task without predicting their performance did equally well on it regardless of which hypothetical outcome they had previously explained. However, when subjects were asked to predict their performance, those who had explained why they might fail did significantly worse than those who had explained why they might succeed. This was because subjects predicted that the outcome they had arbitrarily been asked to explain would actually occur. These predictions, once made, may then have affected subjects' motivation to work hard on the task, leading their predictions to be a self-fulfilling prophecy. In any event, it is clear that asking subjects to predict their behavior did not simply tap into an ongoing process. Rather, it created a phenomenon that otherwise did not exist.

3. In a study by Dweck and Gilliard (1975), males and females were led to experience failure on an initial task, and their perseverance on a subsequent task was then assessed. Before performing this second task, however, some subjects were asked to predict how well they would do on it. Under these conditions, males persevered longer following failure, whereas females persevered less. In contrast, sex differences in perseverance following failure did not occur when subjects were *not* asked to make predictions. Subjects' predictions of their future performance were apparently based in part on their interpretations of why they had failed initially, and these explantations differed as a function of gender. That is, males attributed their initial failure to a lack of effort, and this stimulated them to work harder. In contrast, females attributed their initial failure to a lack of ability, and this in turn decreased their motivation to persevere, on the second task. However, these different attributions did not occur spontaneously. Rather, they occurred only because the experimenter had asked them to predict their performance. Thus, as in the study by Sherman *et al.*, subjects' predictions did not reflect an ongoing process but, rather, created a process that would otherwise not have occurred. (For further evidence that predicting perform-

ance outcomes affects the nature of these outcomes, see Goodhart, 1986.)

The role of attribution in behavior

The studies by Dweck and Gilliard and by Sherman *et al.* raise a more general question concerning the mediating role of causal attributions in behavior and decision making. As noted earlier, the enormous interest in attribution theory and research in the last two decades has undoubtedly been based, at least in part, on the assumption that the explanations one gives to one's own and others' past behavior are determinants of one's subsequent behavior. Thus, our reactions to a colleague's hostile remark depend on whether we attribute the remark to the colleague's disliking of us personally, to our own previous behavior toward the colleague, or to the fact that the colleague is in the process of getting divorced and is generally tense and edgy. However, although such intuitions undoubtedly have some validity, it is nevertheless conceivable that the conditions in which attributions actually have an important influence on behavior are much less common than we often assume.

This possibility has in fact been suggested by Abelson (1976, 1981) and Langer (1978). Persons may form prototypic scripts of "rules of thumb" for responding in certain situations, and may apply them independently of any explanation they have for why the situation occurred. For example, suppose we learn that students think our lectures are disorganized and difficult to follow. We might then decide to distribute outlines of our lectures on future occasions. However, we may do this simply because we have learned the rule: "when people think you are disorganized, provide an outline of the lecture." If so, the same behavior will result regardless of whether we attribute the students' confusion to their stupidity or to our poor teaching ability. Similarly, if we get a series of papers rejected by the editor of a particular journal, we may send our next paper to a different journal. But this might occur simply because we don't like the negative feelings that accompany rejection, independently of whether we think the rejections occur because of the editor's shortsightedness or because our work is inherently of poor quality.

This does not imply that people are incapable of generating explanations for decision-relevant events if they are asked to do so. Indeed, there are undoubtedly occasions in which people spontaneously generate them at the time the events occur (Weimer 1985, Winter and Uleman 1984). Even in these cases, however, behavioral decisions may be driven, not by such attributions, but by factors that are quite independent of them (cf. Nisbett and Wilson 1977). Moreover, as the research by Sherman *et al.* and by Dweck and Gilliard indicates, explicit requirements to generate such explanations, or at least to make judgments that require them, may alter – sometimes very dramatically – the behavior that actually occurs. To this extent, there is some question as to whether attribution research and theory is as useful in understanding the bases for behavioral decisions as one would wish. This does not mean that attribution research is unimportant. However, it may be more limited in its scope than is sometimes realized.

Concluding remarks

We have attempted in this chapter to draw an analogy between the process of acquiring "scientific" social knowledge and the process of acquiring social knowledge more generally. Three components of this analogy were emphasized.

First, people interpret new social information in terms of a previously formed set of concepts. They then process it according to a set of rules that are relevant to their particular objectives at the time the information is received. The particular set of concepts and procedures they happen to select has a major influence on the conclusions they draw from the information and the decisions they make on the basis of it. This is the case with scientific knowledge as well. That is, the interpretation of any piece of data we acquire is highly dependent on the procedures we use to acquire it. Moreover, the conclusions we draw from these data are contingent on which of several equally applicable "scientific knowledge structures" we happen to apply. These scientific knowledge structures can be chosen fortuitously, or they can be chosen with care and deliberation; examples of each were provided throughout the chapter. If the data obtained could speak for themselves, it wouldn't really matter which choice was made. But they don't, and the choice is an important one with ramifications for how quickly true conceptual progress will be made.

Finally, the interpretations made of social information often come to function independently of the information itself, and therefore influence behavior and decisions independently of this information. There is a danger that scientific interpretations may also become autonomous of the data on which they are based. A major objective of our discussion, from the very outset, has been to call attention to this danger. As long as one is clearly aware of the conceptual underpinnings of the interpretations placed on the data one obtains, the possibility of alternative interpretations will also be recognized. And, ultimately, each of these can be checked and our scientific knowledge and understanding will advance. Without this awareness, however, any "understanding" is likely to be illusory.

It is important to emphasize that the conclusions we have drawn do not necessarily have pessimistic implications for the advancement of science. As others (e.g. Weimer 1979) have also pointed out, the theoretical conclusions that are drawn from scientific inquiry, like the beliefs that lay persons derive from their social experience, are almost inevitably based on a set of premises and assumptions that are not the only viable ones. The point to be kept in mind is that these assumptions pertain not only to the relations among the conceptual variables postulated as governing a phenomenon, but also to the procedures used to assess these variables. The former assumptions are typically explicit. However, for scientific knowledge to advance, the latter assumptions must be explicit as well.

In this regard, our urging that investigators make explicit the theoretical premises that underlie their selection of a particular response measure, and that they be cautious about generalizing their findings beyond the interpretational system defined by these premises, recognizes the need to distinguish between (*a*) the objective of verifying the internal consistency of a theory ("within-theory" research) and (*b*) the objective of making comparative tests of the validity of different theories ("between-theory" research); see Greenwald and Ronis 1978, Ostrom 1977. Precise statements of the assumptions underlying the use of a particular response measure or research paradigm are particularly essential in the former case. On the other hand, the latter objective places particular importance on the need for multiple operations (cf. Garner *et al.* 1956), that is, the need to establish theoretical conclusions through several different experimental procedures, thereby eliminating the danger that these conclusions are specific to a given set of procedural assumptions.

In this chapter, we have likened the acquisition of scientific social knowledge to the acquisition of knowledge by the layperson, and have pointed out that a recognition of this similarity sensitizes us to constraints in interpreting scientific information similar to those constraints that confront the layperson in forming beliefs on the basis of everyday experiences. In considering our recommendations for minimizing ambiguities that result from these constraints, it is perhaps interesting to reverse our analogy. That is, just as it is desirable for the scientist to recognize the limits that are placed on his/her conclusions about the meaning of scientific observations, to distinguish between within-theory and between-theory criteria for evaluating data and to engage in multiple operationalism, so may it be desirable for laypeople to apply these considerations in evaluating the beliefs they form from observations they make in the course of daily experience. An elaboration of this possibility, and its implications for an understanding of social information processing, is left for further consideration.

References

Abelson, R. P. (1976). Script processing in attitude formation and decision-making. In J. S. Carroll and J. W. Payne (eds.), *Cognition and social behavior*. Hillsdale, NJ: Lawrence Erlbaum.

Abelson, R. P. (1981). The psychological status of the script concept. *American Psychologist* 36: 715–29.

Allen, R. B. and Ebbesen, E. B. (1981). Cognitive processes in person perception. Retrieval of personality trait and behavioral information. *Journal of Experimental Social Psychology* 17: 119–41.

Anderson, J. R. (1972). FRAN: A simulation model of free recall. In G. H. Bower (ed.), *The psychology of learning and motivation*, vol. 5. New York: Academic Press.

Anderson, J. R. (1976). *Language, memory and thought*. Hillsdale, NJ: Lawrence Erlbaum.

Anderson, J. R. (1977). Neural models with cognitive implications. In D. LaBerge and S. J. Samuels (eds.), *Basic processes in reading*. Hillsdale, NJ: Lawrence Erlbaum.

Anderson, J. R. (1978). Arguments concerning representations for mental imagery. *Psychological Review* 85: 249–77.

Anderson, J. R. and Bower, G. H. (1973). *Human associative memory*. Washington, DC: Winston.

Anderson, J. R. and Reder, L. M. (1979). Elaborative processing of prose material. In L. S. Cermak and F. I. M. Craik (eds.), *Levels of processing and human memory*. Hillsdale, NJ: Lawrence Erlbaum.

Anderson, N. H. (1966). Component ratings in impression formation. *Psychonomic Science* 6: 279–80.

Anderson, N. H. (1970). Functional measurement and psychophysical judgment. *Psychological Review* 77: 153–70.

Anderson, N. H. (1971). Integration theory and attitude change. *Psychological Review* 78: 171–206.

Anderson, N. H. (1981) *Foundations of information integration theory*. New York: Academic Press.

Anderson, N. H. and Hubert, S. (1963). Effects of concomitant verbal recall on order effects in personality impression formation. *Journal of Verbal Learning and Verbal Behavior* 2: 379–91.

Anderson, N. H. and Lampel, A. K. (1965). Effect of context on ratings of personality traits. *Psychonomic Science* 3: 433–44.

Aronson, E., Willerman, B., and Floyd, J. (1966). The effect of a pratfall on increasing interpersonal attraction. *Psychonomic Science* 4: 227–8.

Asch, S. E. (1946). Forming impressions of personality. *Journal of Abnormal and Social Psychology* 41: 258–90.

Baddeley, A. D. (1978). The trouble with levels: a reexamination of Craik and Lockhart's framework for memory research. *Psychological Review* 85: 139–52.

Bargh, J. A. (1984). Automatic and controlled processing of social information. In Wyer and Srull 1984, vol. 3.

Bem, D. J. (1972). Self perception theory. In L. Berkowitz (ed.), *Advances in experimental social psychology*, vol. 6. New York: Academic Press.

Birnbaum, M. H. (1974). The nonadditivity of personality impressions. *Journal of Experimental Psychology* 102: 543–61.

Bransford, J. D. and Franks, J. J. (1973). The abstraction of linguistic ideas: a review. *Cognition* 1: 211–49.

Cantor, N. and Mischel, W. (1977). Traits as prototypes. Effects on recognition memory. *Journal of Personality and Social Psychology* 35: 38–48.

Carlston, D. E. (1980). The recall and use of observed behavioral episodes and inferred traits in social inference processes. *Journal of Experimental Social Psychology* 16: 779–804.

Cohen, C. E. (1977). *Cognitive basis of stereotyping*. Paper presented at the American Psychological Association Meeting, San Francisco, September.

Cohen, C. E. (1981). Person categories and social perception: testing some boundaries of the processing effects of prior knowledge. *Journal of Personality and Social Psychology* 40: 441–52.

Collins, A. M. and Loftus, E. F. (1975). A spreading-activation theory of semantic processing. *Psychological Review* 82: 407–28.

Craik, F. I. M. and Lockhart, R. S. (1972). Levels of processing: a framework for memory research. *Journal of Verbal Learning and Verbal Behavior* 11: 671–84.

Dreben, E. K., Fiske, S. T., and Hastie, R. (1979). The independence of item and evaluative information: impression and recall order effects in behavior-based impression formation. *Journal of Personality and Social Psychology* 37: 1758–68.

Dweck, C. S. and Gilliard, D. (1975). Expectancy statements as determinants of reactions to failure: sex differences in persistence and expectancy change. *Journal of Personality and Social Psychology* 32: 1077–84.

Eich, J. M. (1985). Levels of processing, encoding specificity, elaboration, and CHARM. *Psychological Review* 92: 1–38.

Fazio, R. H. and Zanna, M. P. (1981). Direct experience and attitude–behavioral consistency. In L. Berkowitz (ed.), *Advances in experimental social psychology,* vol. 14. New York: Academic Press.

Festinger, L. (1954). A theory of social comparison processes. *Human Relations* 7: 117–40.

Festinger, L. (1957). *A theory of cognitive dissonance*. Stanford: Stanford University Press.

Fishbein, M. and Ajzen, I. (1975). *Belief, attitude, intention and behavior: an introduction to theory and research*. Reading, Mass.: Addison-Wesley.

Fiske, S. T., Taylor, S. E., Etcoff, N. L., and Laufer, J. K. (1979). Imaging, empathy, and causal attribution. *Journal of Experimental Social Psychology* 15: 356–77.

Galambos, J. A. and Rips, L. J. (1982). Memory for routines. *Journal of Verbal Learning and Verbal Behavior* 21: 260–81.

Garner, W. R., Hake, H. W., and Erickson, C. W. (1956). Operationism and the concept of perception. *Psychological Review* 63: 149–59.

Gillund, G. and Shiffrin, R. M. (1984). A retrieval model for both recognition and recall. *Psychological Review* 91: 1–67.

Goodhart, D. E. (1986). The effects of positive and negative thinking on performance in an achievement situation. *Journal of Personality and Social Psychology* 51: 117–24.

Gordon, S. E. (1982). *The role of trait concepts in the cognitive representation of behaviors.* Unpublished Ph.D. dissertation, University of Illinois, Urbana-Champaign.

Graesser, A. C. , Gordon, S. E., and Sawyer, J. D. (1979). Recognition memory for typical and atypical actions in scripted activities: test of a script pointer + tag hypothesis. *Journal of Verbal Learning and Verbal Behavior* 18: 319–32.

Graesser, A. C. and Nakamura, G. V. (1982). The impact of a schema on comprehension and memory. In G. H. Bower (ed.), *The psychology of learning and motivation: advances in research and theory*, vol. 16. New York: Academic Press.

Greenwald, A. G. (1968). Cognitive learning, cognitive responses to persuasion, and attitude change. In A. G. Greenwald, T. Brock, and T. M. Ostrom (eds.), *Psychological foundations of attitudes.* New York: Academic Press.

Greenwald, A. G. and Ronis, D. L. (1978). Twenty years of cognitive dissonance: case study of the evolution of a theory. *Psychological Review* 85: 53–7.

Grice, H. P. (1975). Logic and conversation. In P. Cole and J. L. Morgan (eds.), *Syntax and semantics*, vol. 3: *Speech acts.* New York: Academic Press.

Hamilton, D. L., Katz, L. B., and Leirer, V. O. (1980). Organizational processes in impression formation. In R. Hastie, T. M. Ostrom, E. B. Ebbesen, R. S. Wyer, D. L. Hamilton, and D. E. Carlston (eds.), *Personal memory: the cognitive basis of social perception.* Hillsdale, NJ: Lawrence Erlbaum.

Hamilton, D. L. and Zanna, M. P. (1974). Context effects in impression formation: changes in connotative meaning. *Journal of Personality and Social Psychology* 29: 649–54.

Hartwick, J. (1979). Memory for trait information: a signal detection analysis. *Journal of Experimental Social Psychology* 15: 533–52.

Hastie, R. (1980). Memory for information which confirms or contradicts a general impression. In R. Hastie, T. M. Ostrom, E. B. Ebbesen, R. S. Wyer, D. L. Hamilton, and D. E. Carlston (eds.), *Personal memory: the cognitive basis of social perception.* Hillsdale, NJ: Lawrence Erlbaum.

Higgins, E. T. and King, G. (1981). Accessibility of social constructs: information processing consequences of individual and contextual variability. In N. Cantor and J. F. Kohlstrom (eds.), *Personality, cognition, and social interaction.* Hillsdale, NJ: Lawrence Erlbaum.

Hintzman, D. L. and Ludlum, G. (1980). Differential forgetting of prototypes and old instances: simulation by an exemplar-based classification model. *Memory and Cognition* 8: 378–82.

Jacoby, L. L. and Craik, F. I. M. (1979). Effects of elaboration of processing at encoding and retrieval: trace distinctiveness and recovery of initial context. In L. S. Cremak and F. I. M. Craik (eds.), *Levels of processing in human memory*. Hillsdale, NJ: Lawrence Erlbaum.

Kraut, R. E. and Higgins, E. T. (1984). Communication and social cognition. In Wyer and Srull 1984, vol. 3.

Langer, S. J. (1978). Rethinking the role of thought in social interaction. In J. Harvey, W. Ickes, and R. Kidd (eds.), *New directions in attribution theory*, vol. 2. Hillsdale, NJ: Lawrence Erlbaum.

Lauden, L. (1977). *Progress and its problems: towards a theory of scientific growth*. Berkeley: University of California Press.

Lichtenstein, M. and Srull, T. K. (1985). Conceptual and methodological issues in examining the relationship between consumer memory and judgment. In L. F. Alwitt and A. A. Mitchell (eds.), *Psychological processes and advertising effects: theory, research and application*. Hillsdale, NJ: Lawrence Erlbaum.

Lingle, J. H. and Ostrom, T. M. (1979). Retrieval selectivity in memory-based impression judgments. *Journal of Personality and Social Psychology* 37: 180–94.

Loken, B. (1984). Attitude processing strategies. *Journal of Experimental Social Psychology* 20: 272–96.

Lynch, J. G. (1981). A method for determining the sequencing of cognitive processes in judgment: order effects on reaction times. *Advances in Consumer Research* 8: 134–9.

Meyer, D. E. and Schvaneveldt, R. W. (1971). Facilitation in recognition between pairs of words: evidence of a dependence between retrieval operations. *Journal of Experimental Psychology* 90: 227–34.

Minsky, M. (1977) Frame-system theory. In P. N. Johnson-Laird and P. C. Wason (eds.), *Thinking: readings in cognitive science*. Cambridge University Press.

Murdock, B. B. (1982). Recognition memory. In C. R. Puff (ed.), *Handbook of research methods in human memory and cognition*. New York: Academic Press.

Nisbett, R. E. and Wilson, T. D. (1977). Telling more than we can know: verbal reports on mental processes. *Psychological Review* 84: 231–59.

Norman, D. A. and Bobrow, D. G. (1979). Descriptions: an intermediate stage in memory retrieval. *Cognitive Psychology* 11: 107–23.

Norman, D. A. and Wickelgren, W. A. (1969). Strength theory of decision rules and latency in retrieval from short-term memory. *Journal of Mathematical Psychology* 6: 192–208.

Nottenburg, G. and Shoben, E. J. (1980). Scripts as linear orders. *Journal of Experimental Social Psychology* 16: 329–47.

Ostrom, T. M. (1977). Between-theory and within-theory conflict in explaining context effects in impression formation. *Journal of Experimental Social Psychology* 13: 492–503.

Picek, J. S., Sherman, S. J., and Shiffrin, R. M. (1975). Cognitive organization and coding of social structures. *Journal of Personality and Social Psychology* 31: 758–68.

Raaijmakers, J. G. W. and Shiffrin, R. M. (1980). SAM: a theory of probabilistic search of associative memory. In G. H. Bower (ed.), *The psychology of learning and motivation*, vol. 14. New York: Academic Press.

Raaijmakers, J. G. W. and Shiffrin, R. M. (1981). Search of associative memory. *Psychological Review* 88: 93–134.

Ratcliff, R. (1978), A theory of memory retrieval. *Psychological Review* 85: 59–108.

Ross, L., Greene, D., and House, P. (1977). The "false consensus effect": an egocentric bias in social perception and attribution processes. *Journal of Experimental Social Psychology* 13: 279–301.

Rundus, D. (1973). Negative effects of using list items as recall cues. *Journal of Verbal Learning and Verbal Behavior* 12: 43–50.

Schank, R. C. and Abelson, R. P. (1977). *Scripts, plans, goals and understanding*. Hillsdale, NJ: Lawrence Erlbaum.

Schwarz, N. and Wyer, R. S. (1985). Effects of rank ordering stimuli on magnitude ratings of these and other stimuli. *Journal of Experimental Social Psychology* 21: 30–46.

Sentis, K. P. and Burnstein, E. (1979). Remembering schema-consistent information: effects of a balance schema on recognition memory. *Journal of Personality and Social Psychology* 37: 2200–12.

Sherman, S. J., Ahlma, K., Berman, L., and Lynn, S. (1978). Contrast effects and their relationship to subsequent behavior. *Journal of Experimental Social Psychology* 14: 340–50.

Sherman, S. J., Skov, R. B., Hervitz, E. F., and Stock, C. B. (1981). The effects of explaining hypothetical future events: from possibility to probability to actuality and beyond. *Journal of Experimental Social Psychology* 17: 142–58.

Srull, T. K. (1981). Person memory: some tests of associative storage and retrieval models. *Journal of Experimental Psychology: Human Learning and Memory* 7: 440–63.

Srull, T. K. (1983). Organizational and retrieval processes in person memory: an examination of processing objectives, presentation format, and the possible role of self-generated retrieval cues. *Journal of Personality and Social Psychology* 44: 1157–70.

Srull, T. K. (1984). Methodological techniques for the study of person memory and social cognition. In R. W. Wyer and T. K. Srull (eds.), *Handbook of social cognition*, vol. 2. Hillsdale, NJ: Lawrence Erlbaum.

Srull, T. K. and Brand, J. F. (1983). Memory for information about persons: the effect of encoding operations on subsequent retrieval. *Journal of Verbal Learning and Verbal Behavior* 22: 219–30.

Srull, T. K., Lichtenstein, M., and Rothbart, M. (1985). Associative storage and retrieval processes in person memory. *Journal of Experimental Psychology: Learning, Memory and Cognition* 11: 316–45.

Srull, T. K. and Wyer, R. S. (1979). The role of category accessibility in the interpretation of information about persons: Some determinants and implications. *Journal of Personality and Social Psychology* 37: 1660–72.

Srull, T. K. and Wyer, R. S. (1980). Category accessibility and social perception: some implications for the study of person memory and interpersonal judgment. *Journal of Personality and Social Psychology* 38: 841–56.

Srull, T. K. and Wyer, R. S. (1986). The role of chronic and temporary goals in social information processing. In R. M. Sorrentino and E. T. Higgins (eds.), *Handbook of motivation and cognition*. New York: Guilford Press.

Sternberg, S. (1969). Memory-scanning: mental processes revealed by reaction-time experiments. *American Scientist* 57: 421–57.

Sternberg, S. (1975). Memory scanning: new findings and current controversies. *Quarterly Journal of Experimental Psychology* 27: 1–32.

Tulving, E. (1983). *Elements of episodic memory*. Oxford: Clarendon Press.

Tulving, E., Schacter, D. L., and Stark, H. A. (1982). Priming effects in word-fragment completion are independent of recognition memory. *Journal of Experimental Psychology: Learning, Memory and Cognition* 8: 336–42.

Tulving, E. and Thomson, D. M. (1973). Encoding specificity and retrieval processes in episode memory. *Psychological Review* 80: 352–73.

Tulving, E. and Watkins, M. J. (1975). Structure of memory traces. *Psychological Review* 82: 261–76.

Watkins, M. J. (1979). Engrams as cuegrams and forgetting as cue overload: a cueing approach to the structure of memory. In C. R. Puff (ed.), *Memory organization and structure*. New York: Academic Press.

Watkins, M. J. and Peynircioglu, Z. F. (1984). Determining perceived meaning during impression formation: another look at the meaning change hypothesis. *Journal of Personality and Social Psychology* 46: 1005–16.

Weimer, W. B. (1979). *Notes on the methodology of scientific research*. Hillsdale, NJ: Lawrence Erlbaum.

Weimer, W. B. (1985). "Spontaneous" causal thinking. *Psychological Bulletin* 97: 74–84.

Winter, L. and Uleman, J. S. (1984). When are social judgments made? Evidence for the spontaneousness of trait inferences. *Journal of Personality and Social Psychology* 47: 237–52.

Wyer, R. S. (1974). *Cognitive organization and change: an information processing approach*. Potomac, MD: Lawrence Erlbaum.

Wyer, R. S. (1981). An information-processing perspective on social attribution. In J. Harvey, W. Ickes, and R. Kidd (eds.), *New directions in attribution research*, vol. 3. Hillsdale, NJ: Lawrence Erlbaum.

Wyer, R. S. and Bodenhausen, G. V. (1985). Event memory: the effects of processing objectives and time delay on memory for action sequences. *Journal of Personality and Social Psychology* 49: 301–16.

Wyer, R. S., Bodenhausen, G. V., and Srull, T. K. (1984). The cognitive representation of persons and groups and its effect on recall and recognition memory. *Journal of Experimental Social Psychology* 20: 445–69.

Wyer, R. S. and Budesheim, T. L. (1985). Person memory and judgments: the impact of information that one is told to disregard. Unpublished manuscript, University of Illinois at Urbana-Champaign.

Wyer, R. S. and Budesheim, T. L. (1987). Person memory and judgments: the impact of information that one is told to disregard. *Journal of Personality and Social Psychology* 53: 14–29.

Wyer, R. S. and Carlston, D. E. (1979). *Social cognition, inference, and attribution*. Hillsdale, NJ: Lawrence Erlbaum.

Wyer, R. S. and Gordon, S. E. (1982). The recall of information about persons and groups. *Journal of Experimental Psychology* 18: 128–64.

Wyer, R. S. and Gordon, S. E. (1984). The cognitive representation of social information. In Wyer and Srull 1984, vol. 2.

Wyer, R. S. and Hartwick, J. (1980). The role of information retrieval and conditional inference processes in belief formation and change. In L. Berkowitz (ed.), *Advances in experimental social psychology*, vol. 13. New York: Academic Press.

Wyer, R. S. and Srull, T. K. (1980). The processing of social stimulus information: a conceptual integration. In R. Hastie, T. Ostrom, E. Ebbesen, R. Wyer, D. Hamilton, and D. Carlston (eds.), *Person memory: cognitive basis of social perception*. Hillsdale, NJ: Lawrence Erlbaum.

Wyer, R. S. and Srull, T. K. (1981). Category accessibility: some theoretical and empirical issues concerning the processing of social stimulus information. In E. T. Higgins, C. P. Herman, and M. P. Zanna (eds.), *Social cognition: the Ontario symposium on personality and social psychology*. Hillsdale, NJ: Lawrence Erlbaum.

Wyer, R. S. and Srull, T. K. (eds.) (1984) *Handbook of social cognition*, vols. 1–3. Hillsdale, NJ: Lawrence Erlbaum.

Wyer, R. S. and Srull, T. K. (1985). *A theory of social information processing: implications and applications*. Unpublished manuscript, University of Illinois at Urbana-Champaign.

Wyer, R. S. and Srull, T. K. (1986). Human cognition in its social context. *Psychological Review* 93: 322–59.

Wyer, R. S., Srull, T. K., and Gordon, S. E. (1984). The effects of predicting a person's behavior on subsequent trait judgments. *Journal of Experimental Social Psychology* 20: 29–46.

Wyer, R. S., Srull, T. K., Gordon, S. E., and Hartwick, J. (1982). Effects of processing objectives on the recall of prose material. *Journal of Personality and Social Psychology* 43: 674–88.

Wyer, R. S., Strack, F., and Fuhrman, R. (1984). *The acquisition of information about persons: effects of task objectives and personal expectancies*. Unpublished manuscript, University of Illinois.

Wyer, R. S. and Unverzagt, W. H. (1985). The effects of instructions to disregard information on its subsequent recall and use in making judgments. *Journal of Personality and Social Psychology* 44: 533–49.

Wyer, R. S. and Watson, S. F. (1969). Context effects in impression formation. *Journal of Personality and Social Psychology* 12: 22–33.

Zajonc, R. B. (1980). Feeling and thinking: preferences need no inferences. *American Psychologist* 35: 151–75.

8 The concept of accuracy in social judgment[1]

Reid Hastie and Kenneth A. Rasinski

Discussions of the nature of human knowledge, how we get it, and its relationship to social psychology inevitably lead to considerations of the accuracy of knowledge. This is an essay on the concepts of accuracy that are used in research on social perception. It is important to distinguish between evaluation of the accuracy of a judgment and research on the manner in which we come to make the judgment. Both topics are important and they are interrelated, but social psychologists have been careless about keeping the two problems separate, and many good studies of how judgments are made are poor studies of judgment accuracy. This essay was written in an effort to clarify the difference between the two problems, to identify the major "logics" of accuracy that are implicit in conclusions about accuracy, and to suggest improvements in the practice of conducting research on accuracy.

The concept of accuracy that will be used in this chapter is close to the commonsense notion summarized in an English language dictionary: "(1) having no errors, correct; (2) deviating only slightly but within acceptable limits from a standard" (*American Heritage Dictionary*, 1983). This definition indicates that an analysis of accuracy requires the consideration of three elements: (*a*) a judgment, response, or assertion; (*b*) a standard or criterion of the truth; (*c*) a rule specifying a correspondence relation between the judgment and the criterion. We define error as the converse of accuracy – the discrepancy or deviation between the criterion and the judgment. We

1 The authors are grateful to Daniel Bar-Tal, David A. Kenny, Arie Kruglanski, Nancy Pennington, and to many colleagues at Northwestern University, at the Center for Decision Research of the University of Chicago, and the participants in the Tel-Aviv Conference on the Social Psychology of Knowledge (June 1984). The authors are also grateful for support from the Center for Advanced Study in the Behavioral Sciences and the Trout Foundation.

will use the term "bias" to refer to systematic error – patterned or orderly deviations from the standard (Einhorn *et al.* 1977).

This review will be restricted to social judgments about the properties of a single target person. These properties would include characteristics such as physical appearance, personality traits, emotional states, enduring attitudes, abilities or knowledge, intentions to behave, or behaviors. We restrict our discussion to judgments of the characteristics of *individuals* and exclude the accuracy of statements about general *classes* of individuals (e.g. "women are more artistic than men"). But this still includes consideration of statements that are generalizations about an individual across instances of his or her behavior and across time (for example, statements about appearance, traits, attitudes, abilities, even intentions and emotions, are generalizations in this sense). We also lean towards an objectivist, correspondence theory-oriented approach to epistemology. Our basic assumption is that two perceivers, a subject and a researcher, are both attempting accurately to judge the real properties of an individual who exists independently of them. Our analysis is nonsense when it turns out that the properties or the individual do not exist.

It is immediately apparent in research on social judgment that our hard-headed, objectivist definition of accuracy may be unwieldy in application. When the object of judgment is as intangible as a personality trait, emotional state, ability, attitude, or intention, or as fleeting as a behavior, must not the establishment of the *researcher's* criterion itself involve a high degree of subjectivity and intersubjectivity? Furthermore, is not the objectivist approach circular, simply pitting the belief of one privileged group of judges (the researchers) against the belief of another defenseless group of judges (the subjects)? Yes and no. We do not think that the judgment criteria can be directly known (even by the "right" people); justification of a criterion is a lot of work, and shares much with the commonsense manner in which everyday beliefs are justified with reference to subjective degree of support and intersubjective consensus. But, no, the objectivist approach is not simply an arbitrary process of labeling the researcher's belief a criterion and the subject's belief a judgment and then proceeding as if disagreement always counted as the subject's error. What the objectivist approach implies for practice is casting the analysis of accuracy in the fundamental judgment–correspondence–criterion framework and then checking each of its ingredients to assess the validity of the overall analysis. Is the subject attempting to make the judgment the researcher has instructed him or her to make? Is there *good reason* to label the researcher's response a criterion? Is the correspondence relationship direct and meaningful? To the degree that each of these ingredients fails, the quality of the overall evaluation of accuracy is diminished.

Why care about accuracy?

Many social cognition researchers are concerned with the relationship between their subjects' judgments (responses) and the cues (stimuli) that control those responses – *how* the judgment is made. We might call this research on "cue utilization", following the distinctions laid down by Brunswik (Postman and Tolman 1959). Research on cue utilization does not require an assessment of the accuracy of judgment. For example, few (if any) experiments in the impression formation literature or the attitude change literature assess accuracy; virtually all concentrate on cue utilization. Nevertheless, it seems to us that a good theory of judgment would provide hypotheses that predict when people will be accurate and when they will be inaccurate, as well as methods to assess accuracy. However, most research on social judgment does not attempt to assess the accuracy of judgment, although many of these studies are used to draw conclusions about accuracy.

One reason to study accuracy derives from the philosophical roots of the field of cognition (Kruglanski and Ajzen 1983). To a philosopher concerned with "cognitivism", the key questions involve what knowledge people possess, how it is obtained, and whether it reflects objective reality. A second reason comes from the assumption that action depends on judgment. Choices and decisions depend on our judgments of conditions in the environment and judgments of our evaluative responses to those conditions. Successful adaptation to natural environments depends on accuracy of judgment, under the assumption that action depends on judgment. Furthermore, research on accuracy may be a special imperative for social psychologists because the "interstitial" character of the field of social psychology puts us in the role of communicators between artificial laboratory environments and naturally occurring settings.

Third, there has been a recent obsession with bias and inaccuracy by experimental and social psychologists (Nisbett and Ross 1980). The research literature is full of conclusions about "vagaries of probabilistic judgment", "fallibility of judgment", "cognitive failings", "pathologies of preference as well as of inference behavior", "startling deficiencies in man's ability to think in probabilistic terms or to integrate probabilities and utilities into his decisions", "dramatic failures of the human mind", statements that "the same organism that routinely solves inferential problems too subtle and complex for the mightiest computers often makes errors in the simplest of judgments about everyday events", and so on (Christensen-Szalanski and Beach 1984). Such conclusions require a rigorous analysis of the accuracy of judgment. Fourth, the development of "debiasing techniques" and "decision aids" to improve judgments requires methodological tools to assess accuracy. The development of "cognitive prosthetics" also requires valid theories of judgment to help us understand the conditions for accurate and inaccurate judgment.

Finally, there is something fundamental, but ineffable, about including an analysis of accuracy in the program of cognitive research. Fields such as memory and perception appear to make the greatest progress in developing models of the mind when they focus on experimental results obtained in research where an analysis of accuracy is central.

Logics of empirical research on accuracy

One approach to understanding research on accuracy is to look at current practice. In a review of empirical research, we discovered that four "logics" underlie all the published analyses or claims about the accuracy (or inaccuracy) of social judgment. The first, most basic logic involves a direct comparison between a judgment response and a criterion value measured independently of the subject's judgments. A large portion of the literature is based on the application of this straightforward logic. Often the research is conducted within the theoretical framework that provides a conventionalized breakdown of the "accuracy score" into components. Examples would be Brunswik's "lens model" (Hursch *et al.* 1964, Dudycha and Naylor 1966); Cronbach's "accuracy score components" (1955); signal detection theory (Swets and Pickett 1982); calibration probability score decomposition models (Yates 1982); information transmission partitioning analysis (Garner 1962); and threshold models for detection (McNichol 1972).

Under this logic the researcher defines a judgment task, measures a criterion, independently measures a subject's judgments, and then compares the judgment with the criterion for each judgment trial. If the judgments and criterion are measured quantitatively, then a judgment–criterion discrepancy index is frequently the basis for a summary of judgment accuracy. If the criterion and judgment are expressed in a categorical form (e.g. yes–no, present–absent), then usually several trials are performed and accuracy is indexed by the proportions of various types of correct and incorrect response. A clear example of the application of this logic is provided in an experiment by Kraut (1978) in which observers attempted to judge whether or not a target subject was lying or telling the truth (see Fig. 8.1). Kraut measured many verbal and nonverbal properties of the stimulus person's behavior, and conducted a correlational analysis to determine which ones were diagnostic of lying (cue validity) and which cues were used by the observers (cue utilization).

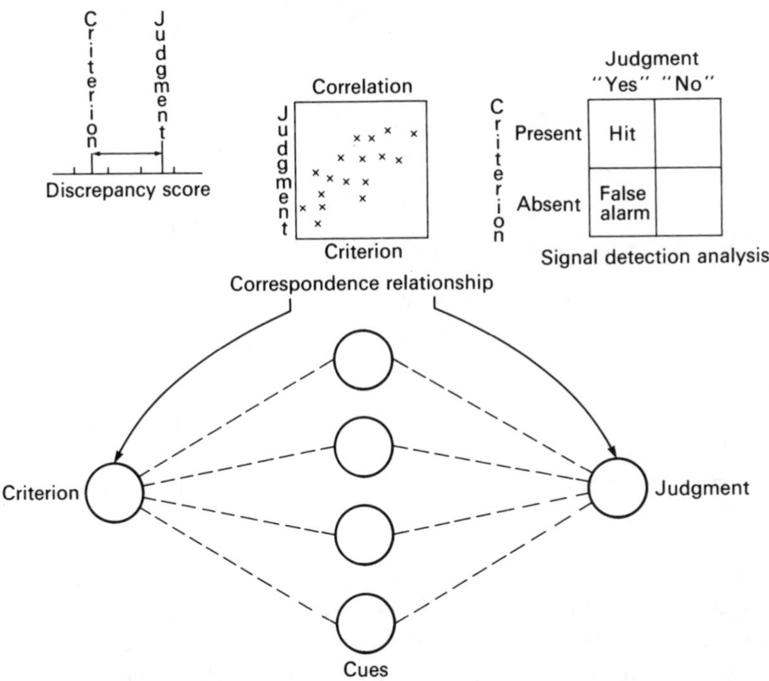

Fig. 8.1. Logic 1: Direct assessment of criterion–judgment relationship

A second logic (see Fig. 8.2) used to evaluate accuracy of performance involves comparing the judgment of one subject with the judgment of a second subject to determine whether the two judges agree. If the two judges disagree, then someone must be in error. Note that this approach assumes that the property the subjects have been asked to judge "exists", and that one value of the property excludes the possibility of other values of the property. Conclusions about accuracy from research on point-of-view effects, actor–observer differences, false consensus effects, and some other person perception phenomena depend on this logic (Dornbusch *et al.* 1965, Bourne 1977, Ross, Greene, and House 1977, Ross, Amabile, and Steinmetz 1977, Taylor and Fiske 1975, Jones and Nisbett 1972, Monson and Snyder 1977). For example, Bourne (1977) found that inter-judge agreement for a single stimulus person was low when members of a group described one another. He concluded that personality did not appear to be an "objective entity" and that accuracy was low. Monson and Snyder (1977) noted that subjects disagree with one another and with psychologists concerning the causes of a stimulus person's behavior, and concluded that subjects' causal attribution judgments are inaccurate.

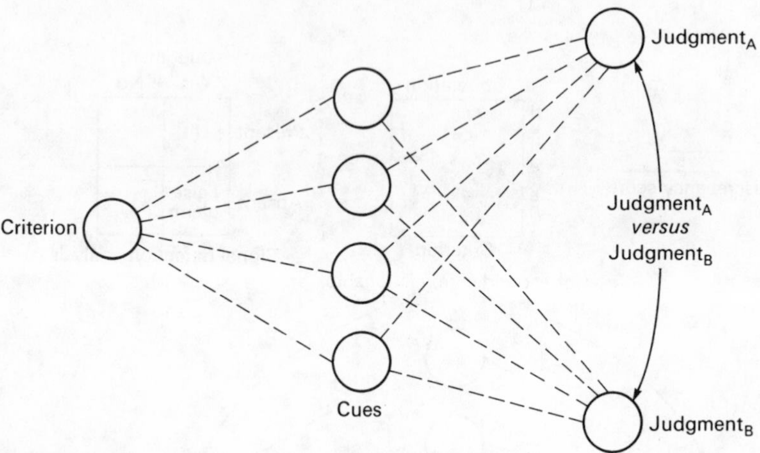

Fig 8.2. Logic 2: Judgment $_A \neq$ Judgment$_B$ → At least one judgment is inaccurate

A third logic (see Fig. 8.3) depends on assumptions or measurements of the relationships among three elements to draw conclusions about accuracy of judgment. The three elements are the judgment, the criterion, and a cue for the judgment. The logic can be summarized as a simple syllogism: (*a*) the judgment is correlated with a cue; (*b*) the cue is not correlated with the criterion; therefore (*c*) the judgment is inaccurate. This "use a bad cue" logic is less common than the other three, but it is represented in a few papers in the literature. One example would be Ross *et al.* 1975, in which the researchers demonstrate that a subject's judgments about his or her performance (criterion 1) or the performance of another person (criterion 2) were correlated with initial false feedback that subjects were given about performance (this establishes term (*a*) of the syllogism). However, the initial feedback (cue) is not correlated with actual performance (criterion), thus establishing term (*b*) of the syllogism. Consideration of these two premises yields the conclusion (*c*) that the judgment is inaccurate. Wells and his colleagues (Lindsay and Wells 1981, Wells and Lindsay 1985, Wells *et al.* 1981) have used the same logic to conclude that mock-jurors' evaluations of eyewitness testimony are inaccurate. In their research mock-jurors relied on cues such as the eyewitness's confidence or the completeness of the eyewitness's reports of trivial details, both uncorrelated with eyewitness accuracy, to evaluate eyewitness testimony.

A fourth logic ("miss a good cue") is closely related to the third logic and, again, involves consideration of the three terms judgment, cue, criterion (see Fig. 8.4). In this case the syllogism has slightly different premises: (*a*) the judgment is not correlated with a cue; (*b*) the cue is correlated with the

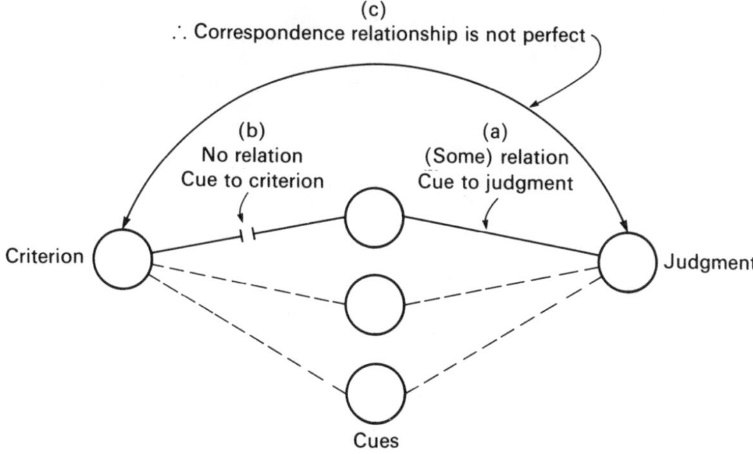

Fig. 8.3. Logic 3: "Use a bad cue."

criterion; therefore, (*c*) the judgment is inaccurate. Many of the experiments which have studied subjects' under-use of base-rate information (cue) conclude that subjects' judgments are not correlated with the base-rate (establishing (*a*) of the syllogism). However, normative model analysis or empirical measurements imply that the base-rate cue information is correlated with the judgment criterion (term (*b*) of the syllogism). Thus the researchers conclude that subjects' judgments are inaccurate (e.g. Nisbett and Borgida 1975).

Shortcomings of research on accuracy of social judgment

Some difficulties arise because the experimenter and the subject do not agree with one another on the task representation. In extreme cases, a subject may understand the task as requiring judgments concerning one criterion value, but the experimenter understands the task as requiring judgments of a different criterion. If experimenter and subject do not agree on the nature of the task (for example, the criterion that is the target of judgment or the goals of optimal or efficient performance), then it would be foolish to draw conclusions about accuracy (Berkeley and Humphreys 1982, Miller and Cantor 1982). The clearest examples of this difficulty arise when the criterion is complex or unfamiliar. For example, some studies should not be cited in support of the conclusion that subjects' judgments of a correlation between target properties are inaccurate because the experimenter's concept of the criterion (Pearson's r) and the subjects' (com-

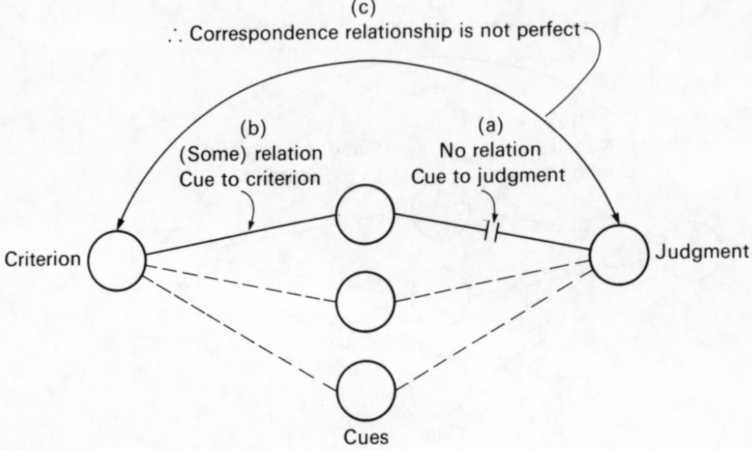

Fig. 8.4. Logic 4: "Miss a good cue."

monsense or instruction-based notion of a relationship) are not the same (cf. Crocker 1981, Beyth-Marom 1982, Oakes 1982, Wright and Murphy 1984). Even tasks designed to simplify the prediction of a future event to a degree that rodents and birds would understand them in the same fashion as human subjects have revealed greater agreement among subjects of whatever species than between human subjects and human experimenters (Estes 1976, Lee 1971). But the typical failures to provide for subject–experimenter agreement on task definition simply occur because the experimenter does not present clear instructions, explaining to the subject the nature of the criterion for accuracy that will be applied when the subject's responses are analyzed.

The literature on optimal statistical decision-making provides two sets of concepts that may help guide theoretical and empirical research on the subject's goals and task representation. First, there is the technical decision theory literature on loss functions and the optimization of judgment performance (e.g. DeGroot 1970). The vocabulary and techniques that have been developed by Bayesian statisticians to describe and to reason about the costs and payoffs associated with decisions may be useful as the basis for a theory of motivation in human judgment tasks. Interestingly, the foundations of Bayesian methods for the elicitation of subjective probabilities explicitly recognize the inseparability of probabilities and values (Ramsey 1931, Jeffrey 1983). The second set of concepts is Einhorn and Hogarth's (1981) generalization of the competence–performance distinction from psycholinguistics to judgment. Social psychologists and other judgment researchers have been far too quick to draw conclusions about the limits of competence from findings that are more properly characterized as describing one (possible) level of performance.

Occasionally it is possible that the experimenter has chosen a "degenerate task" where no cues are available to the subject that would allow "above-chance" levels of performance. For example, an experimenter might ask a subject to judge another person's trait, mood, or attitude but inadvertently not provide cues that could support a judgment at any level of accuracy. Again, it would be foolish to draw conclusions about accuracy from a judgment task in which all performance is forced to the "floor" of accuracy levels.

Sometimes difficulties arise because the subject's judgment response is not easy to measure or summarize. Recent examples of this difficulty occur in assessments of the accuracy of estimates of the probability that an event will occur or the probability that a subject's first-order judgment is correct. "Calibration" methods have been developed to assess the accuracy of probability estimates following an objectivist logic. The criterion is defined as a relative frequency of occurrence of target events in well-specified classes of events. An individual's judgments are aggregated according to the confidence or probability assigned to each judgment and then compared with the corresponding relative frequencies. But, as might be expected, the methods require many judgments to be elicited from each subject under complex, systematically varying task conditions, and the analysis depends on restrictive assumptions (Yates 1982).

All the "logics" assume that the criterion which subjects have been asked to judge "exists" independently of the subject's judgment. However, it is possible that certain properties (personality traits, for example) are psychological "unicorns" that appear in the fairytales of some theoreticians but do not exist as objects for judgment in the real world outside the mind. Alternatively, some logics assume that if one property is possessed by a target individual, then other properties are impossible. Again, for certain properties this may be moot. For example, it is plausible that a person could possess the properties of "sadness" and "joy" simultaneously.

Three of the logics assume that the criterion can be reliably and validly measured by the researcher. However, practical circumstances (for example, where the researcher studies judgments of future behavior but cannot observe the behavior) and measurement problems (for example, the interminable controversies over the definition and measurement of emotions, personality traits, and attitudes) may be obstacles to the establishment of criterion values.

A special class of difficulties which has been prominent recently involves the use of a normative model to calculate a criterion value that is used in a judgment task. Edwards (1968) and his students (e.g. Tversky and Kahneman 1974) have used this approach extensively, calculating a normative criterion value based on the assumption that a mathematical model can be applied to the domain of judgment. We have argued elsewhere (Hastie 1983) that the use of normative models to establish a criterion for accurate judgment can be justified, but the justification is laborious and the procedure is certainly no short cut to easy conclusions about accuracy.

Furthermore, Introductions and Discussions to the contrary, normative model criterion values are almost never calculated in research by social psychologists (Locksley *et al.* 1980 may be the sole exception; see also Rasinski *et al.* 1985).

Other difficulties arise when the normative model does not assume the form of a precisely specified mathematical or logical formulation. For example, some researchers (Kelley 1973; Jones and McGillis 1976) have provided informal "logical baseline" models that might be used to provide a criterion for judgment accuracy. Other investigators have suggested that scientific research by psychologists has yielded laws of behavior that provide normative criteria to assess the accuracy of judgments (e.g. Nisbett and Wilson 1977). We are dubious of the utility of the latter two approaches in research on accuracy.

There are problems with the analysis of accuracy that arise at the level of data analysis. For example, some researchers have attempted to draw conclusions about the accuracy of an individual's judgments from averages of grouped data (e.g. Locksley *et al.* 1980; see Smith and Miller 1978 for a related criticism of Nisbett and Bellows 1977). However, it is difficult, and often impossible, to draw conclusions about an individual's performance from grouped data (e.g. Estes 1956, Stevens 1955).

Researchers studying accuracy are often concerned with "differential accuracy". It is important to keep in mind the entities or conditions that are being compared to determine whether there is differential accuracy. Cronbach's two disciplines of scientific psychology (1975) are still not talking to one another in the area of social judgment. Some researchers focus on individual differences in accuracy, comparing one subject's level of accuracy with another subject's. Other investigators are interested in differential accuracy of performance for a single subject across conditions. What we need is a framework for the assessment of accuracy that applies in a uniform fashion to individual differences and differential performance within the individual across conditions. We also suspect (perhaps a bias from our roots in experimental psychology) that differential accuracy of an individual's judgments across conditions is a better focus of research, at present, than individual differences across subjects. For example, research on judgment of emotional state and lie detection, using verbal and nonverbal cues, has emphasized individual differences across subjects over differential accuracy across conditions (Hall 1978, DePaulo *et al.* 1982). An examination of this literature, however, suggests that individual differences in accuracy are much smaller and less reliable than differential accuracy within an individual across conditions of judgment.

Perhaps the worst habit of researchers studying accuracy in social judgment is the tendency to apply the logics with "all-or-none null hypotheses". For example, logics 2, 3, and 4 (Figs. 8.2, 8.3, 8.4) are usually applied to test the "null hypothesis" of perfect accuracy. If the subject is inconsistent, misses a good cue, or uses a bad cue, the researcher concludes that the subject's judgments are *not perfectly accurate.* On the other hand, the "null hypothesis" that accompanies logic 1 is typically that the subject is performing with zero or chance accuracy. There may be some conditions under which these extreme conclusions, perfect accuracy or zero accuracy, would be of interest. However, it is usually obvious even before data are collected in most social judgment tasks that subjects will be neither perfectly accurate nor totally inaccurate, but that their performance will fall somewhere in between. The goal of empirical analysis should be to determine where subjects' performance falls in the middle between the two extremes. Logic 1 will be the most useful in providing an assessment of the relative degrees of accuracy.

Accuracy and epistemology

How is our analysis of the concept of accuracy related to philosophical discussions of the nature of knowledge and the methods of epistemology? Although our goal in this essay is to review current practices by social psychologists, our discussion draws on philosophical analyses of epistemology and cognition. We have attempted to avoid some of the major problems for philosophical analysis by restricting our subject matter to simple individual subject–predicate propositions, by excluding categorical generalizations across sets of individuals, and by excluding complex counterfactual or self-referential statements. This keeps us out of some philosophical traps, but there are still fundamental problems.

First, our analysis works best in cases in which there is a true criterion. In the examples we considered where the criterion was calculated from a normative model or where contradiction between judgments (logic 2) was the basis to infer (in)accuracy, our discussion was obviously less fluent. Clearly, our correspondence approach to epistemology is inept at handling methods to assess accuracy that are based on a coherence approach (cf. Prior 1967 and White 1967). The solution that we advocate is to restrict the use of the label "accuracy" for analyses that follow the correspondence logics, and deal with judgments that refer to events in the real world. The coherence approaches are useful, but yield an assessment of the consistency or *validity* of judgments, and these judgments do not necessarily refer to reality.

Second, even with our restrictions on the types of simple judgment that will be considered in the present review, the judgments of the subject and the researcher are represented (in our analysis) as propositions (note that we count a subject's mark on a rating scale or list of responses as a proposition, asserting a "predicate" about a target "subject"). Again, we are caught in considerations of the meanings of these propositions that are inextricably tied to concepts of coherence as well as of correspondence. Even if we attempt the detour of interpreting the researcher's judgment as a description of operations to measure a property of the target individual, this description must get a meaning from somewhere, and we are back in the net of coherence considerations. We do not see an easy way out of this complexity.

Third, when all the technical distinctions are made and the studies reviewed, we end up with a simple competition between the subject's judgment and the researcher's judgment. Why do we say that the researcher's judgment wins? Because there is more justification for the researcher's judgment (see Pappas 1979 for a thorough discussion of justification). Fortunately, in most research on social judgment even the subjects agree, when the basis for the researcher's judgment is explained, that the researcher has more reasons and better reasons for his or her judgment. What constitute reasons for a judgment?

(*a*) The researcher often has *more evidence* and *better evidence* on which to base his or her judgment than is available to the subject. For example, in research on personality judgment, the researcher often has direct measurements of the target's personality, self-reports by the targets, ratings by acquaintances who know the target well, etc., while the subject makes judgments based on a few cues that are indirectly related to the target's personality. In this (most common) case, subjects are usually willing to grant that the researcher's judgment is better justified than are their judgments.

(*b*) The researcher often uses a measurement *method* of proven *reliability and accuracy*. For example, research on personality judgments sometimes compares the subject's judgment with the results of a personality assessment procedure (a written test) that has been shown to yield reliable, consistent, and accurate measurements (to some degree). Again, subjects themselves often acknowledge the superiority of the conclusions based on an established assessment method.

(*c*) The researcher often uses a measurement method that is *embedded in a system* of statements about human psychology that is internally consistent and has been validated by tests of its implications for behavior in settings unrelated to the current judgment task. Thus, for the personality judgment example, the researcher may justify his or her judgment with reference to a theory of personality that is supported by prior scientific research.

(*d*) Finally, the researcher can usually muster more *social support* for the validity of his or her judgments, or for the theory or method that underlies them, than can the subject (Wittgenstein 1953, Kuhn 1977, Rorty 1979).

It should be clear that a researcher can justify his or her criterion values along the lines suggested by epistemologists and in a manner that will convince subjects that the researcher's criterion is correct. However, few social psychologists take seriously the problem of justifying a criterion – indeed, few even measure a criterion or attempt to apply logic 1.

Recommendations for better practices in research on the accuracy of social judgment

This chapter has taken a negative stance and contains mostly criticism of current and past practice. What can we recommend to improve future research practices?

We recommend general acceptance of a simple set of definitions, perhaps those we presented at the start of this chapter, for terms such as "accuracy", "bias", and "error".

We recommend the use of the direct comparison logic 1 in research on accuracy because of its straightforward character, and because of the technical developments available to embellish that logic. Furthermore, of the four logics it is closest to permitting an assessment of degree of accuracy or allowing the decomposition of an overall accuracy score into theoretically meaningful components. The extremist version of this recommendation would be a prohibition of all research on accuracy that does not include a specific, independently verified criterion with a report of individual subjects' judgment deviation scores or error rates.

We urge researchers to avoid the "all-or-none null hypothesis" reasoning that has dominated research on accuracy in social judgment. Rather, we exhort researchers to adopt a "parametric" attitude towards research on accuracy, and to attempt to assess degrees of accuracy rather than to quibble over perfect accuracy or total error.

References

American Heritage Dictionary (1983), 2nd college edition. Boston: Houghton–Mifflin.

Berkeley, D. and Humphreys, P. (1982). Structuring decision problems and the "bias heuristic". *Acta Psychologica* 50: 201–52.

Beyth-Marom, R. (1982). Perception of correlation reexamined. *Memory and Cognition* 10: 511–19.

Bourne, E. (1977). Can we describe an individual's personality? Agreement on stereotype versus individual attributes. *Journal of Personality and Social Psychology* 35: 863–72.

Christensen-Szalanski, J. J. J. and Beach, L. R. (1984). The citation bias: fad and fashion in the decision literature. *American Psychologist* 1984: 75–8.

Crocker, J. (1981). Judgment of covariation by social perceivers. *Psychological Bulletin* 90: 272–92.

Cronbach, L. J. (1955). Processes affecting scores on "understanding of others" and "assumed similarity". *Psychological Bulletin* 52: 177–93.

Cronbach, L. J. (1975). Beyond the two disciplines of scientific psychology. *American Psychologist* 30: 116–27

DeGroot, M. H. (1970). *Optimal statistical decisions*. New York: McGraw-Hill.

DePaulo, B. M., Lassiter, G. D., and Stone, J. I. (1982). Attentional determinants of success at detecting deception and truth. *Personality and Social Psychology Bulletin* 8: 273–9.

Dornbusch, S. M., Hastorf, A. H., Richardson, S. A., Muzzy, R. E., and Vreeland, R. S. (1965). The perceiver and the perceived: their relative influence on categories of interpersonal perception. *Journal of Personality and Social Psychology* 1: 434–40.

Dudycha, L. W. and Naylor, J. C. (1966). The effect of variations in the cue *R* matrix upon the obtained policy equation of judges. *Educational and Psychological Measurement* 26: 583–603.

Edwards, W. (1968). Conservatism in human information processing. In B. Kleinmuntz (ed.), *Formal representation of human judgment*. New York: Wiley.

Einhorn, H. J. and Hogarth, R. M. (1981). Rationality and the sanctity of competence. *The Behavioral and Brain Sciences* 4: 334–5.

Einhorn, H. J., Hogarth, R. M., and Klempner, E. (1977). Quality of group judgment. *Psychological Bulletin* 84: 158–72.

Estes, W. K. (1956). The problem of inference from curves based on group data. *Psychological Bulletin* 53: 134–40.

Estes, W. K. (1976). The cognitive side of probability learning. *Psychological Review* 83: 37–64

Garner, W. R. (1962). *Uncertainty and structure as psychological concepts*. New York: Wiley.

Hall, J. A. (1978). Gender effects in decoding nonverbal cues. *Psychological Bulletin* 85: 845–57.

Hastie, R. (1983). Social inference. *Annual Review of Psychology* 34: 511–42.

Hursch, C. J., Hammond, K. R., and Hursch, J. L. (1964). Some methodological considerations in multiple-cue probability studies. *Psychological Review* 71: 42–60.

Jeffrey, R. C. (1983). *The logic of decision*, 2nd edn. University of Chicago Press.

Jones, E. E. and McGillis, D. (1976). Correspondent inferences and the attribution cube: a comparative reappraisal. In J. H. Harvey, W. J. Ickes, and R. F. Kidd (eds.), *New directions in attribution research*, vol. 1. Hillsdale, NJ: Lawrence Erlbaum.

Jones, E. E. and Nisbett, R. E. (1972). The actor and the observer: divergent perceptions of the causes of behavior. In E. E. Jones, D. E. Kanouse, H. H. Kelley, R. E. Nisbett, S. Valins, and B. Weiner (eds.), *Attribution: perceiving the causes of behavior*. Morristown, NJ: General Learning Press.

Kelley, H. H. (1973). The processes of causal attribution. *American Psychologist* 28: 107–28.

Kraut, R. E. (1978). Verbal and nonverbal cues in the perception of lying. *Journal of Personality and Social Psychology* 36: 380–91.

Kruglanski, A. W. and Ajzen, I. (1983). Bias and error in human judgment. *European Journal of Social Psychology* 13: 1–44

Kuhn, T. S. (1977). *The essential tension: selected studies in scientific and traditional change*. University of Chicago Press.

Lee, W. (1971). *Decision theory and human behavior*. New York: Wiley.

Lindsay, R. C. L. and Wells, G. L. (1981). Can people detect eyewitness identification accuracy within and across situations? *Journal of Applied Psychology* 66: 79–89.

Locksley, A., Borgida, E., Brekke, N., and Hepburn, C. (1980). Sex stereotypes and social judgment. *Journal of Personality and Social Psychology* 39: 821–31.

McNichol, D. (1972). *A primer of signal detection theory*. London: Allen & Unwin.

Miller, G. A. and Cantor, N. (1982). Review of Nisbett and Ross 1980. *Social Cognition* 1: 83–93.

Monson, J. C. and Snyder, M. (1977). Actors, observers, and the attribution process. *Journal of Experimental Social Psychology* 13: 89–111.

Nisbett, R. E. and Bellows, N. (1977). Verbal reports about causal influences on social judgments: private access versus public theories. *Journal of Personality and Social Psychology* 35: 613–24.

Nisbett, R. E. and Borgida, E. (1975). Attribution and the psychology of prediction. *Journal of Personality and Social Psychology* 32: 932–43.

Nisbett, R. E. and Ross, L. (1980). *Human inference: strategies and shortcomings of social judgment*. Englewood Cliffs, NJ: Prentice-Hall.

Nisbett, R. E. and Wilson, T. D. (1977). Telling more than we can know: verbal reports on mental processes. *Psychological Review* 84: 231–59.

Oakes, M. (1982). Intuiting strength of association from a correlation coefficient. *British Journal of Psychology* 73: 51–6.

Pappas, G. (ed.) (1979): *Justification and knowledge*. Dordrecht: Reidel.

Postman, L. and Tolman, E. C. (1959). Brunswik's probabilistic functionalism. In S. Koch (ed.), *Psychology: a study of a science*, vol. 1. New York: McGraw-Hill.

Prior, A. N. (1967). Correspondence theory of truth. In P. Edwards (ed.), *The encyclopedia of philosophy*, vol. 2. New York: Macmillan.

Ramsey, F. P. (1931). *The foundations of mathematics and other logical essays.* London: Kegan Paul.

Rasinski, K. A., Crocker, J., and Hastie, R. (1985). Another look at sex stereotypes and social judgments: an analysis of the social perceiver's use of subjective probabilities. *Journal of Personality and Social Psychology* 49: 317–26.

Rorty, R. (1979). *Philosophy and the mirror of nature.* Princeton: Princeton University Press.

Ross, L., Amabile, T. M., and Steinmetz, J. L. (1977). Social roles, social control, and biases in social perception processes. *Journal of Personality and Social Psychology* 35: 485–94.

Ross, L., Greene, D., and House, P. (1977). The false consensus phenomenon: an attributional bias in self-perception and social perception processes. *Journal of Experimental Social Psychology* 13: 279–301.

Ross, L., Lepper, M. R., and Hubbard, M. (1975). Perseverance in self-perception and social perception: biased attributional processes in the debriefing paradigm. *Journal of Personality and Social Psychology* 32: 880–92.

Smith E. R. and Miller, F. D. (1978). Limits on perception of cognitive processes: a reply to Nisbett and Wilson. *Psychological Review* 85: 355–62.

Stevens, S. S. (1955). On the averaging of data. *Science* 121: 113–16.

Swets, J. A. and Pickett, R. M. (1982). *Evaluation of diagnostic systems.* New York: Academic Press.

Taylor, S. E. and Fiske, S. T. (1975). Point-of-view and perceptions of causality. *Journal of Personality and Social Psychology* 32: 439–45.

Tversky, A. and Kahneman, D. (1974). Judgment under uncertainty: heuristics and biases. *Science* 185: 1124–31.

Wells, G. L., Ferguson, T. J., and Lindsay, R. C. L. (1981). The tractability of eyewitness confidence and its implications for triers of fact. *Journal of Applied Psychology* 66: 688–96.

Wells, G. L. and Lindsay, R. C. L. (1985). Methodological notes on the accuracy–confidence relation in eyewitness identifications. *Journal of Applied Psychology* 70: 413–19.

White, A. R. (1967). Coherence theory of truth. In P. Edwards (ed.), *The encyclopedia of philosophy*, vol. 2. New York: Macmillan.

Wittgenstein, L. (1953). *Philosophical investigations*, tr. G. E. M. Anscombe. New York: Macmillan.

Wright, J. C. and Murphy, G. L. (1984). The utility of theories in intuitive statistics: the robustness of theory-based judgments. *Journal of Experimental Psychology: General* 113: 301–22.

Yates, J. F. (1982). External correspondence: decomposition of the mean probability score. *Organizational Behavior and Human Performance* 30: 132–56.

9 On the use of statistical and nonstatistical knowledge: a problem-solving approach[1]

Yaacov Trope and Zvi Ginossar

Introduction

One of the oldest issues in social psychology concerns the accuracy of social judgment. Early research on this issue compared people's judgments of a target's characteristics (e.g. emotions, abilities, and traits) to criteria of self-ratings or expert decisions. In the late 1950s and early 1960s, the lack of factual criteria and the growing recognition that the results of such comparisons depend on numerous extraneous factors shifted research efforts from the judgmental outcome to the underlying process (see Tagiuri 1968). The question then became whether the procedures people employ to arrive at a judgment conform to normative models. Over the years, researchers have used logical, statistical, and decision-theoretic models as standards of comparison.

Recently, the accuracy question received a new impetus from Tversky and Kahneman's seminal work on heuristic judgment (1974). Following this lead, social judgment researchers became increasingly interested in the comparison between intuitive social judgment and statistical models (Higgins and Bargh 1987, Nisbett and Ross 1980, Ross 1977, Sherman and Corty 1985). Heuristic judgment research has uncovered an impressive list of statistical principles that are violated by intuitive judgment (Kahneman *et al.* 1982). Moreover, the violations were not haphazard; they were predictable consequences of people's frequent reliance on nonstatistical heuristic rules.

It seems safe to conclude from a decade of heuristic judgment research that statistical rules cannot provide a complete model of intuitive judg-

1 Preparation of this chapter was supported in part by a grant from the Israeli National Academy of Science to the first author.

ment. This does not mean, however, that people are incapable of pure statistical reasoning. Neither does it mean that a set of nonstatistical heuristics can fully account for judgmental phenomena. Heuristic judgment research has convincingly demonstrated that when statistical and nonstatistical rules are pitted against each other, nonstatistical rules often dominate. However, the dominance is not universal. A considerable number of studies have found circumstances where statistical considerations receive equal weight and even override nonstatistical heuristics (see for example Ginossar and Trope 1980, Kruglanski *et al.* 1984; Nisbett *et al.* 1983). These findings suggest the need for a unified conceptual framework that will delineate the determinants of the relative influence of the two kinds of rule. As an initial step in this direction, the present chapter presents a problem-solving analysis of judgment under uncertainty. First, we briefly describe the heuristic judgment approach. We then present the basic tenets of the problem-solving approach and derive from it a set of general principles that determine the application of inferential rules, statistical or nonstatistical. Finally, we describe a series of probabilistic categorization studies demonstrating the operation of these principles, and discuss the implications of the findings for judgment under uncertainty.

Natural assessments and heuristic judgment

Judgmental heuristics are simple rules of thumb used in making predictions or estimations. According to Tversky and Kahneman (1983), judgmental heuristics are based on *natural assessments*, i.e. perceptionlike impressions that are automatically evoked as input information is processed. These assessments include perception of the causes of events, the representativeness of an individual case with respect to a mental model, and the availability of instances of a category. A judgmental heuristic relies on a single natural assessment to produce the required judgment. Thus the representativeness heuristic relies on the natural assessment of the representativeness of a given case with respect to the prototype of a category, the features of the generating process, or the parameters of a population (Tversky and Kahneman 1982a). For example, the probability that a given student is in medical school is estimated according to the similarity between the information about the student and the stereotype of a medical student. The availability heuristic relies on the ease with which specific instances or associations of a concept are brought to mind (Kahneman and Tversky 1972). For instance, the probability of death by fire is estimated according to the ease with which instances of death by fire are retrieved from memory. Related to the availability heuristic is the simulation heuristic that uses as a basis for judgment the ease with which examples or scenarios can be constructed (Kahneman and Tversky 1982). For example, the establishment of an independent Palestinian state is judged in this heuristic by the ease of imagining scenarios leading to this outcome.

In relying exclusively on natural assessments, heuristic judgment reduces cognitive load and allows fast and relatively effortless responses to judgmental demands. Furthermore, the probability of events is frequently correlated with their representativeness, availability, or ease of simulation. For example, an individual is often more likely to belong to a certain category to the extent that his or her characteristics match those of the category prototype. Consequently, in addition to reducing cognitive strain, heuristic judgment ordinarily provides reasonable probability estimates. However, heuristic judgment does not follow the logic of statistics or probability theory. The facts that affect the probability of an event do not always affect its representatives or availability and vice versa. In probability theory, the probability of a conjunction is always equal to, or smaller than, its constituent events. Yet, it is frequently hard to avoid the impression that the conjunctive event is more representative (Tversky and Kahneman 1983). To use Tversky and Kahneman's example, the constituent event of Bjorn Borg losing the first set of the match is less representative but more probable than the conjunctive event of his losing the first set but winning the match. Similarly, it is hard to avoid the impression of greater availability of the conjunctive —— *ing* class of words than the constituent —— *n* – class of words, despite the latter's greater probability of occurrence.

The reliance on natural assessments thus produces systematic violations of statistical rules. Indeed, over the years heuristic judgment research has demonstrated insensitivity to various statistically relevant factors such as base-rates, sample size, and regression effects (see Kahneman *et al.* 1982, Nisbett and Ross 1980). However, this research has also uncovered instances where purely statistical rules are taken into account and even supersede nonstatistical heuristics. Specifically, under certain circumstances judges were found to be responsive to the conjunction rule (Tversky and Kahneman 1983), statistical reliability (Birnbaum and Meller 1983, Trope and Burnstein 1979, Kruglanski *et al.* 1984), regression effects (Kruglanski and Ajzen 1983, Kruglanski *et al.* 1984), sample size, and sample heterogeneity (Nisbett *et al.* 1983).

A decade of intensive research on the utilization of base-rate information in probabilistic categorization tasks exemplifies this state of affairs. Base-rates are important determinants of the probability of events, but have no effect on their representativeness. By experimentally varying base-rates independently of case information, it was therefore possible to pit representativeness against statistical logic. The typical research problem presents a personality description of an individual supposedly drawn from a group of

100 lawyers and engineers. The base-rate frequency of lawyers and engineers in the group is varied: either 70 lawyers and 30 engineers or 30 lawyers and 70 engineers. Based on this information, subjects judge the probability that the personality description belongs to a lawyer or to an engineer.

A considerable number of studies using this and comparable probabilistic categorization problems have demonstrated that people ignore base-rate frequencies and, instead, base their judgments solely on the similarity between case information and the prototypes of the categories under consideration (see reviews in Bar-Hillel 1980, Borigda and Brekke 1981, Sherman and Corty 1985, Tversky and Kahneman 1982b). Further evidence for the role of representativeness in producing the "base-rate fallacy" was provided by studies showing that base-rates were utilized when they reflected an underlying causal process rather than incidental frequencies (see Ajzen 1977, Tversky and Kahneman 1980). Under these circumstances, an outcome was judged probable to the extent that it was representative of the causal process implied by the base-rates.

However, while many studies have demonstrated the neglect of noncausal, frequentistic base-rates, the neglect is by no means universal. Recent research has shown that seemingly minor changes in the problem can produce marked utilization of base-rates even when they convey noncausal, purely incidental base-rate frequencies. Specifically, Birnbaum and Meller (1983) and Fischhoff *et al.* (1979) found that within-subject variation in noncausal base-rates was sufficient to produce considerable use of the base-rates. Furthermore, Manis *et al.*'s (1980) subjects exhibited marked sensitivity to base-rates when making multiple judgments rather than a single judgment. Finally, Ginossar and Trope (1980) found that the utilization of purely frequentistic base-rates depended on the diagnosticity of the case information. As normative consideration would prescribe, the utilization of base-rates increased as the diagnosticity of the individuating information decreased.

Proponents of the heuristic judgment approach interpreted these inconsistent findings in terms of the specific procedural variables used in the different studies (Tversky and Kahneman 1982b). The general limiting conditions on the dominance of representative case information over statistical base-rates thus remained unspecified. In general, by demonstrating consistent violation of statistical rules, the heuristic judgment approach has amply disconfirmed a purely statistical model of judgment. However, in postulating dominance of nonstatistical heuristics, this approach cannot account for systematic variation in the utilization of purely statistical information. This variation suggests the need to integrate both statistical and nonstatistical reasoning within a more comprehensive theory. The requirements for such a theory were outlined by Kruglanski and Ajzen (1983).

Specifically, it should allow for differences in the *specific contents* of statistical and nonstatistical rules but should also describe the *general processes* that govern the application of both kinds of rules. Guided by this distinction, the present contribution adopts a problem-solving approach to judgment under uncertainty. The basic concepts of this approach and their application to probabilistic categorization problems are presented below.

The problem-solving approach

Problem-solving is a goal-directed sequence of mental operations (Newell and Simon 1972). The definition of the goal can be precise (e.g. solving a word puzzle) or vague (e.g. finding a title for a paper). In recent problem-solving theories (Anderson 1982, Newell 1980) the mental operations are represented by condition–action production rules. The conditions of the production rule specify certain features that the available information should fulfill. If the conditions are met, the cognitive act contained in the production rule is performed on the available information. Productions thus transform one state of knowledge about the problem into another. Problem-solving involves a search for a sequence of productions that will transform the initial state of knowledge about the problem into a state where the goal is satisfied (goal state), without violating the constraints imposed on the application of productions. For example, in a chess problem the initial state refers to the starting positions of the pieces on the board, the goal state refers to mating in a certain number of moves, the constraints refer to rules of the game, and the productions refer to stored rules specifying the moves that should be made to achieve the goal, given a certain arrangement of the pieces.

Production rules change on the basis of past experience. Specifically, prior success and failure in achieving the goal may strengthen or weaken production rules. Feedback from prior applications may also lead to the modification of a rule through the addition of restrictions on its application conditions. Newell and Simon (1972) introduced the distinction between algorithmic and heuristic rules. The former are production rules that are guaranteed to provide a solution but are exceedingly effortful. Heuristic rules are relatively simple and easily performed, but do not guarantee successful solutions. Means–end analysis and working backward from the goal state to the initial state are examples of general heuristic principles. The problem-solving approach suggests that, if stored in long-term memory, a production rule, algorithmic or heuristic, will be utilized depending on several general factors. One is the relationship of the production rule to the current goal. The second is the match between the givens of the problem and the application conditions of the rule (Anderson 1982,

Newell 1980). Given the same degree of match, rules whose application conditions refer to more specific informational contents are more likely to be applied (Anderson 1982). Finally, given that production rules are stored in long-term memory, their utilization also depends on their activation. The activation of production rules, in turn, depends on the frequency and recency of their prior activations (accessibility) and on their concurrent activation by situationally available information (Anderson 1982, Higgins and Chaires 1980, Higgins and King 1981, Smith 1984, Wyer and Srull 1980).

The problem-solving approach is readily applicable to judgment under uncertainty. Considering the case of probabilistic categorization problems, the initial state consists of the information presented by the problem, including case information, the source of this information, the method whereby it was obtained, the base-rate frequency, and the method whereby the individual was drawn from the population. The judgmental process can be described as an application of inferential production rules to the information available at the initial state in order to reach the goal state. The goal is defined as finding the correct probabilities that the individual belongs to the specified categories. To this definition, subjects may implicitly add other features such as the requirement that the probability estimates add up to 100 and that they discriminate between the two categories, i.e., that they are not equal. The application of inferential production rules may be constrained by such considerations as the need to arrive at a judgment without using information obtained by means of an inappropriate method or from a biased source.

The representativeness rule can be described as an inferential production system. Its conditions require information about the individual case and information about a target category, causal process, or population parameters. Given a personality description and familiar target categories, the representativeness rule retrieves the stored representations of the categories, compares the features of the personality description to those of the retrieved categorical representations, computes the similarities to the target categories, and translates these similarity assessments into category membership probabilities.

People's intuitive versions of statistical rules can also be represented as inferential productions. Specifically, people may possess a production embodying an intuitive *sampling rule* wherein the probability of an event is equal to its relative frequency in the sampling space. Judged category membership would then depend not only on the relation between the case information and the target categories, but also on the base-rate frequencies of these categories: the higher the base-rate frequency of a target category, the higher the probability that the individual was drawn from that category (see Nisbett *et al.* 1983).

Whereas the heuristic judgment approach postulates exclusive reliance on representativeness, the problem-solving approach views *both* the representativeness rule *and* the intuitive sampling rule as potential candidates for application. Their actual influence on judgment should depend on the same general principles that determine the application of any production rule, namely the availability of the rules in long-term memory, their accessibility, their concurrent activation, their relation to the goal, and their application conditions. The following sections discuss in greater detail these problem-solving principles, and describe a research program designed to study their influence on the solution of probabilistic categorization problems. All of the experiments used noncausal, purely frequentistic base-rates and representative, concrete case information. Furthermore, base-rates were always manipulated between subjects. Yet the use of the base-rates was predicted to vary as a function of the general problem-solving factors.

The possession and activation of inferential rules

The possession of an intuitive sampling rule

Our initial research attempted to relate the solution of probabilistic categorization problems to the possession of a sampling rule (Ginossar and Trope 1980). Subjects were presented with completely random processes (e.g. drawing a marble from a well-shuffled urn) and were asked to estimate the probability that a randomly sampled case (whose description was not provided) belongs to the alternative categories (e.g. two different colors) given the base-rate frequencies of those categories.

Since the randomness of the process and the sample space were fully transparent and individuating case information entirely absent, subjects' estimates can be viewed as a test of the most elementary comprehension of the sampling rule. It turned out that most subjects (70 per cent of high school graduates) based their estimates on the base-rate frequencies, but a sizable minority did not. More important, this finding suggested to us that the neglect of base-rates in past research was partly due to the fact that some subjects simply did not possess an intuitive sampling rule. To test this possibility, we presented subjects with probabilistic categorization tasks that included both base-rates and individuating case information. As the problem-solving analysis predicts, we found that subjects who possessed the sampling rule exhibited greater utilization of noncausal base-rates than subjects who did not possess the rule.

Accessibility (prior activation) of inferential rules

Given that the majority of subjects possess an intuitive sampling rule, the problem-solving analysis suggests that the actual application of the rule depends on its accessibility. Rule accessibility, in turn, varies as a function of the rule's prior and concurrent activation (Anderson 1982, Higgins and Chaires 1980, Higgins and King 1981, Wyer and Srull 1980). To study the effect of prior rule activation on the solution of probabilistic categorization problems, we varied the opportunity for prior application of the sampling rule (see Ginossar and Trope 1987, experiment 1). Specifically, subjects solved the same *test problem* after initially solving *prior problems* containing either diagnostic or nondiagnostic case information. The rationale for this prior diagnosticity manipulation was based on our earlier finding that subjects ignore base-rates when presented with diagnostic case information, but utilize base-rates when presented with nondiagnostic case information (Ginossar and Trope 1980). Nondiagnostic case information apparently leads subjects to shift from exclusive reliance on the representativeness rule to taking into account the sampling rule. We therefore assumed that the sampling rule is likely to be activated by solving prior problems with nondiagnostic case information (nondiagnostic prior problems) but not by solving prior problems with diagnostic case information (diagnostic prior problems). On the basis of this assumption we expected that the base-rates of the test problem would be ignored after solving prior diagnostic problems but utilized after solving nondiagnostic prior problems.

The lawyer–engineer problem originally used by Kahneman and Tversky (1973) served as the test problem. The problem read as follows:

> Several psychologists interviewed a group of people. The group included 30% (70%) engineers and 70% (30%) lawyers. The psychologists prepared a brief summary of their impression of each interviewee. The following description was drawn randomly from the set of descriptions:
> Dan is 45 years old. He is married and has four children. He is usually conservative, careful, and ambitious. He has no interest in politics and social problems. Most of his free-time is devoted to his many hobbies that include home carpentry, sailing and mathematical puzzles.

On the basis of this information, subjects judged the probability that Dan is a lawyer or engineer. Past research has shown that the personality description in this problem is diagnostic with respect to the lawyer–engineer categories. Before receiving the test-problem, subjects solved either two nondiagnostic prior problems or two diagnostic prior problems. The prior problems were identical to the test problem except for the personality descriptions. The nondiagnostic prior problems contained the following personality descriptions:

Joseph is 30 years old. He is married and has no children. He is highly competent and motivated. Joseph promises to be successful in his field. He is well liked by his colleagues.

and

Benjamin is 35 years old, married, and has one child. He likes orderly systems where each item finds its appropriate place. Benjamin is argumentative, ambitious, and his oral and written expression are excellent. He devotes much of his free time to his hobbies – construction of airplane and ship models.

The diagnostic problems presented the following personality descriptions:

Zev is 39 years old. He is married and has two children. He is politically active. Zev's favorite hobby is the collection of rare books. He is competitive, argumentative, and has excellent oral ability.

and

Moses is 37 years old and has two children. He likes orderly systems in which each item has its proper place. Moses is accurate, introverted, and does not particularly enjoy social contacts. His style of expression is laconic and simple. His main hobby is photography.

These descriptions were selected on the basis of extensive pretesting showing that the diagnostic descriptions discriminate well between the two categories whereas the nondiagnostic descriptions do not.

Let us consider first the solutions of the prior problems. Replicating our earlier findings (Ginossar and Trope 1980), base-rates produced significant effects on the solution of nondiagnostic prior problems, but not on the solution of diagnostic prior problems. These results indicate that diagnosticity had the intended effect on prior utilization of base-rates, but they are also of theoretical interest in and of themselves. Specifically, the problem-solving analysis would suggest that the representativeness rule was insufficient for solving the nondiagnostic problems. Consequently, these problems may have invoked a search for an alternative inferential rule which, in turn, may have increased the likelihood of retrieving and applying the sampling rule.

For the present purposes, however, the importance of these prior solutions is that the prior diagnosticity manipulation induced differential prior application of the sampling rule. The rule was initially applied by subjects who solved nondiagnostic prior problems, but not by subjects who solved diagnostic prior problems. Hence only subjects who solved nondiagnostic prior problems should utilize the base-rates in solving the subsequent test problem. The probability estimates for the test problem fully confirmed this prediction. Subjects who solved diagnostic prior problems essentially ignored the base-rates. Their mean estimates of the engineer probability given the 30 per cent and 70 per cent engineer base-rates were .70 and .73, respectively, thus replicating the base-rate fallacy. In contrast, subjects who initially solved nondiagnostic problems displayed marked sensitivity to the base-rates on the test problem. Their mean estimates for the 30 per cent and 70 per cent base-rates were .59 and .78, respectively.

These findings suggest that the solution of base-rate problems, like the solution of any problem, depends on the prior activation or accessibility of the relevant production rules. Ordinarily, the representativeness rule may have an advantage in this respect and is therefore more likely to be applied to the problem at hand. However, the present study shows that an increase in the accessibility of the sampling rule increases the probability of its application. Our earlier study (Ginossar and Trope 1980) found that people are more likely to utilize base-rate information if they know or comprehend the sampling rule than if they do not. The present study adds to that finding in showing that the utilization of base-rates also depends on the accessibility of the rule.

The concurrent activation of the sampling rule

Theoretically, the retrieval of a production rule depends not only on its prior activation but also on its concurrent or situational activation. Certain elements in the initial state may be associated with the conditions of the production rule. To the extent that these elements are situationally *salient*, they are more likely to activate the corresponding production rule. The implication for the solution of base-rate problems is straightforward: the greater the salience of base-rate information, the greater the likelihood that the sampling rule will be activated and actually applied in solving the problem.

In the probabilistic categorization problems used in past research, base-rates were embedded in the introductory statements leading to the detailed characterization of the individual case. This format may have encouraged subjects to disregard the base-rate and focus on the case information. To test this potential advantage of case information over base-rates, we asked our subjects to judge each of the givens of the original version of the lawyer–engineer problem as to whether it is relevant to the required probability estimates and, if relevant, whether it is indicative of a high or a low probability. More specifically, subjects were asked to make two judgments: first, to cross out any word that does not help in estimating the probability that the described person is a lawyer or engineer; second, to mark each of the remaining words either with an L, if it indicates a high probability of the person being a lawyer, or with an E, if it indicates a high probability of the person being an engineer.

The results were striking. All of the 60 subjects participating in the experiment totally ignored base-rate information. None of them even crossed out this item as irrelevant to the required judgment! Instead, subjects responded only to the personality description. Within this description, some items were judged irrelevant, others as indicative of either a lawyer or an engineer, but none ignored by more than a small minority of the subjects. For example, the item "Dan is 45 years old. He is married and has four children" was crossed as irrelevant by 52 subjects, whereas the fact that Dan's hobby was math puzzles was crossed as irrelevant only by 9 subjects. However, both these items, the highly relevant as well as the highly irrelevant, were ignored by very few subjects (3 and 6 respectively).

It appears, then, that subjects assumed that the personality characteristics, whether relevant or irrelevant to the solution, are the only givens of the problem. The base-rates were seen as an incidental part of the cover story about the two professions. Consequently, the personality description clearly enjoyed a salience advantage over the base-rates. The question, then, is whether an elimination of this advantage of case information will increase the use of base-rate information. To answer this question we presented the lawyer–engineer problem in two formats. One was the original Kahneman and Tversky (1973) format. The other, modified format presented exactly the same base-rate and case information as the original format. However, to equalize the salience of base-rate and case information, the information was presented as a list of distinct statements (see Ginossar and Trope 1987, experiment 2). In this list format, the problem read as follows:

The following is a list of facts on the basis of which you will be asked to estimate the probability that a certain person (Dan) is a lawyer or an engineer:

(1) He belongs to a group composed of 30% (70%) lawyers and 70% (30%) engineers.
(2) He was drawn randomly from the group.
(3) He is 45 years old.
(4) He is married and has four children.
(5) He is usually conservative, cautious, and ambitious.
(6) He has no interest in politics and social problems.
(7) Most of his free time is devoted to his hobbies.
(8) His hobbies include home carpentry, sailing and math problems.

The difference in the format of the problem strongly affected subjects' probability estimates. When presented in the original format, the base-rates produced a negligible effect on estimates of the probability that the described person is an engineer, *M*'s = .69 and .71, for the 30 per cent and 70 per cent engineer base-rates. These results once more replicate previous demonstrations of the base-rate fallacy with the lawyer–engineer problem. However, when presented as a distinct item, base-rates had a powerful effect, *M*'s = .54 and .74, for the 30 per cent and 70 per cent base-rates of engineer.

These results corroborate our predictions. When embedded in the introduction, base-rates apparently drew little attention and therefore could not activate the sampling rule. Consequently, judgment was entirely dominated by the representativeness rule, in that the probability that a person resembling the prototypical engineer remained high even when the base-rate of this category was low. In contrast, the presentation of the problem in a list format increased the salience of base-rates and, thereby, the likelihood of the sampling rule being activated. Indeed, even though the personality description resembled the prototypical engineer, subjects were uncertain about the person's categorization (*M* = .54) when the base-rate of the engineer category was low. In sum, the results of the experiments reported thus far are consistent with the problem-solving view that the solution of probabilistic categorization problems depends on the retrieval of relevant production rules. Like the application of any production rule, the application of the sampling rule depends on its prior and concurrent activation (Anderson 1982, Higgins and Chaires 1980, Wyer and Srull 1980).

Goal-driven application of inferential rules

The most fundamental property of problem-solving is its goal-directedness (Anderson 1982, Kruglanski 1980). A production rule will be selected for application to the extent that it can achieve the goal. In past base-rate research, the representativeness rule was sufficient to achieve the goal of confident judgment about the individual case. Subjects could therefore rely exclusively on representativeness for finding the solution. However, the problem may pose a goal that renders the representativeness rule insufficient. The problem-solving approach would suggest that under these circumstances problem-solvers will broaden their search to other givens of the problem, including the base-rates. This information will be incorporated into judgment via the sampling rule to the extent that it can lead to the judgmental goal. To test this analysis, we employed the traditional problem-solving paradigm where a goal state is defined and its effect on the utilization of different informational aspects of the initial state is examined. Below we describe two experiments using this general paradigm (see Ginossar and Trope 1987, experiments 3 and 4).

The effect of providing a correct solution

The first experiment sought to assess the effect of providing the correct Bayesian solution for a probabilistic categorization problem on the perceived importance of the various givens of the problem. For this purpose, we employed Tversky and Kahneman's (1972) cab problem – a problem that allows the computation of the correct posterior probability by Bayes' Theorem. Since the correct solution cannot be achieved without utilizing the base-rates, it was predicted that subjects who are provided with the solution will assign greater importance to the base-rates than will subjects who are not provided with the solution. The cab problem was presented to all subjects as a list of six informational items as follows:

(1) In a certain city there are two cab companies, a company operating blue cabs and a company operating green cabs.
(2) The blue cab company operates 85 per cent (15 per cent) of the cabs in the city and the green cab company operates 15 per cent (85 per cent) of the cabs in the city.
(3) A cab was involved in a hit-and-run accident at night.
(4) A person who witnessed the accident later identified the cab as green.
(5) The court tested the ability of the witness to discriminate between blue and green cabs under the same visibility conditions that existed on the night of the accident.
(6) It was found that the witness correctly identified each of the two colors 80 per cent of the time and failed 20 per cent of the time.

Subjects rated the value of the six information items for estimating the probability that the cab involved in the accident was blue or green. Before rating the items, some subjects received the *correct* probability that the cab involved in the accident was green whereas others did not receive the solution. The solution was approximately 50 per cent for the problem with 15 per cent green cabs base-rate and approximately 90 per cent for the problem with 85 per cent green cabs base-rate.

The rating of item (2) served as a measure of the importance assigned to base-rate information, and the rating of item (6) served as a measure of the importance assigned to case information. Subjects who did not receive the correct solution assigned greater value to case information than to base-rate information. This is consistent with past research showing that case information dominates subjects' solutions of the cab problem. However, when presented with the correct solution, subjects rated base-rate information and case information as equally valuable.

These results support the problem-solving assumption that the evaluation of the givens of a problem is goal-driven (Newell 1980). In the present study, the perceived value of case and base-rate data depended on their relationship to the goal. When the representativeness rule was sufficient for reaching the solution, subjects assigned little weight to base-rates – perhaps as they habitually do in many probabilistic categorization problems. However, when the provided solution rendered this rule insufficient, subjects apparently searched for additional means, and were thus more likely to recognize the value of base-rate information for reaching the solution.

The effect of the problem-solver's interests

Everyday problems rarely define a precise goal state. This is particularly true of problems of judgment under uncertainty. However, the problem-solver's interests frequently dictate a preference for a particular judgmental outcome (Kruglanski 1980) and, thereby, guide the application of production rules. In probabilistic categorization problems, the problem-solver will apply the sampling rule if it is instrumental for reaching the desired inference. Suppose, for example, that the problem-solver acts as a lawyer for the company whose cab was identified by the witness in the cab problem. Since the case information (the testimony) cannot advance the lawyer's goal, the lawyer is likely to be sensitized to the base-rates and attempt to use them to draw the desired inference.

To test this prediction, we presented our subjects with two versions of the cab problem. One was the original version of Tversky and Kahneman's cab problem (the "uninvolved version"). The other version (the "involved version") presented the following instructions before asking subjects for their probability estimates: "Imagine that you are a lawyer of the green cab company. Suppose the judge asks you to estimate the probability that a green cab was involved in the accident and to explain your estimate." The involved subjects were asked at this point for their "lawyer judgment" as follows: "What is the probability estimate you will give to the judge that a green cab was involved in the accident?" Subsequently, the involved subjects were asked for their "own judgment" as follows: "What is your own estimate of the probability that a green cab was involved in the accident?"

Our involved subjects' estimates of the probability that a green cab was involved in the accident showed very little sensitivity to the green cabs base-rates, *M*'s = .74 and .78 for the 15 per cent and 85 per cent base-rates, respectively. This finding is consistent with numerous successful demonstrations of the base-rate fallacy with the cab problem (Tversky and Kahneman 1982). However, a different picture emerges from the involved subjects' estimates. Consider first the estimates made under the instruction to take the role of the green cab company lawyer, *M*'s = .43 and .65, for the

15 per cent and 85 per cent base-rates. In compliance with this role, subjects biased their estimates downward. However, these estimates were not only relatively low, but also highly responsive to the base-rate: as lawyers, subjects lowered their estimates twice as much when the base-rate was low than when it was high. Consequently, base-rates had a large effect on lawyer's estimates but not on uninvolved estimates. These results suggest that, in addition to biasing subjects' judgments in a goal-congruent direction, the goal also sensitized subjects to the inferential relevance of base-rates for their probability estimates.

Will subjects retain their sensitivity to base-rates when no longer acting as lawyers for the green company? The mean "own estimates" (*M*'s = .56 and .75, for the 15 per cent and 85 per cent base-rates) were considerably *less* biased downward than the "lawyer's estimates". However, they were no less sensitive to base-rate information. Like the lawyer's estimates, own estimates yielded a stronger base-rate effect than did uninvolved estimates. It seems, then, that after recognizing the inferential relevance of base-rates, subjects continued to utilize them, although the preference that prompted their initial utilization no longer existed.

Together, the results of the studies reported in this section suggest that the reliance on the representativeness rule is conditional on the definition of the goal. When problem-solvers cannot reach their inferential goal by applying this rule, they will look for other means for reaching their goal, including the base-rates. This information will then be utilized to the extent that it can lead, via a stored statistical rule, to the desired inference.

Application conditions of inferential rules

We turn now to the third problem-solving determinant of the selection of production rules, namely their applicability to the givens of the problem. This section describes two studies on the effects of the applicability of the representativeness rule and the sampling rule on the solution of probabilistic categorization problems. The first study increased the likelihood that the sampling rule will be applied by reducing the match between the application conditions of the representativeness rule and the givens of the problem. The second study increased more directly the likelihood that the sampling rule will be applied by increasing the match between its application conditions and the givens of the problem.

Reducing the applicability of the representativeness rule

We noted earlier that the conditions of a production rule include restrictions on its application – restrictions that are added on the basis of feedback from previous applications of the rule (Anderson 1982). One factor that may restrict the application of a production rule to problems of judgment under uncertainty is source unreliability (Birnbaum and Meller 1983, Trope and Burnstein 1979). Specifically, the application of the representativeness rule may be restricted by the unreliability of the source reporting the case information. As a result, source unreliability may increase the likelihood that subjects will consider base-rates and will incorporate them into judgment via the sampling rule. To test this prediction, we constructed three versions of the lawyer–engineer problem varying in the reliability of the source of the personality description (see Ginossar and Trope 1987, experiment 5). The source was either (1) a group of trained psychologists who interviewed the target person, as in the original version of the problem, (2) a student who interviewed the target person in one of the first meetings of a course in interviewing, or (3) a palm-reader who examined the target person's palm.

As a check on the reliability manipulation, a group of subjects read only the personality description from the lawyer–engineer problem and were asked to estimate the probability that the description was true given that it was reported by each source. As intended, the judged probability of the personality description being true was highest when the source was a group of trained psychologists ($M = .78$), lowest when the source was a palm-reader ($M = .31$), and intermediate when the source was a beginning interviewer ($M = .59$). The three full versions of the lawyer–engineer problem were presented to new subjects, who judged the probability that the described person is an engineer. We found that base-rates were neglected only in the original version of the problem, the version where the personality description was reported by trained psychologists. When the sources were less reliable, base-rates had a strong impact. Specifically, the mean judged probabilities for the 30 per cent and 70 per cent base-rates of engineer were .59 and .74 respectively when the source was a beginning interviewer, and .47 and .69 respectively when the source was a palm-reader.

This study provides further evidence that the representativeness of case information is not the sole determinant of probability judgments. The representativeness of the personality description remained the same, yet the utilization of base-rates varied depending on source reliability. This result is readily explainable in problem-solving terms. Specifically, the unreliability of the source created a mismatch between the application conditions of the representativeness rule and the givens of the problem. This mismatch prevented subjects from applying the representativeness rule, and instead prompted a search for other informational bases for judgment. This search, in turn, increased the likelihood that base-rates will be attended to and will actually affect judgment via the sampling rule.

Enhancing the applicability of the sampling rule

The problem-solving analysis suggests that the sampling rule will be applied to the extent that its application conditions match the givens of the probabilistic categorization problem. The study we conducted to test this prediction was based on the assumption that the application conditions of the sampling rule are closely matched by games where the sample space and the repeatability of traits is highly transparent (Ginossar and Trope 1987, experiment 6). Specifically, we contrasted the original versions of the lawyer–engineer and cab problems with versions that framed exactly the same information as games of chance.

The game of chance version of the lawyer–engineer problem read as follows:

> In a certain card game, one side of each card indicates the profession of an individual and the other indicates personal information about him. The profession engineer is indicated on 30% (70%) of the cards and the profession lawyer on 70% (30%) of the cards.

Subjects were asked to imagine that a card was randomly drawn from the deck and were then presented with a personality description identical to that presented in the original version. On the basis of this information, subjects estimated the probability that the other side of the card indicated the lawyer or engineer profession.

The game of chance version of the cab problem read as follows:

> Imagine an urn containing colored marbles. Suppose 15% (85%) of the marbles are green and 85% (15%) blue. A person draws a marble randomly from the urn, looks at it, and states that it is green. An eye examination of this person showed that he suffers from color blindness, that he correctly identified green and blue 80% of the time and failed 20% of the time.

On the basis of this information, subjects judged the probability that the marble was green or blue. The results provided strong support for the problem-solving predictions. When presented in their original form, the problems yielded negligible base-rate effects. However, when framed as a game of chance, the same problems yielded robust base-rate effects. Specifically, the mean judged probabilities that the described person is an engineer were .48 and .72 for the 30 per cent and 70 per cent engineer base-rates. Similarly, the mean judged probabilities that the identified cab is green were .41 and .67, for the 15 per cent and 85 per cent green cab base-rates, respectively. It is evident that a difference in framing was sufficient to produce marked utilization of base-rate information.

The results of the two studies described in this section demonstrate that the solution of probabilistic categorization problems, like the solution of any other problem, depends on the applicability of the relevant production rules. In the present case, the impact of base-rate information depended on the applicability of the representativeness rule and the sampling rule. When the applicability of the representativeness rule was reduced or the applicability of the sampling rule enhanced, subjects made extensive use of the base-rates.

General discussion

The heuristic judgment approach has used perception as a metaphor for understanding judgmental processes (Tversky and Kahneman 1974, 1983). Like perceptual illusions, judgmental errors are ascribed to reliance on potentially misleading *natural assessments* that tasks automatically evoke. Thus, probabilistic categorization tasks presumably evoke a case-category representativeness assessment which translates into judgment, irrespective of statistically relevant information such as the base-rate of the target category. Assuming that statistical rules are inherently inferior, the heuristic judgment approach has devoted little attention to the general factors that determine the relative influence of statistical rules and representativeness assessments (Sherman and Corty 1985). Consequently, the heuristic judgment approach could not provide general accounts for systematic variation in the utilization of statistical information (Kruglanski and Ajzen 1983, Nisbett *et al.* 1983).

The problem-solving approach conceptualizes both judgment by representativeness and judgment by statistics as inferential production rules whose application depends on the same general cognitive principles. Our research program systematically investigated the effect of three such principles: the prior and concurrent activation of the rule, its relationship to the goal, and its applicability to the givens of the problem. The experiments employed probabilistic categorization problems in which the case information was always representative and individuating and the base-rates always purely statistical, nonspecific to the individual case, devoid of any causal meaning, and manipulated between subjects. The heuristic judgment approach predicts absolute dominance of case over base-rate information; yet all of the experiments we conducted showed that the use of these sources of information systematically varied as a function of the three problem-solving factors.

Our first study on the activation factor found that prior exposure to problems whose successful solution required application of a statistical rule increased the probability of subsequent application of this rule to a different problem. This experiment adds to our earlier research, showing that the utilization of statistical information depends on people's comprehension of the relevant statistical rule (Ginossar and Trope 1980). It is also consistent with Nisbett *et al.*'s (1983) evidence for the beneficial effects of statistical training on the utilization of statistical information. However, instead of directly coaching our subjects in statistical reasoning, our prior activation experiment merely provided subjects with prior opportunities to apply a statistical rule. This opportunity was sufficient to produce massive utilization of purely statistical information in subsequent problems.

Our second study on the activation factor showed that case information enjoys a clear salience advantage over base-rates. In a subsequent experiment, we manipulated the perceptual salience of the two information sources. As expected, case information carried greater weight when it was more salient; however, when the salience of base-rates and case information was equalized, they carried the same weight in judgment. These results are consistent with Fischhoff *et al.*'s (1979) earlier finding that within-subject variation of base-rates enhanced their utilization (see Fischhoff *et al.* 1979, Birnbaum and Meller 1983). Together, these studies suggest that the influence of statistical rules, like the influence of any production rule, depends on their prior activation (accessibility) and on their concurrent activation (Higgins and Chaires 1980, Higgins and King 1981, Smith 1984, Wyer and Srull 1980).

Two of our experiments demonstrated that the application of inferential rules is goal-driven. One experiment showed that subjects can shift from exclusive reliance on case information to extensive utilization of base-rate information when the latter is necessary for reaching a satisfactory solution. Our second experiment demonstrated marked sensitivity to base-rates when personal interests prescribed a goal whose attainment required the use of base-rates. The superordinate role played by the goal in these experiments suggests that the cognitive processes engaged by judgmental problems can be more aptly described as means that are conditional upon an end than as autonomous impressions of representativeness. These impressions or *natural assessments* may be automatically evoked by case information. However, their actual integration into judgment appears to be contingent on their instrumental value for reaching the desired solution. In this respect, our subjects' inferences seemed to be not only data-driven but also goal-driven (Anderson 1982, Higgins and Bargh 1987, Kruglanski 1980, Kruglanski and Ajzen 1983, Newell 1980, Sherman and Corty 1985, Smith 1984).

According to the problem-solving approach, the application of an inferential rule, statistical or nonstatistical, depends on the perceived match between its application conditions and the givens of the problem (Anderson 1982, Newell 1980). Consistently with this applicability assumption, we demonstrated that the same representative case information dominated judgment when its source was reliable but not when the source was unreliable. Source unreliability thus appeared to act as a restriction on the application of the representativeness rule. Furthermore, we found that the framing of the problem as a game of chance produced marked utilization of base-rate information. Apparently, the representation of the problem in terms of a familiar chance process enhanced the fit between the application conditions of the sampling rule and the available information. These conclusions are consistent with research by Nisbett *et al.* (1983) and Kruglanski *et al.* (1984) showing that the framing of statistical information in terms of familiar random processes enhanced the application of statistical rules. Learning from past experience – a process neglected by the judgmental heuristics approach – plays an important role in determining applicability conditions. As a result of prior successes or failures in using a rule, conditions are added that allow the problem-solver to discriminate between problems to which the rule is applicable and problems to which it is not applicable (Anderson 1982).

The studies reported here are not the first to demonstrate people's utilization of statistical rules in judgment under uncertainty (see e.g. Birnbaum and Meller 1983, Fischhoff, Slovic and Lichtenstein, 1978, Kruglanski and Ajzen 1983, Kruglanski *et al.* 1984, Manis *et al.* 1980, Nisbett *et al.* 1983). The contribution of this chapter is in relating the use and neglect of statistical information to general problem-solving principles. Indeed, our research program has empirically demonstrated that these principles account for a wide range of specific informational variables. As such, the problem-solving approach has the potential for providing the necessary unifying theoretical framework for judgment under uncertainty. Instead of asking whether people are inherently good or bad statisticians, the problem-solving approach points to the general principles that determine the application of any inferential rule, normative or non-normative. As demonstrated in this chapter, these principles include the possession of a rule, its prior activation or accessibility, its concurrent activation, its relationship to the goal, and its applicability to the givens of the problem. These principles link judgment under uncertainty to general cognitive and motivational processes such as the representation of goals and the givens of a problem in working memory, the acquisition of rules, and their retrieval from long-term memory.

References

Ajzen, I. (1977). Intuitive theories of events and the effects of base rate information on prediction. *Journal of Personality and Social Psychology* 35: 303–14.

Anderson, J. R. (1982). Acquisition of cognitive skill. *Psychological Review* 89: 369–406.

Bar-Hillel, M. (1980). The base-rate fallacy in probability judgments. *Acta Psychologica* 44: 211–33.

Birnbaum, M. H. and Meller, B. A. (1983). Bayesian inference: combining base rates with opinions of sources who vary in credibility. *Journal of Personality and Social Psychology* 45: 792–804.

Borgida, E. and Brekke, N. (1981). The base rate fallacy in attribution and prediction. In J. H. Harvey, W. J. Ickes, and R. F. Kidd (eds.), *New directions in attribution research*, vol. 3. Hillsdale, NJ: Lawrence Erlbaum.

Christensen-Szalanski, J. J. J. and Beach, L. R. (1982). Experience and the base-rate effect. *Organizational Behavior and Human Performance* 29: 270–8.

Fischhoff, B., Slovic, P., and Lichtenstein, S. (1979). Subjective sensitivity analysis. *Organizational Behavior and Human Performance* 23: 339–59.

Ginossar, Z. and Trope, Y. (1980). The effects of base rates and individuating information on judgments about another person. *Journal of Experimental Social Psychology* 16: 228–42.

Ginossar, Z. and Trope, Y. (1987). Problem solving in judgment under uncertainty, *Journal of Personality and Social Psychology* 52: 464–76.

Higgins, E. T. and Bargh, J. H. (1987). Social cognition and social perception. *Annual Review of Psychology* 38: 369–425.

Higgins, E. T. and Chaires, W. M. (1980). Accessibility of interrelational construct: implications for stimulus encoding and reactivity. *Journal of Experimental Social Psychology* 16: 348–61.

Higgins, E. T. and King, G. (1981). Accessibility of social constructs: information-processing consequences of individual and contextual variability. In N. Cantor and J. F. Kihlstrom (eds.), *Personality, cognition, and social interaction*. Hillsdale, NJ: Lawrence Erlbaum.

Kahneman, D., Slovic, P., and Tversky, A. (1982). *Judgment under uncertainty: heuristics and biases*. New York: Cambridge University Press.

Kahneman, D. and Tversky, A. (1972). On prediction and judgment. *ORI Research Monograph* 12 (4).

Kahneman, D. and Tversky, A. (1973). On the psychology of prediction. *Psychological Review* 80: 237–51.

Kahneman, D. and Tversky, A. (1982). The simulation heuristic. In D. Kahneman, P. Slovic, and A. Tversky (eds.), *Judgment under uncertainty: heuristics and biases*. New York: Cambridge University Press.

Kruglanski, A. W. (1980). Lay epistemo-logic – process and content: another look at attribution theory. *Psychological Review* 87: 70–87.

Kruglanski, A. and Ajzen, I. (1983). Bias and error in human judgment. *European Journal of Social Psychology* 13: 1–44.

Kruglanski, A. W., Friedland, N., and Farkash, E. (1984). Lay persons' sensitivity to statistical information: the case of high perceived applicability. *Journal of Personality and Social Psychology* 46: 503–18.

Manis, M., Dovalina, I., Avis, N. E., and Gardoze, S. (1980). Base rates can affect individual predictions. *Journal of Personality and Social Psychology* 38: 231–48.

Newell, A. (1980). Reasoning, problem-solving, and decision processes: the problem space as a fundamental category. In R. Nickerson (ed.), *Attention and performance*, vol. 8. Hillsdale, NJ: Lawrence Erlbaum.

Newell, A. and Simon, H. (1972). *Human problem solving*. Englewood Cliffs, NJ: Prentice-Hall.

Nisbett, R. E., Krantz, D. H., Jepson, C., and Kunda, Z. (1983). The use of statistical heuristics in everyday inductive reasoning. *Psychological Review* 90: 339–63.

Nisbett, R. E. and Ross, L. (1980). *Human inference: strategies and shortcomings of social judgment*. Englewood Cliffs, NJ: Prentice-Hall.

Ross, L. (1977). The intuitive psychologist and his shortcomings: distortions in the attribution process. In L. Berkowitz (ed.), *Advances in experimental social psychology*, vol. 10. New York: Academic Press.

Sherman, S. J. and Corty, E. (1985). Cognitive heuristics. In R. S. Wyer, T. K. Srull, and J. Hartwick (eds.), *Handbook of social cognition*. Hillsdale, NJ: Lawrence Erlbaum.

Smith, J. K. (1984). Social inference. *Psychological Review* 91: 301–28.

Tagiuri, R. (1968). Person perception. In G. Lindzey and E. Aronson (eds.), *The handbook of social psychology*, vol. 3. Reading, Mass.: Addison-Wesley.

Trope, Y. and Burnstein, E. (1979). Inferences about others from their reports about themselves. *European Journal of Social Psychology* 9: 291–306.

Tversky, A. and Kahneman, D. (1974). Judgment under uncertainty: heuristics and biases. *Science* 185: 1124–31.

Tversky, A. and Kahneman, D. (1980). Causal schemas in judgment under uncertainty. In M. Fishbein (ed.), *Progress in social psychology*. Hillsdale, NJ: Lawrence Erlbaum.

Tversky, A. and Kahneman, D. (1982a). Judgment of and by representativeness. In Kahneman *et al.* 1982.

Tversky, A. and Kahneman, D. (1982b). Evidential impact of base-rates. In Kahneman *et al.* 1982.

Tversky, A. and Kahneman, D. (1983). Extensional versus intuitive reasoning: the conjunction fallacy in probability judgment. *Psychological Review* 90: 293–315.

Wyer, R. S. and Srull, T. K. (1980). Category accessibility: some theoretical and empirical issues concerning the processing of social stimulus information. In E. T. Higgins, C. P. Herman, and M. P. Zanna (eds.), *Social cognition: the Ontario Symposium*. Hillsdale, NJ: Lawrence Erlbaum.

10 Dimensional versus information-processing approaches to social knowledge: the case of inconsistency management[1]

Patricia G. Devine and Thomas M. Ostrom

Social knowledge is a fuzzy term, as can be seen by the variety of ways it is used in this volume. But despite the sometimes subtle and sometimes substantial differences in definitions of the term, they stem from a common root. They all agree that any analysis of social knowledge must involve considerations of how we acquire and use knowledge about other people, considerations that in turn raise the issue of how such knowledge is mentally structured or organized.

Developing an understanding of another person is a formidable task. This is because behavior is labile; people do not behave consistently over time. They may say one thing and do another. They may behave sympathetically on one occasion and coldly on another. How does the perceiver make sense of these inconsistencies, and what effects do they have on forming a stable and predictable account of people and events in our social world? Answers to such questions are fundamental to our understanding of social knowledge.

When a kind person spreads a nasty rumor about another, the social perceiver is confronted with a perplexing situation. Spreading nasty rumors does not follow from being a kind person. In an effort to make sense of this situation and maintain the belief that there is some stability to the social world, the perceiver seeks a way to resolve this inconsistency. It is through such inconsistency management strategies that the perceiver comes to know and understand his or her social world. Inconsistency management,

1 The authors thank Craig Anderson and Constantine Tsedikies for comments on an earlier version of this chapter. Special thanks are extended to Anthony Greenwald and Thomas Srull for their detailed and insightful comments and suggestions. Preparation of this chapter was supported by a contract from the Organizational Effectiveness Research Group, Office of Naval Research, United States Navy (Code 452) under control number N00014–81–K–0112, NR 170–927.

then, is one of the bedrock problems dealt with in the fields of social perception and social judgment. It is at the heart of social knowledge.

We are arguing, then, that one cannot understand social knowledge without first understanding the processes involved in inconsistency management. This concern is not unique to social psychology. For example, developmental psychologists have long recognized that significant advances in children's cognitive abilities are associated with the child's ability to identify and resolve discrepancies between inconsistent events (for example, acquiring skills of object permanence and conservation) (Piaget 1952).

A conceptual shift in the study of inconsistency management

Our major goal is to show what the study of inconsistency has revealed about the nature of social knowledge. We do this by offering a historical review of how the problem of inconsistency has been construed in the study of impression formation. This review reveals that there has been a fundamental shift in the conceptual approach brought to bear on the study of inconsistency. This shift can be traced to the adoption of information-processing models in the study of person perception. This information-processing orientation is the defining characteristic of the field of social cognition. We argue that this shift is leading to a more comprehensive account of the role of inconsistency in social perception and social judgment.

The late 1970s witnessed a general dissatisfaction with traditional approaches to the study of person perception and, simultaneously, a fascination with the potential application of cognitive information-processing models to the traditional problems in person perception. This has now led to a dramatic shift in how cognitive processes are conceptualized by social psychologists (Ostrom 1984a). The implications of this shift are clear in the study of inconsistency in impression formation research.

The shift in theoretical perspective derives from the information-processing revolution in cognitive psychology, a shift that Lachman *et al.* (1979) have characterized as a paradigmatic shift of the kind described by Kuhn (1962). Kuhn argued that when limitations of a dominant paradigm are identified (e.g. inability to predict or explain empirical outcomes, failure of experiments to replicate, methods derived from existing theory being no longer appropriate to new questions, stagnation in terms of the questions asked) and an alternative paradigm that can resolve the anomalies and shortcomings of the dominant paradigm is available (e.g. the information-processing perspective), a scientific revolution is likely to take place.

During the revolution, scientists come to reject the conventions of the dominant paradigm and accept, in whole or in part, the guidelines of a new paradigm. Commitment to a new paradigm may mean fundamental changes in the discipline's conception of which problems are important, which solutions (methods) are acceptable, and which theoretical language is appropriate to those solutions.

Lachman *et al.* (1979) suggest that the information-processing perspective, with its emphasis on humans as active information-seekers and users of information, has provided psychologists with a fundamentally new way of thinking about people. They contrast this perspective with the more traditional psychodynamic and behavioristic conceptions.

Psychodynamic theories focused on the conflict between rational (societal) and irrational (instinctive) forces as determinants of human behavior and personality. Behavioristic theories conceptualized individuals as conditioned responders, passively waiting for stimuli to impinge on them. Only then do individuals make the response they have been conditioned to make. In contrast to both of these approaches, the information-processing approach focuses on cognitive activity involved in attending to, storing, and retrieving knowledge. As such, information-processing models emphasize the dynamic, categorical, structural, and qualitative features of cognitive systems.

Although many cognitive theorists adopted the information-processing framework and its impact has been truly dramatic, the analogy with Kuhnian scientific revolutions may be misleading. Kuhnian scientific revolutions are typically characterized by the defeat of one paradigm by another (Gholson and Barker 1985). Lakatos (1970) suggests that this perspective, one that views scientific research programs as being incommensurable, does not map onto the history of science. It implies that it is impossible for there to be any real continuity in content from one paradigm to the next.

We believe that it is the continuity between old and new approaches that allows one to identify clearly the advances of new approaches. Although the fundamental questions regarding the nature of inconsistency management (e.g. why and how) have remain unchanged, the old versus new theoretical models used to explain the findings have almost nothing in common. We highlight this shift in the models used for mentally representing person information, and illustrate how the information-processing approach has broadened the kinds of questions researchers ask about inconsistency, the techniques by which they study these questions, and the theoretical terminology that guides their interpretation of findings. Although we believe that the traditional and contemporary models can coexist, our present purpose (and admittedly our bias) is to emphasize the advances in understanding that result from studying inconsistency management from an information-processing perspective.

Early models of inconsistency in impression formation

A variety of empirical approaches have been used in the study of impression formation. In the present analysis we will focus on the dominant task used over the years to study inconsistency. Subjects are given a set of information items about an unfamiliar (and usually fictional) target person. The information items are usually viewed as independent from one another (i.e. they do not form a coherent narrative) and are presented in a single block or sequentially. In the early years the items were usually traits (e.g. friendly, lazy); in recent years they have more often been behaviors (e.g. returned a purse found in the hall, cursed at an old lady who had stalled her car).

Asch's (1946, 1952) classic work on impression formation is the earliest systematic attempt to deal with inconsistency. His work on meaning shift and primacy effects piqued the interest of social psychologists and remains of interest today (Ostrom 1984b). According to Asch, we understand others by forming a holistic organized impression of the other in a manner similar to forming a perceptual gestalt of a visual stimulus. The process of forming an impression, a good gestalt, was presumed to be a dynamic process in which information learned at one point in time can color the interpretation of subsequently learned information.

In a typical experiment subjects were given a list of traits that were said to describe a person. Subjects then wrote a paragraph describing their impression of that person. This was then followed by their selecting from a list of bipolar traits those they felt best characterized the target person. Asch suggested that each trait affects the meaning of each of the other traits, and that the final impression is a dynamic one not predictable from the individual traits taken separately. The whole was greater than the sum of its parts. Asch documented his conclusions by looking at two kinds of data. He was able to show that the qualitative nature of the paragraphs people wrote reflected an active effort to make sense of inconsistencies. Second, the profile of choices from the adjective checklist showed that people selected shades of meanings that produced an overall coherent picture of the target person.

Asch's logic is remarkably contemporary. His conceptual orientation shares with the current information-processing approach a focus on the dynamic, structural, and qualitative features of the cognitive system. Unfortunately, neither his theoretical thinking nor his procedures for analyzing impressions dominated subsequent work on the inconsistency problem. Both were seen as excessively subjective and imprecise.

In an effort to find a quantitative (rather than qualitative) way to study impressions, researchers shifted to a dramatically different strategy. The imprecision in Asch's approach was defined away by construing impressions as the overall level of favorability toward the person, rather than retaining Asch's view that they were the set of beliefs and inferences the perceiver had generated about the target person.

Most work done on the inconsistency problem from the late 1950s to the late 1970s shared the view that all important theoretical features of cognition can be represented in terms of a "point on a continuum". This orientation was parallel to that in the field of psychophysics, in which interest centered on identifying the relationship between the magnitude of physical stimuli and the psychological experiences they produced. In psychophysical studies the stimuli presented to subjects typically vary in terms of a single experimenter-determined stimulus dimension such as heaviness or brightness. And exposure to a physical stimulus is thought to elicit a specific, unitary experience on a subjective sensory dimension. This experience serves as the basis of the overt response to the stimulus.

This dimensional formulation, initially developed for the judgment of sensory attributes, was directly applied to impression judgments (see Ostrom 1981a, for an analysis of the problems created by this dimensional reasoning for the study of attributions). The dimension most often of interest to the early person perception researchers was the likeableness of various personality characteristics. In fact, Anderson (1968) had subjects locate 555 personality trait words on a seven-point likeableness rating scale ranging from "least favorable or desirable" to "most favorable or desirable".

Most of the research during this period involved presenting subjects with sets of Anderson's trait words and asking them to integrate the traits into an overall impression. The implicit impression response was conceived of as falling on a subjective continuum of favorability. The overt rating of favorability was simply a direct rendition of the subjective response.

We can see, then, that there is a direct parallel between the psychophysical approaches and the early cognitive approaches taken by social psychologists to understanding social perception phenomena. The approaches were thought of as being cognitive because they were based on constructs that summarized the "meaning" of information to the perceiver. Just as sensory information could be conceptually represented as a point on a subjective sensory continuum, so could social information be conceptually represented as a point on a social continuum. Just as an overt judgmental response to a physical stimulus could be based on where that point fell on the subjective continuum, so too could the overt response to a social stimulus.

The best exemplar of this kind of point-on-a-continuum theory is N. H. Anderson's information integration theory (1981, 1982). Anderson characterizes the cognitive processes involved in impression judgments as following simple algebraic rules, and postulates that impression responses to trait information can be captured on a single judgment dimension. The final judgment (R) is a function at the same time of how positive or negative the traits are (i.e. their scale values, s_i), of how important the traits are (i.e. their weight, w_i), and of the respondent's initial weighted impression ($w_o s_o$). In the case of person impressions, the most commonly encountered algebraic combination of these elements has been weighted averaging. Mathematically,

$$R = \frac{w_o s_o + w_i s_i.}{w_o + w_i}$$

To produce this algebraic representation, it was necessary to reduce all aspects of the phenomenon (i.e. impressions derived from information) to point-on-a-continuum representations. The "meaning" of information (its scale value) is a point, the relative role in the impression played by each information item (its weight) is a point, and the subjective impression response itself (R) is a point.

Other theorists also generated impression models using the point-on-a-continuum paradigm. For example, Manis *et al.* (1966) showed that judgments of large sets of social stimuli are typically more extreme than judgments of small sets. Theoretically, they suggested that set size acts as a multiplier of the average of the constituent information elements. Fishbein and Hunter (1964) obtained a similar effect, but they preferred to account for it by a summative, rather than an averaging model. This was true despite the fact that the general orientation of these latter authors was derived from general models of concept formation (Fishbein 1967). Other theorists offered similar algebraic models derived from a motivational point of view (Rosenberg 1956) and from a gestalt point of view (Zajonc 1968).

A somewhat different point-on-a-continuum approach was taken by Wyer and Goldberg (1970; see also McGuire 1981). They developed a mathematical model of how subjective probabilities of premises (e.g. a person is friendly and aggressive) combine to determine the subjective probability of a conclusion (e.g. the person is likeable). In this case the continuum on which the information items and the impression response fall is one of subjective probability (from zero to one).

The underlying goal of each of these approaches was to find some general mathematical law, one descriptive of how people integrate information, that would explain the location of judgments on a continuum. Since the algebraic formulation of Anderson (1981, 1982) encompasses many other approaches to the study of person perception (see Anderson 1974), we will focus on it as the prototype of the point-on-a-continuum theories.

Empirical demonstrations of inconsistency

To appreciate fully the subject's task, consider a typical experiment in which subjects are presented with a series of trait adjectives, some of which are consistent with each other and others which are inconsistent. For example, a stimulus person might be described by the traits *honest–considerate–gloomy* (Anderson and Jacobson 1965). In this example, the trait gloomy is evaluatively inconsistent with the other two traits.

Interest centered on how subjects combine such inconsistencies in forming impression judgments measured on a likeability continuum (e.g. Anderson 1967, Anderson and Jacobson 1965, Hendrick and Costantini 1970, Kaplan 1973, Pepitone and Hayden 1955, Wyer 1970, 1974, Birnbaum and Stegner 1979). In general, it has been shown that in the situation in which subjects are encouraged to integrate all available information into a unified impression, they tend to discount the inconsistent elements. Discounting was assumed to occur when the evaluation based on all three adjectives deviated in the appropriate direction from the equal weighted average of each adjective considered separately. Thus in the Anderson and Jacobson (1965) study, under conditions where no discounting occurs, impression judgments of one negative and two positive traits on a likeability scale (where low = 0 and high = 20) averaged 10.38. However, under conditions that encouraged discounting, the negatively valenced trait (e.g. gloomy) is given less weight than the positively valenced traits (e.g. honest and considerate) in the averaging process. This led to a more positive overall rating of 13.84. These means are taken from Anderson and Jacobson 1965.

The dimensional approach was employed to investigate the role of individual differences in discounting. Kaplan (1971a) examined discounting as a function of subjects' predispositions to evaluate persons favorably or unfavorably. He found that those predisposed to think more positively about others will tend to discount (or weigh less) the more unfavorable adjectives, particularly when the traits are provided by a low-valued source.

A second area of application has been the study of source credibility. Research has shown that inconsistent information from a low-credibility source is discounted more than that from a high-credibility source (Rosenbaum and Levin 1968, 1969, Birnbaum and Stegner 1979). The explanations for this discounting, like the explanations offered above, have appealed to the concept of reduced weight in the context of the weighted averaging cognitive algebra model.

The same dimensional models have been used to account for primacy and recency effects when integrating inconsistent information into an impression. A primacy effect occurs when information presented first is more influential in determining the final impression. Thus, when positive information is presented before negative information, the general impression is more positive than when the information is presented in the reverse order (Asch 1946, Anderson and Hubert 1963, Luchins 1957, Stewart 1965). Presumably subjects assign more weight or importance to initial information and de-emphasize or pay less attention to later information. Anderson and Hubert (1963) demonstrated that primacy effects could be eliminated by inducing subjects through recall instructions to pay equal attention to, and presumably weigh equally, each trait. The no-recall instruction subjects evidenced the typical primacy effect.

Several things should be noted about the explanations derived from the combinational, point-on-a-continuum theories. The explanations for how perceivers resolve inconsistency are largely descriptive. The concept of weight merely summarizes the functional impact of an information item on the resulting judgment, but leaves us essentially uninformed about how or why discounting occurs. It provides a way of identifying the factors that lead to discounting in judgment, but does not provide a predictive basis for knowing what new antecedents may be important. It focuses only on the role of discounting in overt judgments, and ignores other potential effects of inconsistency, such as the generation of inferences and the formation of interpretative structures that help to provide meaning and coherence to the information ensemble.

With their emphasis on the assignments of weights and scale values to traits and the identification of a combinatorial rule, point-on-a-continuum theories might well be characterized as theories of a task. That is, the judgment, and thus the continuum, must always be specified first. The weights and scale values are meaningful only in relation to the task-specific continuum. In contrast, contemporary models based on the information-processing perspective take as a starting point a model of the mind (i.e. cognitive system) that can be applied to any task (e.g. forming an impression, resolving inconsistency, forming attributions, etc.).

Early conceptions of inconsistency

The point-on-a-continuum approach had direct implications for how researchers defined inconsistency. Two items of information were inconsistent to the extent that they were located at different places on the favorability continuum. Thus, the magnitude of inconsistency was determined by the amount of their dimensional discrepancy. For example, the words "friendly" and "gloomy" are considered inconsistent because normative ratings of the likeability of the words indicate that they are far apart. "Friendly" has a scale value of 5.19 whereas "gloomy" has a scale value of 1.36 (Anderson 1968). "Liar" would be considered even more inconsistent with "friendly" than is "gloomy". That is, "liar" has a scale value of .26, and as such is farther from "friendly" than is "gloomy".

This definition of inconsistency was termed evaluative (or implicational) inconsistency by Wyer (1974) and pertains to all kinds of information. In the case of behaviors, for example, a stimulus person who returns a lost wallet but also cheats on an exam provides the subject with information that has conflicting implications for the overall judgment.

An interesting logical dilemma emerges from this kind of dimensional definition of inconsistency. Because inconsistency is defined only in terms of discrepancies in scale value, there appears to be no way within this conceptual structure to define denotative inconsistency. Since inconsistency is defined in terms of the distance between scale values, evaluative and denotative inconsistent items of the same distance from a target item are considered equivalent. To define denotative inconsistency one has to consult an extratheoretical source (a dictionary, for example).

A second dilemma also exists. Inconsistency in the dimensional approach focuses on the comparison of one stimulus item with another stimulus item. The approach has difficulties in representing inconsistencies that might exist between a new stimulus item and components of the perceiver's prior impression. The pre-existing impression (or knowledge structure) will certainly contain a variety of components including items of previously acquired information, inferences generated when the earlier information was learned, higher-order structure about the person (e.g. stereotypes, behavioral vignettes, role activities), and (perhaps) an overall impression.

The dimensional approach would represent each of these separate elements and structures with its own scale value, locating all as unique points on the favorability continuum. The dilemma resides in knowing whether a new item of information is or is not inconsistent with the impression. It is almost certain to be consistent with some components of the cognitive representation and inconsistent with others.

As we shall see in the next section, these two dilemmas disappear when the information-processing approach is brought to bear on the problem of defining inconsistency. The concept is no longer solely dependent on the comparison of two or more stimulus items on a single continuum of judgment.

Contemporary models of inconsistency in impression formation

Point-on-a-continuum theories have been primarily concerned with the functional relationship between the properties of a judgment and the properties of stimulus information (e.g. the number of traits, their weights and scale values). These approaches have expressed little concern for the mental operations involved in forming such judgments. The information-processing framework invites a different level of analysis from that of the task-oriented point-on-a-continuum approaches. Point-on-a-continuum models do not have a theoretical framework that allows articulation of information-processing activity concurrent with social judgments, and thus do not provide the level of theoretical elaboration that is possible in the information-processing framework. Empirical and theoretical work in social information-processing has concerned itself primarily with developing alternative mental representations of social stimuli and applying processing models to understanding the formation and change of cognitive structures. They offer a fundamentally different conception of a cognitive element from that provided by dimensional theories. A point in a dimensional space is only one way to conceive a mental representation.

There is a crucial distinction between dimensional models and information-processing models of mental representation (such as semantic network theories). In semantic network models the cognitive element is not viewed as a point-on-a-continuum. Instead, it is viewed as a node in a semantic network, linked to related information (other nodes) via associative pathways (Collins and Loftus 1975). Activation of a node is considered a binary event; that is, a node is either activated or not activated. Related concepts are activated following the spreading activation along the associative pathways. Thus, when activated the cognitive element can have both direct and remote ramifications for the generation of inferences and social judgments.

This representation of cognitive elements in long-term memory permits the theorist to focus on the dynamic, qualitative features of cognitive systems (how cognitive elements interact, for instance) in the formation of judgments and evaluations. In contrast to point-on-a-continuum theories, information-processing models focus on the structure and process of cognitive systems. The information-processing approach has been applied to the problems of person perception under the labels of "person memory" (Hastie *et al.* 1980) and "social cognition" (Wyer and Srull 1984).

The information-processing framework has truly liberated the study of social perception, in terms both of theoretical analysis and of methodological approaches. The impact of information-processing models is particularly instructive in the analysis of how social perceivers manage inconsistency. No longer is the definition of inconsistency bound to a particular experimental context or to the notion of trait weights and scale values. The definition of inconsistency can be expanded to include behaviors being inconsistent not just with one another, but with prior expectations, previous judgments about that person, or any other component of one's cognitive representation. Nor are the theories primarily centered around a single dependent variable, a single judgment continuum. Rather, theorists have taken on the task of examining encoding, storage, and retrieval processes involved in all phases of impression formation.

Most of the early impression formation research dealt with stimulus-based judgments. That is, the dominant methodology involved studying impression judgments made in response to stimulus information present immediately prior to, or simultaneously with, the response scale. So in almost all cases the perceiver was aware of the judgment dimension at the time of receiving the stimulus information.

In contrast to this stimulus-based approach, judgments about other people are often based on memory of previously acquired information about the person or persons being judged. That is, rather than being based on concurrently available information items, judgments are often based on information and inferences (e.g. spontaneous evaluations, prior beliefs, attributions for behaviors) drawn from a cognitive representation of the person that the perceiver has built up over time (e.g. Lingle and Ostrom 1979, 1981, Ostrom *et al.* 1980).

Information processing models can potentially inform us as to what kinds of thoughts people are able to draw upon when they are unexpectedly asked to make a judgment or decision about a person. To what degree or under what circumstances will the specific episodic facts learned about a person be recalled, and how are they related to judgments? We can also ask new questions about how people react to learning new information about a person. Which items are selected for storage in memory, and with which pre-existing thoughts do they become associated?

Another important contribution of information-processing theories is that they offer new methodologies to tap these other aspects of cognitive activity that do not depend on direct self-report of impressions. These include such measures as exposure time (e.g. to examine which items are given the most attention), response time (e.g. which items are most accessible in memory), recall (e.g. what is selectively recalled and how it is structured), and encoding elaborations (e.g. what kinds of thoughts are elicited in response to stimulus items). Point-on-a-continuum theories are essentially mute on these types of response. Unlike the earlier theorists, contemporary investigators are examining multiple manifestations of how inconsistency affects the social perceiver's cognitive system. This point harks back to one of the most important advances of addressing social perception from an information-processing perspective. Rather than developing a theory of a task (i.e. describing how people make ratings on a favorability scale), the long-term goal of information-processing theorists is to develop a conception of the mind, one aspect of which addresses inconsistency management in social perception. Thus, information-processing models are in general more abstract, and consequently more inclusive, than their predecessors.[2]

Research on inconsistency management

Several studies have investigated differential memory for behaviors that are consistent, inconsistent, or neutral with respect to a prior expectancy about the person (Hastie and Kumar 1979, Hastie 1980, Srull 1981, Srull *et al.* 1985, Wyer and Gordon 1982, Hemsley and Marmurek 1982). The typical experiment (e.g. Hastie and Kumar 1979) examined these issues in the context of an impression formation task. Subjects were given a set of traits attributed to a stimulus person (intelligent, bright, clever, smart, quick, etc.) and asked to form an impression. This provided the basis of a cognitively stored expectancy. Subjects were then presented with a series of behaviors performed by the stimulus person. These included consistent, inconsistent, and irrelevant behaviors. Finally, subjects were given a free-recall task, after which they reported their impression of the stimulus person. The most important result in these studies is that circumstances exist where incongruent behaviors are recalled better than congruent behaviors.

The final impression judgment in these studies is comparable to that typically used in point-on-a-continuum research. These judgment data were congruent with the predictions of dimensional models for impression formation (for example, more incongruent behaviors produce a greater shift in judgment away from the initial expectation). In these studies, however, interest went beyond subjects' judgments.

The primary purpose of these initial studies was to determine how inconsistent information was represented in memory. The traditional theories provide no basis for predicting any memory effects. On the other hand, Hastie (1980) and Srull (1981, Srull *et al.* 1985) have offered an information-processing model that predicts that under some circumstances inconsistent items will be better recalled than consistent items. The prediction is based on the associative network conception of memory structure and assumptions regarding undirected search and match mechanisms (Anderson and Bower 1973). The fundamental principle underlying this Hastie–Srull model is that when subjects attempt to form an integrated, unified impres-

2 An additional point is noteworthy in this context. As more and new response measures are examined, they will allow us to address the similarities and differences between social perception and object perception in a way that is guided empirically. This issue, which has been a hotbed of controversy (Ostrom 1984a), could be advanced by such empirically guided efforts.

sion, inconsistent behavioral information will instigate elaborative processing to reconcile the discrepancy between the inconsistent items and the prior expectancy.

When confronted with inconsistent information, subjects attempt to explain its occurrence. These to-be-explained acts spend relatively more time in working memory than either consistent or irrelevant behaviors. As the subject tries to resolve the inconsistency, the inconsistent act is linked through associative pathways to more other behaviors than are the relatively uninformative acts (e.g. congruent or irrelevant acts). The establishment of this rich network of inter-item links between the to-be-explained acts and the other information about the stimulus person produces a memory structure that produces more retrieval routes during recall for the inconsistent items. The point-on-a-continuum theories do not have the conceptual flexibility to explain this finding.

In fact, this result may appear surprising to the point-on-a-continuum theorist; those items that are given the least "weight" (and so in some sense are the least important in the overall judgment) are the best recalled of all items. However, when considered in the light of specific encoding, storage and retrieval assumptions, the apparent anomaly is easily resolved. Information-processing models, such as the Hastie–Srull model, provide a careful and detailed analysis of the nature of the mental representation that allows us to understand the recall advantage for inconsistent information.

In efforts to understand the nature of the presumed elaborative processing, investigators began to take measures of encoding such as attention measures (Hemsley and Marmurek 1982, Erber and Fiske 1984, Bargh and Thein 1985) and cognitive elaboration measures (Hastie 1980, 1984, Devine and Ostrom 1985, Erber and Fiske 1984), in addition to recall and judgment measures. The attention measures have indicated that inconsistent items are allocated more processing time during the initial exposure phase than are consistent or irrelevant items. This finding is congruent with the notion that it requires time to find an explanation. The processing time measures, however, are not unambiguous measures of attention and should be interpreted cautiously. That is, it is not clear whether processing time reflects attention, thinking, inferencing, integration, discounting, or some other cognitively demanding task.

To provide converging evidence that inconsistent items are likely to draw attention and processing time, researchers have also looked at measures of cognitive elaboration. These studies have shown that causal reasoning processes are instigated by the occurrence of inconsistent (or unexpected) events. That is, subjects are more likely spontaneously to seek an explanation for why inconsistent events occur than consistent or irrelevant events (Hastie 1980, 1984, Crocker *et al.* 1983).

These data suggest that subjects need to commit additional resources to explain inconsistent information beyond what would be necessary if the information were congruent. The Hastie–Srull model therefore implies that there are limiting conditions to the finding of preferential memory for inconsistent items. When subjects are prevented from elaborated processing by, say, increasing the load on subjects' available processing capacity, the memory advantage for inconsistent information disappears (Srull 1981, experiment 4). Under such conditions, subjects are not able to produce the associative network structure that produces high recall for inconsistent items.

Bargh and Thein (1985) have examined the implications of the model for individuals who differ in terms of the chronic cognitive accessibility of the trait that served as the basis of the initial expectancy. That is, some individuals have some traits (e.g. honest) readily accessible and ready to use in social information-processing situations, and can do so even under overload conditions. Their data confirmed this prediction. On the other hand, subjects without an accessible category for the trait behaved like the subjects in Srull's (1981, experiment 4) experiment. They showed equal recall of the consistent and inconsistent behaviors. These subjects did not have the cognitive structures to support evaluation of the behaviors at encoding.

Each of these studies suggests that inconsistency management is a dynamic process involving encoding (resource allocation), storage (memory structure), and retrieval processes. Bernstein and Schul (1982, 1983) identified four distinct operations involved in impression formation. These include initial encoding, elaborative encoding, integration, and decision. These processes were identified empirically on the basis of the differential sensitivity to the amount and the consistency of information in a trait description. Bernstein and Schul (1983) found, for example, that traits were processed more slowly with integrated judgment goals (form a coherent impression) than with discrete judgment goals (comprehend the set of traits). Moreover, preferential recall for consistent information was only found when the traits had not been integrated into a unified impression. They suggested that when an impression is formed, the traits are associated with each other via prior knowledge, and thus are represented as a unified structure. Otherwise each trait is stored as a separate piece of information. This kind of model is particularly illustrative of the advances associated with approaching social perception from an information processing framework, as it takes into consideration issues concerning processing, cognitive structure, and the relationship between structure (for example, previous semantically represented knowledge) and phases of the information-processing sequence.

Next, we return specifically to the issues of discounting and primacy–recency effects, phenomena that absorbed the attention of the point-on-a-continuum theorists, and examine how the information-processing approach has contributed to our understanding of these effects.

Discounting and primacy–recency revisited

The early studies on inconsistency were primarily concerned with discounting of inconsistent elements in the overall impression. The fate of these discounted items in memory was not clearly understood, however. Investigators have recently begun attacking these problems from the information-processing perspective (e.g. Devine and Ostrom 1985, Wyer and Unverzagt 1985). The significance of these studies is that they, like the studies on the Hastie–Srull model, were simultaneously concerned with encoding, storage, retrieval, and judgment processes. Thus, their efforts focused on specifying the information-processing mechanisms associated with discounting and primacy–recency phenomena.

Devine and Ostrom (1985) examined the cognitive processes that mediate the discounting of inconsistent testimony from an unreliable source in the context of a criminal trial setting. Subjects read testimony provided by four witnesses. Three impartial witnesses provided testimony consistent with each other (for example, all implied that the defendant was guilty). One witness provided testimony inconsistent with this preponderance. This witness, however, had a special relationship with the defendant that rendered the inconsistent testimony suspicious and potentially discountable (for example, the defendant's sister providing absolving testimony). The impact of this inconsistent testimony from a low-credibility source was examined in two kinds of testimony presentation formats. One facilitated associating sources with the content of their testimony, and the other interfered with this association.

The judgment (i.e. the jurors' verdict) findings of this research are in harmony with the "reduced weight" explanations of the point-on-a-continuum theories. Testimony organization conditions that facilitated jurors associating the inconsistent testimony with the unreliable source led to discounting of the inconsistent testimony. However, the findings went beyond examining the functional effects of inconsistency on judgment.

Devine and Ostrom (1985) suggested that discounting occurs in the context of jurors generating an integrated representation of the trial events. This representation is a function of both the actual testimony items and the jurors' own spontaneous reactions. By measuring jurors' cognitive elaborations at encoding, it was shown that jurors can explicitly take into consideration the source's motives or intentions for providing the inconsistent testimony. Importantly, biased motives were not explicitly presented as part of the testimony, and they thus had to be inferred on the basis of knowledge about social relationships that was previously stored.

Under testimony organization conditions in which it was difficult for jurors to associate sources with the content of their testimony, these inferences of bias were absent. As a result, these jurors did not discount the inconsistent testimony items. These data are important because they suggest that inconsistency by itself was not enough to produce discounting. When jurors did not associate witnesses with the content of their testimony, subjects treated the inconsistent items as valid testimony items, and consequently produced verdicts less congruent with the majority of testimony items. Note that this process is conceptually similar to the process specified by Bernstein and Schul (1983) when comparing integrated and discrete judgments.

Consideration of the recall data from Devine and Ostrom's (1985) research is instructive as well. They found that jurors in both testimony organization conditions evidenced superior recall for inconsistent items, largely supporting the Hastie–Srull model for the processing of inconsistent information. Interestingly, however, the highest level of recall was not for the inconsistent items, but for the items that revealed the discountable nature of the inconsistent testimony – the low-credibility source information (even for those who did not associate this source with the inconsistent testimony). Jurors in both testimony organization conditions recalled the same factual testimony items but imparted very different meanings to the items at encoding; these encoding differences led to different judgments. The encoding elaboration measures supported this analysis.

Thus, again, we have a series of informative and interesting encoding and memory findings that are not derivable from the point-on-a-continuum framework. Perhaps most importantly, the point-on-a-continuum theories offer no *a priori* reasons to expect that selected manipulations of the testimony structure would affect discounting judgments. These theories can only offer *post hoc* explanations which are, at best, incomplete. It was specific processing assumptions derived from the information-processing framework that led to the manipulation of testimony structure to produce conditions in which discounting would and would not occur. And it was the creation of these conditions that highlighted the contribution of assumptions concerning specific processes that mediate discounting of inconsistent testimony.

Another case in point is a recent study by Wyer and Unverzagt (1985). They employed the typical primacy–recency setting studied by point-on-a-continuum theorists. The study examined the effects of instructions to disregard specific information about a target person on likeableness judgments and on the memory representation of the provided information. Subjects were given descriptions of a person's behavior and were asked to form an impression of the person. The first behaviors in the series had implications for one trait, and the last behaviors had implications for a second trait that differed in favorableness from the first.

The instructions to the subjects were designed to have specific effects on the processing of the stimulus information. After having read the first set of behaviors, some of the subjects were told that, because of an error in procedure, they should disregard the first set of behaviors; others were told after reading the entire list to disregard the last behaviors presented. To-be-disregarded behaviors that occurred first in the series had little impact on judgments either of the specific trait to which they pertained or of judgments of the target's likeableness; subjects could, however, recall these items well. In contrast, to-be-disregarded items at the end of the series did influence specific trait judgments but these items were recalled relatively poorly.

Point-on-a-continuum theories do not have the conceptual flexibility to explain such findings. Wyer and Unverzagt (1985) accounted for these results in terms of a general model of social information-processing proposed by Wyer and Srull (1980). The model outlines specific storage and retrieval processes that involve theoretical representations of the to-be-disregarded and to-be-used information in terms of associative structures formed as subjects encoded the information.

When the to-be-disregarded behaviors occur early in the sequence, the subject is able to differentiate these items from the useful items. They are stored separately in memory from the useful items. Subjects start a new memory structure for the useful items at the point at which the instruction to disregard the first items occurs. When they are asked to recall all of the information presented about the target person, the subject searches both memory locations and both sets of items are recalled well.

When the to-be-disregarded items are presented last, however, they become fully integrated with the useful early-presented items in subjects' representation of the stimulus person. Subjects had no forewarning that the last items were to be disregarded, and thus did not create a new memory structure for these items separately from the useful items. As a result, associative pathways were formed between the early, useful and later, to-be-disregarded items. The one memory location contained both to-be-disregarded items and the behaviors subjects have *not* been told to disregard. As a result of interference produced by these latter items, at retrieval the actual to-be-disregarded behaviors are difficult to identify, producing a decrement in their recall. In addition, the implications of the to-be-disregarded behaviors for ensuing judgments are considered at encoding. The to-be-disregarded behaviors, when presented late in the series of behaviors, are for all functional purposes considered relevant to the judgment. Since the subject cannot easily distinguish between to-be-disregarded and useful behaviors, the former also affect specific judgments.

These findings cannot be easily accommodated by point-on-a-continuum (or spatial) models. In an algebraic function, items that are irrelevant to a judgment (e.g. to-be-disregarded items) should be assigned a weight of zero and thus should exert no influence on the resulting judgment. When the items became integrated into a unified impression of the stimulus person, this apparently becomes impossible. In fact, subjects did not manifest high recall for those items, and yet they affected judgments of the stimulus person.

We would like to argue that it is the type of theoretical model suggested by Wyer and Unverzagt (1985) that will lead to an understanding of primacy–recency effects in impression formation. In order to understand which information items will be more influential in impression judgments, we need to take into consideration the dynamic relation between information-processing activities and the way in which stimulus items are represented in subjects' memories. It is not enough to *know* that a primacy or recency effect has occurred, as evidenced by the location of a judgment on a continuum. The goal of information-processing models is to *explain* how and why such effects occur. The general strategy is to examine many aspects of the cognitive activity to shed light on the cognitive dynamics – relationships between encoding, storage, and retrieval processes – that produce the effects.

Concluding comments

As is evidenced in the research reviewed above, the process of forming impressions and dealing with inconsistency is much more dynamic than the point-on-a-continuum theories would have us believe. Point-on-a-continuum theories take a very narrow perspective on the judgment process. The conceptual framework of point-on-a-continuum theories requires *a priori* specification of a judgment continuum, something that is not required by information-processing theorizing. In fact, the theoretical representation of all elements of cognitive algebra (w, s), and the judgment itself (R) are defined as points-on-a-continuum. Point-on-a-continuum theorists focused only on judgment responses, and ignored other aspects of cognitive activity that have proved to be revealing about how and why inconsistencies are managed.

We have argued that there are many aspects of cognitive activity that are outside the scope of point-on-a-continuum theories, and that information-processing models offer the theoretical flexibility necessary to map these cognitive processes. It is this flexibility that has generated renewed interest in traditional problems in person perception research such as discounting and primacy–recency effects (Devine and Ostrom 1985, Wyer and Unverzagt 1985). Furthermore, information-processing models can therefore subsume the data generated by point-on-a-continuum theories. In terms of explanatory power, nothing has been lost and much has been gained by the shift in theoretical focus.

In summary, where point-on-a-continuum theories are theories of a task, information-processing models aspire to produce a theory of the mind that can be applied to many different tasks. In the study of inconsistency, information-processing models accommodate multiple manifestations of inconsistency on cognitive activity (for example, attention, elaborations, recall, memory-based judgments, structure of the memory representation). This point has been nicely made in the chapter by Wyer and Srull appearing in this volume. Thus, these theories embrace a wider range of conceptual issues and empirical domains than was possible for point-on-a-continuum theories.

Implications for attribution and attitude theory

Up to now we have focused almost exclusively on impression formation research. However, it is important to note that information-processing models also have implications for the development of theories of attribution and attitude change. These domains, like the area of impression formation, are central to any study of social knowing (see the chapters by Jaspars, Hamilton, and Zanna and Rempel in this volume).

Attributions

Previous models for how people attribute causality have direct parallels with the point-on-a-continuum models of impression formation. Although the originating theorists did not view them in algebraic terms, most (if not all) early theories of attribution can be modeled by one of Anderson's (1974, 1981) cognitive algebra rules. For example, Jones and Davis (1965) were interested in how unexpected or inconsistent information would influence the likelihood of making dispositional attributions as measured on a continuum. Likewise, Kelley's (1967) ANOVA model can be conceptualized as a dimensional, combinatorial model. The issue for the ANOVA model is how to combine consensus, distinctiveness, and consistency information to provide an internal or external attribution. These attributional judgments were most often regarded as points on a subjective continuum. And as was the case for impression formation research, this emphasis on how stimulus events combine into dimensional judgments led to a narrow conception of the attribution process.

Attribution researchers have recently become acquainted with information-processing theories and have begun to ask new questions concerning the attribution process. As Hamilton's chapter in this volume illustrates, attribution theorists have become interested in the influence of expectations on attributions and on the cognitive activity that accompanies these attributions. Hamilton points out that heretofore most attribution theorists have not considered the cognitive process and representational consequences of engaging in causal reasoning. The conceptual emphasis has shifted from studying only whether a person makes a situational or dispositional attribution to a probing of the cognitive consequences associated with making attributions.

Crocker *et al.* (1983) have shown that the type of attribution elicited by inconsistent behaviors affects whether the inconsistent information is retained in memory and how that information is linked to other information about the stimulus person. Preferential recall for inconsistent information was found following dispositional but not situational attributions. This research, like Hamilton's (this volume), examined the implications of the Hastie–Srull model for attribution research (see also Hastie 1984).

Attitudes

A second area in which inconsistency management plays a fundamental role is in theories of cognitive consistency and attitude change (Abelson *et al.* 1968). A great deal of research was generated to evaluate how people achieve consistency in the cognitive system. Most theoretical approaches were a variant on Heider's (1958) P–O–X system (see Insko 1981). The attitude of a person (P) toward an attitude object (X) was part of a cognitive structure involving P's attitude toward another person (O) and O's attitude toward X. Balance was achieved if two friends (P likes O) had the same attitudes toward X, or if two enemies (P dislikes O) disagreed about X. Other attitudinal structures were imbalanced. They would be unstable, and tended to shift toward a more consistent (or balanced) structure.

This line of theorizing can potentially lead to the kinds of work now being conducted under the information-processing approach. Unfortunately, most previous researchers approach these issues from the point-on-a-continuum perspective. Most research looked only at the effects of imbalance on ratings of attitudes on a pro–con scale (even though Heider's original presentation viewed these bonds as being discrete states of positive or negative). No work was done on the inferences that people made in an effort to resolve the inconsistencies. Perhaps Anderson (1981, 1982) captured this overall orientation best when he observed that the tendencies toward balance and congruity are derivable from the general principle of information integration. Future work on imbalanced structures will doubtless examine the inferences and explanatory structures people develop when such cognitive representations become activated.

Attitude change research has historically faced the problem of how targets of persuasive communications will respond to attitudinally discrepant (i.e. inconsistent) information. Early models of attitude change focused on a set of logical stages involved in responding to a persuasive communication (Hovland *et al.* 1953). Hovland and his collegues organized their studies of communication and attitude change around the question, "Who says what to whom with what effect?" The most important stages involved include attention to the message, comprehension of the message, yielding to the message, and retention of the message. Although this orientation (sometimes referred to as an "information-processing approach" – see McGuire 1968) did not yield a coherent model of the cognitive activity involved in responding to a persuasive communication, it did serve a heuristic function for organizing the research on attitude change.

This early work can be viewed as a precursor of more contemporary models of information-processing. Although the phases of information-processing differ, the approaches have in common a metatheoretical perspective that invites process to be broken down into distinct phases. The advantages of the contemporary models is that they suggest a mechanism for studying the qualitative nature of change in terms of cognitive activity (e.g. encoding, storage and retrieval) and structure. As with the impression formation domain, contemporary models suggest new approaches to old problems.

Contemporary information-processing models offer an analysis of the cognitive activities involved in the question "*Who* said *what* to *whom* with what *effect*?" For example, Devine and Ostrom's research on jurors' evaluation of inconsistent testimony from an unreliable source sheds some light on the *who* and *what* components of the question. Although not specifically an attitude change study, Devine and Ostrom found that different interpretations of the *what* depended on whether subjects were able to link up the *what* (inconsistent testimony) with the *who* that said it (unreliable source). Linking *who* and *what* affected encoding elaboration processes, and produced qualitatively different cognitive representations of the testimony from those produced when the *who* and *what* were not linked.

The *whom* component of the attitude change process invites an individual differences analysis on the part of the target of a persuasive communication. Although variables such as educational level, gender, and cognitive complexity have traditionally been studied (see Petty and Cacioppo 1981 for a review), contemporary models suggest that a self-schema analysis might be appropriate. This approach suggests that different *whoms* may attend to different aspects of a communication depending on their self-representations and general knowledge structures.

Yielding coupled with message retention are prerequisites for successful persuasion in the model by Hovland *et al.* (1953). Yielding was an outcome in this model, but the model provided no clear account of the process by which yielding occurred. In fact the audience members were assumed to be passive recipients of the persuasive communication.

Contemporary work on the cognitive response approach to persuasion replaces this passive audience with an active, thinking audience (Petty *et al.* 1981, Petty and Cacioppo 1981). As an audience member listens to a persuasive communication, she or he generates thoughts that are favorable (e.g. supportive of the communication) or unfavorable (e.g. counterarguments against the advocated position). Persuasion occurs when the number of favorable thoughts generated in response to the communication exceed the number of counterarguments generated. Thus far, most work on the cognitive response approach has proceeded in the absence of explicit information-processing models. But now that the utility of these models has been established in the field of impression formation, we anticipate their speedy adoption in the analysis of cognitive responses to persuasion.

An additional issue of importance to both old and new models is how the respondent generates overt responses to attitudinal inquiries from their covert, cognitive representations. Whereas the message-learning model (Hovland *et al.* 1953) assumed that message retention was a key component of persuasion, the cognitive response model suggests that message retention is not important for the persuasion process. In fact, people seem to access their cognitive responses rather than specific message content when generating attitudinal responses (Greenwald 1968, Petty *et al.* 1981). Note the similarity in this analysis and the analysis offered by Lingle and Ostrom (1979, 1981, Ostrom *et al.* 1981) for how people use previous judgments of a target person when making a current judgment. People preferentially access evaluations generated at the encoding phase of the information-processing sequence, rather than the literal stimulus items, when subsequently asked to make new judgments about the stimulus person. Thus attitude change, like impression formation, is a dynamic process involving more than recall for specific stimulus items and combining them to form a judgment.

More recent research (e.g. Fazio *et al.* 1986, Judd and Kulik 1980, Johnson and Judd 1983, Loken 1984) has focused on the importance of attitude structure in the processing of attitude-consistent and inconsistent information. These efforts have adopted the information-processing perspective examining such issues as the selective processing and recall of attitudinally consistent and inconsistent information. This research is moving us toward a more coherent analysis of the relationship between attitude structure (e.g. as an associative network) and cognitive activity involved in responding to attitude relevant information.

Implications of inconsistency for social knowledge

A primary goal of this volume is to explore the nature of social knowledge. Distinctions can be made between the contents of knowledge, the structure of knowledge, and the processes by which social knowledge is acquired, used, or modified. This chapter has examined two theoretical approaches toward inconsistency management in social knowledge. In this section we compare these approaches on the content, structure, and process themes.

"Content" typically refers to the semantic elements in the cognitive system. These include both items of stimulus information (e.g. behavioral observations and reports from other people) and the inferences or attributions made about the other person. We argue that content does not differ between the point-on-a-continuum theories and the information-processing models. Cognitive elements are represented in both approaches, although in different ways. The weight and scale values are the critical features of cognitive elements in the dimensional approach, whereas their links to other cognitions is the critical feature for the information-processing approach.

The second theme concerns the structure of the elements within the cognitive system. Point-on-a-continuum theories do not deal with structure issues. They view cognitive elements as being independent of one another. Scale values never change as a function of content (Anderson 1981), although weights may shift. Unfortunately, the theory offers no *a priori* basis for predicting weight shift.

In contrast, the information-processing approach suggests that there are many structures possible that link elements in the cognitive system. For example, scripts (Schank and Abelson 1977), schemata (Hastie 1981, Taylor and Crocker 1981, Fiske and Taylor 1983, Rumelhart 1984, Brewer and Nakamura 1984), prototypes (Cantor and Mischel 1979), and stories (Pennington 1981, Devine and Ostrom 1985) have all been proposed as structures used to organize relations among cognitive elements. Wyer and Srull (this volume) suggest three different approaches to exploring the relations among cognitive elements: the feature list approach, the network approach, and the depth of processsing approach (see Markus and Zajonc 1985 for a related review). Also distinct from the dimensional approach, relations among cognitive elements in the information-processing approach can be identified independently of their relationship to any particular judgment continuum.

As process models, the point-on-a-continuum and information-processing approaches differ substantially. Process, according to point-on-a-continuum models, involves assigning weights and scale values to items (a valuation phase) and combining these values according to some algebraic function (an integration phase) to produce an overt judgment. Information-processing models, however, emphasize the dynamics that occur at encoding and retrieval. Researchers working within the information-processing framework articulate specific processing assumptions associated with encoding (e.g. attention, pattern-matching), storage (e.g. how long an item stays in short-term memory, how information is organized in long-term memory), and retrieval (what rules govern the initiation and termination of memory search, what are effective retrieval cues). These issues are discussed further by Anderson (1983), Lichtenstein and Srull (1985), and Wyer and Srull (this volume).

Is the shift really new? – Yes and No

We stated earlier that the information-processing theories have revolutionized the study of social perception, and illustrated the point with research on inconsistency management. Ostrom (1981) suggested that the success of a new theoretical orientation is measured by its ability to *challenge* previously accepted explanations, *resolve* pre-existing controversy, *integrate* diverse empirical topics, *identify* new independent and dependent variables, and *predict* new relationships. Our review of the research on inconsistency illustrates the potential of information-processing models to accomplish all five objectives.

It is clear that the information processing approach has challenged the descriptive, point-on-a-continuum models as explanations for discounting and primacy–recency effects. In addition, it has the potential to integrate diverse areas of social perception including impression formation, attribution, and attitude change. New independent and dependent variables have been suggested, and have proved to be informative regarding cognitive activity involved in social perception. Moreover, this approach has enabled researchers to predict new relationships among variables that were outside the realm of point-on-a-continuum theories.

The information-processing models render tractable important problems in the study of inconsistency that have previously defied rigorous theoretical and methodological solution. Most notable in this regard has been the problem of identifying the different qualitative strategies people might use to resolve inconsistency. For example, Abelson (1959) offered a logical analysis of how people might resolve belief dilemmas. He identified four different modes: denial, bolstering, differentiation, and transcendence. In addition, he offered a set of propositions that attempt to specify which modes will be used under what circumstances.

Abelson's analysis was actually sketched in terms of associative network structures. But it was offered in advance of the development of more formal information-processing models, and so never became fully formalized. Nor did it lead to any empirical research. What research has been published on this problem (Gollin 1954, Asch and Zukier 1984) has been content to provide subjective content analyses of paragraphs written by subjects who were given inconsistent information about the target person.

There is every promise now that researchers will return to the question of modes of inconsistency resolution and the rules governing adoption. The constructs and methods now available from the information-processing perspective should rapidly advance our understanding of these processes.

One of the most enlightening contributions of information-processing models stems from their potential to resolve pre-existing controversies. A longstanding controversy in impression formation research concerned the existence of meaning change, the possibility that a word or event can have different meanings in different contexts (Asch 1946, Kaplan 1971b). It is argued that many words have multiple meanings that may vary from positive to negative in favorability. For example, aggressive can be a positively valued trait (e.g. a go-getter) or can be evaluatively negative (e.g. hostile). Which meaning is activated is likely to depend on the context words (e.g. successful, energetic versus mean, obnoxious).

The alternative to meaning change is that context effects can be explained by a variant of the cognitive algebra rules (Anderson 1981, Anderson and Lampel 1965, Wyer and Watson 1969). This approach assumes that the scale values (s_i) do not change as a function of context. The original debate over the possibility of meaning change was brought to a halt when it was recognized that the lack of theoretical precision and inadequate methodologies prohibited a definitive resolution (Ostrom 1977). The meaning shift controversy is now essentially resolved. The resolution did not occur through a refinement of theory and method, but by abandoning the point-on-a-continuum framing of the problem. It was inherently impossible properly to represent meaning shift within the constraints of the dimensional approach. On the other hand, the concept of meaning shift is an integral part of the texture of the information-processing approach.

Associative networks represent meaning in terms of the set of nodes activated by the stimulus item, and that set is always affected by contextual features. The question is no longer one of whether meaning shift exists, but rather one of identifying the conditions and mechanisms responsible for it.

It seems clear that the paradigm used to study social perception has undergone a fundamental transformation. However, as is evident in our coverage of inconsistency research, most of the underlying concerns have remained unchanged. In fact, if we review the history of research on social perception, we can see the antecedents of information-processing models in the work of Asch (1946), Kelly (1955), Peak (1958), and Bruner (1957). For example, Asch's use of personality descriptions as stimuli and his use of impression paragraphs and trait ascriptions as dependent variables is completely consistent with contemporary models. Unfortunately, the formal models that received the greatest theoretical attention at that time could not accommodate Asch's concepts or dependent measures. As a result, the issues Asch pursued (meaning change, context effects, primacy–recency, discounting) were forced into the theoretical zeitgeist of that time, the point-on-a-continuum theories.

Our emphasis has been on social perceivers as active processors of information who seek knowledge about and understanding of their social world. Social perception involves acquiring information about other people, most often over time. People do not always behave consistently with our expectations about them, and this introduces instability into our social experiences. How the perceiver makes sense of these inconsistencies provides key insights into the processes involved in social knowledge. Inconsistencies provide grist for our cognitive mill. They instigate cognitive activity (for example, causal reasoning to explain the inconsistent event), they drive the process of inference generation, and they influence social judgments. We have just begun to open new vistas of social knowledge with the information-processing approach. Research on inconsistency management will continue as one of the key windows to future understanding.

References

Abelson, R. P. (1959). Modes of resolution of belief dilemmas. *Journal of Conflict Resolution* 3: 343–52.

Abelson, R. P., Aronson, E., McGuire, W. J., Newcomb, T. M., Rosenberg, M. J., and Tannenbaum, P. H. (1968). Theories of cognitive consistency: a sourcebook. Chicago: Rand McNally.

Anderson, J. R. (1983). *The architecture of cognition.* Cambridge, MA: Harvard University Press.

Anderson, J. R. and Bower, G. H. (1973). *Human associative memory*. Washington, DC: Winston.

Anderson, N. H. (1967). Averaging model analysis as a stimulus combination rule in impression formation. *Journal of Experimental Social Psychology* 75: 158–65.

Anderson, N. H. (1968). Likeableness ratings of 555 personality-trait words. *Journal of Personality and Social Psychology* 9: 272–9.

Anderson, N. H. (1974). Cognitive algebra: integration theory applied to social attribution. In L. Berkowitz (ed.), *Advances in experimental social psychology*, vol. 7. New York: Academic Press.

Anderson, N. H. (1981). *Foundations of information integration theory*. New York: Academic Press.

Anderson, N. H. (1982). *Methods of information integration theory*. New York: Academic Press.

Anderson, N. H. and Hubert, S. (1963). Effects of concomitant verbal recall on order effects in personality impression formation. *Journal of Verbal Learning and Verbal Behavior* 2: 379–91.

Anderson, N. H. and Jacobson, A. (1965). Effect of stimulus inconsistency and discounting instructions in personality impression information. *Journal of Personality and Social Psychology* 2: 531–9.

Anderson, N. H. and Lampel, A. K. (1965). Effect of context on ratings of personality traits. *Psychonomic Science* 3: 433–4.

Asch, S. E. (1946). Forming impressions of personality. *Journal of Abnormal and Personality Psychology* 41: 258–90.

Asch, S. E. (1952). *Social psychology*. Englewood Cliffs, NJ: Prentice-Hall.

Asch, S. E. and Zukier, H. (1984). Thinking about persons. *Journal of Personality and Social Psychology* 46: 1230–40.

Bargh, J. A. and Thein, R. D. (1985). Individual construct accessibility, person memory, and the recall–judgment link: the case of information overload. *Journal of Personality and Social Psychology* 49: 1129–46.

Bernstein, E. and Schul, Y. (1982). The informational basis of social judgments: operations in forming an impression of another person. *Journal of Experimental Social Psychology* 18: 217–34.

Bernstein, E. and Schul, Y. (1983). The informational basis of social judgments: memory for integrated and nonintegrated trait descriptions. *Journal of Experimental Social Psychology* 19: 49–57.

Birnbaum, M. H. and Stegner, S. E. (1979). Source credibility in social judgment: bias, expertise, and the judge's point of view. *Journal of Personality and Social Psychology* 37: 48–74.

Brewer, W. F. and Nakamura, G. V. (1984). The nature and functions of schemas. In Wyer and Srull 1984, vol. 1.

Bruner, J. S. (1957). On perceptual readiness. *Psychological Review* 64: 123–52.

Bruner, J. S. and Tagiuri, R. (1954). Person perception. In G. Lindzey and E. Aronson (eds.), *Handbook of social psychology*, vol. 2. Reading, MA: Addison-Wesley.

Cantor, N. and Mischel, W. (1979). Prototypes in person perception. In L. Berkowitz (ed.), *Advances in experimental social psychology*, vol. 12. New York: Academic Press.

Collins, A. M. and Loftus, E. F. (1975). A spreading-activation theory of semantic processing. *Psychological Review* 82: 407–28.

Crocker, J., Hannah, D. B., and Weber, R. (1983). Person memory and causal attributions. *Journal of Personality and Social Psychology* 44: 55–66.

Devine, P. G. and Ostrom, T. M. (1985). Cognitive mediation of inconsistency discounting. *Journal of Personality and Social Psychology* 49: 1–17.

Erber, R. and Fiske, S. T. (1984). Outcome dependency and attention to inconsistent information. *Journal of Personality and Social Psychology* 47: 709–26.

Fazio, R. H., Sanbonnmastsu, D. M., Powell, M. C., and Kardes, F. R. (1986). On the automatic activation of attitudes. *Journal of Personality and Social Psychology* 50: 229–38.

Fishbein, M. (1967). A behavior theory approach to the relations between beliefs about an object and the attitude toward the object. In M. Fishbein (ed.), *Readings in attitude theory and attitude measurement*. New York: Wiley.

Fishbein, M. and Hunter, R. (1964). Summation versus balance in attitude organization and change. *Journal of Abnormal and Social Psychology* 69: 505–10.

Fiske, S. T. and Taylor, S. E. (1984). *Social cognition*. Reading, MA: Addison-Wesley.

Gholson, B. and Barker, P. (1985). Kuhn, Lakatos, and Laudan. *American Psychologist* 40: 755–69.

Gollin, E. S. (1954). Forming impressions of personality. *Journal of Personality* 23: 65–76.

Greenwald, A. G. (1968). Cognitive learning, cognitive response to persuasion and attitude change. In A. G. Greenwald, T. C. Brock, and T. M. Ostrom (eds.), *Psychological foundations of attitudes*. New York: Academic Press.

Hastie, R. (1980). Memory for behavioral information that confirms or contradicts a personality impression. In Hastie *et al.* 1980.

Hastie, R. (1981). Schematic principles in human memory. In E. T. Higgins, C. P. Herman, and M. P. Zanna (eds.), *Social cognition: the Ontario symposium*, vol. 1. Hillsdale, NJ: Lawrence Erlbaum.

Hastie, R. (1984). Causes and effects of causal attribution. *Journal of Personality and Social Psychology* 46: 44–56.

Hastie, R. and Kumar, A. P. (1979). Person memory: personality traits as organizing principles in memory for behaviors. *Journal of Personality and Social Psychology* 37: 25–38.

Hastie, R., Ostrom, T. M., Ebbesen, E. B., Wyer, R. S., Hamilton, D. L., and Carlston, D. E. (eds.) (1980). *Person memory: the cognitive basis of social perception*. Hillsdale, NJ: Lawrence Erlbaum.

Heider, F. (1958). *The psychology of interpersonal relations*. Hillsdale, NJ: Lawrence Erlbaum.

Hemsley, G. D. and Marmurek, H. H. C. (1982). Person memory: the processing of consistent and inconsistent person information. *Personality and Social Psychology Bulletin* 8: 433–8.

Hendrick, C. and Costantini, A. F. (1970). Effects of varying trait inconsistency and response requirements on the primary effect in impression formation. *Journal of Personality and Social Psychology* 15: 158–64.

Hovland, C. I., Janis, I. L., and Kelley, J. J. (1953). *Communication and persuasion*. New Haven: Yale University Press.

Insko, C. A. (1981). Balance theory and phenomenology. In Petty *et al.* 1981.

Johnson, J. T. and Judd, C. M. (1983). Overlooking the incongruent: categorization biases in the identification of political statements. *Journal of Personality and Social Psychology* 45: 978–96.

Jones, E. E. and Davis, K. E. (1965). From acts to dispositions: the attribution process in person perception. In L. Berkowitz (ed.), *Advances in experimental social psychology*, vol. 2. New York: Academic Press.

Judd, C. M. and Kulik, J. (1980). Schematic effects of social attitudes upon information processing and recall. *Journal of Personality and Social Psychology* 38: 569–78.

Kaplan, M. F. (1971a). Dispositional effects and weight of information in impression formation. *Journal of Personality and Social Psychology* 18: 279–84.

Kaplan, M. F. (1971b). Context effects in impression formation: the weighted average versus the meaning change formulation. *Journal of Personality and Social Psychology* 19: 92–9.

Kaplan, M. F. (1973). Stimulus inconsistency and response dispositions in forming judgments of other persons. *Journal of Personality and Social Psychology* 25: 58–64.

Kelley, H. H. (1967). Attribution theory in social psychology. In *Nebraska symposium on motivation*. Lincoln: University of Nebraska Press.

Kelly, G. A. (1955). *The psychology of personal constructs*. New York: Norton.

Kuhn, T. S. (1962). *The structure of scientific revolutions*. Chicago: University of Chicago Press.

Lachman, R., Lachman, J. L., and Butterfield, E. C. (1979). *Cognitive psychology and information processing: an introduction*. Hillsdale, NJ: Lawrence Erlbaum.

Lakatos, I. (1970). Falsification and the methodology of scientific research programmes. In I. Lakatos and A. Musgrave (eds.), *Criticism and the growth of knowledge*. Cambridge: Cambridge University Press.

Lichtenstein, M. and Srull, T. K. (1985). Conceptual and methodological issues in examining the relationship between consumer memory and judgment. In L. F. Alwitt and A. A. Mitchell (eds.), *Psychological processes and advertising effects: theory, research and application*. Hillsdale, NJ: Lawrence Erlbaum.

Lingle, J. H. and Ostrom, T. M. (1979). Retrieval selectivity in memory-based impression judgments. *Journal of Personality and Social Psychology* 37: 180–94.

Lingle, J. H. and Ostrom, T. M. (1981). Principles of memory and cognition in attitude formation. In Petty *et al.* 1981.

Loken, B. (1984). Attitude processing strategies. *Journal of Experimental Social Psychology* 20: 272–96.

Luchins, A. S. (1957). Primacy–recency in impression formation. In C. Hovland (ed.), *The order of presentation in persuasion*. New Haven, Conn.: Yale University Press.

McGuire, W. J. (1968). Personality and attitude change: an information processing theory. In A. G. Greenwald, T. C. Brock, and T. M. Ostrom (eds.), *Psychological foundations of attitudes*. New York: Academic Press.

McGuire, W. J. (1981). The probabological model of cognitive structure and attitude change. In Petty *et al.* 1981.

Manis, M., Gleason, T. C., and Dawes, R. M. (1966). The evaluation of complex social stimuli. *Journal of Personality and Social Psychology* 3: 404–19.

Markus, H. and Zajonc, R. B. (1985). The cognitive perspective in social psychology. In G. Lindzey and E. Aronson (eds.), *Handbook of social psychology*, 3rd edn. Reading, MA: Addison-Wesley.

Ostrom, T. M. (1977). Between-theory and within-theory conflict in explaining context effects on impression formation. *Journal of Experimental Social Psychology* 13: 492–503.

Ostrom, T. M. (1981a). Theoretical perspectives in the analysis of cognitive responses. In Petty *et al.* 1981.

Ostrom, T. M. (1981b). Attribution theory: whence and whither. In J. H. Harvey, W. Ickes, and R. F. Kidd (eds.), *New directions in attribution research*, vol. 3. Hillsdale, NJ: Lawrence Erlbaum.

Ostrom, T. M. (1984a). The sovereignty of social cognition. In Wyer and Srull 1984.

Ostrom, T. M. (1984b). Social cognition. In R. J. Corsini (ed.), *Wiley encyclopedia of psychology*. New York: Wiley.

Ostrom, T. M., Lingle, J. H., Pryor, J. B., and Geva, N. (1981). Cognitive organization of impressions. In Hastie *et al.* 1980.

Peak, H. (1958). Psychological structure and person perception. In R. Tagiuri and L. Petrullo (eds.), *Person perception and interpersonal behavior*. Stanford, CA: Stanford University Press.

Pennington, N. (1981). *Causal reasoning and decision making: the case of juror decisions*. Unpublished dissertation, Harvard University.

Pepitone, A. and Hayden, R. (1955). Some evidence for conflict resolution in impression formation. *Journal of Abnormal and Social Psychology* 51: 302–7.

Petty, R. E. and Cacioppo, J. T. (1981). *Attitudes and persuasion: classic and contemporary approaches*. Dubuque, Iowa: Wm. C. Brown.

Petty, R. E., Ostrom, T. M., and Brock, T. C. (eds.) (1981). *Cognitive responses in persuasion*. Hillsdale, NJ: Lawrence Erlbaum.

Piaget, J. (1952). *The origins of intelligence in children*. New York: International Universities Press.

Rosenbaum, M. E. and Levin, I. P. (1968). Impression formation as a function of

the relative amounts of information presented by high and low credibility sources. *Psychonomic Science* 12: 349–50.
Rosenbaum, M. E. and Levin, I. P. (1969). Impression formation as a function of source credibility and the polarity of information. *Journal of Personality and Social Psychology* 12: 34–7.
Rosenberg, M. J. (1956). Cognitive structure and attitudinal affect. *Journal of Abnormal and Social Psychology* 53: 367–72.
Rumelhart, D. E. (1984). Schemata and the cognitive system. In Wyer and Srull 1984.
Schank, R. C. and Abelson, R. P. (1977). *Scripts, plans, and understanding: an inquiry into human knowledge structures.* Hillsdale, NJ: Lawrence Erlbaum.
Srull, T. K. (1981). Person memory: Some tests of associative storage and retrieval models. *Journal of Experimental Psychology: Human Learning and Memory*: 440–63.
Srull, T. K., Lichtenstein, M., and Rothbart, M. (1985). Associative storage and retrieval processes in person memory. *Journal of Experimental Psychology: Learning, Memory, Cognition* 11: 316–45.
Stewart, R. (1965). Effect of continuous responding on the order effect in personality impression formation. *Journal of Personality and Social Psychology* 1: 161–5.
Taylor, S. E. and Crocker, J. (1981). Schematic bases of social information processing. In E. T. Higgins, C. P. Herman, and M. P. Zanna (eds.), *Social cognition: the Ontario Symposium*, vol. 1. Hillsdale, NJ: Lawrence Erlbaum.
Wyer, R. S. (1970). Information, redundancy, inconsistency, and novelty and their role in impression formation. *Journal of Experimental Social Psychology* 6: 111–27.
Wyer, R. S. (1974). *Cognitive organization and change: an information processing approach.* Hillsdale, NJ: Lawrence Erlbaum.
Wyer, R. S. and Goldberg, L. (1970). A probabilistic analysis of the relationships among beliefs and attitudes. *Psychological Review* 77: 100–20.
Wyer, R. S. and Gordon, S. E. (1982). The recall of information about persons and groups. *Journal of Experimental Social Psychology* 18: 128–64.
Wyer, R. S. and Srull, T. K. (1980). The processing of social stimulus information: a conceptual integration. In Hastie *et al.* 1980.
Wyer, R. S. and Srull, T. K. (eds.) 1984. *Handbook of social cognition.* Hillsdale, NJ: Lawrence Erlbaum.
Wyer, R. S. and Unverzagt, W. H. (1985). Effects of instructions to disregard information on its subsequent recall and use in making judgments. *Journal of Personality and Social Psychology* 48: 533–49.
Wyer, R. S. and Watson, S. F. (1969). Context effects in impression formation. *Journal of Personality and Social Psychology* 12: 22–33.
Zajonc, R. B. (1968). Cognitive theories in social psychology. In G. Lindzey and E. Aronson (eds.), *The handbook of social psychology*, vol. 1. Reading, MA: Addison-Wesley.

11 Context-driven social judgment and memory: when "behavior engulfs the field" in reconstructive memory

E. Tory Higgins and Charles Stangor

In recent years there has been an explosion of research on people's implicit "theories" of the social world, including their social schemata, constructs, beliefs, and expectancies. This line of investigation has demonstrated the remarkable extent to which social judgment is "theory-driven" rather than just "data-driven" (for reviews see Cantor and Mischel 1979, Fiske and Taylor 1984, Hastie 1981, Higgins and King 1981, Markus and Zajonc 1985, Taylor and Crocker 1981). It is well known that two perceivers who are exposed to the same information may pay attention to different details, represent and encode different attributes, and later retrieve different aspects of this information. But the *same* individual may also process the same information in different ways at different times. Thus, a full understanding of the perceiver's role in social perception entails knowing not only why different individuals use different constructs to interpret similar events, but why the same individual will interpret the same information differently in different contexts. One purpose of the present chapter is to consider the extent to which "theory-driven" processing is itself "context-driven".

There is no such thing as a truly "context-free" judgment. Although this is well recognized, little attention has been paid to the implications for social knowledge of the fact that the judgment (or encoding) in judgment-based memory has occurred in some context that may have influenced the judgment. To what extent is the context of judgment taken into account when the judgment is later used to reconstruct the original stimulus information that was judged? One of the most interesting phenomena described in the social perception literature is when "behavior engulfs the field" (Heider 1958) or the so-called "fundamental attribution error" (see Jones 1979, Ross 1977). This phenomenon refers to instances when perceivers' judgments of a target's response focus on the response and fail to take into account sufficiently the impact of the target's circumstances on the response. Given that individuals' judgments of stimulus information are themselves responses, is it possible that individuals sometimes fail to take into account sufficiently the impact of their *own* circumstances on their judgments? And, if so, is this not especially likely to happen when considerable time has elapsed between when they made the judgment and when they use it in reconstructive memory? Another purpose of the present paper is to consider these questions.

The nature of context effects

In order to examine context effects on theory-driven processing, it is necessary to distinguish different kinds of context effect. But in order to do this one must first define "context effects". For our purposes, let us define the general phenomenon of *context effects* as when a difference in context causes a difference in response to the same target by the same perceiver. Whenever a study finds evidence of perceivers responding differently to targets, one can ask what is the source of the differential responding – different targets (i.e. different stimulus information made available to perceivers), different perceivers, or different contexts of perception? To conclude that differential responding is due to a context effect, therefore, one must control for the effects of different targets and different perceivers. Of course, in many studies of context effects comparisons are made between groups of subjects exposed to the same target stimulus in different contexts, with the assumption that the perceivers in the different contexts are the "same" because of random assignment.

The importance of context effects in social cognition have long been recognized by social psychologists (e.g. Asch 1952, Brunswick 1943, Lewin 1951, Mead 1934), but different types of context effects have not been distinguished. The major distinction we propose is between *context effects on the target* and *context effects on the perceiver*. Context effects on the target occur when information about the target's context causes a different response to the target, as in attribution studies where the target's context affects attributions by providing information about factors that may have influenced the target's behavior (e.g. Heider 1958, Jones and Davis 1965). Context effects on the perceiver occur when perceivers process the same target information but the circumstances of the perceivers themselves are different when they process the information. Two subtypes of perceiver context effects can also be distinguished – *perceiver context, data-driven* effects and *perceiver context, theory-driven* effects. The former refers to cases where the perceiver's context affects the proximal stimulus – how the stimulus is registered perceptually. The latter refers to cases where the perceiver context affects which "theories" or constructs are utilized in processing the stimulus.

The major purpose of this chapter is to review evidence of perceiver context, theory-driven effects on social cognition with particular emphasis on our own research in this area. In order to highlight the specific nature of these effects and instantiate our proposed classificatory scheme, however, we will also briefly discuss the distinctions between context effects and non-context effects and the distinctions among the different kinds of context effects. In the concluding section, we will consider whether context-driven processing produces invalid knowledge of the social world.

Context effects versus noncontext effects

The social psychological literature contains various descriptions of "context effects" that would not be considered as such in our scheme. Perhaps the best example is the impression formation literature (see Anderson 1974, Asch 1946, Hamilton and Zanna 1974, Higgins and Rholes 1976, Ostrom 1977). The method of impression formation studies is systematically to vary the attributes used to describe a stimulus person. Typically, some of the attributes are held constant across conditions while other attributes are varied. Subsequently, judgments are made about the target person described by the attributes. In the best-known of these studies, Asch (1946) found that a stimulus person was judged differently depending upon whether the terms "warm" or "cold" were present in the list of traits. Although the results of this and similar studies suggest that the significance of target attributes can vary depending on the other target attributes with which they co-occur, they are not considered "context effects" in the present scheme. In each of these studies, the subjects in different conditions are exposed to *different* sets of attributes describing the target person. Thus, even when the studies demonstrate holistic, "change-of-meaning" effects (e.g. Higgins and Rholes 1976, Zanna and Hamilton 1977), they represent *target effects* and not context effects.

In addition to being distinguished from target effects, context effects must also be distinguished from *perceiver effects*. There are many examples of this type of effect. Most obvious perhaps are individual difference variables, such as self-monitoring (Snyder 1979), authoritarianism (Adorno *et al.* 1950), and cognitive complexity (e.g. Crockett 1965). Also included here are individual social theories (e.g. implicit personality theories, attributional styles), and chronic individual differences in the availability and accessibility of social constructs (see Bargh 1984, Higgins *et al.* 1982, Kelly

1955). When individual differences in orientation or constructs arise from prolonged situational differences, their effects on social cognition could be described as prolonged "context" effects. For example, the effects of poverty on the perception of coins (e.g. Bruner and Goodman 1947) or the effects of hunger on the perception of food-related stimuli (e.g. Levine *et al.* 1942) might be described as prolonged context effects on perception (as mediated by value and need). Judgment and memory effects of individual differences in chronic construct accessibility that arise from individual differences in prolonged exposure to construct-activating events (see Higgins *et al.* 1982) might also be described as prolonged context effects. To do so, however, would blur the distinction between perceiver effects and context effects, since most perceiver differences could be described as prolonged individual differences in context.

This is not to say that only the effects of circumstances that are coextensive with stimulus processing should be considered "context effects". Indeed, as will be discussed later, we consider the judgmental impact of increasing the accessibility of constructs by activating them in a prior task to represent a context effect. The issue is whether the individual difference is temporary and dependent on a current or recent specific context or whether it is chronic and relatively independent of any particular context. If it is the former, then any effects are considered to be context effects; if the latter, then any effects are perceiver effects.

Context effects on the target versus context effects on the perceiver

As discussed earlier, context effects on the target occur when information about the target's circumstances causes a difference in response to the target information. An example of a context effect on the target is Jones *et al.*'s (1961) finding that subjects' trait ratings of a target person's behavior (for example, making statements in an interview that reflected extreme other-directedness – friendliness, cooperativeness, and gregariousness) varied depending on the information they were given about the circumstances surrounding the behavior (the target was trying to appear qualified for a position either as a submariner, which requires the possession of other directed traits, or as an astronaut, which requires the possession of inner-directed traits). Another example of a context effect on the target is Newtson and Czerlinsky's (1974) finding that subjects shown a target person's message advocating a "hawkish" position on the Vietnam war judged the target's true position on the war to be less "hawkish" if they were told that the target's audience was "hawkish" than if they were told it was "dovish" (see also Eagly *et al.* 1978). In such cases perceivers judge a target's behavior differently because the context in which the target's behavior occurs is different. As discussed next, perceiver context effects involve cases where perceivers' judgments are influenced by the circumstances surrounding their processing of the target information; that is, by their *own* circumstances rather than by their knowledge of the target's circumstances. Indeed, some readers may wish to include under "context effects" only those cases involving perceiver context effects.

Data-driven versus theory-driven effects of perceiver context

The circumstances surrounding perceivers' processing of stimulus information can influence their judgments and memory either by modifying how information in the stimulus is registered (i.e. modifying the proximal stimulus), which are data-driven effects, or by modifying which constructs available to them are utilized in interpreting and representing the stimulus, which are theory-driven effects. The difficult, yet not impossible, task of distinguishing these effects is perhaps best exemplified by the work on "contrast" and "assimilation" effects (Campbell *et al.* 1958, Cupchik and Poulos 1984, Manis 1966, 1967, Manis and Armstrong 1971, Sherman *et al.* 1978). These investigations, conducted in both social and nonsocial realms, repeatedly find that judgments of target stimuli may be "contrasted" (judged as more different from the context stimuli than they actually are) or "assimilated" (judged as more similar to the context stimuli than they actually are) depending upon a host of contextual factors. In a classic study, Campbell *et al.* (1958) had clinical judges rate the pathological severity of clinical vocabulary definitions. The ratings showed a contrast effect of context such that midscale (neutral) definitions were rated as less pathological when in the context of many high pathological items and were rated as more pathological in the context of low pathological items.

But how should contrast and assimilation findings be classified? Context is certainly influencing judgment in these studies – the target stimuli remain the same across conditions while only the surrounding field is varied. But does the context influence the actual perception of the stimulus data or only how the perceived data is interpreted or encoded? This is a difficult question to answer because it is usually not clear where in the stimulus-processing cycle the effects are occurring.

Some contrast–assimilation effects probably involve different *perception* of the target stimuli as a function of their context, as when a gray circle is perceived as darker or lighter when placed against a white or black background, respectively (see Gregory 1966). In such cases, although the distal stimuli (target stimuli) are identical, the proximal stimuli are not. Several studies support the notion of perceptual contrast effects, both for psychophysiological (Krantz and Campbell 1961) and social stimuli (Manis 1967, Manis and Armstrong 1971). The results from such studies suggest that they involve perceiver context, *data-driven* effects.

Other contrast and assimilation effects seem to involve perceiver context, *theory-driven* effects. One explanation of contrast-assimilation findings that suggests theory-driven effects derives from the so-called "rubber-band" model proposed by Volkmann (1951) and elaborated by others (Campbell *et al.* 1958, Ostrom and Upshaw 1968, Parducci 1965, Stevens 1958, Upshaw 1962). These theorists emphasize changes in the subject's *subjective scale values*. In this model, the *experience* of the stimuli is always identical – the proximal stimulus is the same in all conditions. Rather, subjects learn the features of the stimuli distribution during their presentation and, at output, stretch the scales that they use to cover the entire spectrum in their experience. In other words, subjects who were given a series of attractive faces but assessed these faces on a rating scale that included an endpoint marked "unattractive" would indeed *rate* some of the faces as somewhat "unattractive."

Phenomenological differences between context effects and target effects and their disappearance over time

Our classificatory scheme has relied on operational definitions to distinguish between context effects and noncontext effects. This has advantages but it also has some obvious limitations, especially if there were no phenomenological differences associated with these operational differences. At least temporarily, however, there are phenomenological differences. In *context* effects on the target, for example, perceivers presented with different information about the target's circumstances can make different causal interpretations of the target's behavior even though their representations of the target features themselves are the same, whereas in target effects the perceivers necessarily have different representations of the target's features. Perceiver context, theory-driven effects also differ from target effects in that perceivers in different contexts can judge the target differently without there being a difference in their representation of the target's features (i.e. the stimulus details). Perceiver context effects can also differ from target effects to the extent that the context is taken into account and represented along with the target information (e.g. "he seemed likeable in comparison to those obnoxious others"; "it felt heavy after lifting all those light weights"; "I made a positive statement about him to his close friend").

These phenomenological differences between context effects and (noncontext) target effects may only be temporary. Consider, for example, the case where the features of a target were initially represented in the same way but the target was judged differently in different contexts. As individuals' representations of the stimulus details decay over time, the target information may be *reconstructed* in terms of the individuals' different prior judgments of the target, thus creating different representations of the target's features. Thus, a target effect, phenomenologically, would be produced. A target effect may also be created over time if individuals remember their judgments but forget the context in which it was made (e.g. "he was likeable"; "it was heavy"; "I felt positive toward him"). To the extent that there is a separation between memory of judgments (e.g. stored with the target in conceptual memory) and memory of context (e.g. stored as events in episodic memory), then the loss of the latter (i.e. its becoming inaccessible over time) would lead to the emergence of a phenomenological target effect that is nondistinguishable from an initial target effect. Indeed, this emergence of a target effect, over time, from an initial context effect is one reason why "context" effects are so interesting, because differences between perceivers exposed to the *same* target behaviors in different contexts become *equivalent phenomenologically* to differences between perceivers exposed to *different* target behaviors in the same context!

Perceiver context, theory-driven effects

The remainder of this chapter focuses on perceiver context, theory-driven effects, which are central to our consideration of the extent to which theory-driven processing is itself context-driven. Two basic kinds of perceiver context, theory-driven effects will be considered – "context-as-foreground" effects and "context-as-background" effects. These two kinds of effects differ with respect to whether context was or was not, respectively, taken into account by perceivers during the processing of the target information. In the case of *context-as-foreground*, perceivers' processing of the target information takes into account (with or without conscious awareness) the features of the context. We will consider this type of context effect by reviewing research on *contextual adaptation* effects, with particular emphasis on verbal encoding-adaptation. In the case of *context-as-background*, perceivers' processing of the target information is influenced by a concurrent or immediately preceding context, but the processing does not take into account the features of the context itself. We will consider this type of context effect by reviewing research on *contextual priming* effects.

Both context-as-foreground effects and context-as-background effects involve the effect of context on the judgment of target information and the effect of the judgment on subsequent memory of the target information. But these two kinds of context effect vary in whether it is the judgment effect or the memory effect that is surprising. In the case of context-as-background, it is the effect of context on judgment that is surprising, because it occurs without perceivers having the context in mind. The subsequent effect of the judgment on memory is less surprising, given that perceivers do not know that their judgment was contextually influenced in any way that would detract from its usefulness as a summary of the input. In the case of context-as-foreground, the effect of context on judgment is *not* surprising, given that the judgment was tailored to take the context into account. Instead, it is the use of the judgment to reconstruct the original target information that is surprising, to the extent that its context-influenced nature is not taken into account sufficiently.

Contextual priming effects

A considerable literature now exists documenting the effects of context on differential *accessibility* of social constructs and the consequences of such accessibility for social information-processing (for reviews, see Bargh 1984, Higgins and Bargh 1987, Higgins and King 1981, Wyer and Srull 1981). Construct accessibility has been defined as "the readiness with which a stored construct is utilized in information processing" (Higgins and King 1981: 71; see also Bruner 1957). The term "availability" has often been used by others (Kahneman and Tversky 1973, Kahneman *et al.* 1982, Nisbett and Ross 1980) to indicate the ease with which stored information is recoverable; for example, the "availability heuristic" is based on the notion that frequency judgments are influenced by the ease with which instances of a class are recoverable from long-term memory. However, "availability" has traditionally referred to the *ability* of an item to be recalled, while the term "accessibility" has been reserved to refer to its ease or likelihood of retrieval (Tulving and Pearlstone 1966, Higgins and King 1981). If an item can be recalled at all, even if this recall comes through an extended memory search or through the presentation of an appropriate cue, then it should be considered *available*. Available information may be more or less accessible, however, depending upon its ease of retrieval or its likelihood of being used as a construct in processing.

Bruner and his colleagues laid the groundwork for investigations into the nature of construct accessibility (Bruner 1951, 1957, Bruner and Goodman 1947, Bruner and Postman 1948, 1949). Although the studies conducted by Bruner's group suffered from problems of interpretation (see Erdelyi 1974 for a review of some of these issues), they did show that accessibility effects were powerful forces shaping social behavior. These early studies concerned the effects of motivation and expectations on the perception of targets, and not the judgmental effects of increasing a construct's accessibility by activating it in a recent context. In the late 1970s, however, studies of contextual priming began to appear in the social psychology literature, as investigators examined the implications of variability in construct accessibility for social judgment (e.g. Higgins 1977, Srull and Wyer 1979). Contextual priming paradigms proved to be a valuable research tool, as different constructs or "theories" could be made relatively more accessible to subjects outside of conscious awareness, allowing manipulations that were free of experimenter demand effects (see Bargh and Pietromonaco 1982, Higgins and Chaires 1980).

Bruner (1957) pointed out that increased accessibility of a construct (1) decreases the perceptual threshold required to recognize the stimulus; (2) reduces the likelihood of recognizing conflicting (but appropriate) stimuli; and (3) causes a wide range of similar stimuli to be interpreted as belonging to the category of the accessible stimulus. There are a number of factors that are known to affect the accessibility of a construct. Bruner outlined two general ways in which constructs could become accessible. First, a construct may become activated and ready to be used because of high subjective probability that it will be encountered as a stimulus. That is, if a given construct is *expected* to occur, functionally it is useful for this construct to be ready for action. Con artists are well known to play upon our expectations. A man in a business suit is expected to be honest at the same time that dishonest possibilities are masked, and ambiguous behaviors are likely to be categorized as honest. Secondly, *motivational* factors (needs, values, attitudes, goals) may influence construct accessibility.

There are now a fairly large number of studies which have shown that expectancies can be manipulated quite outside of the awareness of persons, and that these manipulations can affect subsequent judgments. For example, Bruner and Minturn (1955) conducted a classic *passive expectancy* study. They had subjects view a series of either letters or numbers, and then presented them with a "broken" capital B which had a small separation between the vertical and the curved part of the letter such that it could be perceived as either a "B" or as a "13". When subjects had been previously exposed to letters they called the figure a "B", but when they had been previously exposed to numbers they called it a "13".

Higgins and King (1981) suggested that recent and frequent activation, or priming, of a stored construct also increased its accessibility (see also Wyer and Srull 1981). In a test of this hypothesis, Higgins *et al.* (1977) had subjects form an impression of a target person from a paragraph describing his behaviors (for example, driving in a demolition derby; climbing Mt McKinley). Before receiving this information they participated in an ostensibly unrelated task (a Stroop color-naming task) that required them to use a set of trait names that were either favorable or unfavorable and were either applicable for encoding the targets' behavior (*adventurous* or *reckless*) or were inapplicable for doing so (e.g. *disrespectful*). After reading the behavioral information, subjects characterized the target in their own words and estimated their liking for the person. When the "primed" concepts were applicable for encoding the behavioral information, the primed constructs were more likely to be used to characterize the target person, and evaluations of the target were biased in the direction of the favorableness of the primed constructs. Higgins *et al.* (1977) proposed that trait constructs that were activated by the priming manipulation became more accessible in memory, and were thus more likely to be used when later encoding the target's behaviors. Because the positive versus negative nonapplicable trait terms had no effects on judgments of the target, it was clear that the priming effects on judgment were not due to a mood-induced "halo" effect.

Other investigators have expanded the applications of construct accessibility. Ferguson and Wells (1980) found that priming either consensus, consistency, or distinctiveness information produced attributions that were both faster and more likely to be dominated by the primed dimensions (see also Rholes and Pryor 1982). Bargh (1982) showed that primed constructs were often impossible to ignore and could severely hinder the processing of other conflicting tasks (see also Erdelyi and Appelbaum 1973). Srull and Wyer (1979) demonstrated that it was not necessary to prime a construct using its name, but that priming with behavioral exemplars associated with the construct was sufficient. Finally, Bargh and Pietromonaco (1982) added a new dimension to this literature by showing that it was not even necessary for the subject to be aware of the prime for priming effects to occur.

There is, therefore, substantial evidence that recent contextual priming can influence people's judgments of others through its effects on the accessibility of social constructs. There is also substantial evidence that the judgments in turn influence subsequent responses concerning the original target information (for reviews, see Higgins and King 1981, Wyer and Srull 1981). Moreover, the effects of these context-driven judgments on subsequent responses actually *increase* over time (Higgins and King 1981).

It is also known that the accessibility of a social construct increases as a function of how frequently it has been primed (Higgins *et al.* 1985, Wyer and Srull 1981), and that the impact of priming decreases as the temporal delay between priming and stimulus presentation increases (Higgins and King 1981, Posner 1978, Wyer and Srull 1981). Three kinds of model have been proposed to explain these effects.

Wyer and Srull (1981) proposed a "storage bin" model, where the constructs in each bin are stored in layers in the order in which they were previously used. When stimulus information is interpreted, the relevant bin is searched from the top down so that the constructs at the top are more likely to be retrieved and utilized. When a construct is frequently activated, however, it is more likely to have been recently used and, thus, to remain on top to be subsequently utilized. In this model, therefore, the effect of frequent activation is reinterpreted in terms of its relation to recent activation. Srull and Wyer (1980) report a study that supports this model. They manipulated the time interval between priming of a trait construct and exposure to behavioral information about a target person, as well as the frequency that the trait construct was primed. Subjects' ratings of the target were increasingly related to the primed trait with increases in the number of times the trait had been primed, but were decreasingly related with increases in the length of the delay.

There is a second "battery" model that is implicit in some discussions of priming effects (e.g. Marcel and Forrin 1974, Wyer and Carlston 1979). In this model, a construct is like a battery that is charged by priming, with the likelihood of subsequent utilization being greater for higher levels of charge. Frequency effects in this model would be explained by assuming that the more frequently a construct is primed, the higher is its final level of charge. A third energy cell or "synapse" model of priming effects has been proposed by Higgins and King (1981) and elaborated by Higgins *et al.* (1985). This model proposes that a construct functions like the synapses of vertebrates (see Kandel 1976). In this model, stimulation of a construct through priming increases its action potential to a fixed level, which then slowly dissipates over time. In addition, the more frequently a construct is primed the longer it remains stimulated, and, just as for synapses (e.g. Lloyd 1949), the longer a construct remains stimulated the slower its action potential dissipates.

The major difference between these models concerns the effect of frequent versus recent priming on subsequent stimulus-processing as the delay between final priming and stimulus presentation increases. Higgins *et al.* (1985) conducted a study in which recency of activation and frequency of activation of a construct were independently manipulated in order to test the predictions of each of the above models. Subjects were unobtrusively exposed to both positive and negative primes related to a stimulus description. The stimulus descriptions exemplified the following trait dimensions: independent/aloof, adventurous/reckless, and persistent/stubborn. These pairs were constructed so that the members of each pair differed in social desirability but referred to highly similar behaviors. For half the subjects the positive primes appeared more frequently (four synonyms occurred during the presentation) but the negative prime, which only occurred once, appeared last (i.e., most recently), and for the remaining subjects, the negative primes appeared more frequently but the positive prime appeared last.

After either a 15-second or a 120-second delay during which subjects performed an interference task (counting backwards from 368 by 3s, for example), subjects were presented with an ambiguous description (e.g. "He has risked injury, even death, a number of times. Now he is in search of new excitement. He is thinking, perhaps, he will do some skydiving or maybe cross the Atlantic in a sailboat" for the adventurous/reckless pair) and asked to write down a single word which best described the person.

Judges, blind to experimental condition, rated each of the words generated by subjects with respect to their similarity in meaning to either the positive or negative primes on a scale ranging from "same as positive alternative construct" to "same as negative alternative construct". Subjects' categorizations reflected the "recent" more than the "frequent" construct when the delay between final priming and stimulus presentation was short, but reflected the "frequent" construct more than the "recent" construct when the delay was long. There was no relation between recall of the primes and use of the primes in categorization, which makes it unlikely that episodic memory for the priming events mediated the effect.

The results of this study indicate that when two alternative constructs for characterizing an ambiguous stimulus are made accessible by being either frequently or most recently primed, people will categorize the stimulus in terms of the most recently primed construct if the stimulus appears almost immediately after final priming, but will categorize the stimulus in terms of the frequently primed construct if there is sufficient delay between final priming and stimulus presentation. This finding of a recency–frequency reversal over time is consistent with only the "synapse" model of contextual priming effects (see Higgins *et al.* 1985).

Momentary mood and arousal context effects. Contextual priming effects can occur in ways other than through prior exposure to construct-related stimuli. It is well known that temporary changes in mood or in physiological arousal can influence judgments and memory of target stimuli (see Isen 1984 for an excellent review of this literature). Isen *et al.* (1978) found that positive mood at recall led to better memory of positive than negative trait stimuli as compared with negative mood at recall (see also Postman and Brown 1952). Cantor *et al.* (1975) found that subjects who were still residually aroused after an exercise period, but who did not realize that they were still aroused, reported greater sexual attraction to erotic films. Similarly, Dutton and Aron (1974) found more erotic TAT imagery and more attraction toward a female experimenter in males who were interviewed on a high pedestrian bridge or who were expecting electrical shock than for control subjects. Clark *et al.* (1984) report that aroused subjects were more likely to interpret positive facial expressions as a high-arousal expression (joy) than a low-arousal expression (serenity) than were non-aroused subjects. White *et al.* (1981) found greater attraction to a female confederate when subjects were aroused, regardless of whether the arousal was a result of having viewed a horror film or a comedy film. Other studies have found that targets' attractiveness is rated higher when perceivers are themselves in a positive environment (e.g. Griffith 1970, Maslow and Mintz 1956). A study by Stephan *et al.* (1971) found that sexually aroused males reported females who they expected to date as being more attractive and more sexually receptive than did nonaroused males.

More recently, Stangor (1986) reported a study showing that momentary changes in arousal in combination with an expectancy can polarize judgments of individuals. In this experiment, subjects ran in place for either 2½ minutes (experimental condition) or 30 seconds (control condition). Then subjects were escorted to a separate room for an ostensibly unrelated experiment. At this point, subjects read a story about a target individual. The story contained eight rather neutrally valenced sentences, but each of the sentences was constructed to be interpretable either in terms of a positive or in terms of a negative trait construct. For example, one sentence read "Jerry's the kind of guy who continually makes jokes about everything." This sentence could be interpreted as either *silly* or *humorous*.

Two versions of the same basic story were given to subjects. One began with the sentence "Jerry is the kind of person that nobody can get to like very much" (negative expectancy) and the other with the statement "Jerry is really the kind of person that most people like" (positive expectancy). It was hypothesized that the residual contextual effects of the exercise manipulation would polarize judgments beyond the target effect created by these differential expectancies concerning Jerry's likeability. Indeed, the difference in evaluative trait judgments as a function of these expectancies was significantly greater in the high residual arousal condition. This effect persisted when subjects returned a week later and made the same judgments.

Although the exact mechanisms behind the effects of short-term variability in mood or arousal are still somewhat unclear, one possibility is that the manipulation of mood or physiological arousal increases the acessibility of certain constructs (Clark *et al.* 1983, Higgins and King 1981, Isen 1984).

Contextual adaptation effects

As discussed earlier, contextual priming involves context as a "background" variable in the sense that its impact on subsequent encoding of stimulus information results from passive influences on the accessibility of social constructs, which then automatically affect the processing of subsequent stimulus information. Context in this case is a background variable because the processor does not have the context in mind when processing the stimulus information. Context can also function as a "foreground" variable in the sense that the processor can purposely take it into account when processing the stimulus information. That is, people may purposely adapt or modify their encoding of stimulus information to suit their context. In this section we will review research that has investigated situations in which perceivers actively modify their encoding of target information as a function of contextual goals and/or the audience to whom they are communicating. Included in this section are the effects of contextually activated sets, experimenter-provided goals, audience attributes, and contextual standards on judgment and memory.

Contextual sets. Expectations can be invoked in such a way that the perceiver actively processes information in terms of them (see Posner 1978). In fact, a major manipulation strategy of social psychology has been to manipulate *active expectancies*, often known as *sets*, that directly provide information about a forthcoming stimulus. Two findings of interest have proven to be quite robust in this research. First, contextual activation of a set can produce *distortions* in memory, and, second, they can change the *amount* of related and unrelated information remembered.

Momentary contextual sets to expect an instance of a type of object or person are especially likely to cause distortions in judgment and memory, as in Carmichael *et al.*'s (1932) classic study where the experimenter provided different subjects with alternative labels for an ambiguous drawing (eyeglasses versus dumbbell, for example) prior to its presentation. Carmichael *et al.* found substantial distortions in subjects' reproductions of the original drawings in the direction of the object they were set to see. In another classic study, Kelley (1950) gave students an expectancy that their new instructor was either a "warm" person or a "cold" person prior to the instructor's arrival to class, and this contextual set had a significant impact on the students' ratings of the new instructor.

A well-known study of the effect of expectancies on the *amount* of memory for information related to the expectancy was conducted by Bransford and Johnson (1973) who showed that information was better recalled when it was preceded by a thematic title which related the pieces of information that were to follow. Zadny and Gerard (1974) found that providing subjects with a set for a specific kind of stimuli by telling them that a target student they were about to observe was either a chemistry major, a music major, or a psychology major caused the subjects to recall better those aspects of the students' actions, appearance, and possessions that were relevant to the major. That effects of contextual expectancies can operate both at encoding and at retrieval stages has now been shown in several studies (e.g. Bargh and Thein 1985, Hastie and Kumar 1979, Rothbart *et al.* 1979, Srull 1981, Wyer *et al.* 1982).

Contextual activation of processing goals. Experiments have shown that activating or setting different goals can have a significant effect on the type and amount of information remembered. Hamilton *et al.* (1980), for example, had subjects read about behaviors of target individuals under one of two conditions. In the memory goal condition, subjects were to remember as much of the information as they could, while in the impression formation goal condition they were merely asked to form an impression of what the target person was like. It turned out that subjects in the impression goal condition were able to recall more of the information than were those who were given an explicit goal to remember the information. (But see Hoffman *et al.* 1981 for evidence of better memory in a recall goal condition.) In addition, the order in which the information was recalled varied as a function of subjects' processing objective. Recall was more often clustered around target persons in the impression set condition than in the memory set condition. Evidently, the goal of forming an impression of the target caused subjects to organize their storage of information around the target person, and this organization affected memory. Cohen and Ebbesen (1979) found that subjects attended to different behavioral features of a target, according to Newtson's (1973) unitizing measure, depending on whether they were instructed to form an impression of her or remember the details of the tasks she performed.

The "impression goal versus memory goal" distinction has proved to be fertile ground for investigating the effects of different goals on encoding and retrieval of social information (e.g. Hartwick 1979, Jefferey and Mischel 1979, Ostrom *et al.* 1981, Srull 1983, Wyer and Gordon 1982, Wyer *et al.* 1984). Wyer, Srull, and their colleagues, for example, have found that impression goal subjects are not necessarily able to *encode* all information better than memory goal subjects, but are more likely to *retrieve* information once they have an appropriate retrieval cue. Wyer and Gordon (1982) showed a series of trait adjectives and behaviors to subjects. On a subsequent recall test, the impression goal and memory goal groups did not differ on the number of traits recalled, but the probability of recalling a behavior, given that an associated trait had been recalled, was much higher for the impression goal group. Evidently, processing objectives influence the formation of linkages among items, which then affects retrieval of items from long-term store (see also Srull 1983, Wyer and Gordon 1984, Srull and Brand 1983). Excellent discussions of the social-cognitive consequence of contextually activated goals are presented in Srull and Wyer (1986) and Zukier (1986).

Contextual adaptation effects can occur as a result of contextually provided goals that occur either before or after exposure to the target information. Lingle and Ostrom (1979), for example, displayed an occupation prior to the presentation of a set of target traits and asked subjects to decide whether the target was suitable for the job. Carlston (1980) had subjects read an episode describing the behaviors of a target person (e.g. both "kind" and "dishonest" behaviors), and afterwards had them answer different kinds of questions about the target person. In both studies, all subjects were given the same target information but the context demanded that different initial judgments concerning the target be made. Regardless of whether the contextual demands occurred before or after the target information, these studies found that subjects' subsequent impressions and memory were determined by their contextually adapted initial judgments rather than by the target information alone.

Another area where contextually adapted encoding occurs regularly is when people adapt their verbal encoding of a target person to suit communication goals (see Higgins *et al.* 1981, McCann and Higgins 1984). Although people's encoding of a stimulus person in this situation is influenced by both the stimulus person's attributes (i.e. data-driven target effects) and the communicator's pre-established constructs (i.e. theory-driven perceiver effects), it is also influenced by a variety of contextual factors (for reviews, see Applegate and Delia 1980, Clark 1985, Higgins 1981, Kraut and Higgins 1984). There is considerable evidence that people will modify their message about an issue or about another person in order to fulfill a variety of goals and communication roles (e.g. Grace 1951, Higgins and Rholes 1978, Manis *et al.* 1974, McCann and Hancock 1983, Newtson and Czerlinsky 1974). Most of the research in this area has examined contextual adaptation to the attributes of the audience.

Contextual adaptation to the attitudes of an audience. In a study by Zimmerman and Bauer (1956), an experimenter came to a number of classrooms where she presented herself as representing either an organization promoting economy in government or an organization that favored raising teachers' salaries. She then read a series of statements either supportive of or antagonistic toward pay raises for teachers. Class members were told that they might be asked to give a speech to her organization on the subject of teachers' salaries the following week. The class members were asked to reproduce the statements that the experimenter had read both immediately and after a week's delay. On the delayed measure (but not on the immediate one), subjects recalled more statements consistent than inconsistent with the experimenter's position on the issue. This effect was replicated by Schramm and Danielson (1958).

Manis *et al.* (1974) had subjects simply relay a message to an audience. Subjects heard a message that either favored or opposed the legalization of marijuana. Subsequently, the subjects were asked to communicate a summary of this message to an audience who they knew either favored or opposed marijuana legalization. Independent judges then rated the summaries according to their degree of pro or anti sentiment. These ratings showed that the subjects, especially after a long delay between hearing the message and producing the summary, distorted their summaries to be in line with the attitude of their audience. In a second study, subjects rated several different transmitters. The transmitters were rated more favorably when they transmitted messages that were congruent with the views of the subjects, even though it was clear that the transmitters did not necessarily endorse the content of the message they were transmitting. Manis *et al.* (1974) propose a simple explanation for their results: the transmitters in the first study had tailored their messages toward the attitude of their audience in order to avoid the kind of negative consequences to themselves found in the second study. People are presumably aware of the relation between attitude similarity and liking (Byrne 1971) and thus will attempt to maximize their similarity to potential audiences.

In support of this explanation is a study by Higgins and Rholes (1978). In this experiment, subjects summarized information about a stimulus person who was either liked or disliked by their audience. Subjects who wrote this message significantly distorted the message toward the attitude of their audience. Presumably these subjects were acting under a rule of social interaction that emphasized the goal of "minimizing friction" in their social encounter over the goal of "transmitting information accurately."

Higgins and Rholes (1978) added a new dimension to this research by obtaining subjects' own evaluations and memory of the target person, both immediately and over time, for both subjects who communicated and subjects who did not communicate. At the experimental session, and at a session held two weeks later, subjects were asked to reproduce the information they had read about the target person. Subjects' reproductions over time became more evaluatively consistent with the tone of the message, both through distortions of ambiguous stimulus information in the direction of the audience's attitude and through deletions of unambiguous information that was inconsistent with the audience's attitude. In addition, liking for the target was increasingly related over time to the evaluative tone of the message. Subjects who expected to communicate about the same target person to the same audiences but who did not actually produce a message did not show these effects.

Higgins and Rholes (1978) conclude that subjects increasingly over time remembered and evaluated the stimulus person in a manner matching their message rather than matching the original stimulus information they had received about the person. The fact that this effect did not occur for subjects who did not write the message shows that the presence of the audience affected memory and attitudes by influencing the encoding of the stimulus information rather than by having a direct persuasive effect (see also Higgins and McCann 1984).

Contextual adaptation to suit an audience's knowledge. Another type of audience effect occurs when transmitters modify the contents of their message in order more accurately to communicate their message to an audience who is known to have either more or less topic-relevant information than they do (e.g. Clark and Haviland 1977, Flavell *et al.* 1968, Higgins 1977, Higgins *et al.* 1982). Higgins *et al.* (1982) had subjects read an essay describing the behaviors of a target person after having been assigned the communication role of either speaker or listener. Half of the subjects in each role were told that their partner had received basically the same information about the target person, and half were told that their partner had received different information. Speakers were found to "stick to the facts" more and interpret the target's behaviors less (a *descriptive versus* an *interpretive* orientation) when they believed that their partner had different information about the target than when they believed their listener had the same information.

More importantly, this verbal encoding to suit the communicative situation affected the speakers' own subsequent memory of the stimulus person. Speakers' reproductions of the stimulus information became more accurate and complete after "sticking to the facts" for a listener with supposedly different information about the target, but became less accurate and complete after giving an interpretive account of the target for a listener with supposedly the same information. Thus, although the results of previous studies suggested that verbal encoding to suit the communicative situation *impaired* the accuracy of recall of the original information (Higgins and Rholes 1978, Manis *et al.* 1974), the results of this study suggest that speakers' verbal encoding may sometimes *facilitate* their recall of the original information. The nature of the effects of verbal encoding on recall and judgment thus depends on whether or not the underlying goal of the communicator is to be descriptively accurate.

Contextual adaptation as a function of audience status. Higgins and McCann (1984) showed that differences in the relative social status of individuals affect the nature of the information transmitted among individuals, and that these momentary contextual differences lead to differential memory of the stimulus information. In this experiment, subjects described stimulus information about a target person for an audience of a status either equal to or higher than the subjects, and who purportedly either liked or disliked the target. Half the subjects were low authoritarians and half were high authoritarians who are particularly responsive to a higher-status partner. As predicted, high authoritarians tuned their encoding of the target to suit, especially, the high-status audience. These same subjects also showed the strongest relation between their modified encoding and their own subsequent impressions, evaluation, and memory of the target.

The findings of Higgins and Rholes (1978), Higgins *et al.* (1982), and Higgins and McCann (1984) show that subjects' memory for the stimulus person over time is increasingly influenced by their prior verbal encoding of him, even though their encoding was determined in large part by the context of the earlier encoding (see also McCann and Hancock 1983). These effects were *not* due simply to social or informational conformity to the listener or to public commitment, since they increased significantly over time and disappeared when the contextually adapted encoding was experimentally or statistically removed. Thus, increasingly over time, people use their prior encoding of the stimulus person to reconstruct their knowledge of his or her attributes without taking into account sufficiently the context-induced nature of the encoding.

Effects of a "change of standard" on memory. In a series of studies we have examined the effects of contextually adapted judgments on memory when the salient standard at recall is different than the contextual standard to which subjects' judgments were originally adapted. In a study by Higgins and Lurie (1983), subjects read about the moderate sentencing decisions of a target trial judge, Judge Jones, in the context of other trial judges who consistently gave either higher sentences (harsh context condition) or lower sentences (lenient context condition) than did Judge Jones. Then they judged the harshness or leniency of Judge Jones. As expected, subjects tended to judge the sentencing decisions of Judge Jones as "lenient" in the harsh encoding context condition, and as "harsh" in the lenient encoding context condition. A week later, subjects read about the sentencing decisions of some additional judges who were also either harsher or more lenient than Judge Jones. Thus, over the two sessions either a lenient, a harsh, or a moderate category norm for judges' sentencing decisions was created, depending upon whether the subjects had been exposed to lenient context judges in both sessions, harsh context judges in both sessions, or one set of lenient and one set of harsh context judges across the two sessions. At the end of the second session, subjects were asked to recall the sentencing decisions of Judge Jones that they had read about the week before.

The results showed that subjects recalled Judge Jones' sentencing decisions by interpreting their prior judgments of him in terms of the category norm established over the two sessions, rather than in terms of the original encoding context standard. Thus subjects who were exposed to the same target information in the same encoding context, and initially judged the target in the same way, nevertheless remembered his behavior differently if their category norm was different at the moment of recall. This study represents one kind of "change-of-standard" effect on memory – when there is a change from an encoding context standard to a category norm standard.

Some further studies conducted by the present authors tested additional implications of this "change-of-standard" effect on memory (Higgins and Stangor, in press). In one of these studies, subjects read about the moderate sentencing decisions of the target judge, Judge Jones, in the context of other judges who were either more harsh or more lenient than he. They then judged the sentencing decisions of Judge Jones as "harsh" or "lenient". One week later, subjects returned for a second session where they read about the sentencing decisions of a second set of judges, including a second target judge, Judge Cohen. The sentences of the judges at the second session were always either higher or lower than those of Judge Cohen, while Judge Cohen had the same average sentencing decisions as Judge Jones. Thus, as in the previous study, over the two sessions subjects were exposed to either a harsh, a moderate, or a lenient category norm. At the end of the second session, subjects judged the harshness or leniency of Judge Cohen, recalled the sentencing decisions given by Judge Jones from the week before, and then recalled the sentencing decisions given by Judge Cohen.

As in our previous studies, there was a clear tendency for both Judge Jones and Judge Cohen to be judged as "harsh" when the context of alternative judges at the moment of encoding was lenient (i.e. they had given lower sentences) and to be judged as "lenient" when the context of alternative judges at the moment of encoding was harsh (i.e. they had given higher sentences). We predicted that subjects would recall the sentencing decisions of Judge Jones by using their judgment of him as the basis for reconstructing the original stimulus information. And, consistent with Higgins and Lurie (1983), we predicted that subjects would reconstruct the sentencing decisions by reinterpreting their judgments in terms of the category norm available at the moment of recall, rather than in terms of the first session context standard that had actually determined the judgment. A multiple regression analysis found, as predicted, that subjects' recall of Judge Jones' sentencing decisions was significantly related to both subjects' judgments in the first session and the category norm available at the moment of recall in the second session (as formed by all the information provided across both sessions), thus leading to considerable distortion in recall.

In the Higgins and Lurie (1983) study 1, it was not possible to compare the impact on recall of the "change of standard" effect with the impact on recall of simply contextually adapted judgments. By including a second target judge, Judge Cohen, the present study did permit such a direct comparison. Becaue subjects recalled Judge Cohen's sentencing decisions in the same context in which they judged them, we did not expect any distortions in recall from a "change of standard" effect. We expected, therefore, that subjects' recall of Judge Cohen's sentencing decisions would be quite accurate and, if anything, would show an assimilation to context effect as was found in Higgins and Lurie's (1983) study 2, where the judgment and recall occurred in the same context. And, indeed, subjects' recall of Judge Cohen's sentencing decision was quite accurate (i.e., mean distortion for Judge Cohen = 8 per cent versus mean distortion for Judge Jones = 24 per cent), and was *not* significantly related to their judgments of the sentencing decisions. As predicted, subjects recalled different sentencing decisions for Judge Jones and Judge Cohen even though the target information about both judges was the same (i.e. the same target average and total years of sentencing), the category norm in each condition (i.e. the average of all sentencing decisions to which they were exposed) was the same, and the recall context was the same. The only difference was that for Judge Jones the context of judgment and the context of recall were different, whereas for Judge Cohen they were the same.

The effect of context on judgment and recall is most evident in those conditions where the category norm – the average sentencing decisions of all the judges read about across the two sessions – is the same as the target's sentencing decisions (i.e. fifteen years). In these conditions subjects should recall the correct number of years if they either recall the target's decisions or recall the average decisions of all the judges they have read about. A target judge (Judge Jones; Judge Cohen) × context order (harsh first context/lenient second context; lenient first context/harsh second context) analysis of variance revealed, as predicted, a significant target judge × context order interaction, which reflected the fact that context order had no significant effect on subjects' recall of Judge Cohen's sentencing decisions but had a highly significant effect on subjects' recall of Judge Jones' sentencing decisions. As discussed earlier, for Judge Jones, but not for Judge Cohen, context order reflects differences between the context of judgment and the context of recall, which creates a "change of standard" effect. Subjects recalled Judge Jones' sentencing decisions in terms of their prior judgments of him. For Judge Jones, the context of judgment was the first session context. When the first context was harsh, subjects judged the sentencing decisions of Judge Jones as "lenient" and recalled his sentencing decisions as being less than the category norm (i.e. $M = 13.4$ years, or "less" than 15 years), and when the first context was lenient, subjects judged the sentencing decisions of Judge Jones as "harsh" and recalled his sentencing decisions as being more than the category norm (i.e. $M = 23.2$ years, or "more" than 15 years). However, for Judge Cohen, as predicted, context of judgment was *not* significantly related to recall. Thus, subjects in our first study recalled the same target information differently depending on whether they used their contextually adapted judgments of the information as a basis for recall. This in turn depended on whether the context of judgment and the context of recall were the same or different.

In another study the same general paradigm was used. At the first session, subjects read about the sentencing decisions of three trial judges who were either lenient or harsh. Subjects returned one week later and only then read about the sentencing decisions of the target judge, Judge Jones. In this second session they also read about three additional judges who were either more harsh or more lenient than Judge Jones. Half of the subjects read about and judged the sentencing decisions of Judge Jones *before* they read about the sentencing decisions of the other judges, while the remaining subjects read about and categorized Judge Jones' sentencing decisions *after* they had read about the sentencing decisions of the other judges. The subjects then returned one week later to a third session, when they recalled the sentencing decisions of Judge Jones whom they had read about at the second session.

Once again, subjects in this study recalled Judge Jones' sentencing decisions by reinterpreting their prior judgments of him in terms of the category norm available to them at recall rather than in terms of the context standard they used when actually making their judgments (the "change of standard" effect). But in this study the context standard used for judging the sentencing decisions of Judge Jones was determined by an "accident of timing" – whether a subject happened to judge the sentencing decisions of Judge Jones before or after reading about the additional judges. When it was before, subjects used the first session context of judges as the standard of judgment, whereas when it was after, subjects used the second session context of judges as the standard of judgment.

What is interesting about this study is that all subjects judged the sentencing decisions of Judge Jones in the second session and recalled them in the third session. Moreover, for subjects in the harsh first session context/lenient second context condition and lenient first session context/harsh second session context condition, not only was the target information the same, but the category norm (i.e. the average sentencing decisions of all the judges read about across the sessions) was the same and equal to Judge Jones' average sentencing decision. *Only the timing of judgment was different.* In the harsh first session context/lenient second session context condition, subjects recalled Judge Jones' sentencing decisions as higher if they judged him *after* exposure to the second session context of judges (*M* = 14.5 years) than if they judged him before exposure to the context (*M* = 11.3 years), whereas in the lenient first session context/harsh second session context, subjects recalled Judge Jones' sentencing decisions as higher if they judged him *before* exposure to the second session context of judges (*M* = 17.8 years) than if they judged him after exposure to the context (*M* = 14.7 years), with this crossover interaction being significant.

Because the category norm was the same for these subjects, the differences in recall were due to differences in their judgments of the sentencing decisions of Judge Jones, which in turn were influenced simply by the timing of the judgment – if "before" the second session context subjects used the first session context as the standard; if "after", they used the second session context as the standard. When recalling Judge Jones' sentencing decisions in the third session, however, subjects used the category norm to reinterpret their judgments rather than the context standards that were the basis for their judgments. Thus, even when the target information is the same, the alternative judges are the same, and the context of recall is the same, a "change of standard" can cause differences in recall simply as a function of the timing of judgment.

The results of this study also demonstrated that even when subjects make the *same judgment* of the same target information and recall the target information in the same context (several days after judgment), they will nevertheless recall it differently if the category norm available at the moment of recall is different. Subjects in the harsh first session context/harsh second session context, "before" and "after" conditions, judged the sentencing decisions of Judge Jones as "lenient", as did subjects in the harsh first session context/lenient second context, "before" condition and lenient first session context/harsh second session context, "after" condition. Yet subjects in the former two conditions recalled Judge Jones' sentencing decisions as being significantly higher (*M* = 20.3 years) than did subjects in the latter two conditions (*M* = 13.0 years). Although both groups of subjects judged the sentencing decision of Judge Jones as "lenient", the former subjects reinterpreted "lenient" as less than their harsh category norm (i.e. less than 22.4 years) whereas the latter subjects reinterpreted "lenient" as less than their moderate category norm (i.e. less than 15 years).

Similarly, subjects in the lenient first session context/lenient second session context, "before" and "after" conditions, judged the sentencing decisions of Judge Jones as "harsh", as did subjects in the lenient first session context/harsh second session context, "before" condition and harsh first session context/lenient second session context, "after" condition. Yet subjects in the former two conditions recalled Judge Jones' sentencing decisions as being significantly lower (M = 11.7 years) than did subjects in the latter two conditions (M = 20.5 years). Although both groups of subjects judged the sentencing decisions of Judge Jones as "harsh", the former subjects reinterpreted "harsh" as more than their lenient category norm (i.e. more than 7.6 years), whereas the latter subjects reinterpreted "harsh" as more than their moderate category norm (i.e. more than 15 years).

Thus, even when subjects made the same judgment of Judge Jones, they recalled his behavior differently because they reinterpreted their judgments using their category norms rather than the context standards that were the original basis for their judgments. A "change of standard" from the context of judgment to the context of recall, therefore, can cause differences in recall even when individuals originally judge the *same* target in the *same* way.

General discussion and conclusions: the validity issue

This chapter introduced a classificatory scheme for distinguishing among target effects, perceiver effects, and context effects in social cognition, and, in particular, for distinguishing among different kinds of context effects. Evidence was then presented for a particular kind of context effect – when the "theory-driven" processing of perceivers is itself "context-driven". Context as both a "background" variable (e.g. contextual priming effects) and as a "foreground" variable (e.g. contextually adapted encoding effects) were considered. Our review described how context strongly influences people's judgments of target persons, and how these judgments in turn influence memory of the target information. Thus, people's memory of target information is based in part on context-induced judgments rather than solely on the original stimulus information. And people apparently fail to adjust for the impact of the circumstances surrounding their judgment of a stimulus when they later use the judgment to reconstruct the stimulus. In this sense at least, one might characterize this phenomenon as a case of when "behavior engulfs the field" in reconstructive memory.

One might conclude from these studies that, to the extent that "theory-driven" processing of persons and social events is itself determined by momentary contextual factors, it produces invalid knowledge of the social world. Context influences both judgments and memory of stimulus details, and both these judgments and memory are part of individuals' social knowledge. And to the extent that these judgments and memories are "context-driven", rather than being solely "data-driven", one might assume that they are both invalid. One must distinguish, however, between the issue of whether context-driven judgments are valid and the issue of whether memories based on context-driven judgments are valid. It is our contention that even when context-driven judgments are valid, memories based on these judgments may be invalid.

Let us begin with cases where context-driven judgments are clearly valid. First, consider attributional judgments that vary as a function of target context. Different attributions are made for the same target behavior depending on the circumstances in which the target's behavior occurred. According to attribution theory (e.g. Heider 1958, Jones and Davis 1965), it would be invalid not to vary the judgment as a function of the context. Second, consider the perceiver context effect where verbal encodings of a target stimulus are varied as a function of the context of alternative stimuli from which the target is to be distinguished (i.e. the nonreferent array). According to theories of referential encoding (see Glucksberg *et al.* 1975, Olson 1970), it would be inappropriate not to vary the judgment to suit the nonreferent array. In fact, it would be more difficult for the audience to identify the referent if all the minute details of the target were included in the encoding than if only the distinctive or discriminating attributes of the target were included, where "distinctive" or "discriminating" is always defined *in relation to* the nonreferent array.

These two examples represent cases where context-driven judgments are clearly valid. There are other cases where context-driven judgments may not be valid. But it must be kept in mind that *all* judgments are only summaries of the stimulus information. No judgment can represent all of the individuating, unique properties of the stimulus. The act of identifying a stimulus as an instance of some construct (i.e. making a judgment) necessarily entails recognizing those properties of the stimulus that it has in common with other instances of the construct. Some idiosyncratic properties of the stimulus, therefore, always fail to be represented in the judgment. Thus, the issue is not whether the context-driven judgments we have described fail to represent all of the stimulus' properties, thereby reducing their validity, but whether they fail to represent more of the stimulus' properties than less context-driven judgments. It is not at all clear that this is so.

Consider the case of contextual priming, for example. When individuals have a particular construct activated in a prior context, they are more likely to use that construct to categorize ambiguous stimulus information. But this does not occur unless the construct is *applicable* to the stimulus information (and, at least in that sense, valid). Moreover, the same alternative constructs are used to categorize the target regardless of whether they are primed or not (Higgins *et al.* 1977) and, if not primed, will simply be used as a function of their chronic accessibilities (Higgins *et al.* 1982). Contextual priming simply increases the *relative* likelihood that one of the alternative constructs will be used to categorize the target by temporarily increasing its relative accessibility. Thus, to the extent that these constructs are poor summaries of the stimulus information (e.g. "adventurous" and "reckless" as summaries of Donald's behaviors in Higgins *et al.* 1977), they are poor regardless of the effects of contextual priming. The only difference is that temporary rather than chronic accessibility determines which construct is predominant.

Similarly, the labels that subjects select to characterize a target's behaviors so as to suit their audience's attitude toward the target are the same labels subjects use to characterize the target when they are not adapting to an audience (see Higgins and Rholes 1978). The presence of the audience simply influences which alternative is selected – *not* what the alternatives are, nor the fact that motivational factors influence their selection. In fact, in the Higgins *et al.* (1982) study, the subjects who adapted to an audience which they believed had different information from their own were actually less likely to use labels (i.e. more likely to "stick to the facts") than were subjects in previous studies who described the target in the absence of an audience. Even in the absence of an audience people have goals that influence their decision to use labels, and these goals could originate either from features of the context or from more general individual orientations (see McCann and Higgins 1984).

In sum, a momentary context can influence people's judgments by modifying the relative accessibility of their constructs and their motivational state. But people's judgments will be influenced by the relative accessibility of their constructs and their motivational state in any case. Thus, even if these factors cause judgments to be less than absolutely accurate, they will have this effect regardless of whether the judgments are context-driven. Moreover, these context-driven judgments in themselves need not produce invalid knowledge of the target. Let us turn now to this critical point.

Our account of context-driven judgments is depicted on the top half of Fig. 11.1. As indicated, judgments of the target stimulus information are determined by both the stimulus information and the context of judgment. Let us then assume that individuals represent in long-term memory the original stimulus information, their judgment of that information, and the context of the judgment. To the extent that individuals later remember the target by retrieving their representation of the original stimulus information, their memory for the target will be valid. Thus, the simple fact that their judgments of the target were context-driven does not mean that their memory of the target will necessarily be invalid. Indeed, the results of a

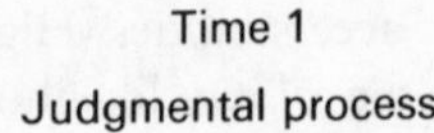

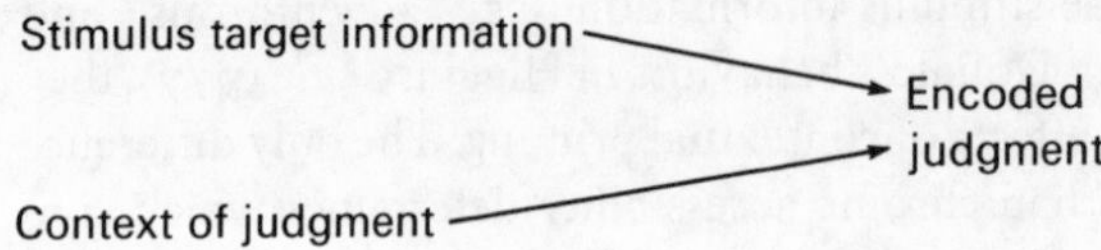

Time 2
Judgment-based memory process

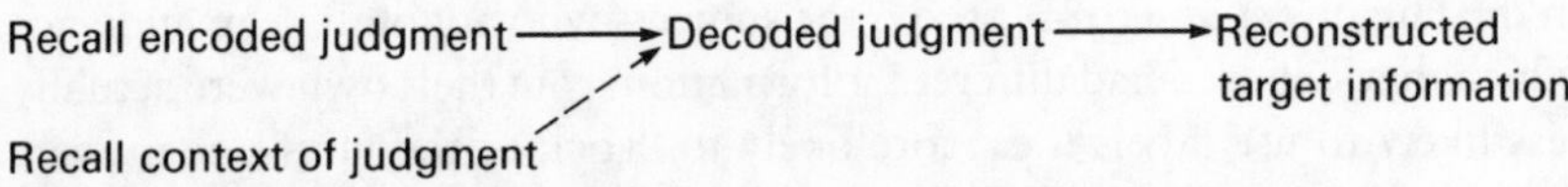

Fig. 11.1. Hypothesized judgmental and judgment-based memory processes

number of our studies suggest that this is precisely what occurs when recall of the target occurs shortly after exposure to the stimulus information (see Higgins and Lurie 1983, study 2, Higgins and McCann 1984, Higgins and Rholes 1978).

But what about instances where individuals' memory of a target is based solely on their prior judgments of the target, as depicted in the bottom half of Figure 11.1? As discussed earlier, this is most likely to occur when there is a long delay between judgment and recall, such that the representation of the original stimulus information has decayed. Even in this case, however, memory of the target need not be invalid as long as individuals' judgment-based reconstruction of the target information reflects *both* determinants of the original judgment – the target information *and* the context of the judgment. That is, if both the original stimulus information and the context of judgment caused the judgment, then a "backwards" inference from the judgment to the original stimulus information is reasonable as long as the effect of the context on the original judgment is taken into account.

More generally, memory based on context-driven judgments can be highly accurate when the context of judgment is taken into account. In fact, it may be more accurate than memory based on context-free judgments. Consider, for example, reading about different judges who presided during the Spanish Inquisition where one of the judges, El Carlos, gave more severe sentences for similar offenses than the other judges. A context-free judgment of El Carlos would compare him to the general category norm of all trial judges, and he would be judged as "extremely harsh". By using the general category norm at both encoding and at recall one would avoid a "change of standard" effect. A context-driven judgment of El Carlos would compare him to the other trial judges of the Spanish Inquisition, and relative to them he would be judged as "harsh". If the context of judgment were not taken into account, then the context-free "extremely harsh" judgment would lead to a more valid reconstruction of El Carlos' behavior based on the general category norm than the context-driven "harsh" judgment. But if the context of judgment were taken into account, then a reconstruction of El Carlos' behavior would probably be more valid if it were based on the judgment "harsh" in relation to trial judges of the Spanish Inquisition than if it were based on the judgment "extremely harsh" in relation to the general category norm for all trial judges.

Memory based on context-driven judgments, therefore, need not be invalid. But to be valid the impact of the context on the original judgment must be taken into account during the reconstructive process. However, as depicted in Figure 11.1 by the broken line from "recall context of judgment" to "decoded judgment," judgment-based reconstructive memory often does not take the context of the judgment into account sufficiently. Failure to take into account the context of the original judgment when using that judgment to reconstruct the original stimulus information means that the reconstructive inference process is faulty, and thus the outcome of this process – the recollection – is invalid. To the extent that the original judgment as a summary of the stimulus information reflects properties of the context in which it was made rather than just the stimulus information itself, the context of judgment must be taken into account in the process of reconstruction. Otherwise the original stimulus information will be falsely credited with possessing whichever properties would have led to this judgment. Such faulty reconstructive inference processes can, and apparently do, lead to invalid social knowledge.

Although it is clear that people often do not take the context of their original judgments into account when later using them to recollect target information, it is not always clear exactly why this is so. In the case of "context as background" effects, such as the effects of contextual priming, it is not surprising that the context is not taken into account because people do not have the context in mind when they make their judgments. However, in the case of "context as foreground" effects, such as the effects of contextually adapted encoding, individuals do have the context in mind (for example the audience's attitude, the nonreferent array) when they make their judgments. What then is the source of invalidity in these cases? One possibility is that people have no understanding of the relevance of the context of judgment for their judgment-based reconstructive inferences. Another possibility is that people do understand the relevance of the context of judgment but often cannot recall it because its representation has decayed or is difficult to retrieve. A third possibility is that prior judgments are more accessible at the moment of recall than representations of the judgmental context, and people only take into account the most accessible information in their reconstructive inferences. Finally, it is possible that people do retrieve the context of judgment and attempt to take it into account, but they do not correct sufficiently for context because they underestimate the impact of the context on their judgment (e.g. Tversky and Kahneman 1974). Answering this particular "Why?" question is critical for understanding the role of context-driven processing in producing invalid social knowledge.

References

Adorno, T. W., Frenkel-Brunswick, E., Levinson, D. J., and Sanford, R. N. (1950). *The authoritarian personality*. New York: Harper.

Anderson, N. H. (1974). Two more tests against change of meaning in adjective combinations. *Journal of Verbal Learning and Verbal Behavior* 10: 75–85.

Applegate, J. L. and Delia, J. G. (1980). Person-centered speech, psychological development, and the contexts of language usage. In R. St Clair and H. Giles (eds.), *The social and psychological contexts of language*. Hillsdale, NJ: Lawrence Erlbaum.

Asch, S. E. (1946). Forming impressions of personality. *Journal of Abnormal and Social Psychology* 41: 258–90.

Asch, S. E. (1952). *Social psychology*. Englewood Cliffs, NJ: Prentice-Hall.

Bargh, J. A. (1982). Automatic information processing and social perception. *Journal of Personality and Social Psychology* 43: 425–36.

Bargh, J. A. (1984). Automatic and conscious processing of social information. In R. S. Wyer, Jr. and T. K. Srull (eds.), *Handbook of social cognition*, vol. 3, Hillsdale, NJ: Lawrence Erlbaum.

Bargh, J. A. and Pietromonaco, P. (1982). Automatic information processing and social perception: the influence of trait information presented outside of conscious awareness on impression formation. *Journal of Personality and Social Psychology* 43: 437–49.

Bargh, J. A. and Thein, R. D. (1985). Individual construct accessibility, person memory, and the recall-judgment link: the case of information overload. *Journal of Personality and Social Psychology* 49: 1129–46.

Bransford, J. D. and Johnson, M. K. (1973). Considerations of some problems of comprehension. In W. Chase (ed.), *Visual information processing*. New York: Academic Press.

Bruner, J. S. (1951). Personality dynamics and the process of perceiving. In R. R. Blake and G. V. Ramsey (eds.), *Perception: An approach to personality*. New York: Ronald Press.

Bruner, J. S. (1957). On perceptual readiness. *Psychological Review* 64: 123–52.
Bruner, J. S. and Goodman, C. C. (1947). Value and need as organizing factors in perception. *Journal of Abnormal and Social Psychology* 42: 33–44.
Bruner, J. S. and Minturn, A. L. (1955). Perceptual identification and perceptual organization. *Journal of General Psychology* 53: 21–8.
Bruner, J. S. and Postman, L. (1948). Symbolic value as an organizing factor in perception. *Journal of Social Psychology* 27: 203–8.
Bruner, J. S. and Postman, L. (1949). On the perception of incongruity: a paradigm. *Journal of Personality* 18: 206–23.
Brunswick, E. (1943). Organismic achievement and environmental probability. *Psychological Review* 50: 255–72.
Byrne, D. (1971). *The attraction paradigm*. New York: Academic Press.
Campbell, D. T., Hunt, W. A., and Lewis, N. A. (1958). The relative susceptibility of two rating scales to disturbance resulting from shifts in stimulus context. *Journal of Applied Psychology* 42: 213–17.
Cantor, N. and Mischel, W. (1979). Prototypes in person perception. In L. Berkowitz (ed.), *Advances in experimental social psychology*, vol. 12. New York: Academic Press.
Cantor, J., Zillman, D., and Bryant, J. (1975). Enhancement of experienced sexual arousal in response to erotic stimuli through misattribution of unrelated residual excitation. *Journal of Personality and Social Psychology* 32: 69–75.
Carlston, D. E. (1980). The recall and use of traits and events in social inference processes. *Journal of Experimental Social Psychology* 16: 303–29.
Carmichael, L., Hogan, H. P., and Walter, A. A. (1932). An experimental study of the effect of language on the reproduction of visually perceived form. *Journal of Experimental Psychology* 15: 72–86.
Clark, H. H. (1985). Language use and language users. In G. Lindzey and E. Aronson (eds.), *Handbook of social psychology*, 3rd edn. Reading, MA: Addison-Wesley.
Clark, H. H. and Haviland, S. E. (1977). Comprehension and the given–new contract. In R. O. Freedle (ed.), *Discourse production and comprehension*. Norwood, NJ: Ablex.
Clark, M. S., Milberg, S., and Erber, R. (1984). Effects of arousal on judgments of others' emotions. *Journal of Personality and Social Psychology* 46(3): 551–60.
Clark, M. S., Milberg, S., and Ross, J. (1983). Arousal cues arousal-related material in memory: implications for understanding effects of mood on memory. *Journal of Verbal Learning and Verbal Behavior* 22: 633–49.
Cohen, C. E. and Ebbesen, E. B. (1979). Observational goals and schema activation: a theoretical framework for behavior perception. *Journal of Experimental Social Psychology* 15: 305–29.
Crockett, W. H. (1965). Cognitive complexity and impression formation. In B. A. Maher (ed.), *Progress in experimental personality research*, vol. 2. New York: Academic Press.
Cupchik, G. C. and Poulos, C. X. (1984). Judgments of emotional intensity in self

and others: the effects of stimulus context, sex, and expressivity. *Journal of Personality and Social Psychology* 46(2): 431–9.

Dutton, D. and Aron, A. (1974). Some evidence for heightened sexual attraction under conditions of high anxiety. *Journal of Personality and Social Psychology* 30: 510–17.

Eagly, A. H., Wood, W., and Chaiken, S. (1978). Causal inferences about communicators and their effect on opinion change. *Journal of Personality and Social Psychology* 36: 424–35.

Erdelyi, M. H. (1974). A new look at the new look: perceptual defense and vigilance. *Psychological Review* 81: 1–25.

Erdelyi, M. H. and Appelbaum, G. A. (1973). Cognitive masking: the disruptive effect of an emotional stimulus upon the perception of contiguous neutral items. *Bulletin of the Psychonomic Society* 1: 56–61.

Ferguson, T. J. and Wells, G. L. (1980). Priming of mediators in causal attribution. *Journal of Personality and Social Psychology* 38: 461–70.

Fiske, S. T. and Taylor, S. E. (1984). *Social cognition*. Reading, MA: Addison-Wesley.

Flavell, J. H., Botkin, P. T., Fry, C. L., Wright, J. W., and Jarvis, P. E. (1968). *The development of role-taking and communication skills in children*. New York: Wiley.

Glucksberg, S., Krauss, R. M., and Higgins, E. T. (1975). The development of referential communication skills. In F. Horowitz, E. Hetherington, S. Scarr-Salapatek, and G. Siegel (eds.), *Review of child development research*, vol. 4. Chicago: University of Chicago Press.

Grace, H. A. (1951). Effects of different degrees of knowledge about an audience on the content of communication. *Journal of Social Psychology* 34: 111–24.

Gregory, R. L. (1966). *Eye and brain*. London: World University Library.

Griffith, W. (1970). Environmental effects on interpersonal behavior: ambient effective temperature and attraction. *Journal of Personality and Social Psychology* 15: 240–4.

Hamilton, D. L., Katz, L., and Leirer, U. (1980). Cognitive representation of personality impressions: organizational processes in first impression formation. *Journal of Personality and Social Psychology* 39: 1050–63.

Hamilton, D. L. and Zanna, M. P. (1974). Context effects in impression formation. *Journal of Personality and Social Psychology* 29: 649–54.

Hartwick, J. (1979). Memory for trait information: a signal detection analysis. *Journal of Experimental Social Psychology* 15: 533–52.

Hastie, R. (1981). Schematic principles in human memory. In E. T. Higgins, C. P. Herman, and M. P. Zanna (eds.), *Social cognition: the Ontario symposium*. Hillsdale, NJ: Lawrence Erlbaum.

Hastie, R. and Kumar, P. (1979). Person memory: personality traits as organizing principles in memory for behaviors. *Journal of Personality and Social Psychology* 37: 25–38.

Heider, F. (1958). *The psychology of interpersonal relations*. New York: Wiley.

Higgins, E. T. (1977). Communication development as related to channel, incentive, and social class. *Genetic Psychology Monographs* 96: 75–141.

Higgins, E. T. (1981). The "communication game": implications for social cognition and persuasion. In E. T. Higgins, C. P. Herman, and M. P. Zanna (eds.), *Social cognition: the Ontario Symposium*. Hillsdale, NJ: Lawrence Erlbaum.

Higgins, E. T. and Bargh, J. A. (1987). Social cognition and social perception. *Annual Review of Psychology* 38: 369–425.

Higgins, E. T., Bargh, J. A., and Lombardi, W. (1985). The nature of priming effects on categorization. *Journal of Experimental Psychology: Learning, Memory and Cognition* 11: 59–69.

Higgins, E. T. and Chaires, W. M. (1980). Accessibility of interrelational constructs: implications for stimulus encoding and creativity. *Journal of Experimental Social Psychology* 16: 348–61.

Higgins, E. T., Fondacaro, R., and McCann, C. D. (1981). Rules and roles: the "communication game" and speaker–listener processes. In W. P. Dickson (ed.), *Children's oral communication skills*. New York: Academic Press.

Higgins, E. T. and King, G. (1981). Accessibility of social constructs: information processing consequences of individual and contextual variability. In N. Cantor and J. Kihlstrom (eds.), *Personality, cognition, and social interaction*. Hillsdale, NJ: Lawrence Erlbaum.

Higgins, E. T., King, G. A., and Mavin, G. H. (1982). Individual construct accessibility and subjective impressions and recall. *Journal of Personality and Social Psychology* 43: 35–47.

Higgins, E. T. and Lurie, L. (1983). Context, categorization, and memory: the "change-of-standard" effect. *Cognitive Psychology* 15: 525–47.

Higgins, E. T. and McCann, C. D. (1984). Social encoding and subsequent attitudes, impressions, and memory: "context-driven" and motivational aspects of processing. *Journal of Personality and Social Psychology* 47: 26–39.

Higgins, E. T., McCann, C. D., and Fondacaro, R. (1982). The "communication-game": goal-directed encoding and cognitive consequences. *Social Cognition* 1: 21–37.

Higgins, E. T. and Rholes, W. S. (1976). Impression formation and role fulfillment: a "holistic reference" approach. *Journal of Experimental Social Psychology* 12: 422–35.

Higgins, E. T. and Rholes, W. S. (1978). "Saying is believing": effects of message modification on memory and liking for the person described. *Journal of Experimental Social Psychology* 14: 363–78.

Higgins, E. T., Rholes, W. S., and Jones, C. R. (1977). Category accessibility and impression formation. *Journal of Experimental Social Psychology* 13: 141–54.

Higgins, E. T. and Stangor, C. (in press). A "change-of-standard" perspective on the relations among context, judgment, and recall. *Journal of Personality and Social Psychology*.

Hoffman, C., Mischel, W., and Mazze, K. (1981). The role of purpose in the organization of information about behavior: trait-based vs. goal-based categories in person cognition. *Journal of Personality and Social Psychology* 40: 211–25.

Isen, A. M. (1984). Toward understanding the role of affect in cognition. In R. S. Wyer and T. K. Srull (eds.), *Handbook of social cognition*, vol. 3. Hillsdale, NJ: Lawrence Erlbaum.

Isen, A. M., Shalker, T. L., Clark, M., and Karp, L. (1978). Affect, accessibility of material in memory, and behavior: a cognitive loop? *Journal of Personality and Social Psychology* 36: 1–12.

Jeffery, K. M. and Mischel, W. (1979). Effects of purpose on the organization and recall of information in person perception. *Journal of Personality* 47: 397–419.

Jones, E. E. (1979). The rocky road from acts to dispositions. *American Psychologist* 34: 107–17.

Jones, E. E. and Davis, K. E. (1965). From acts to dispositions: the attribution process in person perception. In L. Berkowitz (ed.), *Advances in experimental social psychology*, vol. 2. New York: Wiley.

Jones, E. E., Davis, K. E., and Gergen, K. J. (1961). Role playing variations and their information value for person perception. *Journal of Abnormal and Social Psychology* 63: 302–10.

Kahneman, D., Slovic, P., and Tversky, A. (1982). *Judgment under uncertainty: heuristics and biases*. New York: Cambridge University Press.

Kahneman, D. and Tversky, A. (1973). On the psychology of prediction. *Psychological Review* 80: 237–51.

Kandel, E. R. (1976). *Cellular basis of behavior: an introduction to neurobiology*. San Francisco: W. H. Freeman.

Kelley, H. H. (1950). The warm–cold variable in first impressions of persons. *Journal of Personality* 18: 431–9.

Kelly, G. A. (1955). *The psychology of personal constructs*. New York: Norton.

Krantz, D. L. and Campbell, D. T. (1961). Separating perceptual and linguistic effects of context shifts upon absolute judgments. *Journal of Experimental Psychology* 62: 35–42.

Kraut, R. E. and Higgins, E. T. (1984). Communication and social cognition. In R. S. Wyer, Jr. and T. K. Srull (eds.), *Handbook of social cognition*. Hillsdale, NJ: Lawrence Erlbaum.

Levine, R., Chein, I., and Murphy, G. (1942). The relation of the intensity of a need to the amount of perceptual distortion: a preliminary report. *Journal of Psychology* 13: 283–93.

Lewin, K. (1951). *Field theory in social science*. New York: Harper.

Lingle, J. H. and Ostrom, T. M. (1979). Retrieval selectivity in memory-based judgments. *Journal of Personality and Social Psychology* 37: 180–94.

Lloyd, D. P. C. (1949). Post-tetanic potentiation of response in monosynaptic reflex pathways of the spinal cord. *Journal of General Physiology* 33: 147–70.

McCann, D. and Hancock, R. D. (1983). Self-monitoring in communicative interactions: social-cognitive consequences of goal-directed message modification. *Journal of Experimental Social Psychology* 19: 109–21.

McCann, D. and Higgins, E. T. (1984). Individual differences in communication: social cognitive determinants and consequences. In H. Sypher and J. Applegate (eds.), *Understanding interpersonal communication: social cognitive and strategic processes in children and adults*. Beverly Hills, CA: Sage.

Manis, M. (1966). *Cognitive processes*. Belmont, CA: Wadsworth.

Manis, M. (1967). Context effects in communication. *Journal of Personality and Social Psychology* 5: 326–34.

Manis, M. and Armstrong, G. W. (1971). Contrast effects in verbal output. *Journal of Experimental Social Psychology* 7: 381–8.

Manis, M., Cornell, S. D., and Moore, J. C. (1974). Transmission of attitude-relevant information through a communication chain. *Journal of Personality and Social Psychology* 30: 81–94.

Marcel, T. and Forrin, B. (1974). Naming latency and the repetition of stimulus categories. *Journal of Experimental Psychology* 103: 450–60.

Markus, H. and Zajonc, R. B. (1985). The cognitive perspective in social psychology. In G. Lindzey and E. Aronson (eds.), *Handbook of social psychology*, 3rd edn. Reading, MA: Addison-Wesley.

Maslow, A. H. and Mintz, N. L. (1956). Effects of esthetic surroundings: 1. Initial effects of three esthetic conditions upon perceiving "energy" and "well-being" in faces. *Journal of Psychology* 41: 247–54.

Mead, G. H. (1934). *Mind, self, and society*. Chicago: University of Chicago Press.

Newtson, D. (1973). Attribution and the unit of perception of ongoing behavior. *Journal of Personality and Social Psychology* 28: 28–38.

Newtson, D. and Czerlinsky, T. (1974). Adjustment of attitude communications for contrasts by extreme audiences. *Journal of Personality and Social Psychology* 30: 829–37.

Nisbett, R. E. and Ross, L. D. (1980). *Human inference: strategies and shortcomings of informal judgment*. Englewood Cliffs, NJ: Prentice-Hall.

Olson, D. R. (1970). Language and thought: aspects of a cognitive theory of semantics. *Psychological Review* 77: 257–73.

Ostrom, T. M. (1977). Between-theory and within-theory conflict in explaining context effects in impression formation. *Journal of Experimental Social Psychology* 13: 492–503.

Ostrom, T. M., Pryor, J. B., and Simpson, D. D. (1981). The organization of special information. In E. T. Higgins, C. P. Herman, and M. P. Zanna (eds.), *Social cognition: the Ontario symposium*, vol. 1. Hillsdale, NJ: Lawrence Erlbaum.

Ostrom, T. M. and Upshaw, H. S. (1968). Psychological perspective and attitude change. In A. G. Greenwald, T. C. Brock, and T. M. Ostrom (eds.), *Psychological foundations of attitudes*. New York: Academic Press.

Parducci, A. (1965). Category judgment: a range-frequency model. *Psychological Review* 72: 407–18.

Posner, M. I. (1978). *Chronometric explorations of the mind*. Hillsdale, NJ: Lawrence Erlbaum.

Postman, L. and Brown, D. R. (1952). The perceptual consequences of success and failure. *Journal of Abnormal and Social Psychology* 47: 213–21.

Rholes, W. S. and Pryor, J. B. (1982). Cognitive accessibility and causal attributions. *Personality and Social Psychology Bulletin* 8: 719–27.

Ross, L. (1977). The intuitive psychologist and his shortcomings: distortions in the attribution process. In L. Berkowitz (ed.), *Advances in experimental social psychology*, vol. 10. New York: Academic Press.

Rothbart, M., Evans, M., and Fulero, S. (1979). Recall for confirming events: memory processes and the maintenance of social stereotypes. *Journal of Experimental Social Psychology* 15: 343–55.

Schramm, W. and Danielson, W. (1958). Anticipated audience as determinants of recall. *Journal of Abnormal and Social Psychology* 56: 282–3.

Sherman, S. J., Ahlm, K., Berman, L., and Lynn, S. (1978). Contrast effects and their relationship to subsequent behavior. *Journal of Experimental Social Psychology* 14: 340–50.

Snyder, M. (1979). Self-monitoring processes. In L. Berkowitz (ed.), *Advances in experimental social psychology*, vol. 12. New York: Academic Press.

Srull, T. K. (1981). Person memory: some tests of associative storage and retrieval models. *Journal of Experimental Psychology: Human Learning and Memory* 7: 440–63.

Srull, T. K. (1983). Organizational and retrieval processes in person memory: an examination of processing objectives, presentation format, and the possible role of self-generated retrieval cues. *Journal of Personality and Social Psychology* 44: 1157–70.

Srull, T. K. and Brand, J. F. (1983). Memory for information about persons: the effect of encoding operations on subsequent retrieval. *Journal of Verbal Learning and Verbal Behavior* 22: 219–30.

Srull, T. K. and Wyer, R. S., Jr. (1979). The role of category accessibility in the interpretation of information about persons: some determinants and implications. *Journal of Personality and Social Psychology* 37: 1660–72.

Srull, T. K. and Wyer, R. S., Jr. (1980). Category accessibility and social perception: some implications for the study of person memory and interpersonal judgments. *Journal of Personality and Social Psychology* 38: 841–56.

Srull, T. K. and Wyer, R. S., Jr. (1986). The role of chronic and temporary goals in social information processing. In R. M. Sorrentino and E. T. Higgins (eds.), *Handbook of motivation and cognition: foundations of social behavior*. New York: Guilford Press.

Stangor, C. (1986). *Physiological arousal, social interaction, and polarized judgments of others: an expectancy/arousal model of social evaluation*. Unpublished doctoral dissertation, New York University.

Stephan, W. G., Berscheid, E., and Walster, E. (1971). Sexual arousal and heterosexual perception. *Journal of Personality and Social Psychology* 20: 93–101.

Stevens, S. S. (1958). Adaptation-level vs. the relativity of judgment. *American Journal of Psychology* 71: 633–46.

Taylor, S. E. and Crocker, J. (1981). Schematic bases of social information processing. In E. T. Higgins, C. A. Herman, and M. P. Zanna (eds.), *Social cognition: the Ontario symposium*, vol. 1. Hillsdale, NJ: Lawrence Erlbaum.

Trope, Y. (1986). Self-enhancement and self-assessment in achievement behavior. In R. M. Sorrentino and E. T. Higgins (eds.), *Handbook of motivation and cognition: foundations of social behavior*. New York: Guilford Press.

Tulving, E. and Pearlstone, Z. (1966). Availability versus accessibility of information in memory for words. *Journal of Verbal Learning and Verbal Behavior* 5: 381–91.

Tversky, A. and Kahneman, D. (1974). Judgment under uncertainty: Heuristics and biases. *Science* 85: 1124–31.

Upshaw, H. S. (1962). Own attitude as an anchor in equal-appearing intervals. *Journal of Abnormal and Social Psychology* 64: 85–96.

Volkmann, J. (1951). Scales of judgment and their implications for social psychology. In J. H. Rohrer and M. Sherif (eds.), *Social psychology at the crossroads*. New York: Harper & Row.

White, G. L., Fishbein, S., and Rutstein, J. (1981). Passionate love and the misattribution of arousal. *Journal of Personality and Social Psychology* 41: 56–62.

Wyer, R. S. and Carlston, D. E. (1979). *Social cognition, inference, and attribution*. Hillsdale, NJ: Lawrence Erlbaum.

Wyer, R. S., Jr. and Gordon, S. E. (1982). The recall of information about persons and groups. *Journal of Experimental Social Psychology* 18: 128–64.

Wyer, R. S. and Gordon, S. E. (1984). The cognitive representation of social information. In R. S. Wyer and T. K. Srull (eds.), *Handbook of social cognition*. Hillsdale, NJ: Lawrence Erlbaum.

Wyer, R. S. and Srull, T. K. (1981). Category accessibility: some theoretical and empirical issues concerning the processing of social stimulus information. In E. T. Higgins, C. P. Herman, and M. P. Zanna (eds.), *Social cognition: the Ontario symposium*. Hillsdale, NJ: Lawrence Erlbaum.

Wyer, R. S., Srull, T. K., and Gordon, S. E. (1984). The effects of predicting a person's behavior on subsequent trait judgments. *Journal of Personality and Social Psychology* 43: 674–88.

Wyer, R. S., Srull, T. K., Gordon, S. E., and Hartwick, J. (1982). Effects of processing objectives on the recall of prose material. *Journal of Personality and Social Psychology* 43: 674–88.

Zadny, J. and Gerard, H. B. (1974). Attributed intentions and informational selectivity. *Journal of Experimental Social Psychology* 10: 34–52.

Zajonc, R. B. (1960). The process of cognitive tuning and communication. *Journal of Abnormal and Social Psychology* 61: 159–67.

Zanna, M. and Hamilton, D. (1977). Further evidence for meaning change in impression formation. *Journal of Experimental Social Psychology* 13: 224–38.

Zimmerman, C. and Bauer, R. A. (1956). The effect of an audience on what is remembered. *Public Opinion Quarterly* 20: 238–48.

Zukier, H. (1986). The paradigmatic and narrative modes in goal-guided inference. In R. M. Sorrentino and E. T. Higgins (eds.), *Handbook of motivation and cognition: foundations of social behavior*. New York: Guilford Press.

Acknowledgments

Preparation of this chapter was supported by Grant MH 39429 from the National Institute of Mental Health to the first author. We thank Arie Kruglanski, Yaacov Trope, and Henri Zukier for their helpful comments.

12 Constructing the past: biases in personal memories

Michael Ross and Cathy McFarland

> It does us no good to know that the years go by, that youth gives way to old age, that the most stable thrones and fortunes crumble, that fame is ephemeral, our way of forming a conception – and, so to speak, taking a photograph – of this moving universe, hurried along by Time, seeks on the contrary to make it stand still.
> (Proust 1927, p. 1063)

In this chapter, we describe research on people's memories of their past feelings, personality characteristics, and behaviors. Our basic premise is that people are interested in their pasts for a variety of reasons, including entertainment (much of our social interchange with others concerns past foibles and successes), curiosity (you might gaze at your thirteen-year-old kid and wonder whether you were really like that at his age), and the need to achieve self-understanding. Individuals can study the past to learn about their preferences, values, abilities, and so forth.

How do people remember what they were like in the past? The commonsense view is that memories are safely stored away and can be recovered when needed. Unless, of course, the event is forgotten, in which case it cannot be retrieved. Many philosophers, sociologists, and psychologists offer a quite different view of long-term memory (e.g. Bartlett 1932, Berger 1963, Lindsay and Norman 1972, Mead 1959, Taylor and Crocker 1981). They suggest that recall is selective, that the past is reinterpreted and explained over time, and that people unwittingly fill in gaps in memory by inferring events that probably occurred.

What guides people's reconstructions of their past attributes and behaviors? For example, how does a person decide how tidy he or she was five years ago? We emphasize two factors. The first is the person's present standing on the attribute in question. The individual's current status (for example, how tidy he or she is now) is generally more salient and available than is his or her past standing on any particular attribute. Reconstructing the past, then, may consist primarily of characterizing it as either different from, or the same as, the present. The second factor is introduced to explain how people make this judgment. We suggest that people make use of implicit theories of stability and change when attempting to reconstruct their pasts.

What is the nature of these theories? Perhaps the most important theory people possess is one that stresses the unified, stable nature of the self. As many philosophers and psychologists have noted, a sense of personal identity is often derived from the perception of temporal consistency or sameness. In general, I say that I am the same self today that I was yesterday (see the quotation from Proust at the beginning of this chapter). When this consistency principle is invoked, people may view themselves as stable over time, even if change has occurred. Consequently, they may see their current standing on an attribute as an accurate reflection of their past status.

Nonetheless, time does not always seem to stand still. Individuals can maintain a sense of personal unity and still see alterations in themselves. People accomplish this feat of perceiving unity in the face of change by constructing a bridge between the two selves, by explaining how the present state emerged from the earlier one. I may be a better teacher than I used to be because of experience; I may be physically weaker because of age. These examples suggest that people possess implicit theories of change, ideas about the conditions that are likely to foster alterations in themselves and others.

Indeed, we are all walking repositories of such theories. Consider several of the forms they may take. Some are embodied in social-cultural notions of development and change. Suppose you are asked, "How do people change as they get old?" A number of answers probably spring to mind, including that they get more forgetful, conservative, and wise (e.g. Rothbaum 1983).[1] Theories of one's own development may also reflect societal views about shifting trends in the population (for example, North Americans are more concerned about the ecology than they used to be). In addition, some of our social–cultural theories of change are more cataclysmic, as change is associated with the adoption of new roles and entry into new life phases. For example, many of us have some ideas about the impact of puberty, marriage, motherhood, tenure, and retirement on behavior and personality. (A best-selling greeting card contains the following message: "When we first started dating you never belched or farted or picked your nose . . . Marriage has changed all that. Happy Anniversary." We leave it to the reader to intuit whether the intended target of this card is male or female.)

People also possess theories regarding the inherent stability of human attributes such as personality traits, abilities, and attitudes. For instance, people may expect levels of honesty to remain stable in mature adults. An honest person was honest ten years ago and will be honest ten years from

1 These theories are not terribly well articulated, however. For instance, one might hold these expectations and yet not necessarily agree that it is wise to become more conservative.

now. On the other hand, ups and down in happiness and anxiety are to be expected throughout the lifespan. Next, consider abilities and attitudes. They are probably seen as quite stable, but changeable with events and time. In the normal course of affairs, I would assume my tennis ability was the same last week as it is now, but it could have been quite different ten years ago. Similarly, if I dislike a politician now it might be assumed that I disliked him last week; on the other hand, it would not be surprising to find out that I favored and voted for him ten years ago.

We are not arguing for the validity, or invalidity, of such theories. We are suggesting, though, that people hold these (and other) theories and can use them to guide their recall. A tenured professor may infer that she worked harder when faced with the maxim of publish or perish early in her career; a seventy-year-old may assume that, relatively speaking, thirty years ago he was a fool with a good memory.

To this juncture, we have implied that people dispassionately apply theory to data (present standing) and construct a slice of their past. As Freud and others have argued, however, recollections of the past can have implications for current self-esteem and self-views. As a result, people find ways to forget what they would rather not remember. The other side of the coin is that people may construct or select memories that confirm their preferred images of themselves (or the image they wish to project to others if the history is to be made public).

How do we reconcile the idea that reconstruction of the past is guided by people's goals and motives with our contention that reconstruction involves the application of implicit theories of stability and change? There is no necessary conflict between the two views. In any instance a variety of implicit theories may be potentially accessible, for example, population trends versus trait theories. As a result, people can often access a theory that will permit them to reconstruct a past that supports their preferred self-image.

We now consider the relevance of our formulation for interpreting the findings of social psychological research on biases in personal recall. We begin by discussing laboratory research on attitude change. We then turn to recent research that we have conducted in more naturalistic settings. Our analysis suggests that whether people perceive similarity or difference between the present and past will depend, in part, on the theory that they adopt. Consequently, we should be able to show (*a*) that people exaggerate the similarity between the present and the past when they adopt a theory of consistency in the face of actual change, and (*b*) that people overestimate the difference between the present and past when they inappropriately invoke a theory of change.

The perception of consistency over time

A number of studies have examined people's recall of their earlier attitudes after they have experienced a change in opinion (Bem and McConnell 1970, Goethals and Reckman 1973, Ross and Shulman 1973). The general finding is that people exaggerate the consistency between their present and past opinions by biasing their recall of the past. According to our analysis, this finding may be explained as follows. Current attitudes are salient to subjects during the recall phase. They must decide whether they reported a different opinion earlier. In this research, the duration between the two reports of attitude is not very long (a week or so). Typically, people expect attitudes to be stable over such time periods. Moreover, subjects did not enter the study wanting or expecting a change in attitude (as far as we know). Nor did they think that the experiment was designed to alter their views. For example, in the Bem and McConnell study, subjects were led to believe that they were simply helping the experimenter produce a pool of arguments on both sides of an attitude issue.

When people change their opinions in such circumstances are they likely to perceive that they have done so? Perhaps not, because some of the usual cues for a change in attitudes are absent (for instance, a lengthy time period, wanting change, or effort directed toward change). As a result, then, it may not be surprising that subjects in these studies exaggerated the consistency between their present and past opinions. When asked to recall their attitudes, subjects may have used the best available information, their current views, and, adopting a theory of stability, may have assumed that their past attitudes were similar.

This research suggests that people see the past as consistent with the present, even when change has occurred. It is possible to argue that the findings are of limited generality, however. Only attitudes were involved. Would the consistency finding hold for recall of other personal attributes? Also, the results may depend upon deception. By masking the true purpose of the study, the experimenter may have contributed to, or indeed fostered, participants' perceptions that they had not changed their attitudes. Would people see stability when change occurs in the absence of experimental deception?

To answer these questions, we designed a study to assess whether a consistency effect would obtain when changes in people's views of important aspects of themselves develop as they normally do in natural settings (McFarland and Ross 1985a). According to our analysis, the consistency effect in recall should occur primarily on dimensions for which people expect a high degree of consistency over time. We conducted a pretest to select personality characteristics that met this criterion. Subjects in the pretest were asked to indicate the likelihood that a person's standing on a variety of traits would remain consistent over a two-month period. The following attributes were seen by subjects to be highly stable and were used in the subsequent study: honesty, tidiness, reliability, open-mindedness, selfishness, intelligence, good-naturedness, and kindness.

In the main study, subjects reported their impressions of themselves on these dimensions at a preliminary session and then again two months later. At the second session they were also asked to recall their earlier impressions. The results revealed the familiar consistency effect. Subjects whose views of themselves had become more favorable over time recalled their earlier evaluations as more favorable than they were; subjects whose views had become more negative recalled less flattering evaluations than they had provided initially. The results demonstrate that the consistency effect does not depend upon experimental deception, and occurs for personality traits as well as attitudes.

A second line of research examined the impact of attitude change on recollections of past behaviors. When people are induced to alter their attitudes, they overstate the degree to which they have behaved consistently with their new attitudes in the past (Olson and Cal 1984, Ross *et al.* 1981, Ross *et al.* 1983). Once again, it is likely that subjects saw their attitudes as relatively stable over time. Consequently, if they assumed a correspondence between their attitudes and behavior, they could presume that they had already engaged in actions that were consistent with their current attitudes. With some selectivity and reinterpretation, they can readily identify such behaviors in recall.

One further issue has been addressed in this domain. Are revisions of personal history of real consequence or are they simply epiphenomenal? This question has been examined from the perspective of subjects' commitment to new attitudes.

Suppose that you are in the business of attitude change – for example, an advertiser, political leader, or public health official. It may not be all that difficult to alter attitudes temporarily, but it is difficult to produce lasting change (Cook and Flay 1978, Festinger 1964). Festinger reasoned that opinion shifts are unlikely to persist unless they are supported by subsequent changes in the environment or in behavior. These latter changes are often difficult to engineer, however.

Consider an alternative strategy. If you want to increase an audience's commitment to their new attitudes, should you ask them to recall relevant past behaviors, or avoid this strategy at all costs? The argument for avoidance is self-evident. This is a "new" attitude, after all, and your audience may have behaved in ways that are contradictory to it in the past. Focusing people on such contradictory behavior may serve to weaken the new attitude. For instance, attitude change engendered by the message that one's teeth will rot if they are not brushed after every meal may be undermined if people (*a*) perceive their teeth to be relatively healthy, and (*b*) recall brushing much less frequently than was recommended.

But, then again, this is not how memory seems to work. People tend to remember behaving consistently with how they now feel. If I presently think that it is important to brush my teeth after every meal, I will recall brushing my teeth more often in the past than if I think it is less important to do so (Ross *et al.* 1981). In short, past behavior is seen as consistent with current attitudes and hence provides support for the attitudes. This implies a form of self-fulfilling prophecy: new attitudes alter recall which, in turn, may inappropriately bolster a person's commitment to those attitudes.

Research evidence supports this analysis. Subjects who are required to recall past attitude-relevant behaviors after attitude change exhibit greater commitment to their new opinions than subjects who are not required to engage in recall. For instance, behavioral recall increased subjects' intentions to behave in line with their new opinions in the future, increased resistance to an attack on their new opinions, and increased their tendency to recall selectively arguments in favor of their new attitude position (Lydon *et al.* 1983, Ross *et al.* 1983).

The reciprocal relation between new attitudes and behavior recall is likely to occur primarily when people do not realize that they have experienced a change in attitudes. For only then are people likely to assume that their past behaviors are consistent with their current views. We would hypothesize a different outcome when people see themselves as adopting a new opinion. The perception of change should lead individuals to reconstruct past attitudes and behaviors that are at variance with their new views; this may serve to weaken rather than strengthen their commitment to these views.

Do people typically fail to detect a change in their attitudes? There is some indirect evidence that this may be the case. People exposed to persuasive communications in the mass media see them as having a much greater impact on others than on themselves (Davison 1983). For example, respondents perceived television advertising and pre-election news to have a greater effect on others' attitudes and behaviors than on their own. A similar view has been expressed by those custodians of public morality, members of film censorship boards. When Maryland's board of censors was eliminated, its members predicted a sharp decline in the morals of the citizens of that state. However, what was the impact of viewing all that pornography on the censors themselves? To believe their self-reports, it was apparently negligible. "One of them stated that over the course of twenty-one years she had 'looked at more naked bodies than 50,000 doctors,' but the effect of this experience was apparently more on her diet than on her morals. 'I had to stop eating a lot of food because of what they do with it in these movies,' she is quoted as having told the Maryland Legislature" (Davison 1983: 14).

From the above findings, it is not clear whether people are overestimating the effects of mass communications on others and/or underestimating the effect on themselves. One possibility, though, is that people exaggerate the stability of their own attitudes, values, and so forth, and consequently fail to recognize the impact of communications on themselves. If a communication does produce unacknowledged change, then behavior recall should increase people's commitment to their new views.

The perception of change

There is now considerable evidence that people see their past selves as similar to their present selves, even when they have changed. This finding is consonant with the contention of philosophers (e.g. James 1890, Mead 1959), sociologists (e.g. Berger 1963, Kitsuse 1962), and psychologists (e.g. Fischhoff 1975, Greenwald 1980, Snyder and Uranowitz 1978) that people reinterpret the past in light of current knowledge and concerns. For example, Berger describes how divorce leads people to reinterpret their marriage in such a way as to explain the final fiasco and to maintain a unified view of themselves.

Our emphasis on recall being driven by implicit theories of stability and change, however, suggests that consistency should not always rule the roost. Indeed, people's theories may induce them to exaggerate the amount that they have changed. According to our analysis, exaggeration of change should occur when peoples' theories lead them to anticipate change, but little or no change occurs. We have studied two potential instances of this. The first concerns women's theories regarding the menstrual cycle.

Menstrual cycle study

What is the impact of the menstrual cycle on mood and personality? Many women report definite theories about its effect. For example, they expect to become more irritable and depressed during the time of their periods (Moos 1968, Parlee 1974). Given the ubiquity of these beliefs, it is perhaps surprising to discover that the research evidence is quite equivocal (Coppen and Kessel 1963, Golub and Harrington 1981, McCance *et al.* 1937, Parlee 1974, Persky 1974, Ruble 1977).

If, as we suspect, these theories about the impact of the menstrual cycle on mood and personality are largely incorrect, then why don't women reject them on the basis of their personal experience? One answer concerns the perceived relation between physical discomfort and mood. During their periods, women consistently report increased incidence of headaches, backaches, and abdominal pains, among other symptoms (Coppen and Kessel 1963, Moos 1968, Moos *et al.* 1969, Parlee 1974). It is not unreasonable for women to assume that these physical discomforts are accompanied by shifts in mood, personality, and performance. However, women may underestimate their ability to cope with physical discomfort and assume greater shifts on these associated dimensions than actually occur. They may, then, inadvertently derive support for their theory of change in memory. During their period, women may exaggerate, in recall, how well off they were when they were not menstruating.

We tested this hypothesis in the following way (McFarland and Ross 1985b). At a first session, women rated themselves on the following mood and trait dimensions: irritability, loneliness, mood swings, depression, tension, self-critical, romantic, forgetfulness, orderliness, honesty, creativeness, and aggressiveness. They also rated themselves with respect to such physical symptoms as abdominal pains, headaches, backaches, and fatigue. The women returned for a second session, between four and fifty-three days later. For half of the women, this session occurred during their period. For the remainder, matched in terms of the time interval between sessions, the second session was held when they were not menstruating. Women's current evaluations of themselves were obtained on the same dimensions and they were asked to recall their earlier ratings.

Several findings are of interest here. First, women in their period reported more unpleasant physical symptoms than women not in their period. Second, we found no evidence that being in one's period was associated with more negative self-evaluations on the mood and trait dimensions in either within-subject (first session versus second session) or between-subject (period group versus nonmenstruating group at session two) comparisons. On the other hand, when we examined recall, there was an effect for the women in their period, who recalled their earlier ratings on the mood and trait dimensions as being significantly more favorable than they were. Women not in their period exhibited no systematic bias in recall.

Thus women may find support for their theory of the negative impact of their period on mood and trait dimensions by exaggerating how well off they are in its absence. Interestingly, where actual change seems to have occurred, namely on the physical symptoms, no systematic bias in memory was obtained. Bias in memory occurs primarily when a theory of change is invalid.

The data from this study provide an important departure from the findings of previous research. In looking over their pasts, people do not always see consistency with their present states. When a change is assumed to have occurred, people may reconstruct their pasts so as to provide evidence for the supposed transition.

The study skills experiment

Our analysis suggests that people are likely to overestimate change when they invoke a theory of change in a situation of actual stability. Self-improvement programs provide a second setting in everyday life where this may occur. Many different programs flourish in North America. New diet and exercise books head the bestseller lists. Pop therapies and so-called cults such as Scientology and est have large followings. Some of these programs have attracted and seemingly satisfied many, although most are judged by informed professionals to be ineffective or even harmful (e.g. Conway and Siegelman 1979, Polivy and Herman 1979).

There are a number of possible explanations for the contrast between the skepticism of the professional program evaluators and the enthusiasm of the program participants (Ross and Conway 1986). And it is not the case that the professionals' evaluations are necessarily superior. Let us suppose, though, that a program appears to be valid but, in fact, promises more than it delivers. The participants may then believe the promises and inadvertently manufacture evidence that supports the claims. There are two obvious ways in which such fabrication of evidence can emerge. People can distort their postprogram standing and/or revise their impressions of how they were before the program began.

Though both processes undoubtedly occur, it may often be more feasible for people to alter their impressions of their past status than to enhance their present standing. For instance, following a diet, obese people may not be able to convince themselves or a scale that they are now thin. In contrast, they may more readily persuade themselves that, though they are not exactly svelte now, they were worse before the diet.

Conway and Ross (1984) examined the hypothesis that participants in a self-improvement program attribute greater gain to themselves than is warranted by exaggerating how poorly off they were before the program began. The experiment was conducted in the context of a study skills program of the sort commonly offered in universities and colleges. This context was chosen because several well-conducted evaluations of such programs have concluded that they have little merit, even though they are judged beneficial by students who take them (e.g. Chibnall 1979, Gibbs 1981, Main 1980).

The design of this study was as follows. Subjects wishing to participate in a skills program evaluated their study skills at a first meeting and then were randomly assigned to either the skills program or a waiting-list control group. After program participants had attended three weekly skills sessions, both they and the waiting-list subjects returned for a final meeting. All were asked to recall their initial evaluations of their skills, to rate their skills improvement, and to predict their grades at the end of the semester. Recall was examined to determine whether, relative to waiting-list control subjects, participants in the skills program belittled their prior study skills. In addition, we obtained subjects' final grades to compare participants' perceived improvement in study skills with their academic performance. This also allowed us to assess the program's impact on an objective measure of performance.

The results supported the hypotheses. Program participants recalled their original study skills evaluations as being worse than they had actually reported; waiting list subjects exhibited no systematic bias in recall. In short, program participants belittled their prior study skills; waiting list control subjects did not.

In addition to derogating their prior skills, program participants reported significantly greater improvement in their study skills and expected better grades than did waiting list subjects. Participants' expectations were unwarranted. Academic grades were not affected by the program. Interestingly, this did not prevent program participants from subsequently recalling their performance as superior. When contacted six months later, program participants remembered better grades than they had actually obtained in their major for the term during which the program was conducted. In contrast, waiting list subjects did not exhibit a systematic bias in recall.

As opponents of cults, fad diets, and pop therapies have found, it is not easy to persuade participants that a program is ineffective (e.g. Conway and Siegelman 1979). At the end of the study skills experiment, subjects were informed that such programs are generally ineffective. Program participants reacted strongly to this information, emphasizing the potential benefits of the program. Some argued that even if their study skills weren't improved, they had acquired greater self-confidence which would stand them in good stead at exam time. Their reasoning is not supported by the exam results of participants in our own or other programs, however.

Motivational determinants of biases in recall

The research findings presented above reflect conflicting tendencies in autobiographical recall. The findings described in the first half of the chapter contribute to a portrayal of human beings as cognitive conservatives who bias their memories so as to deny change and maintain consistency. The data presented in the last section suggest that people can also be depicted as cognitive radicals who embrace change and exaggerate the amount that they have altered.

Our conceptual formulation for both sets of findings focused on the implicit theory the person invoked to assess whether the past might be similar to, or different from the present. One value of this framework is heuristic. Despite the preponderance of results and theorizing suggesting consistency, our analysis alerted us to the possibility that an exaggeration of change can also occur. More important, our formulation suggested to us the contexts in which we should expect to find either bias.

Earlier, we suggested that recall may also be affected by motivational concerns. We now consider two general sources of motivation that may have contributed to the biases in recall described in the present chapter.

First, perhaps subjects bias their recall to enhance or maintain their self-esteem. For instance, it may violate their self-esteem to see themselves as changing their attitudes or failing to benefit from a self-improvement program. Thus, the memory biases may reflect subjects' efforts to maintain their positive images of themselves.

However, the data from the two McFarland and Ross (1985a, b) studies appear to be inconsistent with a self-esteem interpretation. Revisions that bring the past in line with a current, negative view of oneself do not seem particularly self-enhancing. Nor does the biased recall implying that being in one's period has a negative impact on various personal attributes.

It appears, therefore, that at times, people prefer confirming their theories to maintaining positive views of themselves. In a related vein, Swann and his colleagues have shown that people prefer information that supports their current self-image, even when negative, to information that disconfirms their self-image (Swann and Read 1981, Swann and Hill 1982).

Although the desire to protect self-esteem does not appear to provide a full account of the data, conceivably other motives are operative. It has been proposed that cognitive dissonance might be aroused by a recognition of an inconsistency over time in one's attitudes (Goethals and Reckman 1973). People can reduce their dissonance by forgetting their original positions and assuming that their opinions have not changed.

Let us examine this interpretation more closely. Why would people experience dissonance when they discover that their current attitudes conflict with their previous opinions? Presumably, they feel embarrassment because they expect to be consistent. Yet, as we have seen, people do not always assume consistency. Sometimes they anticipate change. It is possible to argue, then, that dissonance is aroused in two circumstances of relevance to present concerns: (1) when a person's attributes shift over time, but acknowledging change violates a theory that the person holds about him or herself, (2) when a person's attributes are consistent over time, but the failure to change violates a self-theory. In both instances, people may bias their memories (even if it reduces self-esteem) so as to confirm their theories and attenuate or eliminate dissonance.

Thus, our formulation is not incompatible with a dissonance interpretation. Theories of stability or change may contribute to the arousal of dissonance. Note, though, that it is not necessary to posit a motivated, dissonance-induced forgetting to explain the memory data. At the present time, it is not possible to assess how critical dissonance motivation is to the process.

Self-knowledge versus self-deception

One conclusion from the research presented in this chapter is that people are revisionist historians with respect to their personal memories. When we go beyond the psychological literature we find that this is virtually an accepted fact by some philosophers and sociologists.

For example, G. H. Mead (1950) argued that, although there are many novel or unexpected events in our lives, in memory they are reconstructed to appear as part of a connected, continuous process. Mead also suggested that memory is selective, and that the past is reinterpreted and redefined so as to meet current concerns. Similarly, Peter Berger and Hansfried Kellner (1964) in their article "Marriage and the construction of reality" discuss how marriage causes the partners to reinterpret their past. A joint history gets fabricated in the ongoing conversation. One's views and memories of previous relationships are altered in the process.

In his 1963 book, *Invitation to sociology*, Peter Berger is even more emphatic. He suggests that people modify their autobiographies very much as the Stalinists continually rewrote the Soviet Encyclopedia, emphasizing and de-emphasizing the importance of various events and persons. This view is later echoed in Greenwald's (1980) paper on the "totalitarian ego".

It is perhaps time to introduce a note of caution into this discussion. The biases in recall that we have observed in social psychological research seem minor compared with the dramatic alterations suggested by Berger and others. Yes, attitudes influence recall of past behaviors, but so do many other things. For example, people's actions are frequently well practiced, even routinized. As a result, people may be able to recall them without difficulty, not necessarily by remembering each instance but simply by remembering that the activities are performed habitually.

Now, we are not arguing that the biases in recall observed in social psychological research are trivial. They can have long-term, nonobvious implications, affecting for example the durability of attitude change, or the perception of the success of self-improvement programs. We are simply trying to put things into perspective. If we focused on how accurate people are, rather than how inaccurate, we would probably be forced to concede that most of the psychological research demonstrates relatively minor tinkering with autobiographical details.

It is entirely possible, of course, that more major alterations occur in real life. The strength of experimental manipulations certainly pales into insignificance when compared, for instance, with marriage or divorce. Also note that most of the psychological research has focused on recall of specific facts, for example, an attitude or impression reported earlier, or behaviors engaged in. In contrast, researchers such as Mead and Berger were primarily concerned with reinterpretation. Alterations in the significance of an action or in one's view of how or why it occurred are conceivably relatively common. This is different from erasing the record entirely.

At this point, we should also distinguish between bias and error (see the chapter by Hastie and Rasinski in this volume for an incisive discussion of this topic). In our research, the recall of subjects in the control conditions tended to be no more accurate, in an absolute sense, than the recall of experimental subjects. However, the recall errors of control subjects were nonsystematic. For example, waiting-list subjects in the study skills experiment were as likely to enhance their prior study skills in recall as to derogate them. In contrast, experimental subjects exhibited systematic derogation. Thus, the implicit theories that guide the recall of our experimental subjects appear to give direction to the error in recall, rather than alter its magnitude.

Summary and conclusions

We have described a series of studies that focus on an aspect of self-knowledge, memories of the past. Two biases in recall emerged from this research: a tendency to exaggerate temporal consistency and a tendency to exaggerate change. We related both biases to people's theories of self.

The basic finding of biases in recall is quite well established in these experiments. The processes underlying these biases require further clarification, however. We are currently engaged in attempts to assess process data more directly.

Psychologists who study memory can concentrate on how people remember the past accurately or on biases and error in recall. Social psychologists have tended to focus on bias and error. We have maintained this tradition in the present chapter. There are probably two main reasons for such differential attention. First, the study of accurate recall is seen primarily as the province of cognitive psychologists. Second, we believe, as Freud did, that it is the illogic that needs explaining.

Nonetheless, we may have exaggerated the degree of fabrication by focusing on bias rather than accuracy. Also, we should not blame everything on memory. In our experiments, we assessed the validity of subjects' recall by contrasting it with their prior reports. On the other hand, in the examples cited by Berger and others no similar record of the past is available. It is important to emphasize that biased perception and interpretation can occur at every step in the acquisition of social knowledge. For example, participants in troubled marriages may interpret incidents quite differently when they occur. Discrepancies in memory between partners following a divorce may thus reflect the participants' original interpretations, rather than biases in recall. Longitudinal research is required to distinguish between the competing interpretations.

References

Bartlett, F. C. (1932). *Remembering: a study in experimental and social psychology*. London: Cambridge University Press.

Bem, D. J. and McConnell, M. K. (1970). Testing the self-perception explanation of dissonance phenomena: on the salience of premanipulation attitudes. *Journal of Personality and Social Psychology* 14: 23–31.

Berger, P. L. (1963). *Invitation to sociology: a humanistic perspective*. Garden City, New York: Doubleday.

Berger, P. L. and Kellner, M. (1964). Marriage and the construction of reality. *Diogenes* 46: 1–24.

Chibnall, B. (1979). The Sussex experience. In P. J. Mills (ed.), *Study courses and counselling: problems and possibilities*. Guildford, Surrey: Society for Research into Higher Education.

Conway, F. and Siegelman, J. (1979). *Snapping*. New York: Delta.

Conway, M. and Ross, M. (1984). Getting what you want by revising what you had. *Journal of Personality and Social Psychology* 47: 738–48.

Cook, T. D. and Flay, B. R. (1978). The persistence of experimentally induced attitude change. In L. Berkowitz (ed.), *Advances in experimental social psychology*, vol. 11. New York: Academic Press.

Coppen, A. and Kessel, N. (1963). Menstruation and personality. *British Journal of Psychiatry* 109: 711–21.

Davison, W. P. (1983). The third-person effect in communication. *Public Opinion Quarterly* 47: 1–15.

Festinger, L. (1964). Behavioral support for opinion change. *Public Opinion Quarterly* 28: 404–17.

Fischhoff, B. (1975). Hindsight ≠ foresight: The effect of outcome knowledge on judgment under uncertainty. *Journal of Experimental Psychology: Human Perception and Performance*: 288–99.

Gibbs, G. (1981). *Teaching students to learn.* Milton Keynes, England: Open University Press.

Goethals, G. R. and Reckman, R. F. (1973). The perception of consistency in attitudes. *Journal of Experimental Social Psychology* 9: 491–501.

Golub, S. and Harrington, D. (1981). Premenstrual mood changes in adolescent women. *Journal of Personality and Social Psychology* 41: 961–5.

Greenwald, A. G. (1980). The totalitarian ego: fabrication and revision of personal history. *American Psychologist* 35: 603–18.

James, W. (1890). *The principles of psychology*, vol. 1. New York: Holt.

Kitsuse, J. I. (1962). Societal reaction to deviant behavior: problems of theory and method. *Social Problems* 9: 247–56.

Lindsay, P. H. and Norman, D. A. (1972). *Human information processing: an introduction to psychology*. New York: Academic Press.

Lydon, J., Zanna, M. P., and Ross, M. (1983). The effects of behavior recall on the persistence of attitude change. Paper presented at the annual convention of The Canadian Psychological Association, Winnipeg, Manitoba.

McCance, R. A., Luff, M. C., and Widdowson, E. E. (1937). Physical and emotional periodicity in women. *Journal of Hygiene* 37: 571–611.

McFarland, C. and Ross, M. (1985a). *The relation between current impressions and memories of self and dating partners*. Unpublished manuscript.

McFarland, C. and Ross, M. (1985b). Unpublished data.

Main, A. (1980). *Encouraging effective learning*. Edinburgh: Scottish Academic Press.

Mead, G. M. (1959). *Mind, self and society*. Chicago: University of Chicago Press.

Moos, R. H. (1968). The development of a menstrual distress questionnaire. *Psychosomatic Medicine* 30: 853–67.

Moos, R. H., Kopell, B. S., Melges, F. T., Yalom, I. D., Lunde, D. T., Clayton, R. B., and Hamburg, D. A. (1969). Fluctuations in symptoms and moods during the menstrual cycle. *Journal of Psychosomatic Research* 13: 37–44.

Olson, J. M. and Cal, A. V. (1984). Source credibility, attitude, and the recall of past behaviors. *European Journal of Social Psychology* 14: 203–10.

Parlee, M. B. (1974). Stereotypic beliefs about menstruation: a methodological note on the Moos menstrual distress questionnaire and some new data. *Psychosomatic Medicine* 36: 229–40.

Persky, H. (1974). Reproductive hormones, moods, and the menstrual cycle. In R. C. Friedman, R. M. Richart, and R. L. Vandewiele (eds.), *Sex differences in behavior*. New York: Wiley.

Polivy, J. and Herman, C. P. (1983). *Breaking the diet habit*. New York: Basic Books.

Proust, M. (1927). *Remembrance of things past*, vol. 2. New York: Random House.

Ross, M. and Conway, M. (1986). Remembering one's own past: the construction of personal histories. In R. M. Sorrentino and E. T. Higgins (eds.), *Handbook of motivation and cognition*. New York: Guilford Press.

Ross, M., McFarland, C., Conway, M., and Zanna, M. P. (1983). Reciprocal relation between attitudes and behavior recall: committing people to newly formed attitudes. *Journal of Personality and Social Psychology* 45: 257–67.

Ross, M., McFarland, C., and Fletcher, G. J. O. (1981). The effect of attitude on the recall of personal histories. *Journal of Personality and Social Psychology* 10: 627–34.

Ross, M. and Shulman, R. F. (1973). Increasing the salience of initial attitudes: dissonance vs. self-perception theory. *Journal of Personality and Social Psychology* 28: 138–44.

Rothbaum, F. (1983). Aging and age stereotypes. *Social Cognition* 2: 171–84.

Ruble, D. N. (1977). Premenstrual symptoms: a reinterpretation. *Science* 197: 291–2.

Snyder, M. and Uranowitz, S. W. (1978). Reconstructing the past: Some cognitive consequences of person perception. *Journal of Personality and Social Psychology* 36: 941–50.

Swann, W. and Hill, R. (1982). When our identities are mistaken: reaffirming self-conceptions through social interaction. *Journal of Personality and Social Psychology* 43: 59–66.

Swann, W. and Read, S. J. (1981). Self-verification processes: how we sustain our self-conceptions. *Journal of Experimental Social Psychology* 17: 351–72.

Taylor, S. E. and Crocker, J. (1981). Schematic bases of social information processing. In E. T. Higgins, C. P. Herman, and M. P. Zanna (eds.), *Social cognition: the Ontario symposium*. Hillsdale, NJ: Lawrence Erlbaum.

13 Attitudes: a new look at an old concept[1]

Mark P. Zanna and John K. Rempel

The study of attitudes and attitudinal processes has long preoccupied social scientists. Yet despite the concept's venerable and influential history (cf. Fleming 1967), agreement on precisely what an attitude is and how it can be identified has proven to be somewhat elusive (McGuire 1985). There is the general understanding that an attitude has, as its base, an element of evaluation (Ostrom 1969). In his recent work, Fazio (1986) has argued that attitudes primarily fulfill a "knowledge function". Following the functionalist theorists (e.g. Katz 1960), Fazio characterizes attitudes as summary judgments of an object or event which aid individuals in structuring their complex social environments. As such, attitudes can be seen as items of social knowledge, built from the experiences, beliefs, and feelings generated by the attitude objects.

Nevertheless, a number of issues remain unresolved. Briefly, these issues consist of (1) the role played by feelings, beliefs and behaviors in the attitude concept, (2) the dispositional versus episodic nature of attitudes, and (3) the relationship between affect and evaluation. In the following discussion we will present a model of attitudes which will address these various issues. In the process we will consider how an approach to attitudes as knowledge structures can both benefit from and contribute to a more general understanding of social knowledge.

Issues concerning the definition of the attitude concept

We will begin with a more detailed examination of the issues surrounding attitudinal definition. First we turn to the role of beliefs, feelings, and

1 In addition to the editors and each of the participants of the conference at which this paper was first presented, we wish to thank John Cacioppo, Russell Fazio, Connie Kristiansen, and James Olson for their comments on an earlier draft of the chapter.

behavior in the attitude concept. Different theorists tend to advocate definitions which emphasize either a unitary or multicomponent view of attitudes. The most popular definition, at least if one surveys recent social psychology texts, would suggest that attitudes consist of three classes of response (affective, cognitive, and behavioral) to a stimulus, or attitude, object. This view, popularized by Milton Rosenberg and Carl Hovland in the early 1960s (Rosenberg and Hovland 1960), basically suggests that an attitude consists of how we feel, what we think, and what we are inclined to do about an attitude object. Building upon the early work of Ostrom (1969) and Kothandapani (1971), Breckler, in a recent dissertation (Breckler 1983, 1984), has provided impressive evidence supporting this so-called three-component or "tripartite" model of attitudes. Using both verbal and nonverbal measures, Breckler's data demonstrate that affect, cognition, and behavior, though related, do have discriminative validity.

Another common definition of attitudes can be traced back to early attitude theorists such as Thurstone (Thurstone and Chave 1929). This view would suggest that attitudes consist of evaluative or affective responses to attitude objects. More recently popularized by Martin Fishbein and Icek Ajzen (1975), this essentially one-component view proposes that affective responses are based upon cognition.

We believe there are conceptual problems with each viewpoint. One concern we have with the three-component view is that it tends to prejudge the attitude–behavior relation, assuming that, almost by definition, such a relation must exist. The early evidence indicating that the attitude–behavior relation was tenuous (Wicker 1969) may have led theorists not only to feel uncomfortable with the tripartite model but to become unduly pessimistic about the notion of attitudes in general.

The one-component view helps resolve the question of attitude–behavior consistency, by making it a theoretical or even empirical question, rather than a definitional necessity. However, the effort to reduce attitudes to a single component may have resulted in an oversimplification. One concern we have with this view, especially as advanced by Fishbein and Ajzen, is that it seems too narrow in its suggestion that evaluative responses are based primarily (if not entirely) on what we would call utilitarian beliefs. To put it another way, there is as yet little or no emphasis on affective experience *per se* or, for that matter, on past behaviors. And, of course, recent models, as well as data, would suggest attitudes can be based upon affect associated with and/or past behaviors relevant to the attitude object.

Robert Zajonc (1980), for example, has recently proposed that one's preferences can be based on affect *per se* and recent empirical work does suggest that affect is an important determinant of evaluation and/or behavior. In a paper which greatly influenced our own thinking, Abelson and his colleagues (Abelson *et al.* 1982) have demonstrated that affective or emotional states associated with presidential candidates influenced individuals' evaluations of these candidates over and above the conventional beliefs that were held about the candidates. Similar findings, that affect can have a strong and independent effect on attitudes and/or behavior, have now been reported in several other domains, including energy conservation (Seligman *et al.* 1979), health behaviors (Ajzen and Timko 1985), responses to victimization (Tyler and Rasinski 1984), and contraceptive behavior (Fisher 1984).

Daryl Bem, in several influential papers (e.g. Bem 1972), has proposed that attitudes are often inferred from past behaviors, taking into account the conditions under which the behavior was performed. Considerable research has supported this notion (cf. Fazio *et al.* 1977), including a series of elegant studies by Salancik and his colleagues (e.g. Salancik 1974, Salancik and Conway 1975) which demonstratd that subtle manipulations of the salience of past behaviors dramatically influenced individuals' assessments of their attitudes.

Thus the attitude literature is dominated by two conflicting definitions, neither of which seems entirely satisfactory in accounting for the data. By approaching the issue from divergent perspectives, researchers have in effect produced numerous one-component views, each of which emphasizes either cognition, affect, or behavior. By combining the three components into one definition, however, the tenuous relation between attitude and behavior remains problematic.

Some theorists have attempted to deal with the inconsistency among definitions by removing behavior from the attitude equation, and representing attitude as a two-component structure consisting of cognition and affect (Fleming 1967, Zajonc and Markus 1982, Bagozzi and Burnkrant 1979). Others have, in fact, moved toward a loose integration of the one- and three-component views. In this approach, the attitude itself is regarded as a single entity; an evaluative disposition to respond to an object or event in a favorable or unfavorable manner. The three components (beliefs, feelings, and actions) are retained as the three domains in which the attitude is expressed in observable responses (Davis and Ostrom 1984, Ostrom 1969, Ajzen 1984). Greenwald (1968) and subsequently Breckler (1983, 1984) have gone one step further, to argue that the existence of three response categories does not presuppose that they are internally consistent. There is, consequently, no need to assume an *a priori* congruence between attitudes and behavior. Further, these researchers feel that the three components are distinguishable via their developmental roots. Greenwald in particular argues that cognition, affect, and behavioral intentions are coded separately by means of distinct learning processes.

While there is activity among theorists at a conceptual level to move toward integrating the one- and three-component approaches, authors of recent introductory social psychology texts, such as Olson and Zanna (1983) and Myers (1983), have continued to opt for either the one-component or the three-component view. Thus, the distinction continues to provide an important area of conceptual disagreement, at least when presented to an introductory audience.

A second general issue, which is somewhat related to the one-versus-three-component distinction, concerns the extent to which an attitude is dispositional or episodic in nature. Common definitions present attitudes as relatively stable enduring dispositions (cf. Ajzen 1984, Ostrom 1984). In contrast, Bem (1972) has suggested that attitudes may often be the consequence of a relatively superficial inference based on past behavior. From this perspective, attitudinal responses do not reflect an enduring disposition but, rather, indicate a less stable assessment which is more reactive to external cues (see also Salancik 1982). Several researchers have attempted to resolve this controversy by suggesting that superficial attitudinal assessments based on external cues occur when an attitude is either not clearly formed (e.g. Norman 1975, Chaiken and Baldwin 1981) or is inaccessible from internal states (Wood, 1982, Tybout and Scott 1983). Thus these researchers do not assume that an attitudinal response necessarily indicates an enduring disposition toward the attitude object. Further, these views regard issues concerning the internal consistency of the three attitude components as matters to be resolved by empirical investigation.

A final issue concerns the relationship between affect and evaluation. As was mentioned at the outset, most definitions of attitude rely on some reference to an evaluative element. In some cases the evaluative character of an attitude is regarded as isomorphic with the affective component (Ajzen 1984, Zajonc and Markus 1982, Staats 1968), whereas other researchers see the attitude and its affective component as distinct entities (Mills *et al.* 1976, Abelson *et al.* 1982). We believe that part of the confusion stems from a rather broad and imprecise usage of the term "affect". Affect has been used to refer to any thoughts or actions with overtones of pleasant/unpleasant, good/bad, approach/avoidance, etc. These thoughts or actions may be infused with strong emotion, weak emotion or no feeling at all. We suggest that subsequent usage of the term "affect" be restricted to those cases where emotions or feelings are present in an experiential sense, and that these be distinguished from the cognitive categorization of an object or event along an evaluative dimension. Thus, to use an example from Abelson *et al.*'s (1982) research, individuals are likely to have affects (i.e. emotions or feelings) associated with particular political candidates as well as overall evaluations (i.e. assessments of worth or goodness) of the candidates.

Attitudes: evaluations based on beliefs, feelings, and/or past behavior

The definitional issues we have just discussed form the starting-point for our reconceptualization of the attitude construct. Simply stated, we regard an attitude as the categorization of a stimulus object along an evaluative dimension based upon, or generated from, three general classes of information: (1) cognitive information, (2) affective/emotional information, and/or (3) information concerning past behaviors or behavioral intentions.

Let us examine this definition in more detail. First, what do we mean by evaluative dimension? An evaluative dimension is a dimension on which a comparison can be made between the value or worth of the stimulus object and another object or standard. Thus, in its simplest form the dimension itself consists of a minimum of two discrete categories with the object either judged against an absolute standard (good/bad) or a relative comparison with one or more objects (better than/worse than). As the number of categories increases the discrete dimension becomes a continuum (e.g. a scale from 1 to 10).

Second, by categorization we refer to a process with at least some minimal cognitive activity. The stimulus object must be perceived and identified at some level before a value judgment can be made. Thus, although, as we will describe shortly, noncognitive activity may be a basis for an attitude, evaluation itself requires cognitive input.

Describing the attitude concept as cognition is another way of stating that attitudes are, in fact, items of knowledge. Summarizing attitudes at this level of generality, however, masks many of the details which we believe are critical to understanding the implications of the attitude concept. An example may clarify this point. Consider a parent whose child has been killed by a drunk driver. Despite the fact that, when replying to an attitude question toward drivers who drink, the parent is engaging in cognitive activity, the *content* of his or her attitude is, in all likelihood, an intense emotional experience accompanied by a flood of memories containing behaviors and events of the past. The fact that the evaluation is itself a cognitive item of knowledge does not begin to adequately inform the researcher how the attitude is being *experienced*. We argue, therefore, that although it is possible for an attitudinal judgment to be dependent strictly on factual beliefs, attitudes may also be suffused with powerful emotions or may even depend solely on the ways in which the individual has behaved with the attitude object in the past. These sources are not mutually exclusive, of course, and can all be present and acting at the same time. We want to emphasize, however, that beliefs, feelings, and behaviors are more than ways in which individuals can respond to stimulus objects. Rather, they constitute very different ways in which the attitude is formed and subsequently experienced.

This definition of attitudes has a number of important implications for the issues discussed earlier. First, it leaves open the question of congruence among the attitudinal components. It is possible, within this definition, for an individual to have more than one attitude towards the same object if, over occasions, the evaluative judgment is based on a different source of information. Second, this definition reinforces the position that the dispositional or episodic nature of attitudes must be an empirical rather than a definitional question. We suggest that the answer to the stability of an attitude lies, at least in part, with the source that is playing a dominant role in the attitudinal experience. For example, one source (e.g. behavior) may lead to more stability than some other source (e.g. cognition). And an attitude based on congruent sources may be more stable than an attitude based upon incongruent sources. Finally, this definition clearly takes the position that evaluation and affect or emotion are not the same concept (cf. Simon 1982). As was suggested earlier, emotions may be a component, or even the sole basis, of an evaluation, but the two need not occur together.

Given that we are considering an attitude as knowledge based on three sources, the question necessarily arises, why these particular sources? On the one hand we have suggested why subsuming all sources under the more general category of cognition is undesirable. It is a level of analysis which clouds the important elements that may distinguish the experience of one attitude from another. There is, however, the other side of the coin, and that is, why do we choose to focus at the level of three general categories rather than becoming still more specific? We do so because, first, the tripartite distinction has set a strong historical precedent, not only in attitude theory but in Western philosophy as a whole. Such longevity and pervasive influence, it could be argued, attests the utility and heuristic value of such a distinction. Also, using the tripartite framework allows an easy integration of previous attitude theory and research into the present model.

Finally, recent research (Lingle and Ostrom 1981) suggests that the beliefs upon which an attitude is based may not be accessed when the attitude is subsequently activated. If so, it makes little sense to focus on more specific sources such as different types of belief. More generally, this line of reasoning suggests that attitudes not only act as summary statements (Fazio 1986) but are stored as separate cognitive entities, independent of the specific beliefs and, perhaps, of the feelings and/or behaviors on which they were based.

Why then, however, do we concern ourselves with different sources in the first place, if, as implied, these play no subsequent role in how attitudes are stored? This seeming paradox is resolved by noting that while Lingle and Ostrom did argue that an attitude, once formed, can be accessed without "consulting" the specific beliefs upon which the attitude was originally based, they did not propose that these formative beliefs never come to mind once the attitude is activated. To the extent that there are strong associative networks in memory between the attitude and its constituent beliefs, one would expect the opposite to be the case.

While Lingle and Ostrom focused their research on the cognitive domain, we believe their findings may apply to the domains of feelings and past behavior as well. Regarding feelings or emotions, for example, we would argue that the general evaluative response to an attitude object may be stored and persist even though the more specific emotional reactions which led to the overall evaluative judgment are no longer accessible. Nevertheless, when such an attitude is subsequently activated, it would still generate an emotionally based evaluation and a response with emotional content.

Thus, our interpretation of Lingle and Ostrom suggests that it very well may be useful to focus on sources at the general level of beliefs, feelings, and past behaviors, rather than at more specific levels.

In summary, our reconceptualization can be viewed as an attempt to take existing notions and combine them in a new and heuristically useful way. First, we define attitude as the categorization of a stimulus object along an evaluative dimension (i.e. an evaluation). Second, we propose that such evaluation can be based upon three classes of information: (1) cognitive information, (2) affective information, and (3) information concerning past behaviors. We believe these classes of information can determine evaluations separately or in combination. When, however, evaluations are based primarily on (utilitarian) beliefs about the attitude object, the present model can be reduced to something like the formulation proposed by Fishbein and Ajzen (1975). When evaluations are based primarily on affects produced by or associated with the attitude object, the model can resemble the formulation proposed by Zajonc (1980). Finally, when evaluations are based on inferences from past behavior, the model can be similar to Bem's theory of self-perception (1972). Given past research, we feel that our model of attitudes is an accurate reflection of what attitudes actually are. Further, we believe that such a view can both provide a springboard from which more complex attitude-related phenomena can be explored and at the same time offer a general framework into which research on attitudes can be placed.

Understanding past research

If this reconceptualization of the attitude concept is to be useful, it must both help us understand past research and suggest new directions for future research. Let us turn first to past research.

The present model suggests several questions which different researchers, at least implicitly, have addressed in recent years. For example, if attitudes are based on different sources of information, do otherwise equivalent evaluations based on different sources differentially guide (i.e. predict) future behavior? Fazio and Zanna (1981) have been asking just this sort of question. These authors have provided evidence that attitudes based on direct experience with the attitude object predict behavior better than do attitudes based upon indirect experience. In the vocabulary of the current model, Fazio and Zanna have demonstrated that otherwise equivalent evaluations based primarily on past behavior predict future behavior better than evaluations based primarily on cognition. Given the current model's emphasis on three sources of information, an interesting question for future research on direct experience would be whether such experience with an attitude object additionally produces an affective experience, at least under some conditions. That is, does direct experience lead to an attitude based on both past behavioral and affective information?

As mentioned earlier, several researchers have recently demonstrated that one's affects (or feelings) guide behavior, independently from one's cognitions (or beliefs), and perhaps to a greater extent. So, for example, Abelson and his colleagues (Abelson *et al.* 1982) demonstrated that voting preferences were independently (and better) predicted by affects (e.g. whether the candidate made one feel happy or sad) than by cognitions (e.g. whether one thought the candidate was competent or incompetent). In the current model's terms, we would note that evaluations based upon affects seem to guide relevant behavior.

Indeed, a recent series of studies by Wilson and his colleagues (Wilson *et al.* 1984) found that by inducing individuals to analyze the reasons for their affectively based attitudes, the attitude–behavior relation was decreased. According to Wilson, thinking about the reasons why one holds a particular attitude may lead to a reported evaluation based primarily on cognition, rather than upon affect (Wilson *et al.* 1986). If so, and if subsequent behavior continues to be influenced by an evaluation based on one's original feelings, such a "cognitivized" attitude is not likely to guide future behavior.

In future research it would be interesting to determine whether the sort of affect–behavior relation documented by Abelson *et al.* is, in fact, mediated by an overall evaluation (i.e. an attitude). Further, and paralleling the research on direct experience, it would be of interest to ask directly whether the attitude–behavior relation is stronger when attitudes are based primarily on one's feelings rather than on one's beliefs. An intriguing recent study by Millar and Tesser (1985) suggests this question may be put too simply. These authors found strong support for the hypothesis that evaluations based primarily on beliefs about attitude objects (in this instance analytic puzzles) predicted behavior towards the attitude objects only when the behavior (playing with the puzzles) was undertaken for instrumental reasons (i.e. cognitively driven). When the behavior was performed for consumatory, noninstrumental purposes (i.e. affectively driven), it was much better predicted by attitudes based primarily on feelings. Thus, it appears that the strength of an attitude–behavior relation may depend not only on the source of the attitude, but on the purposes of the behavior as well.

In passing, we might note that the present model also provides a way of conceptualizing symbolic attitudes (cf. Kinder and Sears 1981). The present model would suggest that a symbolic attitude might be thought of as an evaluation based primarily on affects associated with symbolic connections to the attitude object. Certainly, our understanding of symbolic attitudes would be enhanced if researchers were to collect direct measures of affects, cognitions, and past behaviors as well as overall evaluations.

The question of what source of information dominates evaluations is also of interest in the domain of social perception. Here the question becomes: what source of information is the most valid indicator of another person's attitude? Research by Amabile and Kabat (1982) has demonstrated that actions do speak louder than words. However, more recent work by Andersen (Andersen and Ross 1984, Andersen 1984) would suggest that the domination of behavior over cognition may only hold for public deeds and words. Andersen, in fact, has demonstrated that private thoughts/feelings are perceived to be more valid indicators of the real self than are behaviors. We believe it would be of interest for future research in the social perception of attitudes to examine all three sources of information in both private and public domains.

Because the model does not assume consistency among the various sources of information, one might ask if consistency among the sources makes a difference in, say, the prediction of behavior. Several researchers (e.g. Norman 1975, Chaiken and Baldwin 1981, Rosenberg 1968) have, in fact, been asking this sort of question. Norman, working from a traditional three-component view, for example, demonstrated that attitudes high in affective–cognitive consistency better predict behavior than attitudes low in affective–cognitive consistency. Individuals with attitudes low in affective–cognitive consistency are not thought to hold very strong attitudes, or, according to Chaiken and Baldwin (1981), are thought to be aschematic with respect to the attitude object. In the current model's terms, we simply suggest that evaluations based on consistent sources of information, whatever the sources, are more likely to predict behavior. Future research might address two general questions. First, how about other inconsistencies – inconsistencies between affect and past behavior or between cognition and past behavior? Second, should attitudes based upon inconsistent information be considered nonattitudes or, more intriguingly, ambivalent attitudes? If such evaluations are highly unstable or ambivalent, what source of information typically dominates? Or, does the weight given to a particular source of information depend, in part, on situational variables? If so, do evaluations based on chronically inconsistent sources of information predict behavior reasonably well when one or the other source is acutely dominant or salient? These questions, and others, left to the readers' imagination, suggest that studying attitudes based on inconsistent information may be at least as interesting as studying attitudes derived from consistent sources of information – if not more interesting. We will return to this issue in the next section.

Implications for future research

In discussing the model's implications for understanding past research we did, in passing, indicate the sort of future research questions we believe are implied by the model. In the present section we would like to go further and suggest three broad directions for future research that, we believe, follow from considering attitudes to be evaluations based on three classes of information. First, because the model focuses attention on the antecedents of attitudes, it would seem to direct research attention to the attitude-formation process (in addition to the attitude-change process), at least to a greater extent than in previous research. Second, because the model focuses attention on the antecedents of attitudes, it would seem to direct research attention to the ways in which various sources of information combine and interact to form overall evaluations, both in a developmental progression over time as well as in specific acute situations. Third, because the model suggests that attitudes may be based on different sources of information, it would seem to raise the general question of whether basic attitudinal processes are moderated, or in some way influenced, as a function of the source of information upon which the attitude is based. Do, for example, attitudes based on different sources of information differentially predict behavior? Are such attitudes differentially susceptible to different methods of persuasion? Thus, in addition to suggesting relatively novel areas of research, the model also has potential for shedding new light on the classic questions of attitude research.

Attitude formation. The model would suggest that more attention might be paid to how attitudes are formed in the first instance. For example, it would be of interest to determine if there are any classes of attitudes that are likely to be based primarily on one source of information or another. Recent research on symbolic attitudes, for instance, suggests that many important attitudes, especially intergroup attitudes, are formed relatively early in life and are based, to a great extent, on affect. In the consumer products domain one might ask if people's attitudes are typically based on utilitarian beliefs, and for what classes of products and/or for what classes of individuals this is not the case. In any event, we believe it would be interesting and relevant to determine the informational bases of attitude formation.

In this context it is interesting to speculate on possible individual difference variables which might induce people to base their attitudes on different sources of information. There are, for example, societal norms and standards urging people not to "judge a book by its cover". In other words, societal or parental pressure encourages individuals to add behavioral experience to the evaluative equation before making an attitude judgment. In addition there may be personality variables such as Cacioppo and Petty's "need for cognition" (1982a) and Jung's distinction between "thinkers" and "feelers" (1923) which may encourage individuals to weigh information from various sources differently or even cause them to seek out different sources on which to base their evaluations. Thus, in deciding which car to buy, some individuals might be more likely to narrow their choice by seeking out reliability information in consumer reports, while others might prefer to rely on their gut reactions to the car's appearance, how loudly the engine roars, or even how many lights appear on the instrument panel.

These possibilities also provide potentially relevant contributions to the understanding of interpersonal conflict. Attitudinal disagreement may be particularly difficult to resolve if the attitudes of the individuals involved are based on different sources of information and provide no common basis for negotiation. One has only to think of the family dinner table to appreciate this possibility. The child's evaluation of green beans may be based primarily on negative affect related to appearance and taste, while the parent's positive evaluation may be based, to a large extent, on cognitions surrounding a green bean's nutritional value.

Consistency of information. The model also suggests taking a more developmental perspective on attitude formation and change, paying particular attention to how the various sources of information influence one another, as well as the overall evaluation, over time.

One major question is whether there is a tendency for the sources of information to become more consistent over time. For example, if an attitude is initially and primarily based on one source of information, will the other sources fall in line and, over time, provide consistent support for the overall evaluation? Further, are such consistency pressures more (or less) likely when attitudes are initially based on one source than on another? Zajonc and Markus (1982) have, in fact, proposed that cognition often follows and justifies a preference which was originally based on affect. They suggest, as well, that a preference originally based on cognition often leads to affect, which then becomes functionally autonomous and loses its original cognitive justification. At this point, we are simply proposing that these sort of intriguing possibilities are in harmony with the model we have presented, and deserve to capture research attention.

A second basic question concerns what happens if, and when, the sources of information have contradictory implications for the overall evaluation. This is a state of affairs we might call ambivalence, as in the case when your "mind" (i.e. cognition) tells you one thing (e.g. that exercise is good for your health) but your "heart" (i.e. affect) tells you another (e.g. that exercise is painful). The interesting question, for us, is how such ambivalence might be resolved. If the sources of information contradict one another, the present model can easily incorporate the notion, proposed most recently by Salancik (1982), that an individual can, in fact, hold more than one attitude toward an attitude object by simply assuming that one source of information can temporarily be made more salient than the others (e.g. Salancik and Conway 1975). Thus, we would suggest that attitudes (and behavior) of individuals with ambivalent attitudes will be highly variable or volatile, and seemingly inconsistent. On some occasions the attitudes will be based on one source while at other times they may be based on another.

In this context, it becomes interesting, as well, to determine which source of information is most likely to be primed or made salient under certain circumstances. Generalizing from a recent hypothesis proposed by Abelson (1982), that deindividuation leads people to act on their symbolic attitudes, we would speculate that conditions of stress or arousal (or perhaps conditions which increase need for structure, cf. Kruglanski, this volume) might result in individuals following their hearts rather than their minds. In addition, it is also possible that the particular behavior an individual is involved in can influence which source becomes dominant.

Attitudinal processes. The model also implies that attitudes based on different sources of information may differentially influence basic attitudinal processes or relations.

In recent years the attitude–behavior relation has received the lion's share of research attention. With the present model it becomes possible to extend this question one step further and ask whether attitudes based on different sources of information differentially predict behavior. As noted, Fazio and Zanna (1981) have demonstrated that attitudes based on past behavior better predict behavior than attitudes based on cognition. Future research could explore the possibility that attitudes based primarily on affect might guide behavior to an even greater extent. Following the early work by Norman (1975), future research could also test the notion that attitudes based on consistent information across all three sources would better predict behavior than attitudes based on information consistent across only two sources.

In a similar vein, the model offers a research approach to questions concerning the persistence of attitude change. Research by Lydon *et al.* (in press), for example, has found that there is more persistence of attitude change when beliefs and past behaviors are in agreement. In general, we would expect greater persistence if change occurs in all three sources.

As another example, we can ask if attitudes based on different sources of information are differentially resistant to persuasive communications. Future research could test the notion that attitudes based primarily on affect and/or past behavior are more resistant to persuasive communications than are attitudes based on cognition (cf. Ross *et al.* 1983). Future research could also explore the possibility that dissonance-induction procedures (e.g. the induced-compliance technique) are more effective when attitudes are based primarily on, say, past behaviors. In general, just as the classic functional theories of attitudes (cf. Katz 1960) proposed different strategies to change attitudes which fulfilled different functions, the present model suggests that different techniques may be differentially successful in changing attitudes based upon different sources of information. As an initial working hypothesis we would propose that persuasive communications, induced-compliance techniques, and emotional appeals (or classic conditioning techniques) are most effective in changing attitudes based, respectively, on cognition, behavior, and affect. Of course, as we previously mentioned, the best practical approach to persuasion may be to try and change all three sources.

In addition to the two basic questions concerning the attitude–behavior relation and attitude change, our model suggests it might also be interesting to explore the possibility that other attitudinal processes are moderated by the source of information upon which attitudes are based. Concerning the attitude–memory relation, for example, could attitudes based primarily on affects lead to greater selective learning, especially if what is to be learned is emotionally charged? Concerning the attitude–attribution relation, might attitudes toward another person based primarily, for example, on affect lead to more attitude-consistent attributions for the person's behavior?

Finally, concerning the attitude–physiology relation (Cacioppo and Petty 1982b), do attitudes based primarily, for example, on affect have more substantial physiological correlates?

While there are undoubtedly more classic questions that could be re-asked, we feel it is time to address the issue of how one might, in fact, attempt to answer these questions.

Research strategies

We have indicated the sorts of research question that we believe follow from this new conceptualization of the attitude concept. Now we would like to suggest possible strategies of research for asking these questions.

First, however, we need to address briefly the question of attitude measurement. The model has implications for the validity of attitude measurement. Recall that in the present view attitudes are not necessarily considered to be stable entities. We therefore urge caution in interpreting attitude measures as indications of consistent and enduring responses towards the attitude objects. Second, the model conceptually requires that evaluation be measured independently from the three postulated sources of information. This implies separate measures of evaluation, affects (or feelings), cognition (or beliefs), and past behaviors. Procedurally, the question arises exactly how to measure each of these constructs, especially since, depending on what source of information is "primed", you might get a different overall evaluation.

For evaluation (or attitude) we would warn of two potential pitfalls to avoid. First, we would recommend *not* asking subjects how they feel or what they think about the attitude object (as in current practice), but instead suggest asking subjects to "rate" or even simply to "evaluate" the attitude object. Second, we would *not* recommend using scales that overemphasize either affect (e.g. pleasant–unpleasant) or utilitarian beliefs (e.g. beneficial–harmful), but instead suggest employing scales more purely evaluative, such as favorable–unfavorable. In this way subjects will self-select their attitudes from whichever sources are most personally relevant.

For measuring affects, cognition, and past behaviors, we would recommend asking subjects directly to rate relevant feelings, beliefs, and past behaviors associated with the attitude object. In addition, following a technique developed by Wood (1982), we would also suggest asking subjects, in a thought-listing type of procedure, to recall material from each of the relevant domains.

Finally, there are domain-specific measures such as a promising technique developed by John Cacioppo and his colleagues (cf. Cacioppo and

Petty 1987) in which a subject's emotional responses are measured by analyzing the pattern of facial muscles excited by exposure to the attitude objects.

Two general research strategies seem to follow from the model, one correlational and one experimental in nature. Let us now turn to the correlational strategy.

Correlational strategy. With independent measures of evaluation, affect, cognition, and past behavior one can use multiple-regression techniques to determine, at least for a given group of subjects, the relative contribution made by each source of information to the overall evaluation. This technique might be especially useful for studying the development of attitudes over time. For example, an attitude initially based primarily on past behavior (as indicated by a relatively large beta weight for past behavior and relatively small beta weights for affect and cognition in the prediction of evaluation) may become, over time, additionally based on cognition (as indicated by an increasing beta weight for cognition) *or* affect (as indicated by an increasing beta weight for affect) *or* both cognition and affect. Thus, it might be possible to track the precise informational bases of attitudes developmentally.

This procedure might also be useful in comparing the informational basis of attitudes for different groups of individuals. It would be possible to discover, for example, that one group's attitude is based primarily on affect while another's is based primarily on cognition. Thus, we could discover that different groups hold the same attitude, but are differentially likely to act on it, because they hold it for different reasons. More likely, we could discover that different groups hold opposing attitudes, each based on different sources of information. For example, individuals in favor of capital punishment might base their attitudes on affect while individuals who oppose capital punishment might base their attitudes on cognition (or vice versa!). (In any case, if opposing camps are found to hold attitudes for different reasons, this may be an additional obstacle to resolving conflict between the groups.)

Experimental strategy. Several experimental strategies come to mind and should be pursued. One could, of course, try to create attitudes in the laboratory based on different sources of information. This strategy has been used with some success by Fazio and Zanna (1981) in their research on direct behavioral experience with the attitude object, and may be useful for creating attitudes based primarily on behavior or cognition. However, it has been relatively difficult to establish attitudes based primarily on affect in laboratory situations. For example, Zanna *et al.* (1970), using a rather powerful conditioning procedure, only managed to establish attitudes in a subset of their subjects. In the domain of person perception, however, Niedenthal and Cantor (1984) have been able to influence subjects' affective reactions toward target persons by varying the size of pupil dilation in slides of the target persons.

Other techniques employing false feedback and misattribution are also possible. Mills *et al.* (1976) used false feedback to induce subjects to believe that their emotional reactions following a communication were either positive or negative. In addition, there is another, possibly more manageable strategy, suggested by the model itself. Recall that the model implies that one can hold more than one attitude toward an attitude object as a function of whether one source of information or another is temporarily salient. This suggests using priming procedures, or saliency manipulations, similar to those originally employed by Salancik (1982), to focus subjects' attention on either their feelings, their beliefs, and/or their past behaviors relevant to the attitude object. This strategy has been used with some success by Zanna *et al.* (1981) in making past behaviors salient, while more recently Andersen and Williams (1984) and Millar and Tesser (1985) have used this strategy to make cognitive and/or affective information more salient. Of course, in future research we would recommend that any experimental manipulation be "checked" by the multiple-regression strategy discussed previously.

Conclusion

In the present chapter we have attempted to present the outlines of a model of attitudes that incorporates the main ideas of past conceptualizations in a way that (1) capitalizes on the strengths of several of the most prominent, current models, and (2) provides a framework for future research. We will have fulfilled our purpose if we have piqued the reader's curiosity by the sort of research questions that we believe flow from the model. It is our hope, however, that these questions will actually capture research attention in the coming years.

By characterizing attitudes as items of knowledge in the form of evaluative summations, we hope to have also added to the understanding of social knowledge in general. Perhaps the most important contribution arises from an examination of the bases or sources of an attitude. In emphasizing multiple sources we suggest that the basis and experience of knowledge in general cannot be simply understood in terms of cognition alone. Rather, social knowledge rests as much on past behaviors and emotions as it does on beliefs. This goes beyond the obvious suggestion that knowledge has multiple sources to argue that the impact a piece of knowledge has on an individual may depend heavily on how it is experienced. In other words, we agree that a study of social knowledge should both give strong consideration to the sources of such knowledge and then go on to consider the impact that such sources have when the knowledge is again called to action.

References

Abelson, R. P. (1982). Three modes of attitude–behavior consistency. In M. P. Zanna, E. T. Higgins, and C. P. Herman (eds.), *Consistency in social behavior: the Ontario symposium* (vol. 2). Hillsdale, NJ: Lawrence Elbaum.

Abelson, R. P., Kinder, D. R., Peters, M. D., and Fiske, S. T. (1982). Affective and semantic components in political person perception. *Journal of Personality and Social Psychology* 42: 619–30.

Ajzen, I. (1984). Attitudes. In R. J. Corsini (ed.), *Wiley encyclopedia of psychology*, vol. 1. New York: Wiley.

Ajzen, I. and Timko, C. (1985). *Correspondence between health attitudes and behavior*. Unpublished manuscript, University of Massachusetts.

Amabile, T. M. and Kabat, L. G. (1982). When self-descriptions contradict behavior: actions do speak louder than words. *Social Cognition* 1: 311–35.

Andersen, S. M. (1984). Self-knowledge and social inference. II: The diagnosticity of cognitive/affective and behavioral data. *Journal of Personality and Social Psychology* 46: 294–307.

Andersen, S. M. and Ross, L. (1984). Self-knowledge and social inference I: The impact of cognitive/affective and behavioral data. *Journal of Personality and Social Psychology* 46: 280–93.

Andersen, S. M. and Williams, M. (1985). *Salience and self-inference: the role of biased recollections in self-inference processes*. Unpublished manuscript, University of California, Santa Barbara.

Bagozzi, R. P. and Burnkrant, R. E. (1979). Attitude organization and the attitude–behavior relationship. *Journal of Personality and Social Psychology* 37: 913–29.

Bem, D. J. (1972). Self-perception theory. In L. Berkowitz (ed.), *Advances in experimental social psychology*, vol. 6. New York: Academic Press.

Breckler, S. J. (1983). *Validation of affect, behavior, and cognition as distinct components of attitude*. Unpublished dissertation, Ohio State University, Columbus.

Breckler, S. J. (1984). Empirical validation of affect, behavior, and cognition as distinct components of attitude. *Journal of Personality and Social Psychology* 47: 1191–205.

Cacioppo, J. T. and Petty, R. E. (1982a). The need for cognition. *Journal of Personality and Social Psychology* 42: 116–31.

Cacioppo, J. T. and Petty, R. E. (1982b). A biosocial model of attitude change. In J. T. Cacioppo and R. E. Petty (eds.), *Perspectives in cardiovascular psychophysiology*. New York: Guilford Press.

Cacioppo, J. T. and Petty, R. E. (1987). Stalking rudimentary processes of social influence: a psychophysiological approach. In M. P. Zanna, J. M. Olson, and C. P. Herman (eds.), *Social influence: the Ontario symposium*, vol. 5, Hillsdale, NJ: Erlbaum.

Chaiken, S. and Baldwin, M. W. (1981). Affective–cognitive consistency and the effect of salient behavioral information on the self-perception of attitudes. *Journal of Personality and Social Psychology* 41: 1–12.

Davis, D. and Ostrom, T. M. (1984). Attitude measurement. In R. J. Corsini (ed.), *Wiley encyclopedia of psychology*, vol. 1. New York: Wiley.

Fazio, R. H. (1986). How do attitudes guide behavior? In R. M. Sorrentino and E. T. Higgins (eds.), *The handbook of motivation and cognition: foundations of social behavior*. New York: Guilford Press.

Fazio, R. H. and Zanna, M. P. (1981). Direct experience and attitude–behavior consistency. In L. Berkowitz (ed.), *Advances in experimental social psychology*, vol. 14. New York: Academic Press.

Fazio, R. H., Zanna, M. P., and Cooper, J. (1977). Dissonance and self-perception: an examination of each theory's proper domain of application. *Journal of Experimental Social Psychology* 13: 464–79.

Fishbein, M. and Ajzen, I. (1975). *Belief, attitude, intention, and behavior: an introduction to theory and research*. Reading, MA: Addison-Wesley.

Fisher, W. A. (1984). Predicting contraceptive behavior among university men: the role of emotions and behavioral intentions. *Journal of Applied Social Psychology* 14: 104–23.

Fleming, D. (1967). Attitude: the history of a concept. In D. Fleming and B. Bailyn (eds.), *Perspectives in American history*, vol. 1. Cambridge, MA: Charles Warren Center in American History, Harvard University.

Greenwald, A. G. (1968). On defining attitude and attitude theory. In A. G. Greenwald, T. C. Brock, and T. M. Ostrom (eds.), *Psychological foundations of attitudes*. New York: Academic Press.

Jung, C. G. (1923). *Psychological types*. London: Constable.

Katz, D. (1960). The functional approach to the study of attitudes. *Public Opinion Quarterly* 24: 163–204.

Kinder, D. R. and Sears, D. O. (1981). Symbolic racism versus racial threats to the good life. *Journal of Personality and Social Psychology* 40: 414–31.

Kothandapani, V. (1971). Validation of feeling, belief, and intention to act as three components of attitude and their contribution to the prediction of contraceptive behavior. *Journal of Personality and Social Psychology* 19: 321–33.

Lingle, J. H. and Ostrom, T. M. (1981). Principles of memory and cognition in attitude formation. In R. Petty, T. Ostrom, and T. Brock (eds.), *Cognitive responses to persuasion*. Hillsdale, NJ: Lawrence Erlbaum.

Lydon, J., Zanna, M.P., and Ross, M. (in press). Bolstering newly-formed attitudes by autobiographical recall: implications for attitude persistence and selective memory. *Personality and Social Psychology Bulletin*.

McGuire, W. J. (1985). Attitudes and attitude change. In G. Lindzey and E.

Aronson (eds.), *Handbook of social psychology*, 3rd ed. Reading, MA: Addison-Wesley.

Millar, M. G. and Tesser, A. (1985). *Effects of affective and cognitive focus on the attitude–behavior relationship*. Unpublished manuscript, University of Georgia.

Mills, J., Jellison, J. M., and Kennedy, J. (1976). Attribution of attitudes from feelings: effect of positive or negative feelings when the attitude object is benefited or harmed. In J. H. Harvey, W. J. Ickes, and R. F. Kidd (eds.), *New directions in attribution research*, vol. 1. Hillsdale, NJ: Lawrence Erlbaum.

Myers, D. G. (1983). *Social psychology*. New York, NY: McGraw-Hill.

Niedenthal, P. M. and Cantor, N. (1985). *Affect-based categorization and category based affect*. Unpublished manuscript, University of Michigan.

Norman, R. (1975). Affective–cognitive consistency, attitudes, conformity, and behavior. *Journal of Personality and Social Psychology* 32: 83–91.

Olson, J. M. and Zanna, M. P. (1983). Attitude change and behavior prediction. In D. Perlman and P. C. Cozby (eds.), *Social psychology*. New York: CBS College Publishing.

Ostrom, T. M. (1969). The relationship between the affective, behavioral and cognitive components of attitude. *Journal of Experimental Social Psychology* 5: 12–30.

Ostrom, T. M. (1984). Attitude theory. In R. J. Corsini (ed.), *Wiley encyclopedia of psychology*, vol. 1. New York: Wiley.

Rosenberg, M. J. (1968). Hedonism, inauthenticity, and other goals toward expansion of a consistency theory. In R. P. Abelson *et al.* (eds.), *Theories of cognitive consistency: a sourcebook*. Chicago: Rand McNally.

Rosenberg, M. J. and Hovland, C. I. (1960). Cognitive, affective, and behavioral components of attitude. In M. J. Rosenberg *et al.* (eds.), *Attitude organization and change: an analysis of consistency among attitude components*. New Haven, CT: Yale University Press.

Ross, M., McFarland, C., Conway, M., and Zanna, M. P. (1983). Reciprocal relation between attitudes and behavioral recall: committing people to newly formed attitudes. *Journal of Personality and Social Psychology* 45: 257–67.

Salancik, G. R. (1974). Inference of one's attitude from behavior recalled under linguistically manipulated cognitive sets. *Journal of Experimental Social Psychology* 10: 415–27.

Salancik, G. R. (1982). Attitude–behavior consistencies as social logics. In M. P. Zanna, E. T. Higgins, and C. P. Herman (eds.), *Consistency in social behavior: the Ontario Symposium*, vol. 2. Hillsdale, NJ: Lawrence Erlbaum.

Salancik, G. R. and Conway, M. (1975). Attitude inferences from salient and relevant cognitive content about behavior. *Journal of Personality and Social Psychology* 32: 829–40.

Seligman, C., Kriss, M., Darley, J. M., Fazio, R. H., Becker, L. J., and Pryor, J. B. (1979). Predicting summer energy consumption from homeowners' attitudes. *Journal of Applied Social Psychology* 9: 70–90.

Simon, H. A. (1982). Comments. In M. S. Clark and S. T. Fiske (eds.), *Affect and cognition*. Hillsdale, NJ: Lawrence Erlbaum.

Staats, A. W. (1968). Social behaviorism and human motivation: principles of the attitude-reinforcer-discriminative system. In A. G. Greenwald, T. C. Brock, and T. M. Ostrom (eds.), *Psychological foundations of attitudes*. New York: Academic Press.

Thurstone, L. L. and Chave, E. J. (1929). *The measurement of attitude*. Chicago: University of Chicago Press.

Tybout, A. M. and Scott, C. A. (1983). Availability of well-defined internal knowledge and the attitude formation process: Information aggregation versus self-perception. *Journal of Personality and Social Psychology* 44: 474–91.

Tyler, T. R. and Rasinski, K. (1984). Comparing psychological images of the social perceiver: role of perceived informativeness, memorability, and affect in mediating the impact of crime victimization. *Journal of Personality and Social Psychology* 46: 308–29.

Wicker, A. W. (1969). Attitudes versus actions: the relationship of verbal and overt behavioral responses to attitude objects. *Journal of Social Issues* 25: 41–78.

Wilson, T. D., Dunn, D. S., Bybee, J. A., Hyman, D. B., and Rotondo, J. A. (1984). Effects of analyzing reasons on attitude–behavior consistency. *Journal of Personality and Social Psychology* 47: 5–16.

Wilson, T. D., Dunn, D. S., Kraft, D., and Lisle, D. J. (1986). *Self-analysis and the cognitivation of attitudes*. Unpublished manuscript, University of Virginia.

Wood, W. (1982). Retrieval of attitude-relevant information from memory: effects on susceptibility to persuasion and on intrinsic motivation. *Journal of Personality and Social Psychology* 42: 798–810.

Zajonc, R. B. (1980). Feeling and thinking: preferences need no inferences. *American Psychologist* 35: 151–75.

Zajonc, R. B. and Markus, H. (1982). Affective and cognitive factors in preferences. *Journal of Consumer Research* 9: 123–31.

Zanna, M. P., Kiesler, C. A., and Pilkonis, P. A. (1970). Positive and negative attitudinal affect established by classical conditioning. *Journal of Personality and Social Psychology* 14: 321–8.

Zanna, M. P., Olson, J. M., and Fazio, R. H. (1981). Self-perception and attitude-behavior consistency. *Personality and Social Psychology Bulletin* 7: 252–6.

14 Mental models of causal reasoning

Joseph M. F. Jaspars
Edited by Denis J. Hilton[1]

1 The logic of Kaspar Hauser

On 26 May 1828, a bewildered and incoherent boy of just sixteen named Kaspar Hauser was brought before the Nurnberg authorities. His birth had been enigmatic. Some said that he was the eldest son of Grand Duke Charles Louis of Baden, but whatever the case may be, he had been placed in the care of a labourer when he was about five months old. Plays, movies, and poems were inspired by him, and recently Werner Herzog made a film based on the life of Kaspar Hauser.[2] In the film the boy is subjected to an interrogation in the presence of his foster mother by a professor of logic who wants to test Kaspar's mental faculties. The professor, a dour and stern character, poses a classic problem in logic for Kaspar to solve. "You meet", he says "a stranger who comes either from village A or from village B. All

1 *Editor's note*: Jos Jaspars died on 31 July 1985. The paper, together with the book editors' comments, was passed on to me for revision. I have made minor alterations and additions to the text itself to clarify and elaborate particular points. I have not, however, made any substantial alterations to the text itself.

However, for those who are not familiar with Jos Jaspars's earlier work on causal attribution, I have added substantial footnotes (particularly 2, 3, and 6) to give relevant background. The best accounts of this work are, of course, to be found in Jaspars 1983 and Jaspars *et al.* 1983. For the later footnotes (7 to 11), I have had to rely more on my memory of discussions I had with Jos on the issues written about in this paper. I have endeavoured to make Jos's thinking on causal logic more accessible by adding Table 14.5 to concretize issues discussed in the text. However, it should be emphasized that this is my addition, not his, and should therefore not be taken as an authoritative rendition of his views. For the same reason, I have indicated which are my footnotes, and which his.

Finally, I would like to thank Alison Roberts for her help in preparing the manuscript, Jim Casey for taking the photograph of the JAM, and Mansur Lalljee for help and advice.

2 The following discourse has been reconstructed from memory. I only saw a brief episode of the film on television, and have been unable so far to verify the exact nature of the discourse. Whatever the exact words were, the general argument is that logical problems can be perfectly solved by making use of knowledge of the real world. (JMFJ)

inhabitants of A are liars, those of B speak the truth. You can ask one question and one question only to determine whether the stranger comes from village A or from village B." "*Also*," the professor says, "what question would you ask, Kaspar?" Kaspar appears to think for a while but no answer is forthcoming. His foster mother complains that the Herr Professor should not ask the poor boy such difficult questions. The professor soon gives up the hope of an answer and starts explaining that he should use the double negative when suddenly Kaspar indicates that he knows another way of finding out whether the person is from A or B. "Impossible," answers the professor "there is only one correct solution." "I would ask", says Kaspar, "whether he is a treefrog." The professor immediately realizes, of course, that Kaspar's question will allow him indeed to solve this difficult logical problem but he protests vehemently, declaring the solution invalid because Kaspar goes beyond the information given, as Bruner (1973) would say.

The example of Kaspar Hauser is interesting because it illustrates vividly one of the most basic problems in the study of human judgement and reasoning: how to combine knowledge of the real world with logical rules of inference. Traditionally, cognitive and social psychology have taken normative procedures for making a correct inference as descriptive models of human reasoning, only to discover that our judgements are full of biases and shortcomings (Nisbett and Ross 1980). We do not make sufficient use of available information, we neglect base-rate information, we are not particularly good at detecting covariation, we confuse opposite conditional probabilities; in short, we seem to be rather poor information-processors.

Various authors have protested against this view of man as a poor scientist. Some have argued that we do not think like scientists at all but use simple rules of thumb or cognitive heuristics (Kahneman *et al.* 1982). Others have suggested that we use a natural logic, which differs from normal logic but is equally valid (Cohen 1977, Braine 1980); and at least one cognitive scientist declares that we can do without any formal rules of inference in deductive reasoning (Johnson-Laird 1983).

These developments in cognitive psychology seems to have bypassed the study of causal attribution in social psychology. The most influential model of causal reasoning proposed in social psychology is undoubtedly Kelley's ANOVA model of attribution processes (Kelley 1967, 1973). The heart of Kelley's model is the effect of informational dimensions such as consensus, distinctiveness, and consistency on causal inferences to the person, the entity, the circumstances, or some combination of these factors. Prior expectations or beliefs and motivational factors are thought to distort the causal inference process, and a large number of studies have been devoted to the question whether such biases could or should be explained by cognitive or motivational factors (Kelley and Michela 1980, Harvey and Weary 1984), but recently Kruglanski and Ajzen (1983) have argued for an integrated theory of the epistemic process that goes beyond this contradistinction. Whichever way one wants to explain such biases as the overattribution to personal dispositions or the neglect of consensus information, it is not at all clear that recent attribution research has presented us with a viable alternative model of how people explain events, in particular their own behaviour and that of others, in everyday circumstances. Clearly people do not seem to make inferences in exactly the same way as scientists who use analysis of variance to interpret the results of an experimental study, but so far attribution researchers have only managed to show by comparison with the "correct" or scientific way of making inferences where ordinary people fail. Heuristics, probability, lay-epistemology are as yet not to be regarded as coherent alternative theories of human judgement or causal reasoning but as statements of apparent biases. Attempts to develop different systematic models of man's ability to understand and explain human behaviour can perhaps be found in Schank and Abelson (1977) on computer simulation of natural language understanding, Hart and Honoré (1959) and Mackie (1974) on causation in the law, von Wright (1983) on practical reasoning and demotic logic, and Johnson-Laird (1983) on mental models.

There is no time or space here to develop exhaustively my reservations about the first set of approaches and the value of the second group. However the research conducted by myself, my colleagues, and my students has been greatly influenced by looking over the fence at work in philosophy, law, and cognitive science. I do not want to claim that we have made an extensive survey of the study of commonsense explanations in other disciplines (anthropologists and linguists must have something to say as well), nor that the approaches mentioned are any better than what social psychologists have to offer. I only mention them to indicate the source of some of our ideas about commonsense explanations and the effect these sources have had in developing a coherent model of commonsense explanations.

2 The erroneous calculus of causality

It is said that the famous German mathematician Leibniz's greatest or ultimate goal in life was to develop a universal calculus of reasoning so that we could resolve human conflict like accountants. He did, as we all know, not succeed, although we do not regret the byproducts of his endeavours in the form of differential calculus and contributions to symbolic logic.

I believe that the significance of normative models of human reasoning may be of a similar kind. Such models have the tendency to be initially much too general and therefore wrong, but they help us to formulate more specific and adequate models of the cognitive processes involved. In attribution theory the same development can be observed. Heider (1958) and Kelley (1967) originally suggested that our naive analysis of action is akin to analysis of variance. Kelley also suggested that, for explanations of behaviour, actors, stimuli, and time or modality of interaction with stimuli are the relevant causal dimensions which vary according to consensus, distinctiveness, and consistency. Several predictions were formulated on the basis of this general conception, but neither the model itself nor its implications were ever fully developed. On the contrary, many studies have been devoted to the attributional "main" effects of consensus, distinctiveness, and consistency without it being realized that these predictions are quite clearly at variance with Kelley's original notion. To add empirical insult to theoretical injury, most of these studies found their incorrect predictions confirmed.

Looking back in surprise, one discovers that the so-called ANOVA model does not specify how information is to be encoded; that the stated rules of inference are not developed fully in the seminal publications of Kelley (1967, 1973), that they are applied wrongly in McArthur (1972), and that in addition the decoding process is nowhere mentioned.[3]

3 The general conception proposed by Heider and Kelley is that causal attribution proceeds through the application of Mill's method of difference. The problem is that Kelley (1967, 1973) did not explicate the full logical consequences of applying Mill's method of difference in his ANOVA derivation. In particular, he failed to specify the *interactional* attributions that would be logically predicted for specific *patterns* or *configurations* of consensus, distinctiveness, and consistency information. Thus the HHL, LHH, LHL, and LLL *configurations* of consensus, distinctiveness, and consistency information would respectively predict: attributions to interactions of the stimulus with the circumstances; the person with the stimulus; the person with the stimulus with the circumstances; and the person with the circumstances (see Table 14.1).

Jaspars's inductive logic model (sometimes referred to as the logical or natural logic model) is thus the logical interpretation of Kelley's (1967) definition of causality, and can be read as the correctly interpreted ANOVA model. Its predictions are detailed in Table 14.1. Confusion arises because the predictions made by Orvis *et al.* (1975) do not strictly follow from Kelley's (1967, 1973) covariational definition of causality.

This is due to the fact that if Mill's method of difference is applied to consensus, distinctiveness, and consistency information to determine whether the target behaviour (explanandum) occurs in the presence of other persons, stimuli (entities), and circumstances (times), then *interactional* attributions are *logically* implied. For example, low consensus, high consistency, and low distinctiveness logically implies an interactional attribution to a *combination* of the person, the stimulus, and the circumstances (see Table 14.1; also Jaspars *et al.* 1983) whereas Orvis *et al.* (1975) predict and find attributions to the circumstances. This is presumably due to Orvis *et al.*'s (1975) failure, shared by McArthur (1972), to explicitly include attributions to a combination of the person, the stimulus, and the circumstances in their response format. When such interactional possibilities are explicitly mentioned in the response format, subjects make the logically predicted attribution (see Table 14.2; also Jaspars 1983).

Table 14.1. *Formalization of McArthur's stimulus vignettes with predictions according to the logical model of causal attributions*

Vignettes		Information combinations							
		Cs $\bar{D}$ Cy	Cs D Cy	$\bar{C}$s $\bar{D}$ Cy	Cs $\bar{D}$ $\bar{C}$y	$\bar{C}$s D Cy	Cs D $\bar{C}$y	$\bar{C}$s $\bar{D}$ $\bar{C}$y	$\bar{C}$s D $\bar{C}$y
	spc	B	B	B	B	B	B	B	B
	sp$\bar{c}$	B	B	B	$\bar{B}$	B	$\bar{B}$	$\bar{B}$	$\bar{B}$
	s$\bar{p}$c	B	B	$\bar{B}$	B	$\bar{B}$	B	$\bar{B}$	$\bar{B}$
	$\bar{s}$pc	B	$\bar{B}$	B	B	$\bar{B}$	$\bar{B}$	B	$\bar{B}$
Conditions for occurrence of behaviour in vignette	s	Su	(Su N)			N	N		N
	p	Su		(Su N)		N		N	N
	c	Su			(Su N)		N	N	N
	sp	Su	Su	Su		(Su N)			N
	sc	Su	Su		Su		(Su N)		N
	pc	Su		Su	Su			(Su N)	N
	spc	Su	Su	Su	Su	Su	Su	Su	(Su N)
Logical attribution		∅	s	p	c	sp	sc	pc	spc
Kelley's prediction		ps	s	p	psc	psc	sc	pc	c

Cs = consensus; D = distinctiveness; Cy = consistency; s = stimulus; p = person; c = circumstance; Su = sufficient condition; N = necessary condition; ø = no prediction possible. Bars (e.g. $\bar{s}$, $\bar{p}$, $\bar{c}$) indicate the absence of a factor.

A causal inference can be made in each case by establishing whether a particular factor (s, p, c, sp, etc.) is a necessary and a sufficient condition for the occurrence of the behaviour in the vignette. If the behaviour occurs when a particular factor is present, the factor is a sufficient condition. If the behaviour does not occur when the factor is absent, the factor is coded as a necessary condition. If the behaviour occurs if and only if the factor is present, the factor is both a necessary and a sufficient condition for the behaviour to occur and hence a causal attribution is made to that factor. These conditions are indicated in brackets in the second part of the table.

The rules of inductive or causal inference themselves suggested by Kelley are however clear. A cause is a condition which is present when the effect is present and absent when the effect is absent (Kelley 1967, 1973). What is not clear is how that condition is to be selected and encoded by the observer. I have suggested elsewhere (Jaspars 1983) an attributional coding for verbal material of the type used in many studies, which, I recently discovered, is essentially a logical truth table to which a test of sufficiency and necessity can be applied.

This inductive logic model of causal attributions has now been tested in

By encoding, Jaspars means encoding consensus, distinctiveness, and consistency information. For example, low consensus is encoded as meaning that the behaviour does *not* occur ($\bar{B}$) in the presence of other people.

The rules of inference use the information about when the behaviour does occur (B) or does not occur ($\bar{B}$) to determine the necessity and sufficiency of the target factors (person, stimulus, circumstances) for the occurrence of the behaviour. (DJH)

Table 14.2. *Proportion of attributions made to each causal locus as a function of consensus, distinctiveness, and consistency**

Locus of causality	Information pattern**							
	Cs $\bar{D}$ Cy	Cs D Cy	$\bar{C}$s $\bar{D}$ Cy	Cs $\bar{D}$ $\bar{C}$y	$\bar{C}$s D Cy	Cs D $\bar{C}$y	$\bar{C}$s $\bar{D}$ $\bar{C}$y	$\bar{C}$s D $\bar{C}$y
Stimulus	0.20	**0.45**	0.08	0.11	0.22	0.14	0.06	0.13
Person	0.23	0.00	**0.48**	0.02	0.05	0.05	0.11	0.00
Circumstance	0.03	0.08	0.03	**0.22**	0.03	0.20	0.06	0.19
Stimulus × person	0.27	0.16	0.17	0.20	**0.44**	0.03	0.17	0.11
Stimulus × circumstance	0.06	0.11	0.05	0.13	0.02	**0.22**	0.02	0.04
Person × circumstance	0.13	0.06	0.06	0.16	0.09	0.14	**0.39**	0.11
Person × stimulus × circumstance	0.08	0.14	0.13	0.17	0.16	0.22	0.19	**0.33**

*Total number of attributions in each condition is 64.
**Predicted loci of causality are set in bold type.
Cs = high consensus; $\bar{C}$s = low consensus; D = high distinctiveness; $\bar{D}$ = low distinctiveness; Cy = high consistency; $\bar{C}$y = low consistency.

several studies (Jaspars 1983, Hewstone 1981, Hilton 1984) and confirmed at a very high degree of statistical significance. The results of a replication of McArthur's study are presented in Table 14.2, which shows a number of interesting results which are at variance with the findings reported in the literature.

2.1

The results presented in Table 14.2 show clearly that the attributions made are a function of the various *informational patterns* (i.e. specific combinations of C_s, D, and C_y) and not of the various types of information in isolation. Still, McArthur and quite a few other authors have reported main effects of consensus, distinctiveness, and consistency, which is not in accordance with the theory. The reason for this remarkable but unnoticed discrepancy is that analysis of variance does not provide us with an appropriate test of the combined effects of the various kinds of information. Standard analysis of variance utilizes contrastive coding of the independent variables which leads to a definition of interaction effects as residual variances after main effects have been accounted for. In particular one should, for example, expect an interaction effect in attribution studies when the effect of the joint presence of two factors is the same as the effect of the joint absence. This is of course not what the theory predicts. A particular attribution is only predicted when a unique pattern of information is present. Coding the levels of consensus, distinctiveness, and consistency as dummy variables (1 or 0) and defining interaction terms in line with the theory, multiple-regression analysis leads to radically different conclusions. In all attributions except one, interaction terms explain most of the variance, as can be seen in Table 14.3.[4]

The one notable exception is formed by circumstance attributions, which is probably due to the ambiguous response format used. Attributing behaviour to the circumstances can mean either the occasion or the particular combination of factors present. In another study (Jaspars 1983) in which a free response format was used, this effect did not occur.

2.2

The second point to be noted about the results presented in Table 14.2 is that the predictions made by Kelley (Orvis *et al.* 1975) and the conclusions drawn in the often-quoted study of McArthur are quite wrong as well. McArthur (1972) did report that subjects did not attribute behaviour to combinations of actor, stimulus, and/or circumstances. Reanalysis of her data shows, however, that one-third of all attributions in her study were made to some combination of these three factors. In our replication of McArthur's study all possible combinations of persons, stimulus, and circumstance were explicitly mentioned in the response format, and this raised the proportion of interactional attributions to 60 per cent.

Comparing the predictions made by Kelley (Orvis *et al.* 1975) and by the inductive logic method, we can see that in four combinations where the two models lead to different predictions, Kelley's model fits the observations less well in three out of four cases, whereas it may be superior in the fourth case, for the high-consensus, low-distinctiveness, and high-consistency (HLH) cell, for the wrong reason, i.e. a reason different from the one suggested by Orvis *et al.* (1975).

2.3

Although the predictions made by the inductive logic model are impressively confirmed, there are nonetheless various reasons for concern. Three of

4 The use of multiple-regression analysis enables the prediction that *patterns* of consensus, distinctiveness, and consistency information cause attributions to be tested, since the dummy variables, constructed out of *interactions* of levels of consensus, distinctiveness, and consistency information, explain most of the variations in subjects' responses, leaving very little to be explained by simple "main" effects of consensus, distinctiveness, and consistency information. Previous studies (e.g. McArthur 1972, Orvis *et al.* 1975) only analysed for simple "main" effects of consensus, distinctiveness, and consistency information on attributional responses, thus failing to test adequately the logically implied interactional predictions of the ANOVA model of causal attribution. As Jos Jaspars once remarked, the incomplete application of analysis of variance to the subjects' responses was an ironic reflection of shortcomings in the interpretation of the ANOVA analogy itself. But, as he put it, two wrongs don't make a right. (DJH)

Table 14.3 *Amount of variance in causal attributions explained by interactions of consensus, distinctiveness, and consistency information*

	Stimulus			Person			Circumstance			P–S			S–C		P–C		P–S–C	
	McA V%	JS1 V%	JS2 β*R	McA V%	JS1 V%	JS2 βR	McA V%	JS1 V%	JS2 βR	McA V%	JS1 V%	JS2 βR	JS1 V%	JS2 βR	JS1 V%	JS2 βR	JS1 V%	JS2 βR
C	5.2	9.3	.08	6.3	4.1	−.04	.30	2.9	.09	.64	1.1	−.03	10.3	.05	0.6	.03	1.1	.08
D	12.1	12.5	.13	21.7	22.1	−.05	7.6	0.9	.00	0	0	.05	6.1	−.08	5.3	.11	5.2	.16
Y	5.9	14.3	.03	15.8	13.6	−.06	41.4	20.3	.72	16.0	10.0	.12	8.1	−.09	11.3	.20	13.2	.34
CD		0	−.06		8.3	.23		0	−.03		17.4	.13	0	.25	1.1	−.17	0	−.07
CY		8.3	.20		3.8	.13		0.3	−.12		0	−.11	0	.34	4.2	−.14	0	−.09
DY		8.3	.21		27.2	.59		0	−.16		10.5	−.10	8.8	.62	6.1	−.14	0	−.05
CDY		1	.33		0	.11		7.4	.39		7.0	.49	2.9	−.31	26.6	.98	0	.34

* The analysis of Jaspars's data shows that the 'main effects' of consensus (C), distinctiveness (D), and consistency (Y) information on causal attributions are largely due to higher-order interactions between levels of consensus, distinctiveness, and consistency information. This was shown by creating regression equations in which 'single' and 'interaction' factors were entered simultaneously to predict attributions. The beta-weights give the amount of variance explained by each factor.

these I have already pointed out elsewhere (Jaspars *et al.* 1983, Jaspars 1983). Even though the Ss attribute behavioural effects very significantly to the "right" cause, they do so overall in less than 50 per cent of cases. The deviations from the logically correct answers appear to be systematic, in that sufficiency is emphasized more in person explanations and necessity in circumstance attributions. The Millian notion of causality is apparently used with some flexibility, but this in itself would not be a reason to abandon the model straightaway.

More puzzling is the fact that Ss happily make attributions in the case where the information pattern implies complete generalization of the occurrence of the behaviour across persons, stimuli, and circumstances, as in the high-consensus, low-distinctiveness, and high-consistency (HLH) information pattern. In the case of high consensus, low distinctiveness, and high consistency there is no covariation in the information given, and still the Ss make attributions predominantly to the person and/or the stimulus.

Why do they do so? Maybe the simple explanation is that they were not allowed to say that they did not know or could not make an inference. In order to test this possibility, we presented the same vignettes to twenty-four Ss for this condition only. Again, the four different types of behaviour used by McArthur were employed (accomplishments, emotions, actions, and opinions) and we included in the response format a category "don't know". In not one out of ninety-six responses did the Ss decide to reserve judgement. They always had an explanation.

It would seem that one can explain this result only by assuming that Ss go beyond the information given and, making use of their knowledge of the real world, rely on configurational information in the sense of Kelley (1973) and perhaps construct a mental model which allows them to draw an inference nonetheless. Precisely how they do so will concern us later, but an immediate test of this hypothesis would be to present Ss with the same informational patterns in a situation where they lack pre-existing knowledge.

3 On causal logic and JAM

In order to test whether Ss would make causal inferences in accordance with the inductive logic model presented, a simple causal inference task was designed which required Ss to detect how a combination of three switches controlled a light.[5]

An apparatus (see Fig. 14.1), using simple electronic OR and AND gates

5 The task itself is suggested in Johnson-Laird (1983) who uses the same procedure to illustrate that Ss do *not* proceed logically in inferring the cause of the "behaviour" of the light. (JMFJ)

was constructed, to vary the control of a light by three switches which were situated on a separate control panel and clearly marked as P, S, and C. The on and off position of the switches was also clearly marked.

A different panel allowed the experimenter to create four different conditions:

Condition A, in which any switch or combination of switches would make the light come on.
Condition B, in which switch P controlled the light.
Condition C, in which both switches P and S had to be in the on position for the light to come on.
Condition D, in which all three switches had to be on for the light to work.

The front of the apparatus had the appearance of a very complicated system because a chaos of crossing cables connecting the various electronic gates was visible. This was done deliberately to create the impression in the S that he or she could not possibly know off-hand how the system worked.[6]

The four conditions correspond formally exactly to the combinations for which the inductive logic model predicts respectively: A: no explanations; B: P attribution; C: P × S attribution; and D: P × S × C attribution.

In the first experiment, Ss were asked to infer which switch or combination of switches made the light go on after they had been shown that the light was on when all switches were on and the effect when each switch was turned off one at a time. The same response format as in the vignette studies was used. The results are presented in Table 14.4, together with the result of the control study. The results show a dramatic difference between the JAM and the control condition for the general "high-consensus, low-distinctiveness, and high-consistency" information pattern. The results are even more clear than Table 14.4 suggests, because the general HLH condition in the case of the electrical circuit produces responses that are almost pathetic. This is because nothing happens when the switches are turned off one at a time, and hence Ss almost never gave an explanation where they *always* do so in the comparable verbal vignette condition which describes human behaviour.

Although it is not immediately obvious, it is perhaps equally surprising that Ss do make the correct inference in the conditions B, C, and D. Just as in all the vignette studies, S in fact receives incomplete information. No scientist would or should make a causal inference after having observed an effect in only 50 per cent of the conditions. For each of the patterns of infor-

6 Following the tradition of labelling machines or programmes in social psychology by pronounceable trigrams (BAM, SAM, etc.) the apparatus was dubbed JAM, which stands for Jim's Attribution Machine in honour of Jim Casey, to whom I owe many thanks for putting it together. (JMFJ)

Fig. 14.1. The JAM (Jim's Attribution Machine)

mation presented there are in fact 2^4 different ways in which the information could be completed, each one implying a different causal inference.[7]

The Ss can only make the correct causal inference because the actual electronic circuit was designed in such a way that the remaining conditions

7 This point relates to the fact that previous tests of the ANOVA model have failed to give subjects complete "experimental designs" (Jaspars *et al.* 1983). In traditional attribution experiments, subjects receive information about whether the behaviour occurs in the

were compatible with the covariation in the information that was presented to the Ss. It was not planned that way, it was just easier to do it that way. In other words, in constructing the apparatus we had simply not considered all the logical possibilities. Starting from the condition that the light always had to be on when all switches were in the on position, we were logically still left with 2^7 (128) possible patterns which could be created with the 7 remaining positions of the three switches (see also Table 14.5, added by the editor). However, in 64 of these, turning a switch or switches off would make the light come on. Of the remaining 64 possibilities only 7 are either single causes or conjunctive combinations.[8]

Provided subjects make the two assumptions that "on" means "on" and that only combinations of positions which form a union matter, they can make the correct inference with incomplete information. These two assumptions are in fact embedded in the empiricist definition of causality. The cause of an effect is said to be "*the* condition which is *present* when the effect is present, etc.", not "either one or another of the conditions which is present or absent when the effect is present, etc.". The possibilities of an effect being caused by the absence of a condition or disjunctive explanations are simply not considered in the covariation model of attribution research. Disjunctive explanations are of course suggested in Kelley's confi-

presence of: this person and this stimulus on this occasion (target event); other persons (consensus information); other stimuli (distinctiveness information); and other circumstances/times/occasions (consistency information). However, to complete the 'experimental design' of a 2 × 2 × 2 analysis of variance due to person, stimulus, and circumstance factors, subjects should also receive information about whether the behaviour occurs in the presence of: other persons and other stimuli; other persons and other circumstances; other stimuli and other circumstances; and other persons, other stimuli, and other circumstances.

The JAM generates 2^4 information patterns via the 2 × 2 × 2 × 2 possible combinations of on/off positions of the light and the P, S, and C switches. (DJH)

8 There are 8 possible positions of the P, S, and C switches. Assuming that having P on, S on, and C on makes the light come on, there are still 7 other possible positions of P, S, and C. There are 2 possible states in each position (light on/light off). There are thus 2^7(128) possible "data patterns" that can be generated by constructing all the possible on/off combinations in these 7 cells. Of course, if we were allowed to consider the possibility that the light is off when P, S, and C are jointly on, then there would be 2^8 possible data patterns.

The truth tables associated with each of the 7 possible types of explanation referring to *single causes* (P, S, C) or *conjunctions of causes* (P & S, P & C, S & C, P & S & C) are given in Table 14.5, added by the editor. These, of course, only account for 7 of the 256 possible data patterns.

In the rightmost column, I have given an example of the data pattern that would be associated with the exclusive disjunction "either P or S but not both". As can be seen, turning S on when P is already on would have the effect of turning the light off. However, turning S on when P is off would have the opposite effect of turning the light on. Hence the problem posed by disjunctive explanations for the traditional empiricist definition of a cause as "that condition which is present when the effect is present and absent when the effect is absent" (Kelley 1967: 154). (DJH)

Table 14.4 *Causal inferences made with incomplete information (N=24)*

	A	B	C	D	C_A
p		*15*	1	1	13
s		1	1		13
c	2		2		2
ps			*17*		34
pc		1			4
sc		3			1
psc	3			22	19
0	*15*	1			0
R	1				2
M	3	3	3	1	7
missing response					1/96

Italic type indicates predicted inferences.
C_A = control condition for condition A using vignette.
O = null attribution (DJH)
M = disjunctive attribution (DJH)

Table 14.5 *The truth tables associated with the seven possible types of explanation, the universal condition, and a disjunctive explanation**

Switch positions	Logical circuits: A	B	C	D					P or S (but not both)
	(Experimental conditions)								
	P or S or C	P	P×S	P×S×C	S	C	P×C	S×C	
1 PSC	on	on	on	on	on	on	on	on	off
2 $\bar{P}SC$**	on	off	off	off	on	on	off	on	on
3 $P\bar{S}C$	on	on	off	off	off	on	on	off	on
4 $PS\bar{C}$	on	on	on	off	on	off	off	off	off
5 $P\bar{S}\bar{C}$	on	on	off	off	off	off	off	off	on
6 $\bar{P}S\bar{C}$	on	off	off	off	on	off	off	off	on
7 $\bar{P}\bar{S}C$	on	off	off	off	off	on	off	off	off
8 $\bar{P}\bar{S}\bar{C}$	off	off	off	off	off	off	off	off	off

P = person; S = stimulus; C = circumstances; on = light on; off = light off.
* In the experiment, subjects were only given the observations in the top left quadrant of the table: i.e. the states caused by switch positions 1 to 4 when the circuit was one of the types 0, P, P×S, and P×S×C used in the 4 experimental conditions.
** The use of a bar superscript (e.g. $\bar{P}$) indicates that the switch is *off*. If the bar is absent (e.g. P), the switch is *on*.

gurational model of causal attributions (Kelley 1973) as the multiple sufficient cause schema, although no clear distinction is made between inclusive and exclusive disjunction or between disjunctive and compensatory schemes (Coombs 1964). Nor does Kelley indicate how such schemes are utilized when there is also covariational information. He does admit, however, that it is one of the most important problems in attribution research (Kelley and Michela 1980). In this respect he is in agreement with notions developing in cognitive psychology and cognitive science in general, where a lively debate is taking place about the way in which information-processing is driven.

Our JAM experiment suggests one possible way in which causal schemata, pre-stored information, or real-world knowledge can be combined with observed covariance. Knowledge of the real world helps us to rule out from the start a number of logical possibilities, so that the logical calculus operates only on a reduced mental representation of the behaviour to be explained.[9] We do not suspend our knowledge of the real world when we look for explanations in everyday life whereas that is exactly what we are asked to do in science or in logic.

This two-stage, construction-inference notion of causal attributions leaves us of course with some very important unanswered questions. The first one, which has been raised amongst others by Higgins and Trope (see chs. 9 and 11 in this volume), is what determines which mental model we will construct of the event, problem, or behaviour we are asked to explain. One can well believe that the context in a general sense is extremely important. It seems to me that some cognitive psychologists like Johnson-Laird (1983) and Tversky and Kahneman (Kahneman *et al.* 1982) have been very clever in getting Ss to construct the wrong model which subsequently leads to biased inferences but, in my experience, also to the invariant feeling on the part of the subjects that they have been tricked. Although these experiments have some value in that they show that in the construction of a mental model, the encoding of information can be manipulated, it would seem more important to know whether certain mental models are more likely to be called upon than others in natural circumstances.

Perhaps we should start, in trying to answer this question, by considering conditions where the two phases of the explanatory process discussed so far can be separated.

9 By assuming that "on" means on and that only combinations of positions (single causes or conjunctive causes) that make a union matter, subjects only have to sample 7 of the 256 possible data patterns. (DJH)

4 Through the looking-glass and the geological metamorphosis

There are two attribution experiments I have not done and do not intend to do. They are "thought" experiments which when carried out may have the immediately convincing quality of some gestalt illustrations. In the first experiment I would like to suspend reality in a way that is obvious to any English-speaking subject but in such a way that the covariance or computational part of the attribution process can still operate. In such a case one almost naturally looks for children's stories, fairytales, and the like because it is in this situation that reality as we know it is often suspended. At Oxford, *Alice's adventures in Wonderland* and *Through the looking glass* seem obvious choices. Here is an attributional vignette which might apply beyond the looking-glass (Carroll 1971):

> The slithy toves gyre and gimble in the wabe. Almost no other toves do gyre or gimble in the wabe, but slithy toves gyre and gimble in almost any wabe although they do so mainly when it is brillig.

Most people I have asked why they think that slithy toves gyre and gimble in the wabe have no trouble in coming up with the person by circumstance attribution, mentioning both the slithy nature of the tove and the brillig (weather) circumstances.

Apparently, preserving the grammatical or syntactical structure of a vignette is sufficient for the covariational calculus of causality to operate. Subjects can apparently suspend reality and make the predicted inferences. How else could we teach or master logic or mathematics? But suspending reality may not be that easy when it is forced upon us. Still, even under such circumstances we may manage to do this when the task is approached with a conscious attempt to disregard reality. In an experiment conducted by Hewstone (1981), schoolboys from an independent (public) Oxford high school were asked to make causal attributions for a number of vignettes in which the behaviour described was either stereotypical or counterstereotypical. The (sex) stereotype manipulation did not have any effect whatsoever on the attributions made. Weaker configurational information such as the verb effects described by McArthur (1972) and Brown and Fish (1983) are generally easily swamped by covariational information in attribution experiments. Alloy and Tabachnik (1984) have recently reviewed the joint influence of prior expectations and current information, and arrive at the somewhat disappointing conclusion that the effect of each depends on their strength. Although they offer some suggestions about the determinants of the strength of prior expectations (directness of experience) and the strength of current situational information (availability, diagnosticity) they do not develop this crucial aspect any further, nor do they deal with the problem of which prior expectancies are relevant. They relegate this question to a footnote (Alloy and Tabachnik 1984).

It would seem that there is more to the integration of prior expectancy and current information than weighing according to strength. To illustrate the difficulties I envisage, let me introduce my second thought experiment. I keep on my desk in the office a collection of rocks which vary according to their chemical composition, the depth from which they were recovered, and the geographical location where they have been found. The grain of the rocks varies mainly as a consequence of the rate of cooling, which is higher for surface rocks than for rocks found at greater depth (Pannekoek 1973). The rocks are exhibited in the form of a three-dimensional display representing depth, location, and type of rock. The grain obviously varies with the representation of the depth dimension (the vertical axis of this geological Kelley cube), but still, when I ask occasional visitors to explain why the top corner in the geological cube is so smooth, they feel unable to come up with a sensible answer and simply get stuck. The covariational information is very clear and presumably has great strength in the sense of Alloy and Tabachnik, whereas there are no prior expectancies because my visitors admit that they do not know anything about geology. So Ss should be able to make use of the covarying information, but apparently they are not. It seems that they get stuck because they are fully aware of the fact that there must be a right explanation, but they also know that they do not know it, and hence they refuse to make an inference. It would seem therefore that it is not just a matter of the strength of prior beliefs and present information, but also the fact that one knows that things happen in the real world in a particular way whatever one's beliefs are. One would suspect that beliefs or expectations which are grounded in direct or indirect knowledge of the real world are particularly strong in their effect on inferences drawn from observed covariation.

Perhaps I can illustrate this point by referring to a third imaginary experiment, which I am currently planning to do. The experiment is concerned with the perception of causality as studied originally by Michotte (1946). Attribution theorists often pay lip-service to Michotte's work apparently without realizing that Michotte's dynamic gestalt notion of causality is at variance with the covariational idea of a cause.

The point is that behind Michotte's psychological findings lie the world of physics and the laws of conservation of momentum and energy. Michotte's formulation of the principle of amplification is essentially a perceptual statement of these laws, as Runeson (1977) and Todd and Warner (1982) have shown. Let us suppose that we would ask a physicist to explain why the second object in the classical "*lancement*" experiment of

Michotte's moves as far as it does. The answer would probably reflect knowledge of the equation:

$$S_b = \frac{m^2_A V^2_A (1 + e)^2}{(m_A + m_B)^2 2 \mu g}$$

where

S_b is the distance travelled by the second object
V_A the velocity of the first object
$m_A V_A$ the momentum of the first object
m_B the mass of the second object
μ is the coefficient of friction
g the constant of gravity
e the coefficient of restitution (elastic (1) vs. inelastic collisions (0))

In words, the explanation will probably be that the behaviour of the second object depends on something about the first object (momentum, elasticity, and mass), something about the second object (mass and elasticity) and something about the circumstances (friction). If we varied systematically the properties of both objects (consensus and distinctiveness) and the friction (consistency), an ANOVA of the behaviour of B would produce exactly such an answer. It would indicate that B would move further the larger A is, the smaller B is and the smaller μ is. The problem is of course that it would not matter for the covariation model whether the observed movements are physically possible. In Michotte's experiments the immediate perception of mechanical causality does not occur when the conventional laws of physics are broken, and Ss typically invoke additional causes to describe their impressions. I would predict that this is exactly what will happen in explaining human behaviour when the effects are not commensurate with the covarying conditions (Jaspars 1983). Covariation in attribution studies works because it does not violate the laws of nature. When it does, as when a slow-moving small object collides with a large object and causes it to move off at great speed, we realize this and look for alternative explanations. If this were not so, the power of magicians to conjure up covariational illusions would hardly be magical.

So far I have suggested, mainly by means of some illustrative examples, that the strength of prior expectations may be based largely upon real-world knowledge of the individual observer which implies that such expectations are generally content-based and depend upon the nature of the event to be explained rather than the context, such as experimentally given covariation information, in which the event is to be explained. It is however important here to make a familiar distinction between a person's explanatory competence and his attributional performance. An observer may very well understand what the causes of an event are, but he or she may be unable or reluctant to attribute the event to a particular cause. Motivational factors can turn an explanation into a justification, and a good deal of recent attributional research has been devoted to this problem. Explanations offered in a particular social context can readily be affected by Gricean communication principles (Lalljee *et al.* 1982) or by the vested interests of the person, as has been observed by Sally Lloyd Bostock in the case of accident victims (Jaspars *et al.* 1983). The controversy about the cognitive or motivational origin of attributional biases could perhaps be resolved by assuming that the former affect competence or understanding whereas the latter may have an influence primarily at the level of performance or attribution.

To support the significance of this distinction I would like to return briefly to the JAM experiment discussed before, and two extensions of it.

5 Understanding, explaining, and attributions

The experiment described in section 3 of this chapter was in fact only the first part of a more elaborate study. After the Ss had been shown the effect of moving the switches one at a time, they were also shown what the effects of the remaining four configurations of the switches were. One half of the Ss were allowed to explore these possibilities themselves, whereas the other half were shown these effects by the experimenters.[10] I will not discuss here the process which Ss used in the four conditions since the primary purpose is to see how completing the covariational information affected the causal inferences they made. The results obtained are presented in Table 14.6.

If we compare the results presented in Table 14.4 with those in Table 14.6, we see that there is hardly a difference in conditions B, C, and D whereas the results for condition A are very different in the second half from those in the first part of the experiment. Whereas Ss said in the first part of the experiment that they did not know the answer, they now correctly give a disjunctive explanation in most cases. Interestingly enough, Ss seem to have more problems with this condition than with any of the other three, since they need more trials before they offer any explanation in the condition where the Ss are allowed to manipulate the switches themselves. It is more interesting to note, however, that quite a few Ss are giving a conjunctive explanation in this case. They do not say that either P or S or C makes the light come on, but that P and S and C do so. Observations and

10 The four positions shown to all the subjects are the left-hand four configurations (1–4) in table 14.5. (DJH)

Table 14.6 *Causal inferences made with complete information (N = 24)*

	A	B	C	D
p		*20**		
s			1	
c				
ps			*16*	1
pc				1
sc		3	1	
psc	5		2	*21*
0	3			
R	5			
M	*11*	1	2	1

* The italicized scores represent attributions falling in the predicted cells. (DJH)
Key: see Table 14.4.

the sequential analysis of the experiment suggest, however, that these Ss did not explain what makes the light come on but what made the light go off. If that is indeed the case they are of course correct, but the interesting question is why they may have answered the wrong question. One possible reason is perhaps that the causal schema we entertain for explaining why things work is generally conjunctive, whereas the causal schema for failure is the complementary disjunctive schema.[11]

Here then is a possible explanation for why Ss in general seem to have so much trouble with disjunctive explanations. Production processes, success, accomplishments, the occurrence of an event are generally brought about by a combination of factors where failure of one of them is sufficient to cause failure, lack of production or performance, or the absence of an event. In order to test this hypothesis, a second JAM experiment was conducted in which Ss were asked either to explain what made the light come on or what made the light go off. In one half of the conditions the experiment started as in the previous experiment with all switches in the on position and the light on. Considering for comparative purposes only condition A (disjunctive configuration), all Ss gave the right explanation when asked to say what made the light go off (all switches had to be off) whereas only one S gave the right answer in the "on" condition and several gave (just as in the previous experiment) the incorrect (conjunctive) answer. This confusion is in fact significantly worse than in the previous study. The

11 Success on a task may require a conjunction of necessary conditions. In Kelley's (1973) terms, success is explained by a multiple necessary causes (MNC) schema. However, failure of any *one* of these necessary conditions implies failure on the task, even if the other necessary conditions still hold. Thus failure, in Kelley's (1973) terms, is explained in terms of a multiple sufficient causes (MSC) schema, as failure of any one condition is alone sufficient to cause task failure. (DJH)

difference is that the subjects were given a fixed-response format in the first study and were told that they could give more than one cause, whereas in the present experiment their spontaneous explanations were recorded, transcribed, and coded. The Ss do seem to understand much better what causes the light to come on than can be inferred from their spontaneous explanations. When given the right response categories they indicate more often correctly the disjunctive nature of the explanation, but when they are left to their own linguistic devices they tend to confuse the "and" and "or" configurations.

6 The non-orthogonality of nature

The experiments discussed so far demonstrate primarily that we are not only capable of making correct causal inferences based on observation of covariation but also that knowledge of the real world in the form of schemata helps us to shorten the inference process. Prior expectations and beliefs apparently do not always produce biases and shortcomings. They may in fact aid the inference process by ruling out logically possible but (under the circumstances) irrelevant conditions. We seem to construct first a mental model of the events or behaviours that we want to explain and upon which the rules of inference can operate afterwards. The fact, however, that not all logically possible combinations of conditions *do* occur with equal frequency in nature suggests that there may be natural categories of causation or prototypical explanations which come much more readily to mind than others.[12]

When the categorization of causal conditions is completely orthogonal it is much more difficult to detect the covariation of cause and effect. The experiments by Bruner on concept attainment, which have been curiously ignored in the attribution literature, show precisely this. In addition, the original concept attainment experiments suggest a causal attribution strategy which is fundamentally different from the process suggested by the ANOVA model. Bruner describes the behaviour of Ss in concept attainment experiments in terms of (focusing or scanning) hypothesis-testing strategies. There are of course some important differences between the concept attainment experiments and current attribution research, but the focusing strategy observed by Bruner can nevertheless explain perfectly how Ss in attribution experiments can reach a correct conclusion when they

12 The ANOVA experimental design is orthogonal, implying independent manipulations of consensus, distinctiveness, and consistency information. However, in nature it may well be the case, for example, that low consensus covaries with low distinctiveness information. For example, a tendency for low-consensus, low-distinctiveness patterns to co-occur would suggest that person attributions are "prototypical" (cf. Orvis *et al.* 1975). (DJH)

are given initially the information that the effect and all the relevant conditions are present and are shown subsequently what happens when one condition at a time is absent, provided that only single conditions or conjunctions of conditions are regarded as possible causes.

It also follows that since certain conceptual configurations do not occur, the presence and absence of causal conditions is no longer orthogonal or uncorrelated and that effects, taking into account only those configurations which actually occur, are unevenly distributed over these conditions. For the explanation of behavioural events this means that behaviour in one situation is going to be correlated with behaviour in other situations, and that behavioural variations in one person across situations are going to be correlated with behavioural variations in other individuals. Which correlations are going to be higher depends to some extent upon the type of behaviour. For achievement-oriented behaviour it seems likely that the former correlations are higher; for emotions one would expect the latter to be stronger.

An interesting and important question is how Ss take the non-orthogonal nature of the attributional information into account in their cognitive representation. I have suggested elsewhere that Ss might construct a mental model by subjectively scaling the information presented to them (Jaspars 1983). This idea implies that Ss can always explain an event by restating all the conditions which are present and proceed by generalizing as suggested in Bruner's focusing strategy. (The difficulty with disjunctive explanations is that one has to change from one mental model to another.)

It would also follow from this model that Ss might be inclined to consider first of all less general explanations, and would pay more attention to information which correlates highest with the behaviour they are asked to explain. In a study of failure in "A"-level examinations (Jaspars 1983), Ss did present a high frequency of specific ability explanations and tended to offer general explanations only in conjunction with, or after the offering of, local explanations. In two subsequent information search experiments (Jaspars *et al.*, in preparation), it was shown that such local explanations had typically a shorter search time and that Ss considered first of all performance in academic subjects which were similar to the one they were asked to explain. Hilton *et al.* (in preparation) have recently shown that subjects regard less general information patterns as more informative. They found, for example, that subjects regard low-consensus information, indicating low generalization of the target behaviour across actors, as being more informative about the target actor than they did high-consensus information, indicating high generalization of the target behaviour across actors.

The results suggest that subjects, when asked to explain a specific behaviour in specific circumstances, look for the behaviour most like it according to their causal model and explain the behaviour as a function of a condition of limited generality. Apparently Ss do not perform something like a mental analysis of variance; in fact, they seem to do almost exactly the opposite. It is as if they perform an intuitive regression analysis, in which the compound variable with the highest correlation is entered first and the explanatory process is stopped when new information does not improve the explanatory power of the variables already entered into the mental equation. In the case of achievement behaviour, this would lead to overattribution to the person and neglect of consensus information. However, far from being a biased procedure, the validity of the predictions which follow from such a process is just as high as that of an ANOVA procedure. The difference is that the hierarchical regression analysis does not allow for generalization, whereas analysis of variance does. If we want to explain a particular event, local explanations have therefore the same validity as explanations couched in general terms and interactions. The problem which might arise from this situation is, of course, that scientists and laymen may not understand each other, not because one group is biased and the other is not, but because each group processes the same information differently in trying to answer different questions. In the study of causal attributions in common sense, the problem is not to explain laughter, but why John laughs at this comedian.

Conclusion

The model of causal attribution processes suggested here is of course far from complete. I have assumed that Ss tend to represent available information about a particular event by constructing first a mental model from which explanations can be derived by making use of simplified rules of inference. However, I have not addressed the question of which model an S will use in a particular case, nor what the variety of models consists of. Since a model has been described so far as a particular selection of all relevant covarying conditions, one might assume, as Kelley implicitly does, that the information is attributionally categorized in terms of its generalization across actors, entities, and occasions. Brown and Fish (1983) have recently added a powerful argument to this point of view. The advantage of such a coding process is, of course, that it allows for the rules of causal inference to be applied in Kelley's configurational attribution model. In a series of studies of explanations of disorderly behaviour in school we have attempted to test this idea by asking Ss (teachers, parents, and pupils) to offer explanations and to describe the behaviour in terms of attributional categories. The results so far show that for certain behaviours the categorization does indeed affect the explanations offered (indifference, disobedience) but in other cases (aggressive behaviour) particular explanations are offered irrespective of the categorization of the behaviour in terms of consensus, distinctiveness, and consistency. It may be that the coding according to the categories suggested by Kelley acts as a default option, which can always be used, but which can be short-circuited when there is hardly any variation in these factors and/or when certain explanations are suggested or excluded by functional determinants of a social or psychological kind.

References

Alloy, L. B. and Tabachnik, N. (1984). Assessment of covariation by humans and animals: the joint influence of prior expectations and current situational information. *Psychological Review* 91: 112–49.

Braine, M. D. S. (1978). On the relation between the natural logic of reasoning and standard logic. *Psychological Review* 85: 1–21.

Brown, R. and Fish, D. (1983). The psychological causality implicit in language. *Cognition* 14: 237–73.

Bruner, J. S. (1973). *Beyond the information given: studies in the psychology of knowing*. New York: Norton.

Carroll, L. (1971). *Alice's adventures in Wonderland* and *Through the looking glass*, ed. Roger Lancelyn Green. Oxford: Oxford University Press.

Cohen, L. J. (1977). *The probable and the provable*. Oxford: Clarendon Press.

Coombs, C. (1964). *A theory of data*. New York: Wiley.

Hart, H. L. A. and Honoré, A. M. (1959). *Causation in the law*. Oxford: Clarendon Press.

Harvey, J. H. and Weary, G. (1984). Current issues in attribution theory and research. *Annual Review of Psychology* 35: 427–59.

Heider, F. (1958). *The psychology of interpersonal relations*. New York: Wiley.

Hewstone, M. (1981). *Social dimensions of attribution*. Unpublished doctoral dissertation, University of Oxford.

Hilton, D. J. (1984). *Knowledge-based strategies in causal attribution*. Unpublished doctoral dissertation, University of Oxford.

Hilton, D. J., Slugoski, B. R., and Turnbull, W. (in preparation). *Subjective norms, informativeness and causal attribution*. Unpublished manuscript.

Jaspars, J. (1983). The process of causal attribution in common sense. In M. Hewstone (ed.), *Attribution theory: social and functional extensions*. Oxford: Basil Blackwell.

Jaspars, J., Hewstone, M., and Fincham, F. D. (1983). Attribution theory and research: the state of the art. In J. Jaspars, F. D. Finchman, and M. Hewstone (eds.), *Attribution theory and research: conceptual, developmental and social dimensions*. London: Academic Press.

Jaspars, J., Spink, F., and Matheson, J. (in preparation). Information search and causal attributions.

Johnson-Laird, P. N. (1983). *Mental models*. Cambridge: Cambridge University Press.

Kahneman, D., Slovic, P., and Tversky, A. (eds.) (1982). *Judgment under uncertainty: heuristics and biases*. Cambridge: Cambridge University Press.

Kelley, H. H. (1967). Attribution theory in social psychology. In D. Levine (ed.), *Nebraska symposium on motivation*. Lincoln, Nebraska: University of Nebraska Press.

Kelley, H. H. (1973). The processes of causal attribution. *American Psychologist* 28: 107–28.

Kelley, H. H. and Michela, J. L. (1980). Attribution theory and research. *Annual Review of Psychology* 31: 457–503.

Kruglanski, A. W. and Ajzen, I. (1983). Bias and error in lay epistemology. *European Journal of Social Psychology* 13: 1–44.

Lalljee, M., Watson, M., and White, P. (1982). Explanations, attributions and the social context of unexpected behaviour. *European Journal of Social Psychology* 12: 17–29.

McArthur, L. A. (1972). The how and what of why: some determinants and consequences of causal attribution. *Journal of Personality and Social Psychology* 2: 171–93.

Mackie, J. L. (1974). *The cement of the universe*. Oxford: Clarendon Press.

Michotte, A. E. (1946). *La perception de la causalité*. Paris: Nostrand.

Nisbett, R. and Ross, L. (1980). *Human inference: strategies and shortcomings of social judgment*. Englewood Cliffs, NJ: Prentice-Hall.

Orvis, B. R., Cunningham, J. D., and Kelley, H. H. (1975). A closer examination of causal inferences: the roles of consensus, distinctiveness and consistency information. *Journal of Personality and Social Psychology* 32: 605–16.

Pannekoek, A. J. (ed.) (1973). *Algemene Geologie*. Groningen: Tjeenk Willink.

Runeson, S. (1977). *The visual perception of dynamic events*. PhD thesis, University of Uppsala, Sweden.

Schank, R. C. and Abelson, R. P. (1977). Scripts, plans, goals and understanding: an enquiry into human knowledge structures. Hillsdale, NJ: Lawrence Erlbaum.

Todd, J. T. and Warner, W. H. (1982). Visual perception of relative mass in dynamic events. *Perception* 11: 325–35.

Von Wright, G. H. (1983). *Practical reason*. Oxford: Blackwell.

15 Causal attribution viewed from an information-processing perspective[1]

David L. Hamilton

From the beginning, the thinking and research of social psychologists interested in how we come to "know" and "understand" other persons has been guided by a conceptual world-view that emphasizes the informational determinants of person perception. Reflecting its long interest in the cognitive underpinnings of behavior (Zajonc 1980), social psychology's explanations for such diverse aspects of "social knowing" as impression formation (Anderson 1981, Asch 1946), stereotyping (Allport 1954), implicit personality theories (Schneider 1973), attitudes (McGuire 1985), and interpersonal relations (Heider 1958) have all included a focus on the individual's use of information in attempting to understand his or her social world.

Although this emphasis on the informational bases of perceptions and judgments has been characteristic throughout the history of research on person perception, we have seen in the last decade a change in what it means to adopt an "information-processing approach" to this topic. There has been a shift in conceptual orientation that has changed the questions asked by researchers, the techniques by which they pursue those questions in their experiments, the theoretical frameworks that guide their thinking about and interpretation of their findings, and even the terminology they use in discussing their results. Specifically, contemporary research on such topics as impression formation and stereotyping is based on a general model of information-processing borrowed from cognitive psychology (Hamilton 1981, Hastie *et al.* 1980, Higgins *et al.* 1981, Markus and

1 Preparation of this chapter was supported in part by NSF Grant BNS–8216813 and NIMH Grant MH40058. The author is grateful to Arie Kruglanski, Diane Mackie, David Messick, James Olson, Eliot Smith, and James Uleman for their comments on earlier versions of this chapter.

Zajonc 1985, Wyer and Srull 1986). In general terms, this model views the person perception process in terms of the acquisition and utilization of information available about others.

An information-processing framework for social perception

The focus of any information-processing approach is to understand the various processes that mediate between (*a*) the information available to the perceiver from the social stimulus environment and (*b*) those judgments, memories, behaviors, etc. manifested by the perceiver in response to that information. These observable outputs become the grist for the investigatory mill, the data from which we attempt to infer the nature and effects of those mediating processes.

For purposes of simplification, these intervening cognitive influences can be viewed as four steps in a sequential chain: (*a*) attentional and encoding processes, (*b*) elaborative processes, (*c*) cognitive representation, and (*d*) retrieval. In addition, each of these steps can be influenced by the particular cognitive structures used at the time of processing. These components, and the relations among them, comprise the basic elements of any information processing model.

First, the perceiver's *attentional and encoding processes* influence what aspects of the available information will be processed and what aspects will be ignored. Given that attention is necessarily selective, this initial stage performs an important "gate-keeping" function that determines what subset of the information available will become the basis for the perceiver's eventual response. Presumably, in most situations the perceiver's attention will be focused on the most important aspects of the stimulus field. However, the research literature indicates that other factors may have an important bearing on attentional processes as well. What one attends to can be influenced both by features of the external stimulus display, such as salient elements of the stimulus field (Fiske 1980, McArthur 1981, Taylor and Fiske 1978), and by the purposes and goals of the perceiver (Erber and Fiske 1984, Zadny and Gerard 1974, White and Carlston 1983). Also relevant to this encoding stage is the research of Newtson and others on unitizing, whereby a continuous behavior stream is "chunked" into discrete units according to which the behavioral information is stored in memory (Newtson 1973, 1976). As was true for selective attention, the nature of the unitizing process can be affected both by properties of the behavior sequence being encoded (Newtson 1973) and by the perceiver's purposes and goals at the moment (Cohen and Ebbesen 1979).

The next step in the sequence represents a variety of cognitive mechanisms by which the perceiver "goes beyond the information given" (Bruner 1957) and *elaborates* upon it. These processes, which seem particularly important in social information processing, have been a popular focus of research in social psychology. Several such processes have been extensively investigated.

Evaluation. As information is processed from the social world, it seems almost universal that the perceiver assesses the evaluative meaning of that information. Zajonc (1980) has identified this evaluation process as one of the hallmarks of social perception and cognition. Its pervasiveness is one of the features that differentiates social and nonsocial information processing.

Inferences. The social perceiver routinely uses the information available as a basis for inferring additional "knowledge" about the behavior, person(s), group, setting, etc. just observed or described. Consequently the stimulus information, as encoded, is the basis for elaborative processing that extends the perceiver's conception of the person, group, or behavior characterized in that information.

Organization. In many cases in social information-processing the perceiver organizes the information as it is processed. The extent to which such organization is imposed on the information, as well as the nature of that organization, will vary depending on the nature of the information available, on how it is presented, and on the perceiver's processing goals at the time (Hamilton *et al.* 1980, Hoffman *et al.* 1981, Pryor and Ostrom 1981, Ostrom *et al.* 1981).

The products of the encoding and elaborative processes described above are then stored in long-term memory in the form of a *cognitive representation* of the person, group, or event portrayed in the stimulus information. When we talk about a perceiver's impression of another person, or one's stereotype of a group, or one's understanding of what transpired in a particular event, we are referring to the perceiver's cognitive representations as stored in memory. Because of the biases associated with the attentional and encoding stage, and because of the ways that elaborative processes can transform the information being processed, it is assumed that these cognitive representations typically will differ to some degree from the stimulus information on which they are based.

In many situations this cognitive representation will be *retrieved* and used as the basis for the perceiver's subsequent responses pertaining to the person, group, or event. That is, in describing his or her impression of another person, or conception of some group, or recollection of what happened in a particular incident, the perceiver refers back to this cognitive representation and draws on the information, evaluations, and inferences that are stored in memory and available for use.

What role does the attribution process play within this information-processing sequence? Attribution refers to the social perceiver's attempt to understand the causes of behavior. When the perceiver engages in intuitive causal analysis, he or she uses the information available to infer what were the causal antecedents that led to the occurrence of a particular behavioral event. Whether such attributional analysis occurs at all, and if so, to what extent, presumably will vary depending on a number of factors. When it does occur, however, it represents another way in which the perceiver extends and elaborates on the stimulus information that initially was available. One of the central arguments put forward in this chapter is that, because of this similarity to other inference processes, it would be highly useful to consider an analysis of attribution processes within the framework of this information-processing model.

In considering the place of the attribution process in this information-processing framework, I hope to establish some points of contact between two research areas that have been enormously productive in the last decade, yet which have remained somewhat distinct and isolated from each other – namely, research on attribution and research on person memory.

The attribution process and memory for social information

Both of these research traditions are concerned with the general question of "social knowing" – how the perceiver gains an understanding of his or her social world. For person memory research, the interest is in how the perceiver uses the information given and his pre-existing knowledge structures to develop a cognitive representation of some person or group. For attribution research, the question is how the perceiver uses the information available to understand causality. The question I want to address is: what role does the attribution process play in developing cognitive representations?

Given the information-processing framework summarized above, where does the attribution process fit in? Making an attribution involves the intuitive analysis of the causes of some behavior one has observed or learned about. Like other interpretive and inferential processes, attribution involves using and going beyond the available information for a particular purpose. That is, confronted with a behavioral fact that needs to be explained, the perceiver draws on what other relevant information might be available as a means of understanding the causal basis for that behavior. As a consequence, information on which an attributional judgment is based will receive extended processing as it is encoded and represented in memory. Thus the very process of engaging in attributional analysis would have an influence on the way information is represented in memory, and should therefore influence the extent to which attribution-relevant information can subsequently be recalled. In sum, in this analysis we are considering the attribution process as one kind of inference that might occur in the information processing sequence, an inferential activity that involves the extended processing of certain kinds of information, with consequent effects on the retention of attribution-relevant information.

To make this analysis more concrete, consider the following example which is typical of the type of stimulus problem presented to subjects in many attribution experiments. Suppose you learned that a student named Bill had complained that his teacher had been unfair in the grade he was given on an exam. Your task is to make a judgment as to whether Bill's complaint reflects something about Bill – a person attribution – or was due to something about the teacher – an entity attribution. To make this attribution, you make use of other information that is presented – what I will call context information. For example, you might learn that Bill doesn't study very much, that he has trouble dealing with people in positions of authority, and that other students consider the teacher to be fair. All of these facts would lead you to think that Bill is a complainer and hence to make a person attribution. On the other hand, if you learn that the teacher has unusually high standards, rarely gives high grades, and thinks students don't work hard, then you might be inclined to interpret Bill's complaint quite differently and to make an entity attribution – the teacher is the "cause" of Bill's dissatisfaction.

A vast amount of attribution research has been concerned with exactly this question – what kind of attribution the perceiver will make under various information conditions (Kelley and Michela 1980, Ross and Fletcher 1985). The information-processing perspective I described earlier suggests that this process may be interesting for other reasons as well. In the course of making the attribution, the perceiver thinks about the various items of context information and considers their implications for understanding the behavior to be explained. The more time one spends thinking about an item of information, the more likely it is that that item will be effectively represented in long-term memory. As the perceiver attempts to interpret the behavior in question in terms of the context information, associative connections will be established among these items as they are cognitively represented. These interitem associations will facilitate later retrieval of that information. For these reasons, then, the cognitive processes involved in attributional analysis lead to the prediction that engaging in the attribution process will enhance memory for attribution-relevant information.

We can carry this line of reasoning one step further when we realize that attribution tasks will vary in terms of how easy or difficult it is to make the attributional judgment. One factor that will influence the ease or difficulty of making an attribution will be the complexity of the context information. If most of that information implies person causation, or if most of it implies situational causation, then making an attributional judgment should be relatively easy and straightforward. On the other hand, if the context information is more complex, such that some of it suggests person causation and some implies situational causation, then intuitive attributional analysis becomes more difficult and requires more thought. In that case, we would assume that information relevant to the attribution task would spend more time being processed and form more associative links with both the behavior to be explained and other contextual items of information. This leads to the prediction that difficult attribution tasks will result in higher recall of attribution-relevant information than will relatively easy attribution tasks.

To test these ideas experimentally, we (Hamilton *et al.* 1987) presented subjects with a series of stimulus problems, each one consisting of a statement describing a behavioral event – for example, "Bill complained that his teacher had been unfair" – along with six additional sentences providing context information. Each context item implied that either the person or the entity was the cause for the behavior. The subjects' task was to attribute the behavior either to the person who performed the behavior or to an entity or some element of the situation in which the behavior occurred.

The key manipulation of this study was the nature of the set of context sentences. In two of the stimulus sets, five of the six context sentences implied that the actor or subject of the behavioral event sentence was the causal agent, with one sentence implying that the situation or object of the behavior was causal. For two other stimulus sets, the opposite was the case – five of the six context sentences implied entity causation, with one person-oriented sentence. In the final pair of the stimulus problems, the context set consisted of three sentences of each type. We can refer to these conditions in terms of the ratio of person-oriented to entity-oriented context sentences. Thus the 5:1 condition will be called the Person-oriented context, the 1:5 case will be called the Entity-oriented condition, and the 3:3 set will be called the Mixed condition. Three replication booklets were developed such that each behavioral event was presented in each type of context for one third of the subjects.

Following each stimulus set, subjects were asked to attribute the behavior either to the actor or to the entity – the typical attribution task used in numerous experiments. They also rated their degree of confidence in their attribution judgment. Then, forty-eight hours later, subjects returned for a second session during which their recall for the stimulus sets was assessed. Recall was measured in two parts. First, subjects were given a blank sheet of paper and were asked to write down as many of the behavioral event sentences as they could remember. Second, they were given a set of pages, with one of the event sentences presented at the top of each page. On these pages they were to write down as many of the context sentences as they could remember. Our prediction was that subjects in the Mixed condition would remember more of the stimulus information for both of these measures than would subjects in the Person-oriented and Entity-oriented context conditions. Our test of this prediction was a within-subjects comparison of subjects' recall across conditions that were equivalent in the amount of context information presented, but differed in the attributional complexity of that information.

The results supported our hypothesis. First, we analyzed recall of the six behavioral event sentences as a function of the context condition associated with the event sentence. As predicted, subjects recalled significantly more of these behaviors that had been presented in a Mixed context than in the other two context conditions. Second, we analyzed subjects' recall of the context sentences that had accompanied these behavioral events. Although there was partial deviation from prediction for one of the three replication booklets, the results on the whole supported our hypothesis. In general, subjects recalled more context sentences in the Mixed context condition than in the other two context conditions.

Taken together, the results of these two analyses provide support for our hypothesis that subjects would be able to recall more of the stimulus information when the context sentences consisted of an equal mix of person-oriented and entity-oriented items. In this condition the subject's task of making an attribution is more difficult, presumably requiring more extensive thought relating these items of information to each other before the attribution decision can be made. As a consequence, these items become linked with each other in a well-developed network as this information is represented in memory. In contrast, when the context information predominantly implies either person or object causation, the attribution task is relatively easy, makes fewer cognitive processing demands, and results in a less articulated cognitive representation of the attribution-relevant information.

The design of this study provided an opportunity to investigate a second issue as well. Research on person memory by Hastie and others (Hamilton, in press, Hastie 1980, Hastie and Kumar 1979, Srull 1981, Srull *et al.* 1985) has shown that, in the formation of an impression of another person, items of information that are incongruent with an initial impression or expectation are more likely to be recalled than are items of information congruent with that impression. In this study we extended investigation of this issue to an attribution paradigm. In two of the context conditions included in our experiment, five of the six context sentences imply one causal agent as being responsible for the behavioral event. The one remaining item, therefore, can be viewed as incongruent – in terms of its casual implications – with all of the other items in the context set. Generalizing from the findings of Hastie and others, we predicted that a context item would be more likely to be recalled if its attributional implications were incongruent with the implications of the other items in the set of context sentences.

To test this hypothesis we analyzed the probability of recall of particular context sentences. Specifically, we compared the likelihood that an item was recalled when it was the only person-oriented (or the only entity-oriented) sentence with the probability that that same item was recalled when it was one of five person-oriented (or entity-oriented) sentences. In other words, we compared the probability of recall of these sentences when their causal implications were congruent or incongruent with the implications of the other items in the context set. This analysis was done separately for the person-oriented and the entity-oriented sentences.

The results of these analyses provided strong support for our hypothesis. A person-oriented context sentence was more likely to be recalled when it was the only such sentence than when it was one of five sentences implying person causation. Similarly, an entity-oriented sentence was more likely to be recalled when it was the only such sentence than when it was one of five sentences implying entity or situational causation.

These findings, then, are parallel to those reported by other investigators who have studied recall of information congruent and incongruent with an impression-based expectancy. To account for their person memory results, Hastie (1980) and Srull (1981) have proposed a network model in which incongruent items develop more associative links with other items. This is due to the integrative nature of the impression formation process, in which various items of information are related to each other as one attempts to understand and develop a coherent impression of the target person. Incongruent items are, of course, more difficult to integrate into the developing impression. Consequently, they spend more time in working memory and hence develop more associative connections with other descriptive items. These associative links facilitate later retrieval of information, producing better recall of the incongruent items. This same process can be viewed as underlying the attribution results obtained in our research. Our subjects were faced with the task of making an attribution for a particular behavior, and were provided with several sentences of context information for use in making that attribution. An item whose causal implications conflicted with those of all the other items would be more difficult to integrate, would spend more time in working memory, and hence would develop more associative links with other items. Again, these associations would facilitate recall of these items and hence would produce the pattern of results we obtained.

Returning now to the major focus of this study, we found that subjects had higher recall performance for Mixed stimulus sets than for the other two context conditions. Our assumption was that the complex pattern of context information presented in this condition created a more difficult attribution task, and therefore would result in more extensive processing of that information before an attribution was made. It is this extended processing that is presumed to mediate the recall difference obtained in this study. If the Mixed context sets pose a more difficult task that requires more extensive processing, it should be reflected in the amount of time it takes the perceiver to make an attributional judgment. Our next experiment tested this assumption more directly.

In its fundamental respects this study was quite similar to the first experiment. Subjects again read stimulus sets like those used in the first study, and again their task was to make a person or an object attribution for each one. In this case, however, the stimulus sets were not presented in booklet form. Instead, all information was presented by a computer on a CRT screen. The sequence of events was as follows. First, the sentence presenting the behavioral event to be explained appeared alone on the screen for four seconds. Then, the six context sentences and the response options appeared on the screen, all at once. When this happened, a timer in the computer was activated, and it was terminated when the subject pressed one of two keys on the keyboard to indicate either a person attribution or an entity attribution. In this way, the computer recorded the amount of time it took the subject to make an attribution for each stimulus set. Our hypothesis was that these response times would be longer when the context information was mixed than when it heavily favored one or the other attributional option.

The results supported this hypothesis. Subjects took significantly longer to make an attribution for the Mixed context sets than in the other two conditions. These findings provide additional evidence for our conceptualization of what is happening as subjects complete these attribution tasks. When the context information is complex, in the sense that the items are mixed in terms of their causal implications, then making an attribution is more difficult and will require more cognitive work before a judgment can be made. This additional processing of the attribution-relevant information produces a more elaborated representation of this information in memory, which in turn produces the higher levels of recall for the Mixed condition that I reported earlier.

Taken together, the results of the experiments I have discussed provide encouraging support for our view of the attribution process as an influential aspect of the information-processing sequence. In this approach we regard the attribution process as a cognitive activity that involves the extended use and interpretation of incoming information. In this respect it is similar to other cognitive operations that we as information-processors perform on the information we acquire, and as such it is a process that has implications for the perceiver's cognitive representation of his or her social world. Our results indicate that the ease or difficulty of engaging in attributional analysis, and hence the amount of time and presumably the amount of thought devoted to attributional analysis, can influence both the *amount* of information and *what aspects* of that information are retained as a part of the perceiver's social knowledge regarding some event.

In our research we have manipulated the difficulty of the attribution task. However, our argument is easily extended to the distinction between situations in which the perceiver does and does not engage in attributional analysis. That is, when the perceiver does engage in causal analysis, he or she utilizes and cognitively operates on information to an extent and in a manner that differs from situations in which attributions are not made. Thus, we see attribution as an inference process that may or may not occur during information-processing, and when it does occur, it may vary in the cognitive task demands that it places on the perceiver. Both of these variations would have implications for how the available information is represented in memory, and hence for the perceiver's "social knowledge" or understanding of the persons, events, and circumstances portrayed in that information.

Spontaneous activation of the attribution process

If attribution is a cognitive activity that may or may not occur during information-processing, then it becomes important to understand when attributional analysis is more likely to occur and the conditions under which this process will be activated. In view of the massive experimental literature on attribution processes, this question of when the attribution process is triggered has received surprisingly little attention. Throughout the 1970s attribution research was largely concerned with questions of how perceivers use information when they do make attributions. Given this focus, the typical research strategy of manipulating aspects of the stimulus information and then asking subjects directly to make a person or situation attribution was quite reasonable. It is only within the last few years that investigators have sought to determine whether and when subjects *spontaneously* engage in attributional analysis, without an experimenter presenting them with a set of possible causes accompanied by rating scales (Berscheid, Graziano, Monson and Dermer 1976; Clary and Tesser 1983,

Enzle and Shopflocher 1978, Hastie 1984, Pittman and Pittman 1980, Pyszczynski and Greenberg 1981, Wong and Weiner 1981).

The difficulty in studying spontaneous attribution, of course, is the necessity of determining when the subject has made an attributional inference without explicitly asking that such a causal judgment be made. A variety of techniques have been used to detect indirectly attributional inference (see Hastie 1984 and Weiner 1985 for discussion of these methods). One particularly useful strategy has been demonstrated by Smith and Miller (1983; see also Smith 1984). In their studies, subjects were shown (on a computer screen) a number of sentences, each one describing an actor as having performed some behavior. Each stimulus sentence was followed by a question to which the subject responded "Yes" or "No" by pressing the appropriate response key. Several questions, corresponding to possible spontaneous inference processes, were included in the experiment. (Although each stimulus behavior was followed by only one question, each question occurred several times in the stimulus sequence and, through counterbalancing across subjects, was paired with all behavior items.) The time required for the subject to answer each question was recorded.

The rationale of this method is as follows. If the question corresponds to a process that occurred spontaneously during the initial comprehension of the stimulus behavior, then the answer to that question will be readily available and the subject's response time will be short. In contrast, if the question asks about something not inferred during the comprehension stage, then the subject must retrieve the relevant information and make the inference itself before responding to the question. These processes take time, so the subject's response time will be longer than in the previous case. Thus, it is assumed that short response times reflect inferences that were spontaneously made prior to the question being asked, whereas longer response times reflect inference processes activated in response to the question itself.

Smith and Miller's (1983) primary use of this method was to compare response times to several questions in order to determine which inference processes likely occur spontaneously and which do not. Their results, for example, support the conclusion that inferences about whether the actor intended to perform the behavior and whether the actor possesses a trait correspondent to the behavior may be made spontaneously during comprehension. In contrast, subjects took significantly longer to respond to questions about whether the behavior was due to personal or situational causes, suggesting that these attributional judgments may not reflect spontaneous processing. The method can also be used, however, to examine what factors influence response times to these questions, and in this strategy, one can attempt to determine the conditions under which particular inference processes are and are not spontaneously activated. This was the rationale underlying the experiment to be reported in this section.

As was mentioned earlier, several studies of memory for person-descriptive information, using an impression formation paradigm, have found that items of information that are incongruent with an initial impression or expectancy are more likely to be recalled than are congruent items (Crocker *et al.* 1983, Hastie and Kumar 1979, Hemsley and Marmurek 1982, Srull 1981, Srull *et al.* 1985, Wyer and Gordon 1982). There are a number of possible explanations for this finding, one of which is relevant to this chapter's concern with the role of the attribution process in person memory.

In the course of forming an impression, the perceiver attempts to integrate each new piece of information into a developing impression. For information that is congruent with an existing impression or expectancy, this assimilation is relatively easy – the congruent information "fits" with what one already knows or believes about the target person. In contrast, when one encounters an incongruent item, incorporating this information into one's impression of the person is more difficult. Faced with information that clearly contradicts expectations, the perceiver might attempt to understand why this incongruent behavior occurred. In other words, an incongruent piece of information may trigger the attribution process, in which the perceiver attempts to explain the cause of the expectancy-disconfirming behavior. If so, then this would constitute additional processing of incongruent, compared with congruent, items, which in turn would produce better recall of those items.

Clary and Tesser (1983) and Hastie (1984) have reported evidence that supports this argument. In both studies, subjects initially received information about a target person that clearly established an impression that the person possessed a particular personality characteristic (e.g. friendliness), and this was followed by behavior descriptions that were either congruent or incongruent with impression-based expectancies. The task for Clary and Tesser's (1983) subjects was to retell the information in a tape-recording, as if to communicate it to another person. In Hastie's (1984) experiment subjects wrote continuations of the behavior-descriptive items. In both experiments the subjects' verbal descriptions were then coded for whether or not they included explanations for the behavior described. Both studies found that subjects were more likely to use explanatory accounts when the behavioral episode was incongruent with the impression-based expectancies.

In our experiment (done in collaboration with Eliot Smith and Pam Kornasiewicz) we tested the same hypothesis using a different methodology. The study essentially followed Hastie's (1980, 1984) paradigm for studying recall of congruent and incongruent behavior items in an impression formation task. In addition, however, we incorporated Smith and Miller's (1983) method for assessing the mediation of attributional inferences.

Subjects in the experiment were told that their task was to form an impression of a person who would be described by a series of traits and behaviors. All stimulus information was presented on a computer screen. Following the Hastie paradigm, a clear first impression was established by presenting, at the outset, a set of five homogeneous trait words defining a single trait dimension. These were followed by a series of twenty-four behavior descriptions, twelve of which were congruent with expectations based on the initial trait ensemble, six of which were incongruent with that impression, and six of which were unrelated to the trait dimension. Each behavior description was shown on the screen for five seconds. It is at this point that our procedure differed from other studies using this paradigm. Each behavior description was followed by one of six questions, to which the subject was to respond "Yes" or "No" by pressing one of two response keys. The six questions are as follows.

(1) Was the action consistent with your impression?
(2) Do you think you would like this person as a friend?
(3) Did the person intend to perform this behavior?
(4) Based on your impression, is the person friendly (intelligent)?
(5) Was the action caused by something about the person?
(6) Was the action caused by something about the situation?

Each of the six questions occurred four times in the sequence of twenty-four behavior descriptions, and across all subjects, each question appeared in conjunction with each behavior description with equal frequency. The computer recorded the subject's response for each item, and also the subject's response time in answering the question.

The six questions were selected because of their relevance to attributions, attribution-related processes, and social judgment, and because of their usefulness in previous experiments using this methodology (Smith 1984, Smith and Miller 1983). The consistency question was included as a manipulation check on the congruency versus incongruency of the stimulus behaviors (subjects answered "Yes" over 90 per cent of the time in response to congruent items, but less than 20 per cent for incongruent behaviors). The liking question was included to assess subjects' overall evaluative judgments. The intention and trait inference questions were included because of the role of these processes in attribution theories. The last two questions, concerning personal and situational causation for the stimulus behavior, involve direct attributional inference and were the central focus of the experiment.

The data of primary interest for present purposes were the subjects' response times in answering the two attribution questions when they followed incongruent, as compared to congruent, behavior descriptions. The rationale was as follows. I suggested earlier that encountering an incongruent item spontaneously sets off the attribution process, in a way or to an extent that does not happen following a congruent item. If so, then when subjects are asked an attributional question following an incongruent item, they should be able to respond easily and relatively quickly, because the cognitive activity necessary to answer the question will already have been done. Previous research has shown that incongruent behaviors are most often attributed to situational causes (Crocker *et al.* 1983). Therefore, since a situational attribution has likely been made, the faster response times for incongruent behaviors should be particularly evident for the question-asking if the behavior was due to something about the situation. In contrast, following a congruent item, responding to an attributional question should take longer because the question of *why* the person performed the behavior has not been considered during the initial processing of the item. Again, this should be especially true of the situation attribution question, since it is particularly unlikely that situational causes would spontaneously be considered during the processing and comprehension of congruent information.

Our analysis of the response time data, then, focused on a comparison of subjects' response times in answering questions when they followed congruent and incongruent items. Our primary interest was in this comparison for the situation attribution question, and response times for the other questions were used as a baseline. The results revealed two findings of interest. First, collapsing across the six questions, there was a highly significant main effect due to the congruency versus incongruency of the behavior descriptions. Overall, subjects' responses to questions following incongruent items took considerably longer than did their responses to those questions when they followed congruent items. To test our main hypothesis, then, we looked for any modification in this general tendency as a function of the question being asked. The second finding of interest – a significant question-by-item-type interaction – revealed just such a modification. Mean log response times in response to each question for both congruent and incongruent items are shown in Fig. 15.1. It can clearly be seen that the general tendency evidenced in the main effect holds for five of the six questions. However, for the situation attribution question – was the behavior due to something about the situation? – a reversal of this tendency was obtained, as we had predicted. In this case, subjects actually took longer to answer this question when it followed a congruent item than when it followed an incongruent item.[2]

2 There is a potentially troublesome confound in these data in that (*a*) for each of the questions subjects responded "Yes" and "No" with different frequencies and (*b*) response times on Yes/No decision tasks are characteristically faster for a "Yes" response. As one means of

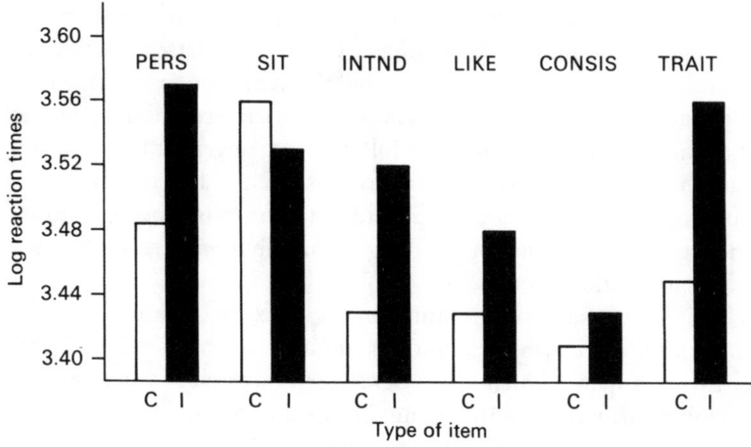

Fig. 15.1 Mean log reaction times to each question for congruent and incongruent items

These findings are consistent with our conceptualization that incongruent information triggers or activates the attribution process, and in particular that it initiates an attributional analysis that most commonly results in a situational attribution. We view these results as evidence of spontaneous attributional activity in response to expectancy-disconfirming information.

What does "attribution" mean?

Another aspect of the results shown in Figure 15.1 is noteworthy. Specifically, response times for the person causation question were quite similar to response times for the trait inference question. The trait inference question asked the subject if the target person possessed the trait (friendly or intelligent) established in the trait ensemble. For a congruent behavior, this question asked for a correspondent inference (Jones and Davis 1965), and subjects almost always responded affirmatively and relatively quickly. Similarly, when a congruent behavior was followed by the person causation question, responses were almost always "Yes," and these responses were slightly slower than those for the trait question. Following a behavior item that was incongruent with expectancies, response times for both of these questions were markedly longer.

Now consider these findings in terms of the argument made earlier that

addressing this problem, we examined the response time data only for "Yes" responses. Although reduced frequencies in some cells precluded statistical analysis, the pattern of response times in this case was similar to that shown in Figure 15.1.

information incongruent with expectations would initiate attributional reasoning during the comprehension phase. Clearly, the person attribution question probes for evidence of attributional thought, so one might expect that, if incongruent items triggered causal analysis, subjects should have responded to this question more quickly following incongruent than following congruent behaviors (paralleling response times for the situation attribution question). The fact that this did not happen is, I believe, informative, and provides a basis for thinking about what we mean when we refer to the "attribution process."

Let us begin by considering the situation on which we focused when we raised the question of what conditions initiate attributional thought, namely, the case in which the perceiver encounters expectancy-disconfirming information. In the paradigm we employed, the subject first receives information, in the form of several trait-descriptive adjectives, that clearly establishes an initial impression of the target person with regard to a particular attribute domain (e.g. friendliness or intelligence). In processing subsequent information about the person, the subject periodically reads a behavior description that is directly incongruent with the initial impression. The subject has difficulty incorporating this piece of information into the evolving impression – it doesn't "fit" with what else is known or believed to be true of the target person. As a consequence, the subject attempts to explain *why* the person performed this behavior that seemingly is so incompatible with his predominant personality characteristics. In doing so, the subject has clearly engaged in explicit causal reasoning – cognitive activity directed at understanding the causal factors that produced the behavior. Typically in this case, the incongruent behavior will be explained in terms of forces external to the person, producing a situational or entity attribution, thereby maintaining the viability of the existing impression. That is, by attributing the contradictory behavior to situational factors, the incongruent information is viewed as unrepresentative of the person and hence has been rendered undiagnostic for the perceiver's goal of understanding the target's personality. The main point here is that the incongruency has activated a process of thoughtful consideration of possible reasons why the behavior occurred, leading to a judgment of probable cause.

Now let us turn to a consideration of what happens when expectancy-congruent behavior is encountered. In this case, the findings (Smith 1984, Smith and Miller 1983, and the present data) indicate that the perceiver very likely makes a correspondent trait inference as a part of the comprehension process. Research by Winter and Uleman (1984, Winter *et al.* 1985), using a totally different methodology, has also shown that perceivers spontaneously make dispositional inferences in the process of encoding behavioral information. As a consequence, subjects in our task are able to respond quickly to the trait question following a congruent item (much more quickly than following an incongruent behavior, the dispositional implications of which conflict with the existing impression and hence create the uncertainty that triggers the attributional analysis discussed above).

If a correspondent dispositional inference is made during the initial comprehension of the behavioral information, then it would greatly facilitate answering the person attribution question following a congruent item. For example, suppose the subject learns that the target person "visited a sick friend in the hospital." The accumulated evidence cited above strongly suggests that, during the encoding of that behavior description, the subject spontaneously infers that the actor is a friendly person, that is, he possesses a dispositional quality that is implied by his friendly behavior. If the subject is then asked "Was the action caused by something about the person?" the answer is readily available because the dispositional inference has been made. The person is friendly, and friendly people do friendly acts, so yes, something about the person caused the behavior. The fact that the response time to the person attribution question was relatively fast, yet still somewhat longer than that for the trait inference question, is consistent with this interpretation. In contrast, the response time for the situation attribution question following a congruent item was considerably longer, presumably because subjects considered the possibility of situational causation for congruent behavior for the first time only after the question was posed. For the person attribution question, having made the dispositional inference, this kind of thought was not necessary.

This intuitive consideration of the psychological processes involved in making attributional judgments for congruent and incongruent behaviors seems to fit with common sense and our introspections about our own experiences in making such judgments. While plausible, this analysis does point out some distinctions and issues that have considerable theoretical importance for understanding the nature of attributional processing.

To begin, notice that there are substantial differences in the processes involved in the way attributional judgments are made for behaviors that are congruent and incongruent with expectations. Attribution is typically defined as the perceiver's attempt to answer the question "Why?", to achieve an understanding of the causes of behavior. Causal reasoning probably occurs only under certain circumstances, and a growing amount of evidence indicates that expectancy disconfirmation is one of those conditions that activates such processing (Hastie 1984, Weiner 1985). As we have portrayed it, encountering incongruent information almost acts as an interruption of routine information-processing. It is as if the perceiver, confronted with a behavior that contradicts expectation, says "Hold everything! I need to think about this one," and begins to engage in explanatory thought in order to make sense of and understand the reasons behind this unexpected event. Causal reasoning is spontaneously activated as the perceiver tries to answer the attribution question "Why?"

Our portrayal of how the perceiver makes an attributional judgment for congruent behavior is quite different. Behavioral information that fits with expectancies is processed easily and, during its initial encoding, is the basis for a spontaneous trait inference that the actor possesses a corresponding disposition. Questions of why the person performed the behavior do not typically arise in processing congruent information, and hence attribution *per se* does not spontaneously occur in this circumstance. On the other hand, if some external factor (e.g. a query from a friend; a task presented by an experimenter) induces the perceiver to consider why the behavior occurred, she can easily make an attributional judgment because the trait characteristic inferred during encoding provides a readily available dispositional explanation for the behavior. However, it is at this point that questions of causality and explanation are considered for the first time.

This interpretation deviates from some views commonplace in the literature which hold that the step of extracting dispositional properties from observed behavior is itself an attributional inference. The present position is that this step does not constitute attributional processing *per se*, and that there are important reasons for recognizing and maintaining the distinction between this type of inference and what we otherwise consider to be attributional analysis. According to the present view, what occurs during this comprehension phase is a simple trait inference, with no attempt to understand the causal basis of the behavior. The inference constitutes a dispositional "summary" of the behavioral information and adds to the evolving cognitive representation, much like other elaborative processes by which the perceiver "fleshes out" the skeleton of information available. From this perspective, then, the trait inference is not itself an attribution, but having been made, it becomes the basis for an attribution when one is needed.

In sum, it is argued here that the attribution *process* itself is fundamentally different for congruent and incongruent behaviors. For incongruent behaviors, a process of intuitive causal analysis is spontaneously activated – a process that takes time, takes cognitive effort, and establishes associations among diverse items of information relevant to the attribution judgment. Because of these properties, the attribution process itself has the potential to contribute significantly to the developing cognitive representation of the information, as was true for the case of "difficult" attributions discussed in an earlier section. For congruent behaviors, extensive attributional thought is less likely to occur as the behavior is attributed to a disposition that was spontaneously inferred from the behavior as it was comprehended during encoding. In this case, the attribution is derived from, rather than contributes to, the cognitive representation of the stimulus information.

In developing this differentiation between the nature of attributions for congruent and incongruent behaviors, it has been argued that simply making a dispositional inference on the basis of some behavioral information does not constitute making an attribution. This point has more general implications for understanding the attribution process as well. Of all the kinds of inferences and judgments a perceiver might make, the defining feature of an attribution is that it concerns causation – the perceiver's attempt intuitively to understand the causal factors underlying some behavior. It seems reasonable, then, to limit our usage of the term "attribution" to those instances where the perceiver is in fact concerned with understanding causation. Inferring a dispositional quality from behavioral information *may* involve such intuitive causal analysis, as when I "explain" a person's temperamental outburst in terms of his emotional nature, and as a consequence of this attributional inference come to perceive the person as (dispositionally) temperamental. In many cases, however, a trait inference based on behavior observation will not reflect causal reasoning. If I observe a person's outgoing and gregarious behavior at a party and infer that she is friendly, I am not attempting to explain why she mingled and chatted with others but am simply summarizing a pattern of behavior and inferring a trait characteristic from it. In making the inference I have implicitly assumed that her behavior is at least somewhat representative of her personality. I may then infer other characteristics of her personality as well, I may have an evaluative reaction to both her behavior and to my impression of what she is like, and so forth. But none of these elaborative processes necessarily involves a concern with understanding *why* she behaved as she did. Dispositional inferences, then, are not necessarily, and often will not be, attributional inferences. (For a related view, see Reeder 1985.)

Once the distinction between dispositional inferences and attributional inferences is recognized, it becomes important to consider the relation between these two kinds of inference processes. In the following discussion two possible relations are discussed. One possibility is the relation assumed by correspondent inference theory (Jones 1979, Jones and Davis 1965). The primary focus of this theory was to understand the conditions under which perceivers are most likely to make inferences "from acts to dispositions," and thereby to assume that an actor possesses a trait or attribute correspondent with some overt behavior. According to the theory, a correspondent inference is made as part of one's attempt to understand the causes for the behavior in question. If an *attributional* inference has been made that an actor's behavior was caused by some internal property, it can lead to a correspondent *dispositional* inference. It therefore seems plausible that correspondent trait inferences would reflect attribution to the actor. Consequently it has become commonplace to interpret evidence that perceivers made correspondent trait inferences as constituting evidence that attributions have been made (e.g. Berscheid *et al.* 1976). In essence, then, correspondent inference theory assumes that extreme trait ratings (particularly when made with confidence) reflect dispositional attributions.

In the present framework we are unwilling to assume this equivalence relation. Extreme trait ratings may reflect the rater's belief that the target person possesses the trait to an extreme degree, or it may mean that the rater is very confident that the target possesses the trait to some degree, or both. Neither of these cases necessarily involves an inference about the causes of behavior. While it is certainly true that, if a behavior is viewed as having been caused by internal forces, then that person attribution would produce a strong dispositional inference, the converse does not necessarily hold. It seems less defensible to assume that strong dispositional inferences are invariably mediated by attributional processing.

A second possible relation between dispositional inferences and attributional inferences is less obvious but, we suspect, more commonplace. As we noted earlier, some recent research indicates that subjects spontaneously make a trait inference about the actor in the process of encoding behavioral information (Smith and Miller 1983, Winter and Uleman 1984, Winter *et al.* 1985). In the language of Jones and Davis (1965), these are *correspondent* trait inferences. These inferences are probably made quickly and with little if any conscious thought, and it is unlikely that they are the result of any process of considering the causes for the behavior described. Rather, these spontaneous trait inferences represent another example of how the social information-processor goes beyond the literal information available in extending his or her cognitive representation of the stimulus person. However, although these inferences are not the product of attributional processes, they have important consequences for attribution. For when an attributional judgment is subsequently called for, the disposition now assumed to characterize the actor (which of course is correspondent to the behavior) provides a readily available explanation for why the actor behaved as he did. Moreover, it is an explanation that does not require that the perceiver retrieve and review other information that might be relevant to the attribution task. It is, therefore, cognitively economical as well. Finally, notice that this process biases the perceiver towards making internal attributions for behavior, a tendency that is quite apparent in the results of numerous attribution experiments (Jones 1979, Ross 1977).

This analysis suggests, then, that the relation between trait inferences and attributional inferences is often the opposite of that implied by correspondent inference theory. That is, rather than being the product of having made an internal attribution for an actor's behavior, correspondent trait inferences are made spontaneously in comprehending the actor's behavior, without attributional analysis, and become an important basis for a dispositional attribution if and when the causal antecedents of the behavior are subsequently considered.

In responding to the viewpoint advocated here, the traditional attribution theorist might acknowledge that dispositional inferences are often made without any deliberate attempt to understand causation, but argue further that those dispositional inferences are themselves made in the service of causal understanding. That is, the reason we make trait inferences from behavior at all – the motivation underlying our attempts to understand a person's dispositional qualities – is to determine the causal basis of the person's behavior. And if we routinely make such inferences in our perceptions of social behavior, then the attribution process would occur almost automatically as that behavior is perceived. In this view, then, an attributional inference is an inherent aspect of any dispositional inference we would make in our observation of others' behaviors. This line of reasoning seems implicit in the way many authors use the term attribution.

There is, however, a difficulty with this position, for it implies that attributional as well as dispositional inferences are made as behavioral information is perceived, encoded, and comprehended. If this were the case, then in Smith and Miller's (1983) studies subjects should have been able to answer a person attribution question as quickly as a trait inference question – the cognitive work relevant for both would already have been completed. Yet in two experiments subjects' response times to answer the person attribution question were significantly longer than those required for answering the trait inference question. These results are incompatible with the view that dispositional inferences are made in the process of arriving at an attributional judgment.[3]

We have discussed two possible relations between attributional and dispositional inferences. They differ in the temporal ordering in which attribution and dispositional inference occur, and this difference has a number of implications for the meaning of how attribution occurs, as we have indi-

3 The present argument was derived earlier in the context of our experiment in which subjects (*a*) were instructed to form an impression of a person (*b*) about whom they had a strong prior expectancy and then (*c*) learned about both congruent and incongruent behaviors. It should be noted, however, that none of these features is crucial to our interpretation regarding the distinction between dispositional and attributional inferences. Relevant to this point is the fact that in Smith and Miller's (1983) research, each stimulus behavior was presented as describing a different person, and subjects did not form an impression based on multiple items. For this reason their results perhaps provide more compelling evidence for the argument advanced in this section than do our own findings.

cated. Both of these sequential relations undoubtedly occur in information-processing and judgment, though under differing circumstances. However, because the nature of attributional processing differs significantly in these two cases, it is important to distinguish between them in understanding the nature and function of attribution.

This distinction between trait inferences and attributional inferences, and our conceptualization of attributional processing, also makes sense in terms of the information-processing framework presented at the beginning of this chapter. If in fact trait inferences are made spontaneously during the initial encoding of behavioral information, and if attributional analysis is a subsequent process that may or may not be activated depending on informational and circumstantial factors, then it is clear that these two kinds of inference processes occur at quite different stages in the information-processing sequence. Given this temporal disparity, then, it would seem unwise to assume equivalence between the two. Moreover, we have characterized the early trait inference process as spontaneous, as occurring without much thought (though not necessarily automatic: see Bargh 1984), and as not being concerned with causation. In contrast, attributional inferences – though they may sometimes be spontaneous and can often occur without much deliberation – are specifically concerned with causation. Our point is that inferences that are not made for the purpose of causal understanding are not attributional in nature, even if, having been made, the products of those inferences provide the basis for subsequent attributional judgments.

Summary and conclusions

One of the primary goals of this chapter has been to view the attribution process within the conceptual framework of an information-processing system, and to consider the implications of such a perspective for understanding the nature of attribution and its relation to other processes. According to the orientation adopted in the introduction, attribution is an inferential process by which the perceiver elaborates on the available information by inferring the causal factors that precipitated a particular behavioral event. As such, attributional inferences share the basic properties of other kinds of inferences – they represent efforts to go beyond the information; they may or may not occur, depending on circumstances; they to some degree consume cognitive resources; they expand the cognitive representation of the stimulus information; they may be based on aspects of the available information, on pre-existing knowledge structures, or both, and so forth. A consideration of attributions as inferences in an information-processing system not only highlights their commonalities with other inference processes, but also draws attention to their differentiating features. The defining property of attributions, of course, is one of content: attributional inferences pertain to understanding causality. By recognizing both the shared and the unique characteristics of attributional inferences, and their place in an information-processing system, it is likely that new and different research questions can be raised about the attribution process that until now have not been explored.

Another goal of this chapter was to provide evidence of the potential usefulness of viewing the attribution process in this broader context. To that end, we have presented two illustrations of experiments originating at the interface of attribution and person memory research. In the first, the attribution process was viewed as a cognitive activity that takes time and consumes cognitive resources, and to the degree that it does so, information relevant to the attributional inference will be effectively encoded and represented in memory. This research showed that the more difficult the attribution task, the more time it takes to make an attributional judgment and the more information relevant to it is remembered by the perceiver. It was also found that an item of information whose attributional implications are incongruent with those of the other information available is particularly likely to be recalled, paralleling findings on memory for incongruent information in an impression formation task.

In the second case, attribution was viewed as an inference that may or may not occur as behavioral information is processed. Again drawing on the person memory literature, we examined the hypothesis that attributional inferences are more likely to occur in response to expectancy-incongruent information, and less likely to occur when the information conforms to prior expectancies. This research also raised questions about what we mean by the term "attributional inference," when it occurs in the information-processing sequence, and whether two distinct processes may have been subsumed in our use of this term.

Both of the research directions we have summarized originated in, and benefited from, a conceptual framework in which attribution plays a role in a social information processing system. It is an important role, for the perceiver's intuitive analysis of causation is an important means by which social knowledge and understanding are achieved. Attribution is a process that occurs in conjunction with other processes in the course of comprehending, understanding, storing, and using information the perceiver acquires about behavior in the social world. We believe our understanding of the attribution process will be enhanced by investigating further its place and functioning within the larger context of this information-processing system.

References

Allport, G. W. (1954). *The nature of prejudice*. Reading, Mass.: Addison-Wesley.

Anderson, N. H. (1981). *Foundations of information integration theory*. New York: Academic Press.

Asch, S. E. (1946). Forming impressions of personality. *Journal of Abnormal and Social Psychology* 41: 258–90.

Bargh, J. A. (1984). Automatic and conscious processing of social information. In R. S. Wyer, Jr. and T. K. Srull (eds.), *Handbook of social cognition*, vol. 3. Hillsdale, NJ: Lawrence Erlbaum.

Berscheid, E., Graziano, W., Monson, T., and Dermer, O. (1976). Outcome dependency: attention, attribution, and attraction. *Journal of Personality and Social Psychology* 34: 987–9.

Bruner, J. S. (1957). On perceptual readiness. *Psychological Review* 64: 123–52.

Clary, E. G. and Tesser, A. (1983). Reactions to unexpected events: the naive scientist and interpretive activity. *Personality and Social Psychology Bulletin* 9: 609–20.

Cohen, C. E. and Ebbesen, E. B. (1979). Observational goals and schema activation: a theoretical framework for behavior perception. *Journal of Experimental Social Psychology* 15: 305–29.

Crocker, J., Hannah, D. B., and Weber, R. (1983). Person memory and causal attributions. *Journal of Personality and Social Psychology* 44: 55–66.

Enzle, M. E. and Schopflocher, D. (1978). Instigation of attribution processes by attributional questions. *Personality and Social Psychology Bulletin* 4: 595–9.

Erber, R. and Fiske, S. T. (1984). Outcome dependency and attention to inconsistent information. *Journal of Personality and Social Psychology* 4: 709–26.

Fiske, S. T. (1980). Attention and weight in person perception: the impact of negative and extreme behavior. *Journal of Personality and Social Psychology* 38: 889–906.

Hamilton, D. L. (ed.) (1981). *Cognitive processes in stereotyping and intergroup behavior*. Hillsdale, NJ: Lawrence Erlbaum.

Hamilton, D. L. (in press). Understanding impression formation: what has memory research contributed? In P. R. Solomon, G. R. Goethals, C. M. Kelley and B. Stephens (eds.), *Memory – An interdisciplinary approach*. New York: Springer Verlag.

Hamilton, D. L., Grubb, P. D., Trolier, T. K., and Carpenter, S. (1987). *Influence of the attribution process on memory for social information*. Unpublished manuscript, University of California, Santa Barbara.

Hamilton, D. L., Katz, L. B., and Leirer, V. O. (1980). Organizational processes in impression formation. In Hastie *et al.* 1980.

Hastie, R. (1980). Memory for behavioral information that confirms or contradicts a personality impression. In Hastie *et al.* 1980.

Hastie, R. (1984). Causes and effects of causal attribution. *Journal of Personality and Social Psychology* 46: 44–56.

Hastie, R. and Kumar, P. A. (1979). Person memory: personality traits as organizing principles in memory for behavior. *Journal of Personality and Social Psychology* 37: 25–38.

Hastie, R., Ostrom, T. M., Ebbesen, E. B., Wyer, R. S., Hamilton, D. L., and Carlston, D. E. (eds.) (1980). *Person memory: the cognitive basis of social perception*. Hillsdale, NJ: Lawrence Erlbaum.

Heider, F. (1958). *The psychology of interpersonal relations*. New York: Wiley.

Hemsley, G. D. and Marmurek, H. H. C. (1982). Person memory: the processing of consistent and inconsistent person information. *Personality and Social Psychology Bulletin* 8: 433–8.

Higgins, E. T., Herman, C. P., and Zanna, M. P. (eds.) (1981). *Social cognition: the Ontario Symposium* (vol. 1). Hillsdale, NJ: Lawrence Erlbaum.

Hoffman, C., Mischel, W., and Mazze, K. (1981). The role of purpose in the organization of information about behavior: trait-based versus goal-based categories in person cognition. *Journal of Personality and Social Psychology* 40: 211–25.

Jones, E. E. (1979). The rocky road from acts to dispositions. *American Psychologist* 34: 107–17.

Jones, E. E. and Davis, K. E. (1965). From acts to dispositions: the attribution process in person perception. In L. Berkowitz (ed.), *Advances in experimental social psychology*, vol. 2. New York: Academic Press.

Kelley, H. H. and Michela, J. L. (1980). Attribution theory and research. *Annual Review of Psychology* 31: 457–501.

Markus, H. and Zajonc, R. B. (1985). The cognitive perspective in social psychology. In G. Lindzey and E. Aronson (eds.), *Handbook of social psychology*, 3rd ed., vol. 1. Hillsdale, NJ: Lawrence Erlbaum.

McArthur, L. Z. (1981). What grabs you? The role of attention in impression formation and causal attribution. In E. T. Higgins, C. P. Herman, and M. P. Zanna (eds.), *Social cognition: the Ontario Symposium* (vol. 1). Hillsdale, NJ: Lawrence Erlbaum.

McGuire, W. J. (1985). Attitudes and attitude change. In G. Lindzey and E. Aronson (eds.), *Handbook of social psychology*, 3rd ed., vol. 2. Hillsdale, NJ: Lawrence Erlbaum.

Newtson, D. (1973). Attribution and the unit of perception of ongoing behavior. *Journal of Personality and Social Psychology* 28: 28–38.

Newtson, D. (1976). Foundations of attribution: the perception of ongoing behavior. In J. H. Harvey, W. J. Ickes, and R. F. Kidd (eds.), *New directions in attribution research*, vol. 1. Hillsdale, NJ: Lawrence Erlbaum.

Ostrom, T. M., Pryor, J. B., and Simpson, D. (1981). The organization of social information. In E. T. Higgins, C. P. Herman, and M. P. Zanna (eds.), *Social cognition: the Ontario Symposium* (vol. 1). Hillsdale, NJ: Lawrence Erlbaum.

Pittman, T. S. and Pittman, N. L. (1980). Deprivation of control and the attribution process. *Journal of Personality and Social Psychology* 39: 377–89.

Pryor, J. B. and Ostrom, T. M. (1981). The cognitive organization of social information: a converging-operations approach. *Journal of Personality and Social Psychology* 41: 628–41.

Pyszczynski, T. A. and Greenberg, J. (1981). Role of disconfirming expectations in the instigation of attributional processing. *Journal of Personality and Social Psychology* 40: 31–8.

Reeder, G. D. (1985). Implicit relations between dispositions and behaviors: effects on dispositional attribution. In J. H. Harvey and G. Weary (eds.), *Attribution: basic issues and applications*. Orlando, Florida: Academic Press.

Ross, L. (1977). The intuitive psychologist and his shortcomings: distortions in the attribution process. In L. Berkowitz (ed.), *Advances in experimental social psychology*, vol. 10. New York: Academic Press.

Ross, L. and Fletcher, G. J. O. (1985). Attribution and social perception. In G. Lindzey and E. Aronson (eds.), *Handbook of social psychology*, 3rd ed., vol. 2. Hillsdale, NJ: Lawrence Erlbaum.

Schneider, D. J. (1973). Implicit personality theory: a review. *Psychological Bulletin* 79: 294–309.

Smith, E. R. (1984). Attributions and other inferences: processing information about the self versus others. *Journal of Experimental Social Psychology* 20: 97–115.

Smith, E. R. and Miller, F. D. (1983). Mediation among attributional inferences and comprehension processes: initial findings and a general method. *Journal of Personality and Social Psychology* 37: 2240–52.

Srull, T. K. (1981). Person memory: some tests of associative storage and retrieval models. *Journal of Experimental Psychology: Human Learning and Memory* 7: 440–62.

Srull, T. K., Lichtenstein, M., and Rothbart, M. (1985). Associative storage and retrieval processes in person memory. *Journal of Experimental Psychology: Learning, Memory and Cognition* 11: 316–45.

Taylor, S. E. and Fiske, S. T. (1978). Salience, attention, and attribution: top of the head phenomena. In L. Berkowitz (ed.), *Advances in experimental social psychology*, vol. 11. New York: Academic Press.

Weiner, B. (1985). "Spontaneous" causal thinking. *Psychological Bulletin* 97: 74–84.

White, J. D. and Carlston, D. E. (1983). Consequences of schemata for attention, impressions, and recall in complex social interactions. *Journal of Personality and Social Psychology* 45: 538–49.

Winter, L. and Uleman, J. S. (1984). When are social judgments made? Evidence for the spontaneousness of trait inferences. *Journal of Personality and Social Psychology* 47: 237–52.

Winter, L., Uleman, J. S., and Cunniff, C. (1985). How automatic are social judgments? *Journal of Personality and Social Psychology* 49: 904–17.

Wong, P. and Weiner, B. (1981). When people ask "why" questions, and the heuristics of attributional search. *Journal of Personality and Social Psychology* 40: 650–63.

Wyer, R. S., Jr. and Gordon, S. E. (1982). The recall of information about persons and groups. *Journal of Experimental Social Psychology* 18: 128–64.
Wyer, R. S., Jr. and Srull, T. K. (1986). Human cognition in its social context. *Psychological Review* 93: 322–39.
Zadny, J. and Gerard, H. B. (1974). Attributed intentions and informational selectivity. *Journal of Experimental Social Psychology* 10: 34–52.
Zajonc, R. B. (1980). Cognition and social cognition: a historical perspective. In L. Festinger (ed.), *Four decades of social psychology*. New York: Oxford University Press.

Author index

Subject index